PROTESTANT THOUGHT:
FROM ROUSSEAU TO RITSCHL

being the translation of eleven chapters of

DIE PROTESTANTISCHE THEOLOGIE
IM 19. JAHRHUNDERT

KARL BARTH

Essay Index Reprint Series

 BOOKS FOR LIBRARIES PRESS
FREEPORT, NEW YORK

Translated by Brian Cozens from eleven chapters of
DIE PROTESTANTISCHE THEOLOGIE IM 19. JAHRHUNDERT,
Evangelischer Verlag A.G., Zollikon, Zürich, Switzer-
land, 1952.

Translation revised by H. H. Hartwell and the editorial
staff of the SCM Press.

INTERNATIONAL STANDARD BOOK NUMBER:
0-8369-2102-X

LIBRARY OF CONGRESS CATALOG CARD NUMBER:
73-142606

PRINTED IN THE UNITED STATES OF AMERICA

CONTENTS

INTRODUCTION

WHEN Karl Barth decided to become a systematic theologian, Protestant historical scholarship lost a man who was potentially the greatest historian of doctrine since Adolf von Harnack. One need not subscribe to the cynical axiom of the historical relativists—that 'today's dogmatics is tomorrow's history of dogma'—to wonder what new insights into the making of Christian creeds and systems might have come from this immense historical and theological talent if Barth had devoted a lifetime to research in the sources of the history of Christian thought. The many historical excursuses in Barth's *Church Dogmatics*, dealing with the history of everything from the doctrine of the angels to the picture of Judas Iscariot, bear witness to the breadth of his erudition and to the depth of his understanding. And the detailed commentary on Anselm's proof for the existence of God which Barth prepared in 1931 illustrates his ability to get at the meaning of a historical text by means of careful exegesis, word study, and the examination of its historical and cultural context.

Yet Barth's most significant contribution to his historical theology is undoubtedly *Die protestantische Theologie im 19. Jahrhundert*, which, like his book on Anselm, owed its origins to Barth's classroom at Bonn. After much gossip, both oral and written, to the effect that Barthian theology was unable to stimulate its disciples in the direction of historical thinking, these two books proved that in his own case, at least, Karl Barth was still enough a pupil of Adolf von Harnack to enter into the theological work of his predecessors with sympathy and perception. Whether or not the epigoni of the Barthian school can manifest a similar capacity for historical imagination without measuring all theology past and present by the norm of their master's *Church Dogmatics* is quite another question—and, incidentally, a question left unanswered by the historical work that has come from this generation. Certain it is, however, that Barth's treatment of the 'ontological argument' in Anselm and, even more, his narrative of the rise of theological liberalism from Schleiermacher to Ritschl gave the lie to the caricature of Barth's position that most of his critics and not a few of his disciples had foisted upon the theological public in Britain and America. An introduction like the present one can perhaps render no better service than to point out some of the features in this book that do not correspond to the caricature and that set it off from much of the literature that has arisen in the history of the history of theology.

Perhaps the most striking feature of the chapters presented here is their willingness to treat the theologians of the past on their own terms. Anyone who expects Karl Barth the dogmatician to become the judge of the quick and the dead when he functions as a historian of theology will find, to his surprise, that Barth has made a genuine effort to comprehend the theologians of the nineteenth century from within their own frame of reference. With his historical evaluations one will feel obliged to argue now and again. Thus it seems to me a vast exaggeration when Barth says of the obscure Reformed theologian, Hermann Friedrich Kohlbrügge (1803-1875): 'We have not been tempted to evaluate a single one of the theologians discussed here according to the criterion of "reformer". It is an indication of Kohlbrügge's greatness that in his case this [evaluation] is unavoidable.' Barth's affinities for Kohlbrügge's thought—or Kohlbrügge's affinities for Barth's thought! —seem here to have outweighed his historical judgment. But even here he is trying to assess the past as the past wished to be assessed, not as a supercilious modern or 'post-modern' theologian thinks the past ought to be assessed. Despite the critical judgments which Barth expresses throughout the book, there are no 'good guys' or 'bad guys' in this history of theology, but only serious-minded thinkers.

The reason for this fairness is not, as it has sometimes been in historians of theology, that Karl Barth is indifferent to the issue of right and wrong in Christian doctrine. Of this he has, to my knowledge, never been accused! But the reason lies in Barth's insistence upon the issue of right and wrong in Christian doctrine, in this instance his realization of what is right and wrong in the Christian doctrine of the Church. As he put it in the introduction to the German edition, 'I believe one holy, catholic, and apostolic Church. And if I seriously intend to listen to a theologian of the past—whether it be Schleiermacher or Ritschl or anyone else—then I must mean this "I believe" seriously, unless I have been released from this obligation by private inspiration! That is, regardless of my myriad opinions I must include these people in the Christian Church. And in view of the fact that I myself, together with my theological work, belong to the Christian Church solely on the basis of forgiveness, I have no right to deny or even to doubt that they were as fundamentally concerned as I am about the Christian faith.' He therefore uses that same introduction to warn his listeners against the tendency to see the history of theology from Schleiermacher through Ritschl to Troeltsch, Seeberg, and Holl as a 'long detour' at whose end 'the dialectical theology' appears as the 'deliverance from all ills which had long been awaited and expected, but which had repeatedly failed to materialize'. From all indications it would seem that such a warning was and still is in place.

Also in place is Barth's disclosure that theology can never escape a dialogue with philosophy, and that it has not managed to escape it when it has pretended to ignore philosophy. The chapters on Kant and Hegel presented here are, in the first place, helpful introductions to the thought of Kant and Hegel. As such, they deserve the attention of readers who are interested in the history of German idealism. Barth's corrections of the standard manuals on this history, especially of those by Lütgert and Korff, are both implicit and explicit throughout his essays on the philosophical background of the nineteenth century. His main interest, however, is in the religious thought of the German idealists and in their influence upon theology. With the insights presented in this book the reader should be able to discern the religious motifs that might otherwise escape his attention in the writings of Kant, Hegel, Fichte, Schelling, etc. He should be able also to identify the presuppositions which the theologians of the nineteenth and twentieth centuries, including and especially Karl Barth, have taken over from Kant and from other philosophers. By his conscientious study of the philosophers Barth has once more reminded theologians of the unfinished business between theology and philosophy which did not reach a settlement, but only a moratorium, during the one hundred and twenty-five years between Kant's *Religion within the Limits of Reason Alone* and Barth's *The Epistle to the Romans*.

Closely related to this recognition of philosophy as the inescapable, if not always welcome, partner of theology is Barth's sensitive portrayal of culture as the inescapable, and often more welcome, setting of theology. The chapter on Rousseau, which was engaging the author just at the time that Hitler rose to power, ranks with the finest writing that Barth has done for sheer grasp, good humour, and insight. After such a chapter it is no shock to find Barth an enthusiastic interpreter of Mozart and even of Michelangelo. Nor is it accurate when some critics of Barth dismiss these forays into art and culture as the stunts of a poseur who is merely trying to show that he can do it too if he wants to—though it must be admitted that the humor in most of these essays does lend some plausibility to such an interpretation. This is, rather, Barth's way of paying tribute to the subtle tension between expression and limitation that has characterized great art and that has been absent among those romantics in whom aesthetics and theology conspired to produce a yearning for the Eternal. It would have been instructive and illuminating if Barth had written for this volume the chapter on Goethe which he had been considering. Even though one may wish very strongly, as I do, that Barth's theology gave more attention to the positive significance of the art, the music, and the liturgy of the Church in precisely this connexion, one must still be impressed by the comprehension he manifests for the sweep and the charm of spirits like Rousseau and Novalis.

With all this historical, philosophical, and cultural orientation, however, Karl Barth never forgets, and never lets his reader forget, that he is a theologian. He probes the men and materials before him for their theological meaning. As he says in his essay on Schleiermacher, the nineteenth century was the era in which men theologized mightily by writing histories of theology. But 'what decides whether theology is possible as a science is not whether theologians read sources, observe historical facts as such, and uncover the nature of historical relationships, but whether they can think dogmatically'. And as the essay on Schleiermacher demonstrates, perhaps better than any other chapter in this book, Barth remains a theologian who can think dogmatically also in his evaluations of the giants of the past. The chapter on Ritschl must, it seems to me, be a disappointment to any reader who has been led by the preceding chapters to expect both fairness and clarity alongside the polemics. It has been said with some justification that in this chapter Barth has treated Ritschl as Ritschl treated the Pietists. But perhaps H. R. Mackintosh's *bon mot* of twenty years ago is still valid: 'Ritschl at the moment belongs, like Tennyson, to the "middle distance": too far for gratitude, too near for reverence.' Perhaps, too, a new emphasis upon historical honesty among theologians, symbolized by this book, will eventually give Ritschl his due.

If this volume helps to destroy the caricature of Barth which has been current among so many otherwise informed people, it may impress upon them a principle which, properly applied, can correct the historical errors there may be in this volume: one can never understand any theologian through reading about him, for there is finally no substitute for the study of the theologian himself. As this is true of Barth, so it is true of the men whom Barth describes. This history of theology will thus perform its assignment if it makes its readers interested (or irritated) enough to open their minds to their fathers and brethren—as well as to their second cousins and even more distant relatives—who have spoken to Karl Barth and through Karl Barth. That is ultimately the assignment of any history of theology.

JAROSLAV PELIKAN

The University of Chicago
February, 1959

I

MAN IN THE EIGHTEENTH CENTURY

IN 1720 there appeared the famous work *Vernünfftige Gedancken von Gott, der Welt und der Seele des Menschen auch allen Dingen überhaupt den Liebhabern der Wahrheit mitgetheilet von Christian Wolffen*.[1] Its frontispiece shows a sun whose powerful rays pierce a mass of black clouds, and spread light upon mountains, forests, towns and villages. The aureole of this sun is obviously not considered to be insupportable to the human gaze, for it takes the form of an exceedingly friendly and pleasantly smiling human face, whose owner seems to be extremely pleased to see the clouds in the heavens and the shadows on the earth dissipate everywhere.

In view of the logic, psychology, cosmology and theology which this book expounds, it is very understandable, and largely in harmony with the author's spirit, that the spiritual movement, whose document the book is, should be termed the Enlightenment, that Enlightenment has been understood to mean man's optimistic effort to master life by means of his understanding ('thoughts'), and finally that the age of that movement, the eighteenth century, has been classified, praised or blamed *a parte potiori* as the age of Enlightenment and that of this kind of Enlightenment. The man of the eighteenth century would then be the champion against prejudices and passions, against vice and hypocrisy, ignorance and superstition, intolerance, partiality and fanaticism; he would honour wisdom and virtue, reason and nature; he would seek his 'pleasure' by finding 'happiness' in the fulfilment of duty, and he would seem to see the supreme goal of the understanding (and therefore of man) as 'utility', personal and general 'welfare', and the supreme spiritual gift as the possession of 'taste' and 'wit', and to see man also as a somewhat tepid, but always very assured and busy believer in God, freedom and immortality.

The man of the eighteenth century would then be such as Gottsched, Nicolai and Basedow, as they lived on in the memory of the men of

[1] *Reasonable Thoughts on God, the World and the Human Soul, and All things in General, communicated to the Lovers of Truth by Christian Wolff.*

the *Sturm und Drang*, and as indeed they were, in large measure. He would be like Wagner, the familiar in Goethe's *Faust* who was so severely judged by his master ('That this dry creeping fellow should disturb this wealth of visions!'), the enemy of all history, enthusiasm, poetry, mystery, as Novalis described him in *Die Christenheit oder Europa* (Christendom or Europe). Or even he would be like that 'divinely Chinese optimist' to whom Kierkegaard in *Begriff der Ironie* (The Concept of Irony) has raised a frightening little monument.

What are we to say of all this? Certainly, that kind of man did exist in the eighteenth century, and perhaps every more or less typical eighteenth-century man in his own way had something of him in himself. But we must not forget that the likeness even of Christian Wolff and his successors is only partially caught in these pictures or caricatures and in the slogans of optimism, moralism, intellectualism and so on. And, moreover, Christian Wolff and his like were not the only bearers of Enlightenment. Voltaire, who was assuredly one, was at any rate no Wagner. Alongside Wagner, Goethe, as Korff justly points out,[1] set Mephistopheles, a figure of Enlightenment, who was not very optimistic, a sceptic—think of the resignation in which Frederick the Great ended—in whom the Enlightenment doubts itself, or at least reaches enlightenment about itself.

But even Mephistopheles is not the only alternative to Wagner. Mozart's *Magic Flute*, first performed in 1791, is certainly also a classic document of the Enlightenment. Here too the group of symbols, sun, light, darkness, plays a decisive part. But who would think of Nicolai or Voltaire in connexion with its mysticism of initiation and its message of the power of music to lead man triumphantly through the night of death? Or what have the architecture and the park of Brühl castle to do with the spirit of Wagner and Mephistopheles? And has not, as again Korff points out, Faust himself, the man of Goethe's time, by a partially almost insensible transition emerged from the man of the Enlightenment, so that we must give the latter the credit for having after all contained his successor in embryo? We shall come to this in our discussion of Rousseau, Lessing and Kant.

But if this is so, what would become of the definition which has been indefatigably repeated by the historians of theology (Stephan, Hoffmann and others), and even maintained by Korff (I, 24), of the Enlightenment as 'culture of the understanding', as 'rationalism', a rationalism to be happily replaced in Goethe's time by a new 'irrationalism'? And how could this pattern fit the great Leibnitz, called 'the

[1] *Geist der Goethezeit* (The Spirit of the Age of Goethe), I, 31.

father of the Enlightenment'? Would it not show a very poor understanding of him, to appeal to an irrational completion of his rationalism? As if he of all people did not understand this dialectic very well!
For it was the problem of his whole thought and life to overcome that
pattern. However when we call Leibnitz the pre-eminent representative
of his century, must we not continue to ask whether the whole concept
of 'Enlightenment', the whole picture of the sun piercing the clouds, is
enough to characterize one aspect of the century—even on the widest
possible interpretation. Could we not with almost as much justice call
it the century of mystery? Is it not one of the remarkable characteristics of that century that the darkness, that is, the spirit, the order and
disorder of the Middle Ages, to which on the one hand it so eagerly
opposed the light of reason and virtue, was something which on the
other hand it both desired and confirmed? Did it not seek freedom and,
in the very search for what it understood by freedom, again and again
re-create the old unfreedom? How could one reduce without remainder
say, the will of Frederick the Great to the denominator 'Enlightenment'? Even in Goethe's time, beside the learned student of Göttingen,
and the worldly-wise student of Leipzig, there was still to be found the
unbroken rowdy and drunkard of Jena, whom the poet and minister
had sometimes to call to order in the theatre at Weimar, in a voice of
thunder and with the threat of the Hussars. All three types are true
children of the age.

But even apart from these connexions with the past, what is the
significance for the Enlightenment that an institution so characteristic
of its spirit as the order of Freemasons, founded in 1717, should assume
the form of an introduction to a mystery religion? One must in fact say
that, on closer inspection, the century possessed, somewhere in the
midst of its consciousness, in spite of and besides its cult of light, but
also in the end in relation to it a peculiar and widespread and various
knowledge and pursuit of the mysterious. The century did not only
have its philosophers (in the traditional sense as well as in its own
special understanding of the word), its historians and naturalists, its
princely and its commoner philanthropists, its schoolmasters and
journalists, but also (entirely out of its own peculiar genius) its mystics
and enthusiasts and pietists, its Rosicrucians and *illuminati*, its al-
chemists and quacks, its Swedenborg and Cagliostro and Casanova.
Count Zinzendorf read and treasured his Pierre Bayle, but this obviously did not in the least hinder him from singing and spreading the
praise of the Lamb. The most eminent scientists of the time, such as
the biologist Albrecht von Haller and the mathematician Leonhard

Euler, were also serious and convinced defenders of traditional Christianity. In the struggle which was fought out at the end of the seventeenth century in the closest entourage of Louis XIV about Quietism, with Madame de Guyon and Fénelon on the one side and Bossuet on the other, typical tendencies of our very age were found on both sides. But what did either of them have to do with 'Enlightenment'? Of course, this expression does have and retains its interpretive significance. But if we really want to see and understand the time from Louis XIV to the French Revolution in its totality, then we must not designate the period as a whole as 'the Enlightenment', but rather interpret it in a more comprehensive way. It is and remains a fact which we cannot ignore that the *Sturm und Drang*, idealism and romanticism, and above all Goethe himself, in dealing with that time, understood it as 'Enlightenment', and that predominantly in the narrower sense of the term. But I do not see how we can understand that discussion by simply appropriating its own terms; rather we must grasp the background and the circumstances in which they have their relative importance. Above all, I do not see how we can reach a theological understanding of the whole situation except by such a procedure.

The sixth volume of Walter Goetz's *Propyläen-Weltgeschichte* (Propyläen—Universal History, 1931), which deals with this period, is entitled *Das Zeitalter des Absolutismus* (The Age of Absolutism). This description probably refers to the well-known structure of the political order of that period, so characteristic of Louis XIV as well as of Frederick the Great and Joseph II. But political structure is at all times and was therefore also at that time no more than an expression of the order of life, the ideal of life in general. 'Absolutism' in general can obviously mean a system of life based upon the belief in the omnipotence of human powers. Man, who discovers his own power and ability, the potentiality dormant in his humanity, that is, his human being as such, and looks upon it as the final, the real and absolute, I mean as something 'detached', self-justifying, with its own authority and power, which he can therefore set in motion in all directions and without any restraint—this man is absolute man. And this absolute man, whether he is called Louis XIV or Frederick the Great or Voltaire, whether he lives the obscure life of a philistine with secret revolutionary thoughts or of a friend of letters with liberal religious or even sceptical tendencies, or of a lady in her castle devoted to the mysticism of Tersteegen, or whether he sails the seas with James Cook or is a watchmaker in Geneva making tiny but useful improvements in the products of his handiwork—for the nature and the degree of the expression he gives to his life is not what matters, nor the extent of his knowledge of how much he shares in the general movement of the time, all that matters is the thing itself—this absolute man is eighteenth-century man, who appears to us more or less distinctly, more or less open or veiled in conventional drapings, in all the human faces of that century which are so different amongst themselves.

We can see this man even in Leibnitz, to some extent. He can be a man of the Enlightenment, but not necessarily, and above all not necessarily in the narrower sense of the term. He is primarily the discoverer, the believer, and the exploiter of the miracle of human power. As such he can be a man of the Enlightenment, but he can also—for he does not need instruction from us about the necessity and beauty of the 'irrational'—become something quite different: Wagner and Mephistopheles and Faust in one, not forgetting: also Nathan and Saladin, Goetz and Egmont, and a 'sensitive soul', Moor the Robber, Don Carlos, and many others. We shall speak in following chapters of the Christianity of this man of the form which theology takes in his world. For the moment he interests us for his own sake, for his sheer humanity. 'Absolutism': this comprehensive key-word which we are now going to enquire into clearly indicates a programme. But where there is a programme, there is also a problem. And where there is a problem we find ourselves recalled, in one way or another, to a reality beyond the scope of programmes. A problem means limits and contradiction, perhaps self-contradiction. This is certainly what we find when we try to come to closer grips with the material which we have provisionally described as 'absolutism'.

Let us begin with some external facts. Eighteenth-century man was the man who could no longer remain ignorant of the significance of the fact that Copernicus and Galileo were right, that this vast and rich earth of his, the theatre of his deeds was not the centre of the universe, but a grain of dust amid countless others in this universe, and who clearly saw the consequences of all this. What did this really apocalyptic revolution in his picture of the universe mean for man? An unprecedented and boundless humiliation of man? No, said the man of the eighteenth century, who was not the first to gain this knowledge, but certainly the first to realize it fully and completely; no, man is all the greater for this, man is in the centre of all things, in a quite different sense, too, for he was able to discover this revolutionary truth by his own resources and to think it abstractly, again to consider and penetrate a world which had expanded overnight into infinity—and without anything else having changed, without his having to pay for it in any

way: clearly now the world was even more and properly so *his* world!
It is paradoxical and yet it is a fact that the answer to his humiliation
was those philosophical systems of rationalism, empiricism and scepticism which made men even more self-confident. The geocentric picture
of the universe was replaced as a matter of course by the anthropocentric.

And European man of the eighteenth century was also, in relation
to the old earth, one whose world had become immeasurably greater
and who nevertheless claimed this world too, even more as a matter of
course, as *his* world. As with Copernicus's discovery, so too he became
fully conscious of the discovery of Columbus and all that followed it in
west and east and south. Atlases and travel books became an indispensable part of the more serious literature, even in bourgeois houses,
afterwards in the world outside—and that already in the seventeenth century there had been a continuous succession of seizures of new territories
following the example of the Spaniards and Portuguese (stimulated
by the rising capitalist trade); these new possessions were ceaselessly
expanded, defended, consolidated, and exploited, making ever fresh
demands on the mother countries, and though with recessions and
disappointments in individual instances yet leading on the whole to
ever fresh successes. Holland—to whom still in 1669 belonged two-
thirds of all seafaring vessels—though gradually being overtaken by
England, led this enterprise in the company of France, while from
1683 to 1717 the Electorate of Brandenburg possessed a colony on the
Gold Coast, and from 1720 to 1727 there was also an Austrian East
India Company in Ostend. Nothing is more characteristic of this
extension of the European horizon and power than the fact that the
attraction of oversea possessions, and what indeed made them possible,
was primarily the slave trade and the possession of slaves. Moral
scruples, let alone Christian ones, were so little in evidence that it was
even possible to say without contradiction of the flourishing town of
Liverpool that it was built on the skulls of negroes.

It was in that same England—though Dutchmen and Frenchmen did
not behave differently—that Milton wrote his *Paradise Lost* and Bunyan
his *Pilgrim's Progress*, and Lord Shaftesbury, on the other hand, developed
the heroic-aesthetic idealism of his *Virtuoso*. The absolute man can and
does do both. One must see the significance of this double activity:
while Gellert was writing his Odes and Kant his *Critique of Pure
Reason*, while Goethe was writing his letters to Frau von Stein, and even
later, the two things were actually being done simultaneously by
absolute man: piety was practised at home, reason was criticized, truth

made into poetry and poetry into truth, while abroad slaves were
being hunted and sold. The absolute man can really do both. But even
within Europe space had both enlarged and diminished. It had enlarged, in the sense that from the time of Peter the Great Russia, from
being an unknown entity, had become one which was at least approximately known. It had diminished, in the sense that ever-increasing
trade had brought nations and lands perceptibly nearer to one another,
and that travel had become a part of education and even a truly
'irrational' necessity for many people. 'One' must have been to Paris
at least once. 'One' begins to wish to see Italy. Not everyone, but
some daring spirits make for the extreme north, or for Alpine peaks.
Mutual visits among like-minded people living far away from each
other become one of the most important means of intellectual exchange.
Pietists and Moravians led the way in that respect, showing themselves in this detail as well as in other ways to be very modern men.
But even without leaving one's own town the entirely new possibility
was discovered of meeting in a *salon*, with tea and tobacco acquiring a
by no means negligible sociological significance. Lastly, the rise of the
printed newspaper, and of the most beloved journals of philosophy, art,
literature, and culture of all kinds, meant the spread from place to
place of new thoughts, which were none the less effective because they
were conveyed in an impersonal way. So Europe, its countries and its
cities, became smaller, more easily seen as a whole, more easily penetrated. And so man too grew in this space in the sense that he unmistakably became more and more master of his existence, though the
space too grew larger and larger.

Further, eighteenth-century man began to become conscious of his
power for science, and of his power through science. The development
at the Renaissance, which had been hindered and reduced for almost
one hundred and fifty years through the period of religious wars, now
began to make immense strides. Once again man, led by a philosophy,
which was only apparently disunited but was in essentials united,
began to be conscious—and more forcibly than before—of a capacity
for thinking which was responsible to no other authority than himself.
This free thought he once more finds related to nature which was just
as freely observed. Mathematics were once more discovered by him to
be the bridge which carried him across in both directions, from concept
to intuition, from intuition to concept. Logic, observation and mathematics were the three decisive elements of the absolute power now
disclosed in science. This absoluteness is symbolized in the undeniable
separation of these elements from the universities, which had hitherto

ranked as the places of science. There did not exist a court with any pretensions which did not at this time found an academy to be the nursery of free research. Even the smallest courts supported at least a local historian, and established a library, a museum of coins and natural history. This free pursuit of science was also followed by the well-to-do bourgeois families in the towns, and in many a manor house and manse in the country. The ideal of a science of history and of natural science, without presuppositions and possessing supreme intellectual dignity in virtue of this very absence of presuppositions, was so firmly established in the minds of that century that it is hard for us to imagine the intensity with which they pursued their activities under the spell of that idea: reading, collecting, observing, experimenting and also perhaps indulging in many a scientific fantasy. And all this went on in circles which long since have learned to spend their leisure again in very different ways.

I take as one example for many the Würtemberg parson Philipp Mattaeus Hahn, a good theologian, in his way, of the school of Bengel and Oetinger. He contrived an astronomical machine of the universe which was much admired, and even respectfully examined by the emperor Joseph II. It also contained a device for stopping it in the year 1836, when, according to Bengel's calculations, the return of Christ and the beginning of the millennium was expected. It is characteristic of the time that alongside the study of the natural world the favourite scientific objects were primarily the study of the nature and activity of the human soul, human customs, and habits new and old, among savages as well as civilized peoples, the 'spirit of laws', as in the title of Montesquieu's famous book, and the various historical possibilities of education, culture, government and society. 'The proper study of mankind is man', said Pope, expressing the conscious or unconscious idea of the whole century in its pursuit of science. The desire to know was so serious that men understood only too well what the old sophists meant, and the best minds understood Socrates and Plato as well. Those who deplore the 'intellectualism' of that time should at least be clear that the human capacity for acquiring knowledge, which had been so long neglected, now began to spread in every sphere like a stream running along dry beds, and produced a movement from whose influence no clear mind could withdraw. And that the achievements of the time were considerable is seen in the fact that even now every science, without exception, has its historical foundations in the eighteenth century. But the amazing scientific spirit of that time which confronts us here was unquestionably one of the manifestations of all-conquering, absolute man, who expressed himself also and with special effect in this field of human activity.

Here we may also suitably call to mind the achievements of modern technique which also come from this time. The curve of progress in this field has not yet risen as steeply as it was to do in the nineteenth century. Here are some dates. In 1684 Hooke invented the optical telegraph, in 1690 Papin, a Frenchman, invented the steam cylinder with which, in 1707, he attempted, though without success, to sail a steam-boat on the river Fulda. The invention of springs for coaches in 1706 made the popular activity of travelling more comfortable. In 1714 Fahrenheit constructed his mercury thermometer. In 1718 Lady Mary Wortley Montagu tried to introduce the practice of inoculation for smallpox, and in the same year Leopold von Dessau invented the iron loading-rod for guns. Metal-boring machines appeared in 1720, accurate spinning machines in 1738. The idea of steam heat appears in 1745. In 1747 sugar was produced from beets. In 1751 the Frenchman Chamette invented a gun which was loaded from the rear, in 1764 James Watt invented the steam engine. In 1770 Priestley discovered oxygen. In 1780 Galvani made his decisive discoveries in electricity. In 1782 the brothers Montgolfier offered Paris the sight of the first balloon flight. In 1786 gas for lighting purposes was first made.

In almost every case we are seeing the first efforts of individual bold pioneers who were followed by the rest of the world only with hesitation, and whose efforts to a large extent were only properly applied much later. And Germany, in this as in the matter of colonies, was obviously a laggard. If we are to understand the feeling of life which surged through the whole of Europe, we must not underestimate the significance of the hopeful excitement which was also stirred by these discoveries too; here too is manifested the existence of the absolute man, the man almost capable of anything.

Yet more significant than science and technique was undoubtedly the political experience of the period. Perhaps eighteenth-century man is in this respect best described negatively: he is the man who no longer has an emperor. Of course, it was not till 1803 that the old empire actually broke up, in the external sense. But inwardly it had already broken up, we can even say, during the Thirty Years War and certainly clearly in the wars with Louis XIV, in which it showed its powerlessness. The image of the Holy Roman Empire which impressed itself on the mind of the young Goethe at the imperial coronation of Joseph II in 1765, and later in a practical form during his work at the imperial supreme law court in Wetzlar, was clearly that of an interesting, honourable, but entirely outdated old age, incapable of any action. The French Revolution was not necessary in order to destroy the real old order in Europe. It was already destroyed long before this Revolution, which was a revolution from below, took place. The Revolution was not the cause but the necessary effect of the destruction. For the Empire had been, ideally, the guarantee, as the means of cohesion and order among the large and small political units of which it was composed, of the hierarchy of relationships which had grown up between these various units. The guarantee of this hierarchy was not a one-way matter, it was not only the guarantee of the might of the higher classes against the lower, but also the guarantee of the right of the lower against the higher. The Empire was the concrete veto on any kind of political absolutism. It represented—imperfectly enough, but still, it did represent, while spanning the oppositions of higher and lower in the individual political units—a third factor, which excluded encroachments within these orders. That is why it was the *Holy* Roman Empire. So the end of the Empire necessarily meant the beginning of absolutism. That was shown both in the separation, in 1648, of the aristocratic republics of Switzerland from the Empire, and in the German principalities. The beginning of absolutism in France also coincides with the practical end of the Empire in Germany. The old French kingdom had corresponded exactly to the German Empire, with its supreme authority both respecting and guaranteeing the existing distances and competences and relationships in a political world with manifold forms. With the extinction of the imperial ideal this French kingdom also came to an end. Only after that was a monarch like Louis XIV possible. He was one type of the politically absolute man. Politically, absolutism means the determination of law by that class in the state which in contrast to the others possesses the effective power. The first type of this absolutism was created when the highest class after the effective elimination of the emperor, namely, that of the princes or the city oligarchs, used their actual power to identify with their own will the law of the political unit which had been entrusted to their leadership. When the king, against the background of this identification, calls himself king 'by the grace of God', no personal religious uprightness or humility which may reside in this kind of confession regarding the origin of his office can alter the fact that he is in effect made to be like God. 'By the grace of God' should mean that he bears the power in common submission with the people before a power which is superior to them both, and therefore that he also recognizes the rights of the people. The concrete form of that superior power had been the Empire. With its fall the prince became absolute and the people were deprived of their rights, while 'by the grace of God' simply masked the prince's resemblance to God. That is the meaning of Louis XIV's famous remark '*L'état c'est moi!*' It is the declaration of the prince, needing no other grounds than those of his actual power to assume the status of law, that right in the state, and the freedom guaranteed by it, are the right established by *me*, and the freedom guaranteed by *me*. The first party to suffer from this was the nobility. It was against their power, that is, against their ancient good right, that the new 'revolution from above' which now started was first directed. This was the meaning of the home policy of Richelieu, of Mazarin and of Louis XIV, and in Germany, in a specially classic form, of the Great Elector of Brandenburg.

Besides this, of course, princely absolutism struck also at the middle classes, who had been steadily rising since the end of the Middle Ages, and at the peasants, who in the sixteenth century had demanded their rights in vain—the first serious sign of the decay of the imperial idea. But it is significant in every respect that there could also on occasion be manifested a certain agreement, a deep community of interests between the absolute prince and the citizens, the class which nourished the rest of society. It is at any rate a fact that this age saw not only the rise of the princes but also—though on a different plane, that of economics and education—the rise of the citizens on an unprecedented scale. 'For reasons of state the princes conceived the idea of a productive bourgeois class . . . and gradually brought them up.'[1] Why did the absolute prince need the power of the unitary state for whose sake he had first to destroy the rights of the nobility? The first answer can only be that he needed this power because—wishing to be an absolute prince, and having in effect no emperor over him—he needed more power. He needed the unitary state, and in it a relatively prosperous bourgeoisie which could provide a regular flow of money to him. He needed money because he needed a standing army which was always at his disposal. He needed the army because his power was 'territorial', as we now say, with other territories alongside it. The existence of other territories openly contradicts the idea of an absolute prince, but this state of affairs could be improved by inheritance, by marriage, by acquisition and—the *ultima ratio*—by wars of conquest. And because the other means had their strict limitations, wars of conquest were the natural method.

War became, therefore, a latent principle. It is not surprising that open war again and again broke out. What is surprising is that it did

[1] *Propyläen-Weltgeschichte*, 6, p. 277.

not happen more frequently. Absolute politics of this kind are outwardly dynastic, cabinet politics; but by an inward necessity, sooner
or later they lead to a policy of conquest. This is the way—the securing
of internal power, that is, a unitary state by revolution from above,
with a view to external power—which was followed by the king of
France in the eighteenth century, as well as by the aristocrats of Berne
and the great and petty potentates of Germany, among whom the
emperor was now only one among the rest, later to be called—logically,
though absurdly—emperor of Austria. Only the clever English—perhaps one of the few nations really gifted politically—foresaw in time
the folly of this development, though they were just as penetrated by
the spirit of absolutism as the rest, and introduced checks which spared
them the catastrophe to which the system by its nature must lead.

This political absolutism from above has, as is known, two variants.
They have in fact crossed and mingled in many ways; their roots are
one, but they may be clearly distinguished. The principle 'through
power to power' had of course also a non-military aspect. This could
consist in the princely display of splendour and pomp at which Louis
XIV was so inventive, even creative, setting a baleful example which
was widely followed. The name of Versailles has thrice had great
historical significance resulting in grave consequences. The first time
it was as the prototype and symbol of a princely attitude to life and
form of life, based on unqualified power. From this life there flowed a
brilliance, like the glory of a god, into architecture, the gardens and
parks, the decoration in the houses, into comforts and enjoyments of
every kind, but above all into the transitory but all the more intoxicating splendour of the festivities. Far beyond the boundaries of France
there arose small and miniature imitations of Versailles whose princely
and noble inhabitants attempted, with more or less luck and dignity
and taste, to emulate Louis XIV.

After his death the Regent Philip of Orléans, then Louis' grandson,
Louis XV, in Germany Augustus the Strong of Saxony, Eberhard
Ludwig, Karl Alexander, and Karl Eugen of Würtemberg, Max
Emanuel and Karl Theodor of Bavaria, Ludwig IX of Hesse, and
many others, were absolute princes of this kind. The notorious immor-
ality, even debauchery, the just as notorious financial transactions, and
the scandalous arbitrariness of justice at all these courts, was perhaps
not the necessary, but as has happened in all similar phenomena in
history the practical, consequence of the representation which one
thought to be owing—and that not without some logic—to the
conception of the prince by divine right.

The idea inevitably presupposed great demands upon the economy of the country, which were made with an astonishing unconcern—not to speak of the sons of Hesse and Brunswick who were sold out of hand to America! And ironically enough the command was in fact often not in the hands of its true possessor, but largely and for all to see in those of a woman—sometimes, admittedly, in those of a woman far from unfitted for such an office, but only in a derivative sense can her rule ever have been described as 'by the grace of God'. But all these things cannot and must not blind us to the tremendous stimulus imparted to economic and artistic life by the fantastic burgeoning of absolutism. Neither must we forget that the luxury these potentates cultivated, though so dubious in many respects, acted in practice as a safety valve and corrective against the possibility of a universal state of war, which should really have been the logical consequence of the general principle 'through power to power' and of dynastic cabinet politics. If it had not been for the Sun-king's notion of the unfolding of power and the relative enervation which was involved herein, Louis himself and all the other God-kings might well with the absolute power they had arrogated have reduced Europe to even greater disasters than those they did in fact cause. Lastly it should be added that anyone who failed to sense not only the pathos imparted by lavishness of ideas, space and materials, but the underlying, unending and truly insatiable yearning in the midst of sensual delight which emanates from every line and form of the art of the age would be guilty of badly misunderstanding those artistic and architectural monuments of that time which still hold a meaning for us. It is this eternal yearning which is the style's inmost beauty, a beauty peculiarly moving for all the horror which is sometimes apt to seize the beholder.

Besides this kind of political absolutism there was another, going by the name of enlightened absolutism. It is possible for the 'through power to power' principle to manifest itself in depth rather than in extent, rationally rather than aesthetically. In that case it takes the form of experiments in social reform—in the technical advance of civilization, in agriculture, industry and in the economic sphere in general, in health measures and policies designed to benefit the population as a whole. There are attempts to improve the state of the law, but also to advance the arts and sciences, to raise the general standard of education—in short all sorts of measures tending to the so-called 'welfare' of the subjects of the state. In chastising a Jew, Frederick William I says: 'You should love me rather than fear me, love me, I say!' As Frederick the Great's famous remark shows, the absolute

monarch can also cherish the wish to be 'the first servant of the state'.
'It is our duty to sacrifice ourselves for the public good'—this was a *mot*
of Louis XIV already, and as proof that it was not just a *bon mot* one
might point to the extensive official activities in the cultural field of his
minister Jean Baptiste Colbert, who is too easily overlooked beside
the more eye-catching figures of a Louvois or of the various great ladies
of Louis' court. Circumstances permitting the absolute monarch might
then, in startling contrast to his princely contemporaries, assume the
rough aspect of a king of ancient Rome or Sparta, as did Frederick
William I of Prussia, or like Joseph II epitomize affability at all costs
and an idealism verging upon folly; or, as in Joseph Emmerich, elector
of Mayence, he might take the astonishing form of a wise prince of an
ecclesiastical state, at once open-minded enough to accept progress in
every form; or, finally, as with Frederick the Great he might be that
almost legendary figure, the 'Sage of Sans Souci' seeming to have his
whole existence centred around a philosophy stripped of illusion yet
rigid upon certain moral points, its purpose being to enable him to be
all the more detached in attending to the business of providing, maintaining and furthering law, order and progress among the people he
happened to be governing. Sarastro, Mozart's strange character in
The Magic Flute, combines elements from all these figures. And we need
only be reminded of Karl August of Saxe-Weimar-Eisenach, the
sovereign who was served by Goethe, to see how sometimes the entire
zest for life of the one kind of prince could be reconciled with the earnest
zeal of the second. It is needless to state that this second interpretation
of the art of kingship at this time and the achievements which sprang
from it command great respect. But let us not forget that although there
may be absolutists in the performing of good they are absolutists for all
that. It is thus with the 'enlightened' absolutism of which we have
been speaking.

We must appreciate this particularly in the classic case of Frederick
the Great. In the preface to his *Histoire de mon temps* he wrote in re-
flective mood: 'I trust that posterity will do me justice and understand how to distinguish the king in me from the philosopher, the decent
from the political man.' Indeed: as king he is no less a 'soldier king'
than his father, and no less a dynastic cabinet politician than Louis
XIV, although and in that he wants to be king and philosopher and a
decent man simultaneously. Temper as one may Lessing's harsh
judgment that the Prussia of Frederick the Great was 'the most slavish
country in Europe' and that 'Berlin freedom' consisted solely in the
right 'to hawk as many anti-religious imbecilities as one wishes', there

is still no escaping the fact that the enlightenment which Frederick desired had absolutely nothing to do with freedom—as freedom of the press, for example, it was a hollow pretence, and it was a foregone conclusion that freedom was not applied to the army or anything connected with the army, e.g. the administration of justice in the army. There is no blinking the fact, either, that Frederick's state had to be a welfare state—a Frederick naturally sees farther than the usual run of despots—in order to be—precisely as welfare state—a state worshipping power, an absolute state. The fact remains that the measure of wisdom and rectitude with which the king happened to be endowed, together with the limitations imposed upon these qualities by his highly individual character, his taste and his whims—limitations common to every mortal—had the significance of destiny for his people, his country and for every individual within his realms—a destiny which like God could bless or punish, might cherish or destroy, and could do so without let of appeal to any higher law. Lessing certainly had nothing to thank King Frederick for, nor did his loyal subject Immanuel Kant, nor did Leonhard Euler, and they were all misjudged for reasons which they and all the people they lived among had to accept as if these reasons represented the impenetrable will of God. The things he found uninteresting just didn't interest him, and the things he didn't like he just didn't like. The remark about 'the first servant of the state' is good, but what practical significance has it if this very first servant is alone from first to last in decreeing every policy of state, if every counsellor, be wise as he may, must ever fear him like a slave? The same might equally be said of Joseph II and his entirely well-intentioned and frequently beneficial innovations. He did much for his people and had in mind to do much more. But once again the highly personal limits of his circumspection and temperament were, like those of fate, the limits of the goodness and usefulness of the things his radicalism had created. His achievements stood with him. It was inevitable that with him they should also fall—to make way for the will of his equally absolutist successor, which chanced to have different objects. In short 'enlightened' absolutism also consisted essentially in 'revolution from above', and could provide no substitute for what the imperial idea had once stood for, or had been intended to stand for: the policy, which not only exercises dominion, but bestows freedom, which not only dispenses favours, but establishes justice, and establishes it by means of justice, a policy whereby the best possible is done for the people with the people, and therefore as a matter of principle just as much through the people as through the king; a policy therefore in whose eyes as a matter of principle no person is merely an object; again, a policy subject not only to an abstract responsibility, but to a concrete one—a policy therefore which might well deserve the title, 'by the grace of God'. Those who do not happen to be in power, who are subjected to an absolute monarch, whether he be enlightened or unenlightened, are bound to look upon him with that rather distant and nervous awe exemplified in the form of the great prayer of the Church at Basle to be found in the liturgy of 1752, a prayer to be offered for 'the wise and worshipful first citizens, counsellors, judges and officials of our Christian town and district of Basle': 'Guide them, O Lord, with the spirit of wisdom and understanding, with good counsel and courage, with the knowledge and fear of thy holy name, that in their care we may lead a peaceful and quiet life in all honour and righteousness.'

It is of course possible to question whether that other policy, pursued in the Middle Ages in the name of the imperial ideal, ever became a reality anywhere. But there was at least a chance that it might be realized while it was still at least an active point of reference (questionable in itself but at least fairly well-defined) within the framework of the imperial ideal. It was when this fell away that the realization of such a policy became impossible. For when the prince's power was made absolute, a step which brought with it the death of the imperial ideal, the prerequisite of such a policy, the very notion of a concrete responsibility, of a higher authority, was removed also, and in its place there arose the state without a master, or alternatively the state governed by an arbitrary master, beneath whose sway, even if he were the best of all possible monarchs, justice was a matter of pure chance.

We have taken the one kind of political absolutist, the absolute prince, as the first for discussion. The second kind, his perfectly legitimate brother, his *alter ego*, following in his footsteps as inevitably as the darkness following the light, as the thunder following the lightning, is the absolute revolutionary—or perhaps it would be better to say, since his predecessor was already a revolutionary—the revolutionary from below, the representative of the lower class, who conceiving those above him to have injured him in his rights, and even to have deprived him of them, takes steps to defend himself by snatching the power lying in the hands of the governing princes in order that he might now determine without let of appeal what is right and just, because he in his turn has the power in his hands. The *rôles* are reversed. Whereas before it had been the prince who had declared himself to be identical with the state, it was now the people, the 'nation', as it at this time began to be called, who assumed the title by means of a simple inversion of

Louis XIV's dictum. This happened true to type in Paris on the 17th June, 1789. The representatives of the so-called third estate, who were, be it remembered, the delegates of that section of the population of France which was in the overwhelming majority, formed themselves into a 'National Assembly' and three days later declared with a collective oath, that they were determined in the teeth of all opposition never to disband until they had given the state a new constitution. Everything that happened afterwards, up to the execution of Louis XVI and beyond, was a direct result of this event. Its inner logic is, however, as follows. (We shall restrict ourselves in the following to the two classic revolutionary documents, the Declaration of Independence of the United States of America of June 1776 and the Statement of Human and Civil Rights ratified by the French National Assembly in August 1789). According to the revolutionary doctrine there exists a self-evident truth which can and must be recognized and announced *en présence et sous les auspices de l'être suprême*:

1. All men are equal, i.e. created with equal rights (Am.), or alternatively (as in the Fr.), born with equal rights.

2. These equal rights are of nature, inalienable, sacred (Fr.), endowed by their creator (Am.).

3. Their names are freedom, property, security and the right to protect oneself from violence (Fr.) or: life, liberty and the pursuit of happiness (Am.). The French statement goes on to make a special point of saying that freedom consists in being able to do anything which does not harm anybody and is not as such forbidden by law. And it also considers the right to property important enough to describe it in a special last article as *inviolable et sacré*.

4. It is in order to protect these rights that *governments are instituted among men* (Am.). *Le but de toute association publique est la conservation des droits . . . de l'homme* (Fr.).

5. Governments *derive* their just authority from *the consent* of the governed. *Le principe de toute souveraineté réside essentiellement dans la nation.* All authority exercised by individuals or corporate bodies stems expressly from the people (*en émane expressément*).

6. The law is *l'expression de la volonté générale* so all must have a part in making it, all are equal in its eyes and every office and honour for which it provides are as a matter of principle open to all.

7. Whenever a form of government becomes injurious to the aims of the state, i.e. to the upholding of the rights aforementioned it is the people's right to remove it and replace it by a government more conducive to their *safety and happiness*. It will be advisable not to proceed too

hastily in such an event, but once it has become plain that a government is seeking to establish *absolute despotism* it is not only the citizen's right but his duty to free himself of its yoke.

The subtle differences of emphasis revealed by a comparison of these two documents are of considerable interest: the French version is clearly distinctive by virtue of the fact that, apart from the mention of the *être suprême* in the preamble, the theological note has entirely disappeared, together with the implicit notion still to be found in the American document that at least in the beginning there could have been a 'government among men' that was not created by the will of the people; a notion that the revolution itself was not only the exercising of a right, but something like the fulfilment of a duty; that this right and duty was of a transitory nature, and that while the authority of a government might rest upon the consent of a people, this was not quite the same thing as the people's will. In contrast to this the French statement is explicit in taking the state to be an *association*, its sovereignty to be the sovereignty of the nation as a whole, and the authority of its laws to be contained in the will of all, i.e. in the generality of the individual possessors of the human rights. The Calvinism gone to seed of the American document still distinguishes itself favourably from the Catholicism gone to seed of the French one. But these fine variations of meaning only reveal the sources and aims common to both versions. They both think of the state in terms of the individual, or the sum of the individuals forming a nation. Both of them show that those who drew them up imagine that they were standing before an ultimate reality, and indeed before a reality beyond which no man would ever see. Face to face with the supreme Being, or self-evidently, man knows according to both documents that he has a right to life, liberty, property and so on. For the sake of these universal rights it is necessary to have a state, and this state comes into being and subsists by virtue of general recognition of these universal rights, and in case of need, should it be found that this right is in effect being suppressed, by the strength of the majority it is actively called into being. It is this which forms the revolution. Such was the line of thought upon which the third estate in 1789 based its declaration that it was identical with the 'nation', and resolved come what might to undertake the transformation of the state.

This then is the essentially unanimous confession of faith of the second kind of absolutist in politics, diametrically opposed to the first kind, the enlightened or unenlightened princely absolutist. Diametrically opposed? Indeed he is, and yet he is himself confined within the same vicious circle. The *Déclaration des droits de l'homme*, in the form in which it was first printed and sold in Paris in 1789, bears over its title a picture of the radiant eye of God, enclosed within the usual triangle, which even here calls to mind the Trinity. At the foot of the page, admittedly, there are to be found the words, *L'œil suprême de la raison qui vient de dissiper les nuages qui l'obscurcissaient*. But beneath the title there is the ingenious symbol of a snake biting its own tail. The snake, unfortunately, is not explained: but it can hardly have any other meaning but that the time was ripe for doing the same as the princely absolutist had done though in reverse: *L'état c'est moi!* That section of society which holds the power (or that which at the moment is striving to acquire it) determines according to its own particular standards what is right for society as a whole. He knows what is right! Why shouldn't he? And why, if he knows, shouldn't he determine for the whole? He needs only to overcome his diffidence to place his conception of freedom, life, property, etc., on the absolute plane with the greatest of ease: and what is there then left to him but to place his will also on a level with them? All this the *ancien régime* had also done, the only difference being that it employed the phrase 'by the grace of God', whereas the revolutionary spoke rather more badly of the Creator, or simply maintained that everything relating to the subject was *naturel, inviolable, sacré*, and *self-evident*. Thus on both sides the same thing happens: the same usurpation and entry into the same vicious circle.

There are as we saw fine distinctions of attitude also within this new kind of absolutism; it is possible within the revolution from below to adhere more to the conservative or more to the radical side. It is possible to place the individual as such, who forms the state, more in the centre of things, or the nation which unites within itself all individuals: this means that there will now be a liberal movement with a nationalist movement as its antagonist, and a liberal-nationalist movement at any point between the two. In short, the nineteenth century can now begin. Occasionally, as in the time of the restoration, and as was perhaps inevitable in any monarchy—it has also been known to happen in a modern republic—a feeling of repugnance against the whole state of things created by the French Revolution, a romantic nostalgia for monarchical absolutism and for the glorious days before 1789 might spring to life and begin to take effect over against both liberalism and nationalism, and in their efforts to combat this reactionary tendency both the liberals and the nationalists would find themselves compelled to invoke ever more and anew the exalted spirit of 1776 and 1789, and oppose reaction by being themselves reactionary. And so one way **or** the other, whether people prefer the 'Marseillaise' or the 'March of Hohenfriedberg', or even if they wish to combine both in one anthem, the snake is for ever biting its own tail. One way or another, either as individuals or, taken collectively, as a nation, the men who assume that they have 'rights' and experience the desire to assert them by violence stand, almost like God, very much alone, thrown upon themselves in a way for which, with due regard for the imperfections of the human state, there was never any true necessity. The empire, it is true, was a concrete political authority, but its authority was higher than the state, and therefore had once made the absolute state impossible in any form; again, it had once in spite of all its political ambiguity not been completely without eschatological significance, drawing attention to the existence of a law that neither princes nor peoples could give themselves, and that therefore they could not play off one against the other; all this, however, is completely foreign to the political world of the eighteenth century. Has man, either as a prince or as man generally, really such a right as the political absolutist thinks he is justified in assuming, whether he tends to the left or the right? Is it really 'right' which they seize in each particular case? Does not right cease to be right whenever it is seized? Is not right possible only in a relationship which presupposes peace and excludes the thought of revolution because its basis is a commandment? Is it not this relationship which alone forms the basis for distinguishing the bearer of office just as it alone forms the basis for the equality of all men? It is of course a relationship which, when destroyed, makes revolution and counter-revolution an absolute necessity, because when it is destroyed everything is bound to become absolute and abstract, and all things fall together like a pile of skittles. It was in fact the destruction of this relationship in the eighteenth century which made inevitable the appearance of the two kinds of political absolutism, the appearance, that is, of the possibility of taking the law into one's own hand and making the state omnipotent. The first kind and the last! And what is more—the consternation and the lamentings of the legitimists were very much misplaced—the second kind was brought about by the first. For political man as he appeared upon the scene in 1789 had been the same man for a long time before, albeit in a different guise. The whole century in fact thought as he did; and so did even the circles which were to fall victim to the revolution. The tyrant will secretly always be a conspirator against himself. If this is not realized the lightning outbreak of this upheaval and its tremendous repercussions throughout Europe will never be understood. By virtue of the same fiction of the contract which constitutes the state whereby the kings of Europe had justified their rule, they now found that rule had been snatched from them again. They themselves, as we saw, had encouraged the growth of the bourgeois, not because they loved him, but because they needed him. And now he was there, just as they had wanted him and shaped him to be, except that at this point he suddenly found that he could do with a little more of the *liberté*, *propriété*, happiness, etc., which the others accorded themselves in such generous measure—more than the others were in fact ready to grant him—and except for the fact that the bourgeois now suddenly discovered that he was in the majority, and that he had only to reach out and seize the power to achieve what he wanted forthwith. Upon which, of course, it became immediately apparent that he who invokes death to tyrants is also always something of a tyrant himself and will reveal himself to be one soon enough.

To show not only the connexion, but the essential unity of the things we have been discussing it will be significant if in conclusion we cast a glance at the political philosophy which first of all nourished the princely absolutist and then provided an equal delight to the palate of the bourgeois. It was truly not without good cause that their tastes were similar. It is the political philosophy of Thomas Hobbes, which stems, it is true, from well back in the seventeenth, but is in effect standard for the whole of the eighteenth century. According to his teaching in *de cive*—part of *Leviathan*—the significance of the state is as follows: the ultimate reality to be reckoned with in man is his instinct to preserve himself and enjoy his life accordingly. He follows this instinct in everything he does, and he is perfectly right to do so. Nature has in actual fact given to all men the same claim to all things, the only restraining factor being that to bring this instinct into play indiscriminately would benefit no one, as its necessary consequence would be universal war. Reason, therefore, backed by the fear of death and the desire for rest, will counsel man to adopt self-imposed restrictions. Thus subjective right in itself seeks an objective kind of right, which is created by way of a transference of law (*translatio iuris*). Agreement is reached and each one of the parties transfers a part of his rights to the state. The state, however, is a *persona civilis*, representing the unity of the general will and possessing power over all: *persona una, unius voluntas ex pactis plurium hominum pro voluntate habenda est ipsorum omnium*. In return this single person affords all men protection, and with it promises to each his own: *Suum cuique!* and in so doing provides the first possibility for all to live a truly human life. Who is this single person? According to Hobbes he can just as easily be represented by monarchy as by an aristocracy or a democracy. (His personal choice was for a monarchy.) The only essential thing is that he should be understood as being one person, whose will is law subject to no condition, and who is alone in determining and sanctioning what is good and what is bad. There exists nothing either good or bad in itself apart from the state, but the public law is the citizen's conscience, just as originally it emerged thence. Free thought exists only in respect to the Church, i.e. in respect to the question that remains of the inevitable fear of the unseen powers. But, while the subject is permitted to adopt what attitude he pleases to the Church, there *is* a fear of invisible powers which is officially sanctioned by the state, and from which, as from the faith which is right in all circumstances, it is superstitious to deviate—from which to deviate would not only mean superstition, but revolution, and which therefore cannot be tolerated. Thus speaks Hobbes.

It is usual in this context to make mention of John Locke's *Two Treatises on Civil Government* (1690). But his political philosophy would seem to be of less significance than Hobbes', because in it the philosophy of revolution from below, the doctrine that force has its source in the people, already preponderates and makes his work one-sided. Hobbes' political philosophy is great by virtue of the fact that it rises above this antithesis and is therefore capable of presenting a comprehensive view of the ideology of politics obtaining in his time.

Hobbes' train of thought leads like a corridor to princely or to bourgeois absolutism, to the arrogation of God-like powers in politics by the individual or by the community, as Hobbes himself says: to the omnipotent monarchy or to the omnipotent republic. Either way it is essentially the same process. In actual fact the eighteenth century took both courses, and it is this which is characteristic for the political experience it gathered.

We have considered the political problem presented by the eighteenth century in particular detail because it is from the political angle that the eighteenth century can be seen most clearly as a whole. Let us now proceed to the attempt to comprehend it under two other aspects which present a less definite picture—the inner and outer forms imparted to life by man as he lived at that time.

By that external form which life has in any age I mean that particular element in its cultural aims and achievements which is evinced fairly consistently throughout its various expressions. Consequently it is possible to identify, with some precision, from the documents of any one of the expressions of this element, the tendency, nature and spirit of its other expressions, and so of the culture of the time as a whole. If there is such an external cast for the eighteenth century, and one that we can identify, it is perhaps most allowable to comprehend it in terms of a striving to reduce everything to an absolute form. Inanimate nature especially, in all its realms, but man's somatic existence too, the sound that could be spontaneously called forth, with all the possibilities for coloration and different rhythmic patterns which it presented, human language in all its adaptability as a means of expression, social inter-course, individual development and the individual in relation to society—all this abundance of things provided is in the eyes of eigh-teenth-century man a mass of raw material, of which he believes himself to be the master. This material he confronts as he who has all the know-ledge: knowledge of the form, the intrinsically right, fitting, worthy, beautiful form for which all the things provided are clearly intended to be the material, for which they are obviously crying out, and into which, as is plain, they must be brought with all the speed, artistry and energy man has at his command. It is easy to become ironical about this, but we must fight against the temptation if we wish to understand the true irony contained in such an attitude.

Eighteenth-century man, at least at the higher levels of society, had very close ties with nature, and they were far from being simply of the kind which lead man to study nature scientifically and exploit it for gain; they could also be felt and enjoyed aesthetically. It is however—let it not be said too quickly—a rationalized, but rather a humanized nature, a nature which has been put to rights and formed in accordance with man's sensibility and enjoyment, an idealized, and most preferably a visibly idealized nature, which is meant: the stream as a fountain, the lake as a clean and tidy pond, the wood as a park reduced to visible order, the field and the bushes and flowers as a garden, the tree shaped with the garden-shears, all these things reduced to harmony, which inevitably means to geometry, more or less; the tamed, groomed and trained animals, shepherds and shepherdesses whose nice prettiness and grace really left them no alternative but to turn eventually into those little porcelain figures; a nature which even after the grooming it has had to endure is really beautiful only when there is a Greek temple, a statue or a bust somewhere about which quite unequivocally serves as a reminder of the lords of creation. It was the time of Goethe which brought about a decisive inner change here but the external change took much longer and was slower in asserting itself: it would seem, as we can see from the *Elective Affinities*, for instance, that the game of 'creating' nature in the eighteenth-century sense was indulged in for a long time and on a grand scale in Weimar too. The man who expresses an attitude to nature such as this must be unusually conscious and certain that he knows how he feels and that his feeling is valid in the sense that it is the true feeling.

The same determined and absolute will for form is conveyed by the architecture of the time. The domineering way in which building materials were handled is evidenced in works like the stairway of Brühl castle. Stone may no longer be stone, nor iron, iron, nor wood, wood. Every material must be transposed (hence the particular fondness that arose at this time for plaster, so obedient to the forming hand!) according to the imaginative though lucid and logical form, which man felt he ought to impose upon space. This form was that of the perception which he held significant and valuable enough to justify its projection into the materials, regardless of everything in them contrary to its own nature. Think too of the way they dared to build whole cities in those days—not with the help of a natural rise in the ground or following the course of a river, as the builder of the older towns had built them, but as in Karlsruhe, Mannheim and Ludwigsburg, with a fully deliberate use of the ruler and compasses and with a mathematical and to that extent harmonious form in mind, absolute enough to be capable of taking shape not only in one building or group of buildings, but on occasion in complete towns. And in this there is as little true contrast in the attitude to life between the relative immoderacy of the so-called Baroque style, with its almost wildly sweeping and intersecting lines, its exuberant ornamentation, and its human and angel statuary imbued with the whole gamut of the human passions, and the Rococo moderation which tended to revert to a kind of tranquil cheerfulness or cheerful tranquillity, as there is contrast in the attitude to life of the ordinary absolutist and his enlightened counterpart, as there is for that matter between pietism and rationalism. The buildings which are most characteristic of that time are precisely those which represent the transitional period between the two styles, and it is only from them that either can begin to be understood. It is just as irrelevant to condemn the one on the grounds that it is bombastic and overladen as to condemn the other for being stiff and affected, unless we have first appreciated in both the boldness of feeling behind them—feeling which took itself entirely seriously and whose entire striving was therefore for an adequate means of expression. What other age has dared to make architecture of its inmost heart to the extent that this one did? But this was an age which simply had to, for its inmost heart *was* precisely this idea of man as one taking hold of everything about him and subjecting it to his will. It is an idea so big and so ill-starred that we do better, especially when confronted by the art it bodied forth, to see and hear and stay silent, instead of saying the all-too obvious things which might well come to mind.

It must also be granted to eighteenth-century man that he did not, still in accordance with the same absolute will for form, spare himself his own personal outer appearance, either. We have only to think of the fashion of the eighteenth century. There is no need for me here to describe the dress, the coiffure, both for men and for women, the forms of intercourse, sociability, play and dancing. One cannot look too attentively at the portraits of the time, the contemporary illustrations of historical and social life, and also at the caricatures, if one is bent upon finding out what it was exactly that these people who thus adorned and comported themselves were trying to express (unconsciously, and therefore all the more revealingly, as is always the case with fashion). What they were certainly not trying to say was that like the lilies of the field we should not care for our attire. And they were certainly not saying that no man can increase his height by an ell. What they were expressing the whole time, from top to toe in actual fact, was this: that man carries in his soul an image of himself which in comparison with his actual figure is still much more noble, much more graceful and much more perfect, and that he is not at a loss for means to externalize this image and render it visible. No age, perhaps, has made this confession of faith so systematically as man of the eighteenth century. As to its results, they need not concern us here. We need only note the following: when man, as happened at that time, proceeded to take himself (that is to say, his idea of himself) seriously, in the grand manner, without humour, but with a certain logic, all the things emerged which now cause us astonishment in the matter of men's and women's dress and in the manners of the age. Man felt bound to weigh himself down in these respects with all the burdens and discomforts which an absolute will for form apparently demands—but at the same time he was able to achieve all the dignity and charm to which eighteenth-century man did without doubt achieve.

Man in the eighteenth century affirms his attitude to nature and to material objects in his relationship to history, and the world of much more profound contrasts inherent in it. H. Hoffmann is quite right to protest against the habit of describing the time of the Enlightenment as deficient in a sense of history, and to refute it by pointing out what close attention the eighteenth century in particular bestowed upon the near and the distant past, the industry and care with which it pursued researches in these fields. But in one important sense the accusation is true, and not disprovable by a reminder of the historical research done in the eighteenth century, a reminder which far from discrediting the accusation in fact corroborates it. H. Hoffmann says it himself: in that century began that highly problematical affair which we call 'critical study of history'. But what else can this mean but that it was in the eighteenth century that man began axiomatically to credit himself with being superior to the past, and assumed a standpoint in relation to it whence he found it possible to set himself up as a judge over past events according to fixed principles, as well as to describe its deeds and to substantiate history's own report? And the yardstick of these fixed principles, at least as applied by the typical observer of history living at that age, has the inevitable effect of turning that judgment of the past into an extremely radical one. For the yardstick is quite simply the man of the present with his complete trust in his own powers of discernment and judgment, with his feeling for freedom, his desire for intellectual conquest, his urge to form and his supreme moral self-confidence. What historical facts, even, can be true except those which to the man of the age seem psychologically and physiologically probable, or at any rate not improbable? How, in face of such a firm certainty about what was psychologically and physiologically probable and improbable could eighteenth-century man conceive of the existence of historical riddles and secrets? And what else in fact could the past consist of than either of light, in so far as it reveals itself to be a preparation and mount for the ever-better present 'You'll pardon me—it is my great diversion, to steep myself in ages long since past; to see how prudent men did think before us, and how much further since we have advanced'—or simply of darkness—a warning counter-example and as such, if you like, a welcome counter-example—in so far as the past had not yet sensed the right road to the future, or had even actively opposed it. The third thing which this attitude precluded was that the historian should take history seriously as a force outside himself, which had it in its power to contradict him and which spoke to him with authority. One way or another the historian himself said that which he considered history might seriously be allowed to say, and, being his own advocate, he dared to set forth both aspects of what he alleged history to have said, its admonitory and its encouraging aspect.

What was the inevitable effect of this criterion when it was applied to antiquity, to the Middle Ages, and also to the time of the Reformation, and indeed to the immediate past? An answer is to be found in

Gottfried Arnold's *Unparteiische Kirchen-und Ketzerhistorie* (Unbiased History of Churches and Heresies). The author, according to the preface 'wishes most heartily that love might settle my spirits in this work to a sweet harmony and tranquillity, so that all my sentiments might be held as far as is possible in perfect balance and that every requisite of a proper, true historian might be conferred upon me'. It was Arnold's wish to maintain an attitude of detachment towards the view of history held in earlier times, which had been dictated by church dogma, and he was in fact thoroughly successful. It was this which made him all the more certain and unconditional in elevating to the measure of all things his own and his sympathizers' mystically inclined Christian belief, whence he arrived very naturally at the conclusion that the whole history of the Church after the time of the 'first Love', that is, after the end of the first century, was with very few exceptions one single, monstrous decline: 'a hotchpotch of violence and error', as Goethe quite rightly later put it when describing his impressions of the book. It is fundamentally the same evil eye with which not only the Encyclopaedists and Voltaire (in his history of Louis XIV, for instance), but also the German disciples of the Enlightenment later saw and mastered history, the only difference between them being in the distribution of light and shade. And this way of mastering history was also axiomatic in cases where the modern consciousness gave the beholder of history a wider scope than was possible for Arnold or Voltaire, for example. It was employed whenever historians found it fitting to abstract from the past all sorts of exemplary heroic tales; in particular from classical antiquity, preferably for instance, from the history of Sparta, but also from Reformation history. It must be said of this race of historians, those who seemed to dismiss the past either in whole or in part as one whole night of wickedness and folly, as well as those who lavished all their love and praise upon one particular aspect of it, that although as a race they were very learned in historical matters, they were at the same time singularly uninstructed, simply because their modern self-consciousness as such made them basically unteachable. But they were far from imagining themselves impoverished by this attitude, by the abandonment of all attempt at historical objectivity. On the contrary; they felt themselves to be enriched and powerful. It was again the sovereign will for form that looked upon history, as it did upon nature, as just so much raw material; which was therefore not at all 'unhistorical' but simply found only raw material, only light and shade, which obviously were the light and shade of its own deeds and aspirations.

If we remember this we cannot be surprised that the eighteenth century was most emphatically also a century of educational theories. The new educational points of view which distinguished it decisively from the preceding age gradually asserted themselves in this century. All those who were active in this field in the manner of their age: the long line from A. H. Francke on the one hand to J. B. Basedow on the other, were agreed about these ideas. They can be summarized as follows:

1. There was now an ever-growing conviction that education is a business resting upon a possibility over which mankind has been given complete command. It follows that it can and must be made the subject of particular thought. There is now a belief in teaching the teacher, so that it was this age which saw the beginnings of a real literature on the theory of education and the beginnings of a real education for teachers: the first teachers' training colleges.

2. There was now the conviction that the young person can be introduced to actual life through the medium of a comprehensive education. He can be brought to 'true godliness and Christian wisdom' (A. H. Francke). Thus the study of ancient languages and of antiquity in general, which had been the alpha and omega of the teaching of previous times, had now to give place to the study of the mother-tongue, of modern languages and of French in particular, and even more to technical studies including manual and physical training of all kinds—only to be deliberately taken up again in the course of a later development from a completely new point of view—a development similarly characteristic of our own time. This was that the classical writers were, after all, 'the greatest people and the noblest spirits who have ever lived' and from them could be learned criteria for both art and ethics, facility in expression and a host of good maxims which improve both the will and the understanding (Matthias Gesner, 1691-1761). As to what precisely was meant by the 'real life' to which the children were to be introduced; this was a point concerning which there was a divergence of opinion between the educators of the pietistic and those of the enlightened school. They did however agree that this introduction was a matter over which they were quite capable of taking control.

3. There was now also the conviction that a communicable method of correct education exists. Hence—mirroring the two philosophic doctrines that dominated the age—on the one hand the more or less correctly understood Socratic method, that of imparting the desired knowledge by skilfully eliciting it from the children themselves through questioning, and on the other the principle of demonstration and

handicrafts-teaching, were now discovered and made to bear fruit in many ways.

4. The faith of educators in the possibility of teaching was now such that they believed—just as it was believed possible to take man generally as a completely explicable object of study—that they, as adults, have it in their power to see the child as a child, and to understand and treat it as such. Hence the spate of methods and experiments designed to enable the teacher to approach the child in a childlike way carefully suited to the child in its various ages, to bring it to the desired goal by a wise descent to its own thought and feeling, as these were then understood, by all sorts of ingenious punishments and amiably enticing rewards, by disguising the dire process of learning as a merry game, by bringing home to it as unobtrusively as possible, and therefore all the more effectively, the 'moral of the story' both in theory and in practice. Thus the eighteenth century really was, in this sense at least, already the 'century of the child'. This is perhaps one of the most noteworthy manifestations of its absolute will for form: that it so confidently believes that it understands that greatest of mysteries presented to man, the child.

5. People were now so completely convinced that the attempt to educate is both feasible and worth while that they wanted no one to be without its benefits. This is shown by the fact that the state now began to take some interest in schools. The enlightened of the absolute princes, Frederick II and Joseph II chiefly, but their predecessors Frederick William I and Maria Theresa too, included schools in their programmes for the betterment of the state, making them one of their most important points and providing very extensively for them. It was Fénelon (*De l'éducation des filles*) who had for the first time in 1687 pointed out in principle the importance of education for the female sex too, and in 1698 it was A. H. Francke once again who was the first to advance to the founding of a '*Gynaeceum*'. In 1717 Frederick William I introduced compulsory schooling for all in Prussia, and during his reign two thousand new schools came into being. Thus the government school now became an accepted principle. It now came to be regarded as being an essential general part in a person that he can be educated, and therefore that it is every person's duty (a duty which must be imposed if need be) that he should allow himself to be educated.

6. Finally, the sense of conviction concerning aims, possibilities and achievements in this field was so strong that education progressively dared to esteem itself more and more independent of, nay even superior to, the revealed gospel; the school, in fact, felt superior to the Church.

'What's more exalted than the teacher?' At first for a long time humbly, but then with mounting self-assurance, and finally turning the tables and attempting to snatch the highest honour himself, the schoolmaster now steps up beside the parish priest as one who has something of his own, something special—something different and indeed much better —to say and offer to all the world: his immortal prototype, this very J. B. Basedow, who not for nothing looked upon the doctrine of the Holy Trinity as his personal enemy. And if all the other convictions of the age about education are valid then it must in fact be admitted that education is a task in itself. This does then prompt the question whether it might not in fact be the superior task: as opposed to the proclamation of the Gospel, the real and true one of the two, and whether it might not be as well for the Church first to make room for the school next to it, then to regard it with respect, and then to look up to it even more respectfully before finally, conscious of its own superfluity, allowing itself to be completely merged with it, or alternatively itself becoming a school, just one more educational establishment among many others.

The commanding way the age took up the problem of education has its equivalent in the freedom with which it treated the problem of the forming of associations. Let us bear in mind that all the associations that had existed until then might be described as associations formed by necessity, such as the natural communion of marriage and family life, the professional association of the guild and the corporation, and the associations, partly geographical, partly political, of the village, the township and the state. Embracing all the others, and not so much formed as instituted, the community of the Church, and that of the empire too, which found its ultimate sanction in the Church, united in the *Corpus Christianum*, stood guarantor for the necessity and sanctity of all those other associations which had come into being by necessity. And the sole voluntary institution which the Church did actually create, the Catholic men's and women's orders, by virtue of its integration in the Church, as a deliberately sanctioned exception hedged about with every imaginable proviso, could ultimately serve only to prove the rule. Its purport was that while there might well be *ordines* there was in fact no such thing as a *societas*. The fact that the Jesuit order specifically assumed the title *Societas Jesu* and not that of an *ordo*, and showed itself to be a *societas* by its whole form and conduct, was one of the seeds of a course of development which found its full fruition in the eighteenth century. The discovery had been made that association could be created, and indeed that association in its true and really living sense had to be created. The old obligatory institutions, the Church included, now began to lose their influence in a way most peculiarly their own—and who would claim to be able to give the final reasons? Imperceptibly but irresistibly they began to sink in the esteem of ever more numerous groups of people to the point where they came to be looked upon as the simple product of nature and history with which one must of course comply, but which could not be sufficient; to the point where they were regarded as the mere visible sign of community—all too visible, in fact—and for this very reason not worthy to be considered its true expression. Within, beyond and beside the old institutions, it was felt, one must seek to find the proper, true, living, invisible community, and right through them all discover, work and build that proper community. Once again it is the expression of the age's absolute will for form, a will to which all the things we find existing about us are mere material to be moulded by man. The meaning of a *societas*, as distinct from an *ordo*, is *Gesellschaft*, that is to say it is an association of companions who meet by their own free choice, independently of the old institutions, seeming to respect them, but inwardly, in some way and at some point doing quite the reverse— united by some common feeling, and for the achievement of some common aim. This feeling, it was thought, did not pulse, or at any rate only feebly pulsed, in the members of the old institutions, and men no longer expected—or little expected—the old institutions to strive after and achieve that aim, whereas in the new, free associations they were in good heart and full of confidence on both counts. It is now that we hear 'He is a prince—but more, he is man!' in *The Magic Flute*. And it is now that the name 'Brother' becomes a freely conferred title of honour.

What does this mean? It means that an entirely new dividing principle, an entirely new way of distinguishing between the lower and higher orders of men, between those who should be taken seriously and those it is safe to ignore, was now coming into effect whereby the old distinctions became relative. The man who does not belong to the same family, class, state or Church could now become an associate and hence a friend, and hence a brother, as and when he belongs to the sacred circle of common views and common aims; and the man belonging to the same family, class, state, and Church can be reduced to one of the anonymous herd, the ignorant masses, as and when he is not included, but shut out from the new, free society's point of view. We have already seen how significantly the theory of man's right to form free associations had affected his conception of the state, and how, once it had taken effect, the political development which led either to monarchical or to liberal-national absolutism was possible. Or was it rather that absolutism formed the root for the new theory of association? Be that as it may, it *was* absolutism, which expressed itself in the idea that association could be created in the form of a community of feeling and aims, and that this community was the true, real and living one. It was a completely non-political manifestation of absolutism, and indeed deliberately non-political—a belief in the limitless nature of man's capacities, and in this, as it were, personal and private form absolutism experienced in the forming of associations now began in all manner of ways to underpin (or shall we say rather, undermine?) the ramparts of the old social institutions.

Suffice it to say that this new, free form of association now existed, and was to prove itself characteristic of man in the eighteenth century. It established itself at every point within the old institutions and, if the truth be known, set them their limits. It provided at least a temporary refuge against a feeling that the old institutions were inadequate—it was available whenever the outside world became too cold and desolate. But within it one could await better times, and in expectation of a better future do many things in the company of fellow-conspirators, and make many preparations against the day. It was a complete world within the world, in which, in contrast to those living outside, men confronted whatever else might happen, God or destiny or the future —face to face, directly and not indirectly—directly by virtue of the fact that the place for the encounter had been freely chosen, a place which after all was invested with the entire strength of human community.

It was this course of development that gave birth, or rebirth, to a counterpart of the Society of Jesus, secular, but only too similar to it in kind. That counterpart originated from a body scarcely distinguishable from the regular orders, the 'Bauhütten' (the corporation of the builders) of the Middle Ages; the order of Freemasons, all bathed in the splendour of the invisible, and for this very reason, the real and true Church, the veritable Church of mankind. Here long before the revolution, the enlightened of the absolute princes, Frederick the Great at their head, had begun to join with their bourgeois antagonists in the peaceful building of temples. 'The search for truth, a life of virtue, heartfelt love for God and man; let these our watchword be!' the masons' song declaims. And again, in *The Magic Flute*, 'be steadfast, patient and discreet!' is the cry to the adept. And what other comment is there than that contained in the same work: 'Who finds no joy in this our plan, does but demean the name of man!'? But the uniting influence and momentum of the esoteric doctrines imbuing the lodges of the eighteenth century must be construed as greater and more widespread than may appear from such professions of faith, whose purpose was after all to pave the way and dispel the general disquiet. Let us hear what Goethe was already saying on the subject (in his *Symbolum* of 1815):

> The mason's searching
> Is life's whole mirror;
> The aims he strives for
> The perfect seeming
> Of human behaviour.
>
> The times imparting
> Their joy and sorrow
> Are slow to follow,
> But not desisting
> We hasten onward.
>
> In awesome distance
> A veil hangs gleaming;
> Above the beaming
> Soft stars' insistence,
> And tombs are beneath.
>
> Regard them closer,
> And see! they invest
> The heroes' breast
> With stealthy terror
> And solemn feeling.
>
> But beyond are sounding
> The phantom voices,
> The masters' voices:
> Delay not in aiding
> The powers of good!
>
> Here crowns are woven
> In endless silence,
> A gift of abundance
> To garland the chosen!
> We conjure you, hope![1]

This was the heart of the matter. And why should it surprise us. It must have been utterly exhilarating to countless people to know that this *was* in fact the matter, and that it could now be contemplated regardless of state boundaries, church precincts or any class distinctions, in an association which had arisen freely and stood freely; that

[1] Cf. Appendix p. 399.

is to say, in a league of free men, and therefore in a league which was genuinely fraternal. Anyone, however, who sought still stronger forms of communal secrecy or secret community could find what he was looking for by joining with the Rosicrucians, just as anyone who had determined upon a more energetic offensive against the existing powers of Church and state could find an answer to his needs in the society of the Illuminati. If, on the other hand, he desired less mysticism, something a little less potent and inspired by more practical feeling and aims, he could engage in what appealed to him in one of the numerous societies for the furtherance of knowledge and the common good which were springing up. A further point to notice in this connexion is that the old universities now found new rivals as centres of research in the academies instituted in accordance with social theory. Neither must we forget that the eighteenth century was the time which saw the formation of the student associations in the ideological and sociological form which still characterizes them today. 'He who guides the stars in the canopy of the heavens' now had many banners to hold. And of course we must on no account overlook here the pietistic movements and especially the founding of the Moravian brethren. Surely the end of all things—for the first time, at any rate on German soil but with a universality unprecedented even elsewhere, they implemented the idea of a free connexion between all the churches, based on their common 'love of the Saviour'. This notion was the all-absorbing interest of Count Zinzendorf. Especially in the first half of the century, everyone who seriously wished to be a Christian, whether or not he was one of the Moravian brotherhood, felt himself a little at home, not in Wittenberg, not in Geneva, but in the invisible *Philadelphia* which was yet everywhere assuming tangible form. In spite of all the diversity of their forms it is impossible not to recognize the single unifying intention, spirit and conviction underlying all this building of free associations of feeling and aim: the conviction that it is possible to create community. This is the exact parallel to the conviction that it is possible to educate. It is this freely formed community, not that already known and in existence, which is alone in possession of the truth, and therefore of the future—or of the joyful, assured prospect of the future. We might well ask ourselves whether the French Revolution would not have broken out very much sooner, had not these convictions and the numerous bodies they created satisfied for a time so many desires tending towards an absolutist sociology, and in so doing temporarily tied up—or engaged—so many energies in relatively harmless activities.

A quick glance at the field of eighteenth-century language, literature and poetry will show us that it too was subject to the absolutism of the will for form as the phenomenon which did most to shape the picture presented by the life of the time. The decisive event here—we are of course speaking of the time before Goethe—was, I suppose, the all-embracing claim made on behalf of the mother tongue in opposition to the language of antiquity which had dominated the cultural life in the Middle Ages and continued to do so even well into the seventeenth century. It was now the mother tongue which was explored, given literary and poetic form, moulded and developed in all its possibilities. This also started happening at first simply because people had become aware that in this sphere there was an enormous mass of raw material to hand, which was clearly inviting conquest, mastery and the imposition of form. They had become aware of an unknown land in the closest proximity and the fact that it had up to then been untouched tempted a generation of such expansive sensibilities simply by virtue of the law of the *horror vacui*. The wildness and barbaric lack of form of this land now gradually became a source of shame, but its rich possibilities at the hands of those with the impulse to activity seemed to give promise of limitlessly fruitful fields.

It is well known that it was France in the great era of Louis XIV which preceded the other nations in transforming the vernacular with all its possibilities into a classical language. The fact that the measure and model of the classical style which the great French formal masters took as their weapon in the task was none other than that provided by antiquity, is a subject apart. They were in something of a hurry and took up the rules of form where they found them. The inner relationship of the French genius with the Latin genius in particular made this form the choice that seemed by far the most natural and obvious one. And the energy of the highly original and peculiar French will to impose form did ultimately prove strong enough to produce a classicism which, even by the aid of a borrowed instrument, succeeded in emerging as something new and peculiarly French, a structure now in its turn impressive enough to serve as a model for the same development to which the German language was subjected at a somewhat later date.

There are no doubt profound reasons, which this is not the place to discuss, why German literature in the first half of the eighteenth century produced no classical literature but only works imitating classical forms: why it produced no Racine, Corneille or Molière, but only a Johann Christian Gottsched, who in spite of the noteworthy collaboration of his spouse Luise Adelgunde Viktoria, née Kulmus, found it quite impossible to achieve fame as a poet, and was only of note as a professor of the German language. But it was not, as it happened, his sterile subservience to French models which in the new period beginning with Klopstock and Lessing gave rise to the violent reaction against the aims he pursued and the works he wrote. It was, on the contrary, the very thing French classicism, so ingenious in its own way, and the patently uninspired German classical style had in common which made his work significant, and later an object of hatred; the conviction, that the language should and could be mastered, the will to achieve a German 'art of language' (grammar), 'art of speaking' (rhetoric) and 'art of composition' (poetics), as the titles of Gottsched's chief works typically indicated. Gottsched wanted to make Leipzig, of all places, for Germany what Paris was to France: a central forum in questions of good taste relating to German language, literature and poetry. The fact that it only managed to become a 'little Paris', as we may still learn among other things from Goethe's *Faust*, does not, however unfortunate this may have been, seriously affect the issue. The true issue was Gottsched's supreme and all-too supreme confidence in the German artistic will as such; and it was this that first called J. J. Breitinger of Zürich—another professor—and then the entire body of inspired youth, into the lists against him. It was his misfortune even if it was certainly no accident that he was doomed to compromise his cause by an all-too conspicuous personal vanity, which led him to play the dictator in his Paris on the river Pleisse, that he was plunged all-too deeply into the shadow of the Titans who were following after him, and that he was therefore doomed even at the height of his fame, to be transformed into a kind of comic figure. But his widely-ranging endeavours on behalf of the early and earliest language and literature of the Germans can bear witness, in a way that commands a certain respect, to the professorial but sincere earnestness with which he furthered his cause. We have mentioned Gottsched here as the typical exponent of the German classical style, which together with French classicism, provides evidence of the dictatorial manner that eighteenth-century man was bold enough to adopt also in his approach to work in the literary sphere.

Let us now conclude our survey of the external form imparted to the life of the age by a few reflections upon its music. Here we touch upon a region which we have to confess is extraordinarily difficult to comprehend even a little, either historically or in any other kind of thought. It is, however, the fact that, with everything else, this century was musical as well and perhaps above all else; more musical certainly than any age that had gone before and perhaps than any since. And there is something in the way in which it was musical which is so characteristic of the whole spirit of the age, that if we wish to understand this spirit we simply cannot escape making some reference to it. We can study the history of a past age, we can contemplate its architectural and other works of art, its portraits and its dress, and we can read the books it gave us, but we cannot hear the voices of the people then living—and this imposes a tremendous limitation upon our understanding—except as they are transcribed and laid before us in their music in so far as it has been handed down to us. Is not this form of communication perhaps the most intimate we can hope for from a past age? How many extraordinary generalizations and judgments on the eighteenth century would have been quite out of the question if only those who made them had recalled that this was also the century of Bach and Handel, Gluck and Haydn, and had remembered just a few notes from the works of any one of them before once again setting pen to paper with their diffusions on the 'one-sided intellectual civilization' of that age and various other catchwords. For Frederick the Great was not only the victor of the battle of Leuthen or the friend of Voltaire, and not only the intellectual author of the Prussian national code of laws. All this is no doubt very important, but Frederick was also an ardent flute player and we may at least ask whether there should not be intensive historical study with the task of investigating whether he might not have been more truly himself in this than in anything else he did. How intently, nay devotedly, people practised music at this time, and—what may show even more clearly how intensely musical they were—how intently they listened. But in the attempt to see them in this aspect of their nature, we must be careful to concede them their own kind of musicality. This discussion is barred to anyone who is familiar only with the modern world and will therefore brook no argument in taking as his yardstick the lyricism of Beethoven or Schubert who simply *are* part of this completely different modern world; to anyone whose ideas in assessing J. S. Bach are like those of Richard Wagner: 'Bach is like the sphinx. The noble head struggling forth from the periwig resembles the human face in its first emergence from the animal body.' On the other hand it is barred too to anyone who thinks Bach should be revered as a true saint of Protestantism, and immediately imagines that he hears in the Passions and Cantatas a complete expression of Luther's theology, and then again to anyone who applies to him the saying, in itself unanswerable, that like all great music Bach's is truly human and therefore timeless. It is moreover debatable whether a true modern feeling for music, would treat the true musicality of a former age in this way. Would it not rather seek to discover and honour its timelessness within and not outside the very qualities which made it a part of its age?

If we hold this to be the true way then the problems which present themselves are such that we can only briefly touch upon them. I would consider it suitable to take as our starting point the fact that all the minor musicians of the eighteenth century *and* the great ones, and perhaps especially the great ones, were not either in their own sight or in that of their contemporaries what we today describe as artists or composers, but quite simply craftsmen of the profession concerned with honouring God and delighting the heart of man: a profession which primarily consisted in the mastery of one or of several musical instruments. And the significant fact we must realize is that the musician of the eighteenth century preferred these instruments to be the piano or its predecessors current at that time, and the organ; the instruments, which were polyphonic in intention. Art was in those days still most definitely the product of technical ability. Art was proficiency. It was this proficiency which first made Bach famous, and kept him famous right up to the time when, as 'old Bach' he was the object of Frederick the Great's admiration. It was this proficiency which made the young Mozart the wonder of Europe. But at that time the art of composing was looked upon by great and small merely as a means of applying, of widening and deepening the scope of the art of professional musicianship, as a means of proving the perfected skill which, in this as in all things, reveals the master. Not sensibility, not experience, not mystique and not Protestantism, but art as a skill, as proficiency in the manipulation of the most exacting rules—not without 'invention', certainly, as it was then called, but invention continually inventing a new necessity, invention in the expression not so much of what the composer himself found personally stimulating, but rather of general laws—this was needed to write a fugue. And the quality which distinguished a good fugue from a bad one in composition and performance was, in the opinion of no less a man than Bach himself, the art which was revealed in the craftsman's skill. The beautiful, so to speak, had to follow as a matter of course (unsought and not to be sought in the abstract) from that which was properly done from the craftsman's point of view. Inspiration on the composer's part was also essential. What emerged would certainly be 'beautiful' too. But an informed admirer like Frederick the Great would admire only the beauty of the skill and style which the work causes to become audible, and not, specifically not, the beauty of the piece in itself. The steadfast conviction that art, understood in this way, would of itself result in the glory of God and the delight of the soul was the first quality peculiar to the typical music of the time.

But what was the mastery which these musicians sought and practised? I should say that it consisted of the sovereign attitude which they had first of all towards the instrument producing the sounds and then to the abundance of possibilities inherent in these sounds. It was the full and joyous awareness of this sovereignty which made them prefer the polyphonic instruments and polyphonic composition. It was for them a question of humanizing, so to speak, the rough amorphous mass of possible sounds—of forcing, imposing and stamping upon it not any individual style as such, but rather the law known to each individual human being, the order of sounds which he 'invents', i.e. finds already within himself as an objectively valid order—until there is no longer merely sound, but sound existing as musical tone. Further, it was for them a question of evolving harmony from the confused mass of possible combinations of sounds and, from the equally confused mass of possible sequences of sounds, something that was henceforth to be a singing cosmos, put forth by man and penetrating space. The man who can do that, who knows the law involved in doing it, and also knows how to handle them in spite of their deep secrecy and bewildering diversity, is a *maestro*. Bach did not consider himself a genius, nor did his contemporaries, as is well known, treat him as one. But both he and they were united in the awareness that he was a master of his art in the sense we have just described, and it was this which they appreciated in him. Making music means subjecting the sound to the laws. That is the second peculiarity of the music of the time: the straightforward way its practitioners believed as a matter of course in the existence of these laws, in the possibility of their being recognized and applied; and the absolutely impartial way they applied them.

We can then go on to ask in what way we can understand this way of making music as serving the glory of God and the delight of the soul in the spirit of the age, and what precisely we should take to be its whole aim and extent? My answer would be that the whole aim and extent of this music was really immaculate playing, not in spite of, but because of the virtuosity expected both in the art of composition and the art of execution. This cannot be said in the same way of the music of any other century. Once this mastery of the world of sound had been achieved, eighteenth-century music-making, with its background of exacting labour, seemed to assume a form which enabled it to attain in an even more unqualified way a totally superior and at the same time totally disinterested ability to deal with the possibilities of that world. *Res severa verum gaudium!* It was only on the basis of this craftsman's mastery of the art of transforming the world of sounds into music that the game of making music could be played. But on the basis of this transformation and re-creation it could be played with assurance and in accordance with the laws of necessity. And it was this playing which was looked upon as the be-all and end-all of the entire process. Here and only here the beauty of the music as such was accorded any place. For its beauty consisted in the freedom founded upon subjection to the law, the freedom upon which we hear the musician embark. It was Goethe who said perhaps the profoundest thing it is possible to say about Bach's music: 'As if the eternal harmony were discoursing with itself, as might perhaps have happened in the bosom of the Lord just before the Creation; so I was moved inwardly and felt that I no longer needed ears, nor eyes the least of all, nor any other senses.' Let the words: 'just *before* the Creation' be noted. There is as we know a passage in the Bible according to which something like a conversation of the eternal harmony with itself takes place, just before the Creation, with a similar reference to playing, i.e. Prov. 8.27-31: 'When he prepared the heavens, I was there: when he set a compass upon the face of the depth: when he established the clouds above: when he strengthened the fountains of the deep: when he gave to the sea his decree, that the waters should not pass his commandment: when he appointed the foundations of the earth: then was I by him, as a master workman: and had delight continually, playing always before him; playing in the habitable part of his earth; and my delights were with the sons of men.' Would it not be the revelation of a supreme will for form, a will for form manifesting perhaps only in this sphere its utmost absolutism, if the music of the eighteenth century sought to emulate the wisdom even of the Creator in its results and in the abandonment and superiority which cause us to forget all the craftsmanship behind it? Be that as it may, all earlier music is still too much involved in the struggle to subdue the raw material of musical sound, and it must be said that the later music, from Beethoven onwards, desired and loved the world of sound too little for its own sake, to be capable of looking upon it in the same unequivocal way as a game. The music of the eighteenth century, the music of absolutism, plays, and for this reason it is in a peculiar way beautiful and that not only in its great exponents but in its minor ones too. Something of the glow of freedom which is peculiar to this age in this particular sphere rests upon all who come to our mind, be they German, Italian or French.

There is something else in the realm of music which is still greater, or at any rate more eloquent than this freedom. It makes its appearance whenever the riddle of human existence appears over against full musical freedom; for it is impossible to explore and resolve this riddle completely by any earthly play. When this happens the play of the sounds which have become entirely transformed into musical tone, which have been quite humanized, breaks like the sea against a rocky shore. It is still the sea, not the infinite sea, which after all only seems infinite, but the sea bounded, as it truly is. If my view—or hearing—of the matter is correct, this cannot be said either of Bach or Handel, or of Gluck or Haydn. As musicians they were naïve children of their century. Their music is like the sea at a point where no shore is in sight. There was one musician who had all the things which distinguished the musicians of the eighteenth century from all those who had gone before and from all those who came after, but who had in addition something entirely personal to himself: the sadness or horror inherent in the knowledge of the border before which absolutist man, even and particularly when cutting his finest figure, stands in blissful unawareness. Like his Don Giovanni, he heard the footfall of the visitor of stone. But, also like Don Giovanni, he did not allow himself to be betrayed into simply forgetting to go on playing in the stony visitor's presence. He still fully belonged to the eighteenth century and was nevertheless already one of the men of the time of transition of whom it will be our chief task to speak in this survey of the antecedents to our story proper. I am referring to Wolfgang Amadeus Mozart.

Before we proceed, almost at once, to the subject of our next chapter we shall discuss the form of the inner life of eighteenth-century man. I mean the thing which is regularly recurrent in the make-up of the great number of individuals of that time who are known to us, and which is therefore characteristic in the attitude they ultimately seem to adopt towards themselves, the world, and the Deity. I do not think we shall be guilty of being too schematic if we surmise that such a common denominator, let us say a psychological common denominators, exists in visible and comprehensible form in every epoch of human events that is recognizable as a unity, such as the eighteenth century, and to which the existence of all those who shared in such a time can in some sense ultimately be reduced, in spite of the abundance of variety and contradiction that may exist. It is an inner analogue to the form of their outward life. With both of them together we can find no actual explanation, certainly, but an instructive light upon the historical experiences (of which we have spoken in, the first half of our chapter) of man at this time. Let us first try to state in simple terms what there is still left to see:

1. All the people who are truly representative of the eighteenth century have a naïvely strong conviction that their self-awareness as human beings is superior to the totality of those things which differ from it, which are in some way outside it. They know that the things outside can certainly be got at in some way by means of human apprehension, willing and feeling. Their relation to them is a free one and they, the men, are the masters. It was not for nothing that one of the favourite figures in the literature of the time was Robinson Crusoe, the man thrown completely upon his own resources, who in spite of this and for this very reason was able to take care of himself so triumphantly.

2. Corresponding to this subjective conviction there is the objective one, that this outside world of things is in itself suited and even planned, and appointed—in a manner which cannot be sufficiently wondered at —to become the object and scene of this expansion of human self-awareness. 'The world is good' means it is good as the object and scene of the deeds of men.

3. In view of this admirable concordance between the inner and the outer world the man of the eighteenth century believed (with few exceptions) in a God who is common lord of both of them, but who of course stands nearer to man and the human world. God is the quintessence, the perfection, unapproached and unapproachable, of that wisdom and goodness with which man is confident enough to approach the world, and which clearly meets him in the world. God is the highest *motive*—as regards the degree of reasonableness which man and the world can produce, for what is possible in the advancement of knowledge, the extension of the sphere of the will and a deepening of the feelings on man's part, and further revelations on the part of the universe. And at the same time God is the highest *quietive* in respect to the effective limits of human self-consciousness which are to be conceded: these limits are as much a part of it in itself as imposed by the mysteries of the universe which are as yet unsolved or might prove altogether insoluble.

4. Man knows that he is linked with, and ultimately of the same substance as, the God significant for him in this double function. God is spirit, man is spirit too. God is mighty and so is man. God is wise and benevolent, and so is man. But he is all these things, of course, infinitely less perfect than God. Man's way of being these things is confused and

fragmentary, but it *is* the same way. And hence that which outside in the world man finds already imbued with reason, or makes reasonable by the exercise of his will, is also, in all its imperfection, of one substance with God.

5. The conviction that God exists thus justified and ensured the conviction that human self-awareness is superior both in the valiant enthusiasm which is necessary to it and in its equally necessary humble acquiescence. This conviction concerning man rests firmly on the conviction about God. The latter, it is true, does not in itself rest firmly upon anything, and it must for this reason from time to time be reaffirmed, if only for the sake of the other conviction. The conviction that God exists and holds sway must from time to time be justified and guaranteed anew. How is this to be done? The proof will be conveyed by a renewed confirmation of the existence of this wonderful concordance between man and the world he inhabits. It is by this means that man will once again be fired with a belief in God, and it is this renewed confirmation which must serve as instrument of the theodicy.

6. The theodicy—that is, the renewed confirmation of this concordance, which is necessary for the sake of the anthropodicy—can indeed also be established theoretically, but the decisive factor will always be that man actually experiences it. But he experiences it in taking up the normal position which he must take up in relation to the world at large, i.e. in acting virtuously. For he can act thus, and in doing so he experiences and apprehends this concordance and in it God, and in God the necessary motive and quietive governing his own mode of existence. The theoretical theodicy is only a paraphrasing of this practical one.

7. But what is meant by acting virtuously? Fulfilling the will of God? Certainly, but what is the will of God that must be fulfilled? Clearly a correct understanding of ourselves and a correct understanding of the world is bound to tell us what virtuous conduct is, as surely as both the world and we ourselves are sprung from God. The correct understanding, will, however, be the natural way of understanding, that is to say, the understanding of ourselves and of the world in their quality as sprung from God. We must therefore allow Nature (and this is within our power) to tell us what is good. We need only allow ourselves to be told by subjective reason, as the elemental voice within every man, and by objective reason, as the elemental voice speaking to every man. For the right understanding of these voices we have only, if at all—for they are assuredly plain to us—to talk of them or alternatively be instructed about them in order to realize that we are quite able to remember what they say. He who hears the voice of reason and

obeys it is acting virtuously and thus finds the theodicy he was seeking and together with it the anthropodicy he was more truly seeking.

But has not man in fact asked himself and himself given the answer he apparently really wished to hear from some other source? This is the question of which, thus expressed, man in the eighteenth century was not aware. This was the absolutism also inherent in his inner attitude to life; he assumed it to be self-evident that in taking himself to account, and himself answering the account, and then acting in obedience to it he was also showing the existence of God, justifying and guaranteeing anew his relationship with God and thereby affirming that his own existence was possible. He believed—even in this inmost place we find him a prey to a strange vicious circle—that by virtue of the reality of his own existence he could vouch for God and in so doing for the possible existence of God. This may have been the secret of his inward attitude in outline.

We can now call to mind a historical connexion. The eighteenth century was without doubt a revival (a very peculiar one, admittedly) of the sixteenth-century Renaissance, or, if you would rather, a recrudescence of that Renaissance. The nature of this Renaissance is however explained by the idea of humanism, the latter to be understood in its widest sense. And the idea of humanism was that the perfect life consisted in the complete autarchy of rational man in a rational world on the basis of the existence and dominion of a Deity guaranteeing this association and thus too man's complete autarchy. It was transplanted from antiquity into the soil of Northern Europe in the late middle ages and became the ideal of England, France and Germany: from antiquity—we should say, from late antiquity, and more precisely still, from that spiritual world which had found its philosophical exponents in the schools—which were in conflict and yet only too united —of the so-called Stoics and the so-called Epicureans. This humanism had been thrust into the background at first by the Reformation and the upheavals which followed it, but it had always remained alive, especially in England. And in Germany too it had only, so to speak, hibernated. For it was a fact which was bound to have some effect eventually, so that—only too faithfully in accordance with the instructions of Melanchthon himself—a whole series of generations of future theologians, philosophers, lawyers, scientists and statesmen and other educated men had been fed at the most impressionable age on Cicero and Plutarch, and then again on Plutarch and Cicero, *ad infinitum*. This seed was now sprouting. There are no doubt deeper reasons why it chose this particular time to sprout, but there is no disputing the fact that the inner attitude to life of the eighteenth century, reduced to its simplest formula, ultimately consisted only of the fact that Cicero and Plutarch were now taken seriously. The attitude of mind of eighteenth-century man makes it quite clear that the man, the citizen, the hero, the sage, the virtuous and the pious man he held before his mind's eye as his model and his measure, as the frame into which he set his own picture, was the man of late pre-Christian or extra-Christian antiquity of quite a definite stamp: the Stoic with a dash and sometimes with a lot more than just a dash of Epicurianism in his make-up. If it is to make sense, the title 'the philosophical century' which has been applied to the eighteenth century can only mean that at this time there were hundreds and thousands of people everywhere to whom philosophy was what it had been to countless numbers of people in the time of the emperors of Rome, namely a practical teaching of life, nay more: a whole attitude to life based on this complete authority of rational man in a rational world with a religious background. In the 'philosopher of Sans Souci' this historical connexion, his place in philosophy somewhere in the middle between Zeno and Epicurus, is quite plain for all to see. But it is also possible to recognize immediately a successor to Seneca and Epictetus in a man as devout and pious in his way as Gellert. And the young Goethe was still firmly rooted in this same soil, and on his own confession started from there for the rest of his way. And strangely enough it continually reappears, either in hidden or in patent form, in the utterances of many a pietist.

The purest form to which this new humanism rose already is in the early eighteenth century—its transfigured form, so to speak—was embodied in the personality and philosophy of Gottfried Wilhelm Leibnitz. This is not the place even to attempt to represent and assess it. Throughout the outline I have just given, I have continually had the thought of this man in mind. It is the thought of a man who was at the same time one of the most typical and one of the most individual men of his age. His life's work represents as in a microcosm all the tendencies of his time, showing how numerous and yet at the same time how similar they were. If we prefer to put it another way, he was in a great manner and most comprehensively what nearly all his contemporaries were capable of being only in a small way and in particular. He was philosopher, theologian, lawyer, politician, courtier, mathematician, naturalist, historian and linguist in one, and was fairly well possessed of the same detailed knowledge, and achieved the same success, in all of them. At one moment he was planning to lay before Louis XIV the Napoleonic idea of a conquest of Egypt, the so-called *consilium Aegyptiacum*; and at another conducting a violent political pamphlet war in the defence of the German emperor and empire against this very same king. At one moment he invented a calculating machine and at another he was at least the co-inventor of the modern infinitesimal calculus. For years he was concerned with the problem of whether it would not be better to drive the pumps in the Hanoverian mines in the Harz Mountains by windmills instead of with water. He then wrote a history of the Guelphs based on the widest possible research into the historical sources. At one moment he formed a plan for the conversion of the heathen and at another he conceived one, and brought about negotiations based upon it, for the reunion of the Catholic and Protestant Churches, or at least of the Lutheran and Reformed Churches. At one moment he was able to write a pre-history of the Earth, and at the next to found, together with many others, the Prussian Academy of the Sciences which is still in existence today. As a most genuine philosopher of the age, he never presented his philosophical teaching in the form of a system, but only in fragments of information quickly and surely set down while actually at grips with one or other of his contemporaries or, as with his theodicy, at the personal wish of a woman of enquiring mind, Queen Sophia Charlotte of Prussia. But it was in this philosophical teaching that, in pursuing lines of thought which were highly original and endowed with a splendour all of their own he at the same time most perfectly revealed the ideal of the inner attitude to life which prevailed in his time. Or are we mistaken in thinking that we can recognize eighteenth-century man in Leibnitz' teaching of the monad, for instance? This simple and utterly individual, indeed unique spiritual substance is the fountain-head of all reality. The utterly self-sufficient monad is an emanation, an image, a mirror of God himself and is therefore nowhere limited by things outside it, but only in its own being; which has no windows, and changes only by its inner principle, its own most peculiar striving; which is always the best it is possible for it to be, and which can therefore transform itself by the tendency of its own most peculiar nature; but it cannot be destroyed, cannot perish, and is immortal like God himself who created it? And do we not meet again that wonderful concordance of man with the world surrounding him when we hear from Leibnitz that between the monads themselves, but also between the monads and the bodies together with which they are effected, there exists a pre-established harmony (*harmonie préétablie*)? That there is a pre-established harmony between body and soul, between form and extension, between the purposive and effective cause, between the dynamic and the mathematical principle, between *vérités de raison* and *vérités de fait*, between chance and necessity, between the sphere of wisdom and the sphere of energy, and between grace and nature? That this is like the harmony between two synchronized clocks constructed in the most artificial manner imaginable for this very purpose; that therefore the relationship of the monads to one another and to the physical world is a piece of work worthy of God, and of God alone? Do we not meet God again, God who guarantees and justifies that concordance and therefore man in the teaching that it is in fact God who is the creator of this best of all possible worlds as a whole, but that he allows each monad to be the best it possibly can and should be, whose world is the best possible one because it is the most suited to the building of his kingdom? Surely this kingdom is the kingdom of the spirit, and that means of the spirits of which each individual one is summoned to be, after his fashion in his particular place, the whole, and the king of this whole? And is not the converse question which inevitably arises here, namely the question concerning the truth of the existence and dominion of God, who vouches for the whole and for the single parts in the whole, answered by way of referring man to himself? Do we not find a theodicy here which decisively refers man to himself? I mean, a converse question and a theodicy in the form of the direct call to man to accept both freely and humbly his individuality and the position it occupies in the plan of the whole, to fill this position as if only God and the soul existed (the soul willed by God precisely in its self-determination and autonomy), and thus to discover that the physical and the moral evil in the world which he imagines to be actively opposed to him contain in truth nothing positive, but are, so to speak, only a shadow fleeing before the light; an inevitable result of the term of life imposed upon all things which are not God, but as such a determining factor also for the harmony of the whole which God created? And may we not ask, to return to the historical connexion, whether all this does not represent Stoicism in its most sublime form, in a form more sublime than ever existed in ancient Greece and Rome; a Stoicism which is a triumph of humanism, which can itself find the answer to every question and seems not to know of a question which might be posed to it? The shape which Christianity was bound to take in this world, which spiritually perhaps found its liveliest and most eloquent embodiment in Leibnitz, we shall have to discuss.

II

ROUSSEAU

WITH Jean-Jacques Rousseau, in the middle of the eighteenth century, the new age begins which we call the age of Goethe, the age which presented Protestant theology after Schleiermacher with the problem with which it chose to concern itself, and which also largely supplied the answer it thought fit to give. The new age in the middle of the eighteenth century! There are two things implied here from which follow significant principles which must be borne in mind in interpreting Rousseau. Not to understand him as a child of his century, who for all his individuality could not help but participate very energetically— after his own fashion—in its general and characteristic trends, would be to understand him falsely. But we would be understanding him even less if we failed to realize that it was precisely as a child of his century that he fought, passionately and radically, against its most typical tendencies, and consummated a completely different new movement in opposition to them. We must be so careful in assessing him because as an event he contains a paradox. He was not merely incidentally a man of the eighteenth century. He was one very definitely, in a way which made him both bolder and more consistent than almost all those about him, and it was precisely in this way that he contradicted and rose above eighteenth-century man and, on the other hand, he contradicted and rose above eighteenth-century man in no other way than this that it was in Rousseau himself that eighteenth-century man achieved fulfilment. There are similar things which we shall have to say later of Lessing and Kant. They must be stated with particular emphasis in the case of Rousseau because as a historical figure he is attacked much more from both sides; and indeed he is much more open to attack.

It is very easy to see Rousseau almost involuntarily from the standpoint and according to the standards of his own age. For this age lives on in us, and Rousseau contradicted it so flatly that it is still possible for us simply to take his contemporaries' idea of him and assessment of him for our own. And what then remains but Rousseau the dreamer, Rousseau the idler, the subjectivist, the barren critic of civilization, the author of a voluminous treatise on education who consigned his five illegitimate children to the Foundlings' Home without ever seeing or wishing to see them again, the author of the *Contrat Social* who had not the faintest notion of how to fit himself to be a citizen or a member of any society and who even in private life was quite incapable of keeping on good terms for any length of time with anyone, however well-intentioned towards him he might be? Anyone who is inclined to dismiss Rousseau lightly for these and other similar obvious reasons, for these moral reasons, let us say, is in a position to claim that he has indeed understood the eighteenth century perfectly. But he has completely failed to understand Rousseau. For it was just in this way that all his typical contemporaries understood him; the only thing they did not understand was that Rousseau was still ultimately and at the deepest level at one with them in—and in spite of—this deviation of his from all they held most holy, and for which they condemned him. He was in fact at one with them as the man in whom all they held most holy was given a future; he had experienced their inmost feelings, the spirit of the old time in a completely new way had reproduced it in a new form and was proclaiming it in a new language; he was the man in whose deviation the time should have been able to recognize, for all its astonishing nature, the embodiment of its own hopes. He was recognized as such in and in spite of his deviation by those of his contemporaries who were not merely typical, but who as contemporaries also bore within them the restlessness of a coming era. In and in spite of his deviation they recognized him as the best exponent of their age.

On the other hand it is very easy to assess Rousseau from the standpoint and according to the standards of our own time, for instance, in so far as our time now in many ways presents a complete contrast to the eighteenth century. For Rousseau was so completely a man of the eighteenth century! What is easier for us than to see in his teaching that human nature was fundamentally good, the height and apotheosis of the Pelagian humanism which was triumphant in the eighteenth century; in the educational teaching of his *Emile*, which ultimately consisted simply in liberating the child in the right way and was the last word of that optimism in educational theory which distinguished that century before all others; and in his teaching of the social contract, above all the individualism and rationalism which knew of no history, i.e. boldly wished to make history solely and alone and according to which there was nothing given, no destiny, and hence no inequality, and no authority because in the last resort there exists neither sin nor grace? What is easier than to dismiss Rousseau on the grounds that we have dismissed the ideals of the French Revolution, of which, as we well know, he was thought to be the chief expounder? What is easier than to regard him as the really classic example of absolutist man, who belongs for us to the past, to the eighteenth-century past? But if we did this we would only show that while we might have understood ourselves we had once again completely failed to understand Rousseau. For we would be overlooking the fact that Rousseau's humanism had the significance of a revolutionary attack upon that which had been esteemed and cultivated as humanism since the Renaissance; that the man's final dislike, which again and again rises to the surface, was reserved for precisely the spirit of his time which was incorporated in the philosophy of men like Voltaire, Diderot, d'Alembert and Hume; that both his political and educational theories were not intended to be a continuation of, but a radical challenge to the political and educational theories of his time and were indeed understood in this sense; that there is something lyrical behind his theories of politics and education, and at the back of this an attitude to life and a feeling for life which surely have their place in the line of development leading from Louis XIV to the French Revolution only in so far as they represent a breakthrough, or an attempt, at least, to break through it. While Rousseau had the same aims as those who followed this line of development he was also developing in quite another direction. From that position he then actually rejected the aims of the line of development from Louis XIV to the French Revolution. He is the first of those men of whom it must be said that the nature of eighteenth-century man, which they did not completely discard, which indeed they perhaps brought to the point where it could be truly honoured, had been reduced in them to nothing but a loose outer garment. Anyone who embarks upon an attack upon Rousseau's individualism and rationalism must realize that this involves attacking all these men, including Hegel and Goethe. A criticism of Rousseau from this point of view which was not on principle also relevant to Hegel and Goethe could hardly touch Rousseau either. If he was an individualist and a rationalist then he was these things in exactly the same sense as they were and it was not the eighteenth-century sense. Rousseau was already a man of the new era, in eighteenth-century garb.

I can make plain the paradoxical conjunction of both these ages in Rousseau by means of an example which should be all the more convincing because it is fairly far removed from the subject of our chief question, the theological problem, and from the other favourite fields of those who engage in research into Rousseau. Rousseau once wrote the following on the nature of genius in music: 'Do not, young artist, ask what genius is! If you have it then you will sense what it is within yourself. And if you have not genius you will never understand it. Musical genius subjects the whole universe to its art. It paints in harmonious sounds all the pictures that it sees. It makes even silence eloquent. It conveys ideas in the form of feeling, feeling by means of accent. And in giving expression to passions it awakens them in the depths of the heart. Through it desire itself acquires new charms; the sadness it awakens calls forth cries of anguish. It burns unceasingly yet never consumes itself. It can burningly express the frost and ice; even in depicting the horrors of death it sustains within its soul that sense of life which never forsakes it, and communicates it to the hearts which are capable of feeling it. But alas! it can say nothing to those who have not its seed within them, and its wonders do little to impress those who cannot emulate them. You want to know whether some spark of this consuming fire glows within you? Hasten then, fly, to Naples and hear the masterpieces of Leo, Durante, Jommelli and Pergolesi. If your eyes fill with tears, if you feel your heart violently beat, if you are shaken by sobs and breathless with delight, then find yourself a poet and set to work; his genius will fire yours and you will create by his example: that is what the genius does, and soon other eyes will pay you the tribute of the tears the masters have caused yours to shed. But if the charms of this great art leave you unmoved, if you feel no ecstasy nor delight, if you find merely beautiful that which should move you to the depths of your being, how dare you ask the meaning of genius? The sacred name should not so much as pass your lips, low creature that you are. What possible concern of yours to know it? You would be incapable of feeling it: confine yourself to—French music.' The passage is to be found in Rousseau's *Dictionnaire de musique*, which he published in 1764, a book of instructive articles under the headings of the technical and scientific musical terms. For Rousseau's profession, in so far as he can be said to have had one in regard to society, might best be described as that of musician, in the craftsmanlike meaning of the word which was typical of the eighteenth century. He acquired a certain significance in the history of French opera through his *Le Devin du Village*, which was actually given a performance before Louis XV in 1752. His chief occupation as a musician, outwardly at least, was quite simply that of copying scores, and it was thus that he earned or supplemented his living during whole periods of his life. As a young man he invented a new musical orthography and urged its acceptance publicly, albeit in vain. And we know that until he was well advanced in years he was fond of singing for his own amusement, accompanying himself on the spinet. And then there was the technical and scientific aspect of the matter which the dictionary presents. So far nothing in Rousseau's musicality exceeds the limits which we have come to know were characteristic in this field of the old time. But then suddenly in the middle of this dictionary we find this article *Génie s.m.* (substantive masculine!), of which there is only one thing to be said: this is not the eighteenth century any more, it is not the genius of Bach nor the genius of Haydn (quite apart from the fact that a book of instruction in accordance with their way of making music could scarcely have contained an article on 'genius' at all), it is not Mozart either, but it *is* unmistakably Beethoven, Schubert and Mendelssohn, line for line. Music which holds the universe in thrall, which reflects ideas in the form of feeling, which aims at expressing and awakening the passions, which as feeling for life addresses itself in a mysterious way to the feeling for life, music which does not wish to be understood as beautiful, but as enchanting and only in a delirium, music which according to whether it moves one or not, reveals a kind of predestination to blessedness or damnation—all that might very well be found in Schleiermacher's *Address on Religion,* but not in any book previous to the age of Goethe, nor in any heart or head either. Anyone who read this article in those days was immediately called upon in the field of music to decide whether to receive the new message, that art is prophetic of feeling, as something rich with new promise or as something in the nature of a declaration of war; and whether he should welcome or hate it accordingly. Anyone who found himself in a position to agree perfectly with Rousseau must, like him, have belonged to both the old and to the new age.

I should like now to give a short account of Rousseau's life, as some knowledge of it is indispensable if we are to understand his work and its significance. Jean-Jacques Rousseau was born the son of a clock-maker in Geneva on 28th June 1712. His early education was pietistic in spirit. The first things he read were Plutarch and the heroic novels of the seventeenth century. At the age of sixteen he ran away from the engraver to whom he had been apprenticed and also abandoned his native city. He became a Roman Catholic in Turin in order to live, but not without having gained his knowledge of the Roman Catholic Church through people who made a great impression upon him; and shortly afterwards he came under the influence of Françoise Louise de Warens, née de la Tour, from the Canton of Vaud. She was twelve years older than he, and influenced him over a long period, and to a certain extent throughout his whole life. Like him rooted in Pietism, and like him a convert, she seems to have presented an extraordinary mixture of theoretical free-thought and practical devotion—she fled across the lake from Vevey taking with her—Bayle's *Dictionnaire*! She also combined the highest degree of spirituality and deep moral feeling with an almost incomprehensible thoughtlessness in erotic matters— in any case, an amazing personality. In the last lines which Rousseau ever set on paper, shortly before his death, he still thought of her as *la meilleure des femmes* and dedicated moving words to her memory. From 1728 to 1741 he kept abandoning all sorts of positions (as house-servant, music teacher, private tutor and government employee) in order to return to her. The last three years formed the climax of this period. He spent them with Madame de Warens on her estate, Les Charmettes, near Chambéry. It was these years also which seem to have been most truly those of his education, using the word in its narrower sense. It was at this time and at this time only that he was fully himself, as he puts it in that last description of his association with Madame de Warens: doing in perfect freedom only those things which he enjoyed doing, in the quiet of solitude, in the close proximity to nature afforded by country life, and in the presence and possession of a woman after his own heart. *J'ai joui d'un siècle de vie*.[1] The year 1741 saw the end of this idyll. Rousseau moved to Paris. He made the acquaintance and even won the friendship of several of the men who were most influential in the intellectual life of Paris at that time: Voltaire, Diderot, Grimm, Holbach and Buffon. It was during these years that he was probably in closest touch with the spirit of the age. But this close association did not last. A stay in Venice as secretary to the French Ambassador there ended unhappily. The year 1745 saw the beginning of his association with Thérèse Le Vasseur, which forms a remarkable parallel to that between Goethe and Christiane Vulpius, in particular also in this respect that he also raised it later to the status of a legitimate marriage. The decisive turning-point in Rousseau's life was in fact the year of Goethe's birth, 1749.

It was in that year that the Dijon academy set the question for a prize dissertation: 'Has the advance of the sciences and the arts helped to destroy or to purify moral standards?' Rousseau later described the effect the question alone had upon him in a style which bears all the hall-marks of an account of a religious conversion: he

---

[1] *Rêveries du promeneur solitaire, Xme. promenade. Œuvres complètes de J.-J. Rousseau,* Basle 1793-95, Vol. 20, p. 341.

read the announcement of the question for a prize competition in a newspaper while he was on the way to visit his friend Diderot, who was at that time in prison in Vincennes. 'If ever anything resembled a sudden inspiration it was the emotion which arose in me as I read this: all at once my mind seemed dazzled by a thousand lights, a throng of fertile ideas presented themselves there at the same instant with a force and a confusion which plunged me into a state of inexpressible excitement; my head swam with a dizziness akin to drunkenness. I was oppressed by the violence of my beating heart and by a swelling of my breast; being unable to draw breath any more while walking, I threw myself down beneath one of the trees beside the avenue, and lay there for half an hour so agitated that on picking myself up again I found my whole shirt-front wet with the tears I had not even noticed shedding.'[1] Diderot has given us a slightly different account of the event, maintaining not only that he made Rousseau acquainted with the question which had been set, but that he also suggested the answer which Rousseau afterwards gave. But however it came about it was not in Diderot's life that the question was seized upon and the answer provided, but in Rousseau's. He himself said of his answer that it gave the lie to everything which was an object of wonder to his age and that he was therefore prepared for its universal rejection. The answer ran: the sciences and the arts have always been harmful to morality because they have always decomposed and destroyed the natural virtue of the human heart, and also the virtues of the good citizen which spring from it. Rousseau's expectations were at first disappointed. Or rather: the expected disavowal of the man who dared to outrage his own time in such a manner, then, as at all times, first took the form of admiration and enthusiastic applause of the novelty of the thing he had produced, and of the brilliance with which, like all those who have something really new to say, he had been able to say it. The dissertation received the prize in 1750 and its author was famous at a blow, although, or perhaps directly because, his work found no lack of distinguished opponents. But he nevertheless demonstrated that he took his own thesis seriously by giving up the bourgeois employment in which he was then engaged in order henceforth to procure by copying scores both the inner peace and the economic freedom necessary to further reflection and literary production, and signalizing his entrance upon a monk-like existence in his outward appearance too, by laying aside the usual sword, white stockings and wig, and above all his watch—he could not rejoice

[1] *Letters to Malesherbes*, 12. I. 1762, Basle edition, Vol. 16, p. 245.

enough later in the liberating effect upon his soul which just this act had brought him—and assuming a 'good coarse, coat of cloth'. Later, for reasons of health, or rather of illness, he exchanged this garment for the dress of an Armenian, and it was thus clad that he busied the tongues and eyes of his contemporaries and has lived on in history. 'A great revolution took place within me, a different moral world revealed itself to my gaze, and caused me to see the absurdity of human prejudice.'[1] Solitude now became a necessity of life for him which could not be denied, because it was the quintessence of that which had been revealed to him as the one necessary thing, and which he now believed he should announce to his time at large. For solitude means a retreat into the original, simple and natural form of human existence in obedience to the dictates of the heart, such as he himself had come blissfully and unforgettably to know, in approximation at least, in Madame de Warens' orchard, and such as he thought he would surmise to be the lost *status integritatis*, the essential thing underlying the forms of human culture and society which are never anything but hidden.

In 1754 he once again answered a prize question set by the Dijon academy: *Concerning the origins and reasons of inequality among men.*[2] The answer, more radical than his first one, was as follows: The natural state of man (*qui n'existe plus, qui n'a peut-être point existé et qui probablement n'existera jamais*) is the state in which no man has need of any other, neither for good nor for bad purposes, neither in friendship nor enmity, because, sitting peacefully beneath an oak and drinking water from a spring, he is outwardly free of all tools and inwardly free of all reflection. It is with tools and reflection, with property and the cultivation of the soil that he becomes a social being. 'The first man who staked out a piece of land and dared to say: this belongs to me! and found people foolish enough to believe him—was the founder of bourgeois society.' It is precisely at this point and thus with society itself that inequality begins, but inequality means the possibility of unfreedom, tyranny and slavery, the possibility of the fateful *amour propre* in opposition to the neutral, and for this reason innocent, natural and good *amour de soi-même*; it means greed, and evil passion. Presupposing the inequality which has now obtruded there is now no other way of protecting each man from his neighbour except by the second-best possibility, which is only a second-best possibility, of the contract of the state, which by the establishment of positive law tries to a certain extent at least to make

[1] *Rêv. 3me. prom.*, Basle ed., Vol. 20, p. 202.
[2] *Œuvres de J.-J. Rousseau*, Amsterdam 1769, Vol. 2.

C

amends for what has been lost for ever by man's abandonment of natural law of that *véritable jeunesse du monde*. Voltaire's well-known mocking phrase, that Rousseau made him feel like going down on all fours, while supplying the most obvious comment there is to make to all this, completely fails as an attack upon Rousseau's position. Where *is* the famous *Revenons à la nature!* ? I have never been able to find it in any of Rousseau's writings. It was not the return to this natural law which was the sense of what Rousseau considered to be his insight here and the conclusion he drew from it, but rather the necessity of basing positive law upon the natural law, that is to say, of keeping the natural law in view as an ideal when establishing the positive law and not starting from a natural law which was no true natural law at all, the right of the strongest, for instance. Hence there was no contradiction involved in Rousseau's dedicating the work in question to the municipal council of Geneva, his native town, of which he says that its political constitution was still the best of all those in existence, so that if he were not a citizen of Geneva already it would certainly be his wish to be allowed to become one.

His next work, the *Discours sur l'économie politique*,[1] in 1755, shows us that he has quite logically taken the next step by advancing to a discussion of the positive doctrine of the state: he now expressly presupposes man's sociability and the right to property. But man's original equality and freedom should not be lost sight of. The state is thus to be understood as arising out of and being sustained by and on behalf of the general will (*volonté générale*), in which one stands for all, but all also stand for one, and in which therefore it is the law that establishes and ensures freedom just as freedom establishes and guarantees the law. The wisdom of a government consists in its (1) teaching the people to love the state, i.e. the law as something which is their most personal concern; (2) making it clear to the citizen that the state with its laws is his mother, who wants only what is best for him. His own existence is a part of the existence of his native country; indeed correctly understood the two are identical. Thus he may and indeed must love it as in the best sense he loves himself; (3) the government must take care that the burdens which the state imposes upon the individual do truly not exceed the extent of the sacrifice which it is fitting each should make for his participation in the general will. This is to be accomplished by means of a just financial and taxation policy, which, especially, must be enforceable among the higher members of the society.

[1] Amsterdam ed., Vol. 2.

Incidentally, Rousseau had returned to Geneva in 1754 and had renounced his conversion. He would have stayed there but that his sojourn in his native town was marred for him by the proximity in Ferney of Voltaire and the prospect of the conflicts to which this might give rise. He therefore returned to Paris. The time from the day of his return until 1762 was on the one hand the period of his most important literary labours and on the other a time of difficult personal entanglements from which, in spite of his principles, he found it impossible to free himself. Their effect was to make his belief in his principles still stronger. Two more feminine influences came into his life: Madame d'Epinay, who probably loved him but whom he was not in a position to love, pressed him with the gift of a home which she intended to prepare for him in a country house which she called a hermitage, as well as with the duty she made conditional upon it that he should participate in the social and intellectual life she cultivated. In her house he came to know her sister-in-law, Madame d'Houdetot, and in her, already bound by another love as she was, the great love of his life. He not only respected the other bond, but in admiration of the love which he encountered in it, loved Madame d'Houdetot as one who was so bound and thus denied to him. But his connexion with his circle, one of whose chief members, unhappily for Rousseau, was the German Friedrich Melchior Grimm, was terminated by an open break, and Rousseau moved to Montmorency castle, owned by the Duke of Luxembourg and his wife, where he was permitted to live as he liked.

It was here in 1758 that he wrote the great Open Letter to d'Alembert.[1] D'Alembert, in the Encyclopaedia article 'Geneva' had proposed to the citizens of that town that the introduction of a theatre might be desirable, a suggestion which at once made Rousseau espouse the cause of the Calvinist tradition which in this matter was still unbroken in his native town. The necessary occasions for a people's pleasure should also be presented in union with the infallible voice of Nature, and Rousseau thought he could show that this was better achieved by a continuance and development of the old Genevan customs and behaviour than by that useless and corrupting modern institution, the theatre. Voltaire, who perfectly agreed with d'Alembert, treated Rousseau from then on as if he were a madman, and found a way of annoying both him and the old city of Geneva by opening a theatre just outside the town boundaries, which did then in fact contribute to the death of the tradition originated by Calvin and defended by Rousseau.

In 1760 Rousseau published his 'Proposal for a lasting peace'[2]

[1] Amsterdam ed., Vol. 3.   [2] Amsterdam ed., Vol. 2.

which was in fact written rather earlier, and had been inspired by the writings of the Abbé de Saint Pierre. This political work too reckons quite realistically with the existence of the state based on power politics and with the likelihood of rivalry between such states. It was however Rousseau's aim to confine this rivalry within its proper limits, and he points to the *Droit public germanique*, to the Holy Roman Empire, that is, which was still an active force in Germany, he says, and a far more important idea than the Germans themselves realized. What was needed to avoid further war was a way of making war impossible by rendering it useless. And this could be achieved by establishing a confederation—what he had in mind was without doubt the very idea of a Pan-Europe or United States of Europe which we have in mind today—a confederation including all the sovereign states of Europe, from the Holy Roman Empire to the Republic of Venice, from the Tsar to the Pope, with a central government presided over in turn by each member of the league, with its Supreme Court of Law, with a common army to oppose the Turk or any other external or for that matter internal enemy of the Union, which was above the state, with a guarantee to each member state that its borders and sovereignty within them, and its freedom of movement within them, would be respected on the basis of the Peace of Westphalia, together with a strict prohibition of an armed attack by one member state upon another. All that was required to allow the implementation of the project was the consent of the sovereigns concerned and in demanding this, Rousseau says, he is not imagining that they would have to be good, noble and selfless men, intent upon the general well-being for humanitarian reasons. Thus the usual observation that it is the sinfulness of human nature which makes the realization of such a plan impossible does not apply to Rousseau. He only presupposes, he says, the kind of man who is sensible enough to wish for something that will be useful for him. If, however, his project should prove incapable of fulfilment, let it not be said that it was merely fanciful: *c'est que les hommes sont insensés et que c'est une sorte de folie d'être sage au milieu des fous.*

The first of the three great literary ventures upon which Rousseau embarked during these years was the epistolary novel *Julie ou la nouvelle Héloïse*, which was written between 1757 and 1759 and carried the sub-title: *Lettres de deux amans, habitans d'une petite ville au pied des Alpes.*[1] The little town is Vevey, home of Madame de Warens. But even if the true hero of the story, Saint Preux, the lover, at first happy then unhappy and finally resigned is, as is doubtless the case, Rousseau

[1] Amsterdam ed., Vols. 4-6.

himself, Julie is not Madame d' Houdetot, as was widely assumed at the time, but a pure invention of Rousseau's heart and imagination, the quintessence of his dreams in regard to the woman he desired, in whom he believed without possessing or even knowing her. So we find Rousseau, in this as in no other of his works, thrown on his own resources as the lyric poet who inwardly torn can yet find satisfaction by putting into poetry what his suffering meant to him before, when he was inconsolable—a God had given him the power to tell what he had suffered—and this is the way by which he guards himself against this sorrow.

The opening words of the preface are as follows: 'Big cities need theatres and corrupted nations need novels. I know the moral habits of my time, and therefore I have published these letters. Why did I not live in an era when I would have had to throw them into the fire?' Here also then we are well involved in the complex of problems which we also encounter in Rousseau's political writings. We have to take note here of a dialectic both of form and content. It is without doubt his intention to give expression in these love-letters to the voice of the heart that is to say, here, to the power of love which is absolutely free and strong, and which binds and frees not only as a force of nature, but by virtue of the whole dignity owned by the original human nature. And thus in the first part of the work we see the two lovers, who, because of their station in society, love without hope, drawn to one another in defiance of the world like steel to the magnet, like the magnet to the steel. But Rousseau is aware that here, as in other things, the state in which complete obedience to the voice of the heart is the normal thing, has been lost and that it is therefore no longer the sole determining factor. Here too his desire is not for a return or advance to a state of nature, which would in this case perhaps be the sphere of free-love. The laws of society are valid and continue to be recognized even if they are on occasion infringed. Hence in fact the free motions of the power of love are, even in this first part of the novel, everywhere interrupted and held in check by insights and principles which are also those of the lovers themselves, and especially of the women involved, and which are put forward with due emphasis by both. And when Julie subsequently becomes the wife of another this is not only accepted by both as their fate, albeit in the course of a severe inner conflict, but honoured as a new inevitable law to which their love (which is, however, undiminished) is now subject. Rousseau has his hero respect this law so much that the second half of the book becomes a very hymn to the praise of marriage and the family, these states, of course, representing not the fulfilment but the limit of the power of erotic love. We are reminded of the tendency which moved Goethe too in writing the *Elective Affinities*. It is just that the death of Julie, with which the work closes, and the energetic denial of the possibility that Saint Preux, reduced now to solitude, might himself marry, make it quite clear that an honest outward recognition of the social order is not capable of reducing by one iota the strength contained in the inner truth of the power of love, which is outwardly condemned as impossible.

The second dialectic of the book, that of form, arises directly from the dialectic of content. Why does Rousseau think that in a better time than his own he would have had to burn the book instead of being able to publish it? Why does he even go on to say in his preface that a chaste girl should abstain from reading it at sight of the title alone? If she did not do this, but read only one page, she would be showing by this act that she was not chaste, but *une fille perdue*, in which case she might just as well read the whole thing straight through. What does this mean? It apparently means that the representation of this broken power of love—broken by the necessary recognition of the law—is the only way in which it can be written about in that century, that is to say, within modern European society, and cannot be a pure comment upon love, as it should really be presented to a young girl and as Rousseau would really like to write it. Just as he would like to withhold the theatre from the good city of Geneva, so he would like to withhold from a girl who perhaps still has a belief in love the only novel, *rebus sic stantibus*, which it was possible for him to write. The novel cannot be chaste precisely because it must allow the conventions to triumph outwardly over love and can therefore show love only as it is inhibited by convention. Rousseau's contemporaries positively devoured the *Nouvelle Héloïse*. He once told the story of a lady who, while engaged in reading it, was due to attend a function to which she had been invited. She let the coach wait for hours before her door and finally read on in the coach until four o'clock in the morning, finishing the book only at daybreak. How did the people of Rousseau's time interpret and misinterpret the dual dialectic which the work contained? It must be admitted that of all Rousseau's works the *Nouvelle Héloïse* is the obscurest in its intention, and yet we feel bound to say that of all his works it is the one which it was most necessary for him to write and which most directly reveals his personal dialectic. And about this work in particular we can most definitely say that neither those people who were outraged at its sublime lasciviousness nor—much less—those who revelled in it succeeded in understanding what was actually taking place there: the rapturous shout of the man who had discovered himself deep down beneath all the human contrivance in which the age believed with such a passionate ardour, and the same man's cry of despair at finding that he cannot and does not wish to escape human contrivance, and is thus at a loss to know what to do with himself, simply because beyond all human contrivance he had only discovered himself. Such was the new Héloïse. And such was the complete Rousseau.

The second work of this period was the great treatise *Du contrat social ou Principes du droit politique*,[1] 1762, which was divided into four parts. This work in particular which today is perhaps relatively the best-known of Rousseau's writings, could not have become the political ogre it in fact was for many people, on the strength of its title alone, if only they had taken the trouble to read it in its place within the scheme of Rousseau's work as a whole and with an understanding of his peculiar position in relation to his own age. It is not true to say that its author makes the mistake of deducing the state from the abstract principles of the liberty and equality of the individual, while ignoring the realities of human history. Indeed the very first lines of the book, which are there for all to read, state that it is Rousseau's aim to understand man as he is, and the laws as they can be. The demand for political justice arises from the insight into the original freedom and equality of individual men but this demand itself constitutes in Rousseau's doctrine of state only the weft introduced into the warp of the undeniably very 'historical' factor which he calls here 'interest' or 'advantage': in man's present no longer natural state (*l'homme est né libre, et par-tout il est dans les fers*, at once master and slave) which here also Rousseau presupposes as only the second-best state, his survival demands a *convention*, a means of regulating the mutual relationship between the lordly slaves or slavish masters. This convention is fundamentally and generally that which Rousseau calls the force exerted by society (*Contrat social*), and the point which he is trying to make in his doctrine of the state is this: that this convention, which he admits is necessary, things being as they are, should not be arrived at without due consideration for the demands of justice, i.e. without any thought being given to man's original state of freedom and equality. 'I seek to unite what the law allows with that which interest prescribes, so that justice and what is expedient might not ever remain divided.' It is thus nonsensical to say, as P. Wernle says[2] that we find ourselves transferred in the *Contrat social* from the atmosphere of freedom, the pure inwardness and lyrical

---

[1] Amsterdam ed., Vol. 2.   [2] Vol. 2, 63.

subjectivity of the *Nouvelle Héloïse* into a completely different world, that, namely, of the Jacobin state governed by compulsion. For the *Nouvelle Héloïse* does not simply convey the 'atmosphere of freedom' any more than the *Contrat social* is simply an account of the 'state with compulsory rule'. The theory and practice of the form of government arising from the French Revolution—the theory as laid down, for instance, in the Declaration of the Rights of Man of 1789—although later in time (*post hoc non propter hoc!*) belonged just as much to the time before Rousseau as did the theory and practice of the absolute monarchy of his time. Likewise in the opening pages Rousseau presents, in opposition to force from above and the force from below which repels it, the social order (*l'ordre social*) as a superior order whose right, although not a 'natural' one, is nevertheless 'holy'. Might, while it may very well be able to create facts, can never create right. Even the power which is ordained of God is, in so far as it is in fact only might, not necessarily right. And an agreement such as Hobbes had in mind, in which nothing but authority is given to the one side and nothing but the will to obey to the other, would not be an agreement at all and would destroy the idea of man as one capable of political action, and indeed the idea of man altogether.[1] The problem of the state is rather how to bring about a union between men which by its corporate might shields every individual in such a manner that he is at once one with the whole and yet free, and free—i.e. obeying himself alone—by virtue of this very consent. The basic act which represents the answer to this problem is an act of submission, the complete transference by the individual of all his rights to the community as such. It is precisely by everyone giving himself completely—not to somebody but to all and not to all as the sum of every individual, but to all as the public person which has arisen by their union—it is precisely by this act that the weft of justice is introduced into the warp of interest, which, *rebus sic stantibus*, is what is needed to make an agreement possible: for it is by the one giving himself to all that the only possible form of freedom and equality, *rebus sic stantibus*, is preserved by him and by all. Participation in the *volonté générale* which arises in this way thus essentially consists in an act of submission and distinguishes the *citoyen*, *civis*, πολίτης from the mere *bourgeois*. And the presence of such a general will distinguishes the *cité*, *civitas*, πόλις, the *république* or the *corps politique* from the mere *ville*: understood in the passive sense it is identical with the concept of the state, in the active sense it is identical with the idea of the sovereign, and understood in its relation to its

[1] I, 3-4.

equals it is identical with the idea of power, *puissance*. The whole body of those who as individuals are united in the state or as sovereign in their own right is the people, and individuals as such are *citoyens* because they share in the sovereignty and *sujets* because they are subject to the laws of the state.[1] The sovereign can therefore by his nature never act in a way which would be harmful to his subjects, but only in their favour, just as the citizen by his nature can never be against his sovereign, but only for him, and, moreover, if he understands his freedom rightly, can imagine the constraint which the sovereign imposes only as leading to his, the citizen's, own freedom.[2] For: 'Freedom consists in an obedience to the law which has been self-imposed.' The citizen will therefore subordinate himself, both in the rights to which he is entitled as regards his own person and in his property rights as a landowner, to the right of the generality. He will, that is to say, regard himself only as a guardian and trustee appointed by the generality, and in this way he is the legitimate owner of these rights, *possesseur* of his person and property.[3]

The sovereignty which is based on such precepts is essentially non-transferable, i.e. it can be exercised by certain individuals but cannot be irrevocably conferred upon certain individuals.[4] And it is essentially indivisible, i.e. it cannot be split into a legislative power and an executive power effectively separate from it.[5] According to Rousseau the formation of political parties constitutes an injury to the rights of the sovereign or state.[6] The sovereign power over the individual is limited because while the sovereign can command the services of the individual in every respect—even the sacrifice of his life (capital punishment and war!) he can command them only as a sovereign, i.e. on behalf of the generality.[7] The way in which these services can be commanded is regulated by the law, whereby a people lays down its rules for itself.[8] We would, of course have to be gods and not men in order to recognize the laws which are best in all circumstances, since the law which was to be imposed upon a man and which was at the same time to proceed from him would have to be powerful enough to bring about nothing more nor less than his transformation from a mere individual into a social being. The *esprit social* which was the law's intention must have been in effect even while the law was being set up. Blessed are the peoples to whom it was granted, like Israel, to hear a Moses, or, like Geneva, to hear a Calvin![9] It is necessary when engaged in legislating for a particular people to take into most careful consideration the special nature of the people and country, and to

[1] I, 6.   [2] I, 7.   [3] I, 8-9.   [4] II, 1.   [5] II, 2.   [6] II, 3.
[7] II, 4-5.   [8] II, 6.   [9] II, 7.

appreciate what exactly is its state of historical development. It is this appreciation which distinguishes the true legislator from the tyrant.[1] In any case it is essential that the legislative power, the power, that is, which brings a certain law into force, should, as a matter of principle, be the people, whether it be for constitutional, civil, or criminal law.[2]

Concerning government as such the situation is somewhat different. The government, it is true, is not sovereign either, but derives from the sovereign, i.e. from the people. But it is truly thus derived, i.e. as servant of the sovereign it is a link endowed with its own real existence and its own will between the people as the generality of citizens and the people as the generality of subjects. It receives from the people as representing the sovereign the commands which it has to pass on to the people as representing the state; but it is precisely in its quality of receiving and imparting spontaneously that it is for its own part a subject—not indeed of the sovereign power, but in exercising the sovereign power as the sovereign intends.[3] As to the form which the exercise of this power should take, this according to Rousseau depends most of all upon the size of the state in question and upon the material resources at its disposal: a large and prosperous state requires a strong form of government and therefore one where all the power resides in the hands of one person, the monarchical form in other words; in a state more limited in means and extent the exercise of power can safely be placed in the hands of several people, so that an aristocracy would be found suitable; the affairs of a small and impoverished state can be conducted more or less directly by the people itself, and so could be a democracy. In historical reality the form of government will inevitably be some sort of mixture of these three.[4] But Rousseau's inclination, quite apart from this practical distinction, was never for a more or less pure democracy: *Il n'a jamais existé de véritable démocratie et il n'en existera jamais*, he states very definitely; it is only very seldom that the right conditions for it exist, and the dangers of constant internal unrest are far too great with this form of government. *S'il y avoit un peuple de dieux, il se gouverneroit démocratiquement. Un gouvernement si parfait ne convient pas à des hommes.*[5] But the Jacobins and the modern exponents of political liberalism evidently thought otherwise. Rousseau it is true, also finds several objections to the aristocratic system and a great many to the system of monarchy. For it will not be in the personal interest of a king to regard the plenitude of power with which he is entrusted as merely expressive of the *volonté générale* as he ought to. Another evil is

[1] II, 8-11.   [2] II, 12.   [3] III, 1.   [4] III, 2-3.   [5] III, 4.

that he will not actually rule personally, but through his ministers; and yet another the fatal fact that the monarchy is hereditary, which means that it is possible for a child, a monster or an idiot suddenly to become king. And lastly there is the fact that the continuity of government is in no way ensured every time the throne changes hands. Rousseau would like to see this better preserved, as it is with a senate like that of Venice or Berne.[1] How is a good government to be recognized? Not by the form of government, for the same form of government can be the best possible for one people and the worst possible for another. By the magnificence of the government then, perhaps, or the prosperity of the people? Or by the preservation of peace at home and abroad?—No, says Rousseau in all sincerity, not by these things, but quite simply by the increase in population of the territory in question: it is this which will show that men have achieved what they intended in forsaking the state of nature for the social state, namely the collective preservation of their life, even if it should perhaps be attained in circumstances of the utmost general wretchedness and possibly of great violence and bloodshed.[2] The abuse of government and subsequent death of the state always occurs at the point where the state loses its meaning because the convention upon which it is based has been mangled by the establishment of some kind of tyranny.[3] But tyrannical also is the conception of the legislative power which causes a people's chosen emissaries to feel and behave like representatives (*représentants*) of the people, instead of feeling and behaving—just like the wielders of the executive power—like their delegates (*commissionaires*). The instant a people appoints representatives for itself it is no longer free; it is no longer even a people. For the instant a man, thinking of his representative in parliament, can say, politics are nothing to do with me, the state as such is doomed. Rousseau also very logically maintained that the institution of taxes was a more than dubious substitute for its underlying institution of co-operative labour (*la corvée*), which was alone worthy of a true *cité*.[4] Thus we can hardly defend or attack what we know today as the parliamentary system as something towards which Rousseau's ideas might have been tending. If a people adopts a system of government embracing a legislative and an executive power, then this does not, according to Rousseau, signify the concluding of a second social contract (just as on the other hand the social contract as such did not for him, as Hobbes thought, simply mean the appointment of a government), but the execution of the first and only contract, beside which there can be no other. In the course of that execution

---

[1] III, 5-6.   [2] III, 9.   [3] III, 10-11.   [4] III, 14-15.

the people, far from retiring into inactivity, is and remains as active as it possibly can be.[1]

From this it follows that it is impossible for the sovereign to determine by an irrevocable act either the form of government or which people are to be entrusted with it. These things must again and again be made the subject of his free decision. The instance of the general will which has again and again to be consulted, i.e. the will of the body politic or of the people as such, is proof against destruction by any attempt of the government to seize excessive power or any attempt by individual citizens to set up a state within the state.[2] This general will is by no means the will of the majority; the only purpose served by the majority is to determine what the general will actually is on a given point. The purpose of the vote is not to ask the citizen whether he is in agreement with a certain law or not, but to ask him whether in his opinion this law is in accordance with the general will. The healthier the political life of a country is the more its political decisions will come under the sign of unanimity. But anyone who has entered into the social contract has thereby expressed his readiness to accept in advance also those decisions which are not passed unanimously or which run counter to his convictions or interest. In this event he will not say to himself that he has perhaps erred in his convictions or in his judgment of the matter in question, but that he has probably erred in his assessment of the general will, and he will not wish, for the sake of his own freedom, which, properly understood, is based upon the true general will, for the result to be different. Rousseau at this point applauds the custom of the old republic of Genoa, which was to inscribe the very word *libertas* over the gates of prisons and on the chains of those condemned to service in the galleys 'Cette application de la devise est belle et juste'. It is precisely for freedom's sake, and for the sake of his own freedom, that the citizen who has encountered the severity of the law makes his way to the prison or the galley![3] As for elections, Rousseau is inclined to prefer the method of electing by lot, so that it may be quite clear that appointment to an official post is not a distinction, but signifies the imposition of a special burden for the citizen concerned, an imposition which in any case in a complete democracy—if such a thing existed— it would be best to leave to pure chance.[4] Finally, in accordance with strict logic, Rousseau finds it possible to attribute a good significance even to the two very illiberal political institutions of dictatorship and censorship. It is the will of the people to preserve the life of the state in all circumstances. But it is possible for circumstances to arise in which

[1] III, 16.   [2] IV, 1.   [3] IV, 2.   [4] IV, 3.

the existing laws, which cannot perhaps be changed immediately, become a danger to the state. In such cases the people's sovereignty must in its own interest be suspended, or alternatively suspend itself for a moment, by being temporarily placed in the hands of one or more persons, a state of affairs which can of course only be transitional if it is not to degenerate into a form of tyranny. And according to Rousseau the formation and cultivation of public opinion (*opinion publique*) in questions of morals and taste is no less a political matter and thus the government's task, than the formation and protection of the laws. The task of a wise censorship in the way in which it has always been exercised by princes and magistrates of note, would be not to create, sway and determine public opinion in these matters, but certainly to ascertain it and give it expression, and by thus propounding the laws which are unwritten constantly provide the written laws with the support they need.[1]

Rousseau ends the book with a strange disquisition on *la religion civile*, which is, it must be admitted, also remarkable for its inconsistencies and lack of careful thought. According to him religion and politics originally went hand in hand; every people had its gods in having its state, and lost them when its state was lost. The message of Jesus about the kingdom which is part of another world dispelled this unity. The pagan persecutors of the early Christians were not completely wrong in scenting political rebellion in the proclamation of this kingdom. With the Roman Papacy it actually became rebellion. The Church managed to establish itself as a political body in its own right, independent of the state, setting up a new social contract based on the benefit of communion and the threat of excommunication (*un chef d'œuvre en politique!*) whose power has proved itself to be greater even than that of the civil contract. We are faced with the two interrelated facts that the state has always had need of some religious basis, and that Christianity has in effect always been more harmful than beneficial to the state. We should really, thinks Rousseau, distinguish, first, *human religion*, which he describes as the purely inward cult of the highest God, which has no visible manifestation in a Church, which is bound up with the recognition of the eternal duties imposed by morality, and which he thinks he may identify with the 'pure and simple religion of the Gospel' or with the 'true theism' or with the 'natural religious right' (*droit divin naturel*); and, secondly, the *national religion* of pre-Christian times, the positive religious right (*droit divin civil ou positif*) whose dogma and cult were prescribed by the law and made the duty of the

[1] IV, 6-7.

citizen; and, thirdly, *priestly religion*, which demands of a man that he
should recognize two separate sources of law, two governments and
two fatherlands, and thus makes it difficult for him to be believer and
citizen at once; a religious right for which, according to Rousseau, there
is no name whatsoever (he expressly states that he is referring to Roman
Catholicism) and which he therefore declines to discuss further.
'Anything which shatters social unity is worthless. Every institution
which sets a man at loggerheads with himself is worthless.' It seems at
first that there are all sorts of things to be said in favour of national
religion, of the theocracy, from the political point of view. But it is
based upon a lie, makes peoples as such intolerant in matters of
religion, and places in the hands of those thus incensed the dreadful
weapons at the disposal of the power-state. Thus we must dismiss it
also from its place in the discussion. There remains human religion,
'Christianity, not that current today, but the quite different Christianity of the Gospel', the 'holy, sublime and true religion'. If only it
were not for its one bad failing: that it is incapable, without being
essentially connected with a state on earth, of lending strength to the
laws of a state on earth, but must rather loose the hearts of the citizens
from their state as it does from all earthly things. It is said, that a people
composed of true Christians would form the most perfect society. But
should it not be borne in mind that a society of true Christians would
no longer be a human society at all? And even assuming the possibility of such a society, would not that 'deep indifference' with which
it is alone possible for a Christian, whose homeland is not upon
this earth, to discharge his duties in the state, would not the ease,
with which he can accept bad conditions too, would not his fear of
becoming intoxicated with the glory of his country, would not his
readiness to bow beneath the hard yoke of God, would not all these
things be bound eventually to constitute a danger to the state in spite
of all the good political results which they may have as well? Will not
Christian soldiers believe not in victory but in God, and will they
then achieve what the pagan Romans achieved? Is it not inevitable
that they should fare badly in face of so inspired an enemy? Is there
in fact any such thing as a 'Christian soldier'? Is not a 'holy war' an
impossibility from the Christian standpoint? Is there a 'Christian
state' (*une république chrétienne*)? Or does not each of these words exclude
the other? Is not Christianity with its teaching of submission and
dependence an all-too favourable prerequisite for tyranny, which has
in fact never neglected to exploit it accordingly? Thus, according to
Rousseau, this third possibility, that of human religion, must also be

ruled out of the discussion. But the fact remains, that the state needs a religion, in order that its citizens might love their duties. It thus demands of them a civil profession of faith (*une profession de foi purement civile*), to be formulated by the state itself, containing the *sentiments de sociabilité* (the convictions on whose account a general will is necessary) without which it is not possible either to be a good citizen or a loyal subject. It demands a dogma concerning the existence of a mighty, wise, beneficent guiding and providing Deity, a future life with rewards and punishments, the sacred nature of the social contract and the Laws; its articles are to be few, simple and clear but—in order not to give rise to theological dispute—on no account too closely defined or even provided with a commentary. All else is conjecture (*opinions*) and this is no concern of the state or of the citizen of the state as such, and the individual should be left to ponder it freely. Anyone who does not accept this civil religion is to be banished; anyone who, after he has accepted it, behaves in a manner contrary to it commits the crime of giving the lie to the law and is to be punished by death. And every intolerant religious form is excluded at the outset, for wherever the principle 'without the Church there is no salvation' is thought valid, an alien sovereign power is in fact set up within the state in worldly political affairs (in questions concerning contracts of marriage, for example), which is set higher than the state, and constitutes an attack which the state can meet only by being for its own part intolerant. The only course for every honest man (*tout honnête homme*) is to renounce the Roman Catholic Church. Such are the last words in this book of the former convert Rousseau.[1]

Rousseau's third chief work of this period, a novel tracing its hero's mental growth and development and entitled *Emile ou De l'education* (1762)[2] is also an answer to the problem of how human life should be moulded in spite of and in its quality of being far removed from its original and natural state. But now the problem is presented in individual microcosmic form. It is now the moulding of a single life which is in question. Rousseau had been approached by a worried mother for advice in matters affecting education: the few short precepts he originally gave then grew into the now famous work which embraces five whole books. It begins with the words: 'All things are good as they proceed from the hands of the Author of all things; all things degenerate in the hands of man. . . . Man wants nothing to be as nature has made it, not even man. Because this is the present state of all things the child and the adolescent cannot simply be left alone, but are in

[1] IV, 8. [2] Amsterdam ed., Vols. 7-8.

need of education. But the significance of this education must then be, in contrast to all the demands of society, class and future profession which are meant to influence the young, and in contrast to the existing customs and prevailing ideas of the adults surrounding the child: educating him to be a man, and indeed an *homme abstrait*,[1] a man, that is, who is as free as possible, and as far as possible acts in accordance with his true nature.

The first lesson which we learn from the book is that mothers should feed their infants themselves and not wrap them in swaddling clothes! The child's education is meant to provide him with room for himself, for the way of life which the child himself must shape and bring to perfection. *Vivre est le métier que je lui veux apprendre.*[2] Such an education will therefore have to consist in taking care that the child is allowed to develop as freely as possible those potentialities lying dormant within him which are quite distinct from the external factors which help to determine and influence it, in ensuring that he can acquire his own experience as freely as possible, and ensuring finally that he should be allowed to come to terms in the most natural way possible with the historical factors conditioning his existence. That is why Emile, the model Rousseau uses to present his ideas, is brought up far removed from society, in the country, and indeed he is educated from infancy not by his parents, but by a tutor. The first aim of education is to free the child of fear, commanding greed and bad behaviour by disposing of the false attitude to the things which can awaken such feelings. The child should be made aware automatically, so to speak, of the moral concepts of obedience, duty and obligation and further of virtue by himself experiencing his own strength and weakness, and necessity and compulsion. Learning and reading should be allowed to proceed from the child's interest in things around it, which is to be aroused first, and on no account should this sequence be reversed. Thus the development and exercise of the five senses is far more important at first than book learning. Instruction proper then follows quite simply upon the child's curiosity and its growing desire for knowledge, and therefore takes as its subject the things by which the child is surrounded, the house, the garden and the stars in the sky, and only finally the books, the first and most important of these being Robinson Crusoe, because like Crusoe the child should arrive at the point where it can decide his requirements for himself and be able to set about procuring them. It is to encourage him in this that Emile is given handicraft lessons even while he is still very young. Only when he is past fifteen is it time to introduce him to

[1] I, p. 12.   [2] I, p. 11.

foreign languages, and to history also, with the aim of paving the way for him to form an independent moral judgment on the basis not of the false speech, but of the deeds of men. And similarly his religious instruction is not to introduce him to the catechism of one particular faith but to enable him to choose that religion to which the best use of his reason must necessarily lead him. The purpose of a stay in the city is to allow the pupil to clarify and establish—in opposition to the bad taste prevailing there, be it understood—his own feeling for the truly beautiful. And then he is to be made acquainted with classical literature too. But the time when he becomes engaged and the first years of his marriage, are also part of the period of his education, a fact rather surprising in retrospect as we learn in the fifth book that Rousseau did not think a corresponding education, far from the parental home and society, necessary for the female sex, but considered the instilling at home, of a little knowledge of music, housekeeping and sewing, the virtue of cleanliness and an unfeigned propriety sufficient for a girl. The essential things to be demanded of a wife are that she should please her husband and have learnt how to make life pleasant for him.

The part of the book which really determined its reception was the *Confession of faith of a Vicar of Savoy*,[1] which was interpolated in the fourth section. The Vicar is a cleric of the type which Rousseau had encountered in Savoy during his stormy youth, and into whose mouth he now put his own theology, or philosophy of religion. Some *bon sens*, a love of truth and a simple heart, in short *la bonne foi*, i.e. an opinion honestly held, seem to him to be the sufficient prerequisites of such an undertaking: he is confident that even any error into which he might fall could not be attributed to him as a crime provided he has adhered to these principles. Neither the Church's call to faith nor any philosophy, be it systematic or sceptical, the confession begins, can allay the mistrust of all truth in the heart for the immediate reason that those representing the Church or a philosophy are far too zealous and fundamentally lacking in objectivity in wishing others to accept their own opinions as the right ones. I must therefore begin at the very beginning. I start by establishing my own existence and with the fact that I am related to a being distinct from myself by virtue of the twofold, the passive and the active power of feeling and judging. Judgment is something other than feeling: in judging I am not passive but active in relation to the things about me. In judging I attribute something to them: existence, size, number, relationship, etc., something which I know not only by awareness of the object concerned but from within

[1] Amsterdam ed., Vol. 8, pp. 13ff.

myself. But I must now attribute exactly the same activity to the objects themselves: it is freedom and not only necessity in the movement by which I apprehend them. How do I know this? I know it from direct experience. *Je vous dirai, que je le sais, parce que je le sens.* It is of my own free will that I make this present motion of my arm. No artifice of reasoning can destroy this certainty within me. It is *plus fort que tout évidence; autant vaudroit me prouver que je n'existe pas* (p. 28). But if now, as I suppose, the universe is not, like myself, a living being, and if movement does not reside in the world as a whole and is even less a property of matter, then I am provided with my first dogma or article of faith, in explanation of the movement in the world, as: the recognition of a will which moves the world from outside. And from my insight into the causal and teleological connexion between all forms of movement, by virtue of which each single movement can at any time be considered as central to every other, I am given to recognize that this will is endowed with intelligence and wisdom. The Being which is possessed of this highest will and therefore, as is apparent, of this highest ability, and which therefore exists in itself—this Being I call God. *Pénétré de mon insuffisance* (note what theological principle comes to light here—) *je ne raisonnerai jamais sur la nature de Dieu, que je n'y sois forcé par le sentiment de ses rapports avec moi* (p. 39). We are evidently taught by nature herself to marvel at him, to worship and love him: a feeling of thankfulness towards him is the consequence of our love for ourselves which suggests itself first of all. But what a contrast there is, in the world created by God, between the peace and happiness of nature and the chaos of the world of men! For man is the slave of his senses and passions. But he is not only that. He is also free, capable, that is, of elevating himself to the level of the 'eternal truths'. Just as he can judge of what is true, so he can also, he who was created in the image of God, judge of what is good, and experience the desire to live up to this judgment. Thus moral evil and the physical evil which follows it stem from us, not from God, and not from our God-created nature. Take away our calamitous progress, take away our mistakes and our vices, take away the work of man, and all is good! *Sois juste et tu seras heureux!* (p. 51). And if in spite of this I see the wicked triumph and the just man suffer? It is precisely this which affords me proof of the immortality of the soul, of man's thinking nature, the dissolution of which is inconceivable to me, and whose preservation God owes less (!) to the deserts of man than to his own goodness (one senses none the less in this fateful sentence something like a lingering echo of the theology of old Geneva, in Rousseau's recalling here Psalm 115, verse 1: 'Not unto us, O Lord, not unto us, but unto thy name give glory!' p. 55). But Hell, the punishment of the wicked which corresponds to the heavenly reward of the good, I should not be inclined to seek in some everlasting Beyond, but in the hearts of the wicked, and then—for is not the wicked man also my brother?—rather hope for peace for them too in the world to come. I should consider spirituality, eternity, wisdom, goodness and righteousness, as qualities of God, to be absolute and attributable only to him as the Creator and therefore not think that they are to be comprehended by means of my corresponding notions of them. I shall say to him: 'Being of all beings, I am, because thou art; in thinking of thee without cease I understand also my own origin. And that is the noblest use to which my faculty of reason can be put, in recognizing that beside thee I am as nothing.' But to what else shall I now devote my life? Nature has inscribed it in indelible characters upon my heart: *Tout ce que je sens être bien est bien; tout ce que je sens être mal est mal* (p. 60). For if good is really good, then it must dwell within us for ever and cannot be lost. To be good, then, must simply mean to be healthy, i.e. to be in a state corresponding to the nature of goodness. How could admiration for good deeds and men, and revulsion at the sight of evil, be possible for all of us, how could pity be possible even for the criminal, if we were wicked in the depths of our nature, if we did not stem from goodness? Thus the form of the moral imperative can only be: *obéissons à la Nature!* (p. 65). In the depths of our souls (*au fond des âmes*) over and beyond all our principles, there dwells always an agent which passes judgment: the conscience, not as a prejudice, and not as an idea we have had grafted on to us by education and custom, but as an evidently innate *a priori* of all moral ideas which has manifested itself in the manners and history of every people at every time. *Nous sentons avant de connaître . . . Quoique toutes nos idées nous viennent du dehors, les sentimens, qui les apprécient sont au-dedans de nous. . . . Exister pour nous c'est sentir. . . . Nous avons eu des sentiments avant des idées* (p. 69). This *sentiment*, however, which is innate and thus inseparable from our existence, and which enables us to recognize good, and spurn evil, is in fact the conscience. 'Conscience! Conscience! Divine instinct; immortal and celestial voice; assured guide of a being who is ignorant and pressed hard, but intelligent and free; infallible judge of good and evil, it is you who make man resemble God; it is you who are responsible for the excellence of his nature and the morality of his actions; without you I sense nothing within me which raises me above brute creation, except the unhappy privilege of straying from error to error by means of a gift of perception which is unregulated, and a gift of reason which has no principle.

Heaven be praised, we are now delivered from all the terrifying apparatus of philosophy. We can be men without being scholars! (p. 71). Why then are there so few men who heed this guide? This is simply because he speaks the language of nature, which the whole world conspires to have us forget. But does the man exist who has not at least once in his life yielded to the tug of the heart which is so natural and sweet and not in doing this found virtue lovable in spite of the difficulties it presents?

But what is virtue? What is goodness? It is placing oneself in relation to the whole, instead of placing the whole in relation to oneself, as the wicked do. The wicked man makes himself the centre of all things, the good man fits himself into an order where God is the centre of all created things, and these form the periphery about him. I put myself of my own free will at God's disposal as his work and as his instrument to the fulfilment of his will, and it is in this legitimate use of my freedom that I have at once my desert and my reward (p. 76). If a man chooses evil instead of goodness that is attributable to the man himself, and most certainly not to God. But in this event the choice of good also depends upon myself alone. I shall be fortified and held in this good choice by contemplating and meditating upon the universe, not with the aim of idly systematizing, but of worshipping and marvelling at its author. I have nothing to ask of him. What, even, should I ask for? For miracles on my behalf?—I, who yet love his order of things as it is immutable? Such a prayer would merit punishment! Or am I to pray for strength to desire the good and to do it? How should I ask for something he has given me already: namely conscience, reason and freedom! *He* demands of *me* that my will should be otherwise than it is— it is not I who have to demand it of him! 'O good and merciful God, fount of justice and truth! In my trust in thee my heart's supreme desire is that thy will be done. In allying my will to thine I am doing as thou dost, and acquiescing in thy goodness; I feel that I am partaking in advance of the supreme joy which is the reward of such a will' (p. 79). I certainly have cause to doubt myself. Certainly I am not infallible. Certainly all the views I hold could be so many lies. But I have done what I could; how could I be held guilty for not having achieved more?

But how is all this now in relation to revelation, Scripture and dogma? It is certain that the answer to this must also be determined by the reasoning power of each individual: *cherchez la vérité vous-même!* Is any other religion but the natural religion, which has just been developed, really necessary? Am I likely to incur guilt in simply following the light which God himself has given me in my reason and conscience? What truth or injunction which is important to the glory of God, the good of society or my own advantage could I possibly miss in following this course? 'Our most sublime notions of the Deity come to us through our reason alone. Gaze upon the spectacle of nature, give heed to the inner voice. Has not God said everything to our eyes, our conscience and our judgment? What is there left for men to tell us?' (p. 82). What purpose will their revelations serve but to reduce God to an all-too human form? What purpose their dogmas but to create new obscurity? They have made man haughty, intolerant and cruel, and brought war instead of peace to the earth. *Je me demande à quoi bon tout cela sans savoir me répondre.* If we had only ever heeded what God says in the heart of man there would only be *one* religion on earth, the religion, namely, of the heart. But now every man, when asked which is the true religion, answers—mine! And how does he know that?—God has said so! he replies. And how does he know that God has said that?—My parson told me, and he should know.

But have we not a right to demand that the true religion should be distinguished by means of some quite unmistakable criterion? How can I be expected to believe on the authority of a man, who after all is in exactly the same position as myself? 'When I believe what he says, I don't believe it because he says it, but because he proves it. The evidence provided by men is therefore fundamentally nothing but that given me by my own reason and adds nothing to the natural means of recognizing the truth which God has given me.' *Apôtre de la vérité, qu'avez vous donc à me dire dont je ne reste pas le juge?* God has spoken to man, you say. Bold words, indeed! But why then have I not heard him? Why has he apparently spoken only to certain other men? Why must I above all else believe again in the miracles which are to attest that these men are speaking the truth? And why before all else in the books in which these miracles have—by men!—been handed down to us? *Quoi! toujours des témoignages humains? toujours des hommes, qui me rapportent ce que d'autres hommes ont rapporté? Que d'hommes entre Dieu et moi!* (p. 88). Must I now ponder, compare and verify? Could God really not spare me this labour? How learned I must be to seek through the whole of antiquity, nay through the entire world for the truth of the prophecies, revelations and miraculous events which are claimed! What critical abilities I must possess to distinguish the true documents from the false, to weigh the theses and counter-theses against each other, the originals and translations, the reliable and not so reliable historical witnesses! And all this as a mere preliminary to deciding whether the reported miracles are really miracles, the reported prophecies really prophecies. For there are also seeming miracles and prophecies which have some natural explanation. And when I have found the confirmation of their authenticity, then that in its turn is but a preliminary to the question: just why did God select such means for the confirmation of his word, as if he were purposely avoiding the simplest method, means which are themselves so much in need of confirmation? Is it credible that God should have given such signs to this or that particular man, and in so doing have made all the rest of mankind dependent upon them? Is it not too strange that every sect ultimately calls such signs to witness, so that all things considered—if all things were correct—there must have been more miraculous events than natural ones! And so that we should regard it as the greatest wonder of all if somewhere at some time no miracle should come to pass among some group of persecuted fanatics! No, I believe in God too much to believe in so many miracles unworthy of him (p. 90). Why do they not happen now in the broad light of day? Why did they all take place somewhere in a dark corner? Why are such and such a number of eye-witnesses necessary to make them credible? And even if they were credible to us, has not the Devil also worked miracles, according to the Bible itself? Is the true doctrine not once again necessary to prove the true miracle, which we were told should for its own part prove the true doctrine? The latter must, however, in any event be recognizable by bearing the 'sacred character of the divine', i.e. by the fact that it at the very least does not contradict the basic concepts of natural religion which it has brought with it. A wrathful, jealous, vengeful, factious God I could not acknowledge as being my God: He is not the good, gentle God my reason has already revealed to me. Further I would beg leave to demand of the dogmas of a revealed religion that they should be clearer, simpler and easier to comprehend than those of natural religion, and not perhaps even more mysterious and contradictory. 'The God whom I worship does not dwell in the shadows; he has not given me understanding to forbid me to use it. To demand of me that I should subject my reason is to insult its Author. A servant of truth would not tyrannize over my reason but enlighten it' (p. 93).

These then are my principles in testing a revealed religion. But would it then be enough to test one of the revealed religions in this manner? To be fair should we not have to look into all of them, and into every religious faction, comparing and weighing them one against the other, and not only by means of their literature but in our own person? Have we, for instance, done justice to the Jews and the arguments they advance for their religion? Have Christian and Mohammedan ever listened quietly to what the other has to say? How in justice can we regard as damned the millions of the heathen, whom no mission has yet reached? What guilt has the heathen incurred who happens to die on the evening before the arrival of the first mission to his district? What fault is it of his that he knew nothing of what is supposed to have happened in Jerusalem on the other side of the globe eighteen hundred years ago? That same Jerusalem, incidentally, where the people even today seem no better placed as regards that event than he himself! And what allegedly revealed religion is there to which the same objections could not be raised! (p. 108). If there were really only one religion which alone is able to grant salvation then, since everyone must test for himself in this matter, it would be everyone's first duty, regardless of age or sex, to ask all these questions and institute the enquiries necessary to answer them. The earth would be swarming with pilgrims wandering in all directions at vast expense and under the greatest difficulties in order to test their religions and find the true one. Then farewell to craftsmanship, art and science, and every social employment. There would then be no striving except for the true religion. And the best that could happen would be that the healthiest, the most zealous, the shrewdest and oldest man will get far enough to discover in his old age in retrospect which religion he *should* have taken as his guide in life. Anyone rejecting this method must grant the son of the Turk the right he concedes to the son of the Christian: the right to abide by his father's religion without being threatened with perdition. So far as I myself am concerned, I can reject this method because I have decided to take as my one and only guide the book of Nature which lies open before the eyes of all men, that is at my disposal come what may as a source for the recognition of God, and from which I learn more than all men can teach me (p. 110).

My attitude to the allegedly revealed religions is, however, neither approving nor disapproving, but one of respectful doubt: I see that there is much to be said for the various religions, but also that there is much to be said against them. Once again, I do not consider myself infallible. But I must think for myself. It may be that someone who can declare himself for a particular religion is gifted with better powers of judgment than I. Thus I certainly condemn no man, but I can imitate no man either: it is just that his judgment, superlative as it may be in itself, is not my judgment. This must be also my attitude in relation to Christianity. 'I gladly confess that the majesty of the Bible evokes my admiration, that the sanctity of the Gospel speaks to my heart. Philosophers for all their splendour are small beside it. Can a book at once so sublime and so simple be the work of men? Can he whom it describes be a mere man? Is his speech that of the enthusiast or of the ambitious founder of a sect? How sweet, how pure his ways! (*quelle douceur, quelle pureté dans ses mœurs!*) What moving grace (*quelle grâce touchante*) in his teachings! How noble his maxims! (*quelle élévation dans ses maximes!*) How wise his discourses! What aptness, finesse and justice in his answers! What command of his passions! What strength and self-denial in his sufferings!' (p. 112). Socrates cannot be compared with him, for just as certainly as his morality was something quite new in his surroundings—whereas Socrates' was but the affirmation of familiar Greek virtues—so his death was incomparably much harder than Socrates' death. *Si la vie et la mort de Socrate sont d'un Sage, la vie et la mort de Jésus sont d'un Dieu.* His story cannot have been invented. In that event its inventors would have had to be more astonishing than their invention. But it must be admitted that this Gospel is also full of things not worthy of belief, contrary to reason, and unacceptable. As far as these are concerned one can only withdraw to the attitude of silent but non-committal respect. This also holds good for the dogmas in so far as they are not relevant to life or to morality. 'I look upon all the individual religions as salutary institutions in so far as they are in each country the uniform means of public worship. Their reasons for being as they are may be in the climate, in the government, in the spirit of the people (*génie du peuple*) or in some other local cause which might make the one preferable to the other, according to the time and the place. I believe they are all good provided they allow God to be worshipped in a fitting manner, that is to say by rendering God the essential service of the heart' (p. 114).

God will certainly not reject any service rendered unto him, whatever its outward form. And now, the Vicar of Savoy declares, I shall make it my task to discharge my duties as a Roman Catholic priest, and especially those of the Mass, which formerly I took lightly, with all the inner conviction and outward punctiliousness I can muster, exactly as the Church prescribes, and to invest the words of the sacraments with all my belief in the highest Being. 'Whatever there is about this inconceivable mystery (the sacrament), I am not afraid that I shall be punished at the day of judgment for having profaned it in my heart.' And for the rest I shall obey the spirit of the Gospel more than the spirit of the Church, and therefore preach virtue to men, and dogma only in so far as it is of help to them in that respect. But one dogma I shall keep from them altogether, namely that of intolerance, which is cruel and immoral. Thus I shall play no part in attempts to convert people who hold another faith (p. 116f). The Protestant who has become a Roman Catholic is to be advised to return to the religion of his forefathers—we do not know if Rousseau was in fact so advised by a Roman Catholic priest—if only because it is morally still the purest and intellectually still the most modest of religions. In any case the true duties of religion are independent of the human religious institutions. The only essential thing is the *culte intérieur*, and it is in this sense that the saying 'no virtue without faith' may well be valid (p. 122). The teachings of philosophical scepticism and atheism which threaten us are just as bad as the teaching which we have to expect from the Churches. As they are even more dogmatic in their approach than the Church, they deprive man of everything he finds worthy of reverence, and thus rob the unhappy of their last comfort, the happy of their only warning, the criminal of the chance that he will repent, and the virtuous of hope. Fanaticism is at least a great passion, whereas this philosophy is tolerant only because of its indifference to good, and creates a state of quiet which can only be called the quiet of death. Both extremes of superstition and unbelief are therefore to be avoided (p. 126). 'Dare to profess a belief in God to the philosophers; dare to preach humanity to the intolerant!'—such is the confession of faith of the Vicar of Savoy and the confession of faith of J.-J. Rousseau.

It was this part of *Emile* which was to prove disastrous for the life of its author. Both Church and State found cause to take action with some speed after the book had appeared, particularly because of this section. Christophe de Beaumont, Archbishop of Paris, promulgated a severe pastoral letter against *Emile*. As a result of a decision and order by the Parliamentary Court of Justice in Paris the book was publicly burned on 11th June 1762 and an order was made for the arrest of its author. The latter step, however, was a vain one, for Rousseau's influential friends had caused him to flee in good time. At first he wanted to return to his native land, but on reaching Swiss soil he was horrified to learn that his book had been condemned and burned in his Protestant native city, Geneva, as well, and that he was threatened with arrest there too.

These events were a turning-point in Rousseau's inner life. From then dates the decline in his inward frame of mind and attitude which threw him on to the defensive, breeding pessimism, misanthropy and even persecution mania. Rousseau was never, even in his early youth, what might be called well-balanced. Judging by his own account of his life one can distinctly see the beginnings of a mental crisis already in his personal experiences between 1756 and 1762. From 1762 onwards he became in his own eyes increasingly the misunderstood, persecuted and suffering Jean-Jacques. He now imagined all the dishonesty and prevarication, all the harshness and cruelty, all the injustice, intolerance and spite of which he had so often accused man in his fall from the state of nature, to be an attack directed against himself personally. In the beginning it was of course a real attack to which he was subjected, an actual attempt at injury, which occupied his mind for some time— an attack by the Catholic and Protestant Churches, which had after all themselves been assailed by the remarks of the Vicar of Savoy, with the aim of defending themselves against his ideas. But he became progressively less conscious of this, so that he did not, as might have been expected, become specifically anti-clerical. He lost sight, so to speak, of this particular foe, that is to say, of the Church, in the ranks of the general front which he imagined was aligned against him, consisting of philosophers, academicians, literary men, politicians, the educated and uneducated public in general, and in short man as he was at that time, the same in all these varied forms. Contemporary man did not understand him because he understood him only too well, because he felt that Rousseau was arraigning him, and for this reason hated and persecuted the arraigner. That is why Jean-Jacques was now, at every turn and no matter with whom, a prey to a passionate mistrust which was likely to flare up at every second, a suspicion that he was being victimized, that he was faced by a general conspiracy, systematically conducted from the highest places and employing the most cunning methods. That is why from now until the end of his life he worked himself more and more into the rôle of the righteous sufferer, indeed into a kind of Christ-character, a rôle in which it would doubtless not have been possible for him to suffer subjectively more severely than he did if it had not been a merely assumed rôle. And indeed it was not entirely assumed—what Rousseau had to endure in the years immediately after 1762 was in fact hard and harsh. It was just that he insisted on investing his experiences with the character of a myth and suffering them accordingly, whereas the conditions of life he had to endure—taken by themselves—were not in fact of an unprecedently dreadful kind, as compared with those of other genuine martyrs.

This inner development is not of significance merely as a source of clinical biographical data, but constitutes together with the problems it presents the background without which we should fail to understand the man who is seemingly so optimistic in the things he wrote from 1756 to 1762, so completely in accord with his age, even hastening

impetuously before it along the path it was treading. This was the man
who saw himself as the hated and hating enemy of this age. But it was
only gradually that this came to light, under the weight of the blows of
fate which later fell upon him. It was with the feeling that with the
confession of faith of the Vicar of Savoy, of all things, he had written
the best and most worthwhile book of the century[1] that he fled from
Paris. Indeed he then felt he was the only man in France who believed
in God.[2] But he also had then the feeling: *ma carriére est finie*. Prevented
from returning to the town of his birth, and banished also from the
Bernese territory, where he had at first set foot at Yverdon, he turned
to the principality of Neuenburg, which was at that time Prussian. He
sent a letter to Frederick the Great beginning with the words: 'Sire, I
have said many bad things about you and shall probably say more',
and shortly afterwards thanked him in a second letter for the asylum
which had been granted him by bluntly demanding that he should
put an end to the Seven Years War.[3] He did in fact find at first at
Neuenburg that the Prussian governor, Field-Marshal von Keith, was
well disposed towards him, and found a lodging at Môtiers in the Val
de Travers. It was from here that he settled his score with his opponents in Paris, in the letter to Monseigneur de Beaumont[4] which
appeared in November 1762, and with those in Geneva in the Letters
from the Mountain in 1764[5]. The core of the charges made against
him by both sides had been that he denied revelation in favour of
natural religion, or in favour of human reason. It is obvious that
Rousseau was in the stronger position polemically not only with the
Archbishop but with the theologians of Geneva, because they were
both, the former with his Thomistic 'reason just as much as revelation',
and the latter, the pupils of one J. A. Turrettini, with their rational
orthodoxy, treading the same path which he had after all only naïvely
and logically trodden to its end in his *profession de foi*, and because it
was fairly easy for him to show—taking into account the moral enthusiasm of his age—that he, with his untroubled rationalism and
Pelagianism was only doing honestly, completely and logically what
they were doing half-heartedly and certainly not for any good reason.
It was he—he, the true, simple, truth-and-virtue-loving Christian
and disciple of Jesus—who retorted to the Archbishop,[6] and who said
to the Genevans that he understood what the Reformation was:

[1] Letter to Beaumont, Amsterdam ed., Vol. 9, p. 53.
[2] Letter of 7th June, 1762, Basle ed., Vol. 26, pp. 1f.
[3] Letters of September and October 1762, Basle ed., Vol. 27, pp. 47f.
[4] Amsterdam ed., Vol. 9.   [5] Vol. 9, second half.
[6] Vol. 9, first half, p. 54.

namely the interpretation of the Bible on the sole basis of free conscience and free reason.[1] As for the things both the Roman Catholic and the Protestant sides complained about in his attitude to revelation but also to the doctrine of original sin, to Christ and miracles, his position was unassailable, not because he was right, but because his opponents were not so right in all these things as to be entitled and able to put him in the wrong. The triumph of the answer this logical rationalist and Pelagian was capable of giving especially to the Genevans was payment for the course which Protestant theology had pursued since the beginning of the century. It was in fact only by acting hypo-critically or in great self-deception that the Geneva of the younger Turrettini could find cause for the burning of *Emile*. We can understand to some extent the anger with which Rousseau, applying his teaching that in an emergency it was possible to contract out of the social contract, informed Geneva in 1763 that he intended henceforth to renounce his rights as its citizen.[2]

But this counter-offensive now made Neuchâtel too attentive to his person and heresies. The local priest at Môtiers, F. G. de Montmollin, with whom Rousseau had at first been on good terms, and who had even at his own request allowed him to take Holy Communion, turned from him and became his opponent. Behind him there was the assembled clergy of Neuchâtel as a class, behind them again the theologians of Geneva and Berne, and behind them the mighty arm of these two states. And remarkably enough it is most probable that among others Voltaire, of all people, had a hand from Ferney in the hounding of Rousseau which was now to be resumed. In the night of 6th to 7th September, 1765, the irate villagers of Môtiers bombarded his lodging with stones and he had to take flight again. He thought he had already found a new sanctuary on St Peter's Island, which belonged to the town of Berne, in the Lake of Biel. The two months of autumn which he spent there must once again have been a climax, reminiscent of the time at Chambéry in his remarkably intimate relationship to plants, animals, landscape and atmosphere. The winter was just beginning when the high bailiff of the neighbouring district of Nidau informed him that the Council of Berne had evicted him from here also. And only a day later he was disappointed once again in thinking that he had found a refuge, at least for the winter, in the town of Biel. He left Switzerland on 31st October, 1765.

The fate that was prepared for him in that year by Geneva, Neuchâtel and Berne can in no way be described as a glorious page in the

[1] Vol. 9, second half, pp. 42f.   [2] Amsterdam ed., Vol. 26, p. 58.

history of the Reformed Churches there. Rousseau was invited by Frederick the Great to come to Prussia, but preferred, to his great subsequent regret, to go to England. The philosopher David Hume had encouraged him to do so, and introduced him into English society, found somewhere for him to live in Wootton in Derbyshire and even managed to procure for him a fairly generous pension from the King. It was at this time that the disturbance of his mental balance was to become visible in an unmistakable way. For he suddenly rounded on Hume himself, without any justification whatsoever as far as can be seen, and accused him of being the one who was the worst-disposed of all towards him, and of being engaged on behalf of his extensive league of enemies in making his mental and physical life utterly impossible. At last he broke with Hume, an action which, judged by anything like normal standards, made no sense at all. Rousseau abruptly rejected the offer of the royal pension. From afar his friends in France pleaded with him in vain. The only thing they achieved was to fall within the sphere of his mistrust themselves; Rousseau thought they were probably involved in the general conspiracy against him too.

Nevertheless, it was during his stay in England that he wrote the first part of his famous *Confessions*, an autobiography which had in common with Augustine's work of the same name an utter frankness and a very deliberate method of presentation. Strangely enough this first part, the history of Rousseau's life until 1741, until the parting with Madame Warens, gives us in content and mood a perfect picture of one reconciled and content with God and the world, and above all with himself. Engrossed in this period of his past its author seems to have forgotten all the unpleasantness and hallucinations of his present. There he finds himself once again in a state of nature, so to speak, before entering into society and thus in innocence of all wickedness and evil. Thus we are surprised, and yet we should not really be at all surprised when we read later on, at the beginning of the second part, that he wrote the first in a state of most tranquil and happy composure. This could not be said of the second part if only because its subject was the years of activity and conflict which brought him towards all the sufferings of the present.

Rousseau returned to France in 1767, where for the last eleven years of his life, afflicted by bodily ills as well, he was scarcely heeded by those about him, much less menaced, but was inwardly condemned to the most painful instability and torment. In 1768 he married his Thérèse Le Vasseur, prompted probably more by gratitude for her loyalty than by love. He lived first at one place and then at another, maintaining himself by the proceeds from his books and by the score-copying which was the strange object of his affection, at the same time pursuing the tranquil pleasure he received from dabbling in botany, and generally going for walks and yet more walks, a pastime of which he never tired. But inwardly he was still—and now more than ever—a volcano. He could not be kept in any one place for long, for everywhere he lived in fear of snares. At the same time he was charged to bursting point with the indictment against a humanity which he imagined he had seen through to the very depths of its stupidity and wickedness, and he could not but conceive of himself, his own existence, as its quite special victim.

Apart from completing his *Confessions* in the manner just alluded to— one very contrary to their beginning—and writing a book on botany, he also composed at this time the strange dialogues *Rousseau juge de Jean-Jacques* in which he talks with a third party about himself, his sad and disputed position, his character and his works: always with the intention of pointing out this general conspiracy against him, its cruelty and senselessness, and of making protest upon protest against the society which thus misused him, and of begging over and beyond this for the right to his own existence and for the right to have room to move and be heard—which it implied. He has done this in a way which, in spite of all its overtones of vanity and self-pity and all the head-shakings it calls forth, instinctively moves the reader. He had the fantastic plan of placing this work on the high altar of Notre Dame, entrusting it to 'Eternal Providence', together with a letter to the same, so that it would be sure to be passed on to posterity, but he found himself—it was 24th February, 1776—forestalled in some mysterious manner. He eventually entrusted it to the care of a travelling English-man, who made its existence publicly known after his death. It would not be true to say of this manifestly pathological piece of writing either, that it is solely of biographical interest. How often have the *Contrat Social* and *Emile* been misconstrued by people who understood nothing of the vibrant sensitiveness or of the tensed-up bitterness or of the con-suming longing for peace and yet for love, too, as they were in this man, and which he expressed in so defenceless and exposed and therefore in so concrete a form perhaps only in this impossible polemic of his old age. But above all it must not be forgotten that this was not his last work, and that the mood in which he wrote it was not the one in which he departed this life. The idea that Rousseau committed suicide, which was believed for some time in the eighteenth century, has long since been proved to be without foundation.

It may only have been a relatively short time before his death, but yet it came: a time in which the state of conflict and tension he had experienced for fifteen years (he himself states this figure several times) was eased somewhat at least, and when at least something of the inner peace of which he had so often defiantly boasted and to which he had at once given the lie by the unrest in which he lived, seemed somehow to have become a reality after all. This last time saw the writing of *Les rêveries du promeneur solitaire*, in which he endeavours once again, for the third time now since the *Confessions*, to look back upon his life and to see and understand himself. In form, language and content these reveries may well be described as Rousseau's most beautiful piece of writing. They have this quality for the simple reason perhaps, if not for any other, that he did not write them with the idea of publishing them, but only for himself, and thus dispensed with all, or nearly all, rhetoric. It is certainly the most moving of all his works. Once again and now in a somehow still truer and more tangible form than in the *Confessions* we seem to catch in these calmer observations of the old man something like a reflection or echo of the young days at Chambéry that had had such a singular significance for him. Or did they only now assume the quite specific glow which his words about them emanate even now? Did he only now endow them with this splendour in a kind of creative act of remembrance? Be that as it may one is tempted to say that it is these reveries that bring his life full circle. The great struggle lies behind him, not done away with, not settled, it is true, but unforgotten, still alive within him, still part of the present, still capable at every moment of stinging him into pain or anger—and yet rumbling only in the distance like a receding thunderstorm, settled into its place in his life as a whole. Was it not his wish to be alone with nature in those days around 1740? The man of 1778 was alone with nature; he had achieved this very differently, and by way of quite different sufferings and disappointments from those he then imagined were in store for him. In the meantime he had also paid his due to life in society, to life in its unnatural form. He paid it in daring and because he had dared to challenge this life, in obedience to a highly necessary but also highly dangerous impulse, because he had dared to oppose to it as a corrective, and indeed as a secret court of judgment, the other life, the life of nature and solitude, and had dared, as a missionary coming from the true homeland of all life, to direct it into another course, namely that leading back to its origins. He had failed in this mission. He himself had been plunged into the condition he had wished to destroy, had been caught in the bonds from which he had sought to set society free. He let himself be infected to the point of madness by the thing he said we should on no account allow to infect us. But he let himself be infected so thoroughly, he took the perverted life of society and its unnaturalness so bitterly and radically to heart, that of necessity he yet found himself in the end back where he had started. He had only to lay down the weapons of the battle with society, the weapons which, after all, it pained him grievously to use, to find that, as in a re-awakening, he was once again thrown back upon solitude, upon himself and into the realm of nature. From here he now made no more warlike excursions. Now he only dreamed of his quarrel. The reality was peace—the peace following defeat, but peace all the same. Thus he let all his experiences pass before his mind's eye once again, but he could linger only upon those which were of ineffable beauty: those at Chambéry, on St Peter's Island, and a few in the neighbourhood of Paris. We should not wonder at finding everything which gives us cause for astonishment in Rousseau contained once more in this last work of his. His childish vanity, naïve egotism, downright ruthless moral optimism, his desire to have people tell him he is right, his rationalism and Pelagianism; all these are still there and bear new fruit on nearly every page of this his final work. There is no trace of heightened religious feeling or of anything like it. Rousseau never reformed or even improved. He is unmistakably the old sinner Jean-Jacques even in this his finest piece of writing, and there could be every reason to find this calm after the storm, this lonely peace, with himself and nature his sole companions, which formed the final tenor of his days, more suspect from a theological point of view than all the rest of his life. But it might be more fitting for us not to brandish any theological weapons at this point. Rousseau stands too rounded and complete before us—rounded and complete precisely in the complete vulnerability of his attitude and teaching—for us not to be glad to remain silent. If we understand what Rousseau seems never to have understood; that no one can live from anything but forgiveness, then we cannot be interested in establishing a fact which it is all too easy to establish; namely that this man was certainly a sinner of a quite unusual order. Nobody commands us to follow in his footsteps. It might in fact be advisable not to. All the less reason for us to feel that it is our duty to throw a stone at him. It might even seriously be doubted, whether the man who does not feel impelled to hail him as a figure lovable for all its tragi-comic doubtful quality—being somehow moved by the things which moved him so violently—is doing him any kind of justice. Rousseau died in Erménonville on 2nd July, 1778.

We shall now turn to a brief consideration of the significance of the phenomenon of Rousseau, for the question which here concerns us. If we are to see all that is to be seen on this subject, it is essential above all that we should choose our point of departure correctly. Even judging simply by what we have heard of his life it could not possibly be right to level the charge against him that his great literary fight, the fight which was to affect his life so much, was a fight against the Catholic and Protestant theologians—the orthodox ones from his point of view, that is. The Rousseau of the Vicar of Savoy, the letter to Beaumont, and the *Letters from the Mountain* is—and this is in itself significant enough— the fulfiller of the religion and theology of the human heart and under- standing, the man who boldly trod the path of eighteenth-century theology to its end in advance of all the orthodox. As such the things he says are final, and it is because of this that in this respect too the world strains to catch every word he says, and that in this respect too he evokes such passionate applause and opposition. But he does not say any first things, any new things. It is certainly inherent in the one uttering the new word that he should at the same time be the one uttering the last old word, but if we now wish to hear Rousseau as the speaker of the new word we must not persist in listening to him in his *rôle* as a fighter for religious progress and freedom. For we have seen how this matter did not play the commanding part in his own mind which the theologian viewing his work is tempted to ascribe to it. Further, we must certainly not have as points of departure the political and educational structures he planned in the *Contract* and in *Emile*, and what might be called the morality of the *Nouvelle Héloïse*. It was, to be sure, an inner necessity for Rousseau to dare to erect these struc- tures. They were more directly connected with what he essentially had to say and with what was new in him, because they were more positively connected with it than was his opposition to the old denomi-ational Churches. In them he used his new and essential characteristics to contribute as far as ever they could to the striving of his own time. It is no wonder that with such a basis they com- pletely dwarfed the contributions of most of his contemporaries, and that, even taking into account the nature of his age, they had the effect of a revelation. But they were in fact his contribution to the striving of his time and as such did not represent the dawning of a new era or the essential thing he had to say. They were, as we saw, sugges- tions as to how a second-best solution might be reached, which Rousseau had become resigned to making. It is precisely the resignation behind them which is without doubt part of the secret of their effect. But it also

D

directs our gaze to things beyond it. In this respect too Rousseau, seen from the point of view of his own time, might well have uttered conclusive words, but it was precisely because they were the last words that they were not yet, or perhaps no longer, the first, the new word which he meant by them and which he actually wanted to utter.

We might now feel tempted to make our point of departure the lyricism of immediate feeling for himself and the world about him which sounds especially in Rousseau's autobiographical works, but also in the *Nouvelle Héloïse*; man's lonely communion with nature which formed the beginning and ending of Rousseau's course in life. Fairly shrewd commentators have often stopped there. Why should this not prove to be the gateway leading directly to his secret? Why should it not be the vantage-point which yields a clear view forward to Goethe, Idealism and Romanticism? This side of his life and work must certainly be understood and appreciated before one can understand and appreciate how he could yet write the *Contract* and *Emile* and become a pioneer of the new human religion. But this side too of Rousseau's life and work can still be interpreted as a last word of the old time, of the age of absolutism, which in point of fact it was. We have constantly stressed the point that the age of Goethe, of which Rousseau was the first great representative, was also the peak of eighteenth-century absolutism. But it was not only its peak but also its end. There is not only continuity between it and the eighteenth century but also discontinuity, a break, and I am inclined to think that it is this break, as it was completed, in the last assessment, simply in Rousseau's biography, in his more or less pathological method of existing as such, which is the essential thing we have to consider in him. I think that this is the point of departure from which everything else about him which singled him out from his contemporaries first becomes clear, clear as something new which was already contained in this age as a coming age—an age struggling to be born.

From the point of view of Rousseau's biography, of his own idea of himself, it would be completely impossible—he himself felt the contrast so violently—to conceive of his being the culmination and last word of the era of absolutism. This need not, however, deceive us into thinking that he was not that as well. It does compel us however to think of him from another angle at the same time. It was not just an impudent lout who fled from his apprenticeship in Geneva in 1728, but at the same time someone who was quite aware of what he wanted, whose intention it was to escape from the bourgeois moral world of his century. It was not merely from some form of ethical chaos, but from an inner world which was strange and new to the accustomed behaviour and ideals of his time that Rousseau returned from Madame de Warens' orchard to Paris society in 1741; he returned not merely as a somewhat useless and unpractical dreamer, but at the same time as the apostle of a new kind of historical reality, which, admittedly, could not at first find any place in his time. It was not only a delight in a cleverly discovered and pointed antithesis which led him in the answer to the prize dissertation question of the Dijon academy in 1750 to begin his impetuous onslaught upon the value of art and science. It was a force which was actually alive within him, sharply opposing the things which his time most greatly and highly esteemed. It is not only by listening to the psychologists and psychiatrists that we shall reach an understanding of the fifteen years' persecution mania which followed 1762; it is not just a case of someone with a grudge against life on whom we must bestow our pity: no matter how delusory Rousseau's grounds for hating and for thinking he was hated were in these years, it was a delusion which had some meaning in so far as it represented a protest in him against the entire inner and outer structure of life in his time, a protest which made itself very definitely felt, and one which within this structure had perhaps inevitably first to make itself felt as a delusion. It is just from here that we cast an involuntary glance in the direction of Goethe. In the first days of December 1777, six months, that is, before Rousseau's death, Goethe made his 'Winter journey in the Harz', and amongst the verses in which he poetically described it, there are to be found the following:[1]

> Easy following Fortune's
> Carriage; one of that
> Leisurely train on the
> Re-made highway concluding
> The monarch's entry.
>
> O, how cure his torments
> To whom balm is now poison?
> Who drank in his hatred
> In fulsome delight!
> First spurned, now despising,
> Consuming in secret
> His own true merit
> In tortured self-love.
> But who walks there apart?
> His path is lost in the bushes,
> The foliage noiselessly
> Closes behind him,

[1] For original see Appendix, p. 400.

The grasses unbend,
The void engulfs him.

If, Father of Love, there be
One note of Thy psaltery
To his ear attuned
Then cheer his heart!
Clear his clouded gaze
That thirsting he may see
The thousand springs
In the desert!

Every word could not only refer and be addressed to Friedrich Plessing, who was its actual subject, but to Rousseau. But would it not also have been relevant to Goethe's Werther, and to his Faust, the man who no longer knew what to make of art and science, as he reached for the phial of poison early on the morning of Easter day? And therefore relevant to Goethe himself in his early days—and perhaps not only as he was in his early days? What else are his Götz von Berlichingen and Schiller's Karl Moor but Rousseau translated into manly, and heroic terms with a capacity for action, a transformation of the protesting, the deluded Rousseau? To be sure, Goethe and his age stand at a point beyond the conflict and tension in which Rousseau was involved. Anyone who can thus take him as a poetic subject has absorbed him and his protest and delusion, his 'Storm and Stress'; they are no longer something vital, but something which has been overcome. But Goethe would not have been Goethe if he had not passed through the period of storm and stress himself, if he had not carried it within him all the days of his life as a protest which, although no longer vital to him, was yet part of him and had taken shape within him; as a madness which had found rest and peace—if Goethe had not himself been a Rousseau, albeit a victorious and comforted Rousseau, but a Rousseau none the less and if Goethe had not been the man who, while he brought the eighteenth century to its culmination, was yet its most embittered opponent. Indeed, we have seen that at the very time when Goethe was writing those lines Rousseau himself was at least on the way to achieving for his part the comfort they offered. The contrast between the two men, which must certainly not be overlooked, is a contrast within a homogeneity which is more important and more powerful than the contrast, and they belong together at any rate also in their contrast with the eighteenth century. Thus the days of bitterness which Rousseau tasted to their end, his illness, were not even in themselves matters of pure chance. The time he lived in was his disease, and the fact that the age that was to come had not yet arrived, the time of which Goethe then became the master not *only* in a sick fashion but much more in a healthy fashion: the master in whom the sickness was overcome by good health. Without Rousseau's negation the affirmation of this new time would not have been possible. Rousseau's cups of bitterness had something of the nature of birth-pangs and it is for this reason that they are the primary and essential thing to which we should devote our attention in studying him, especially if it is our aim to understand him in relation to his time, and to approach his time through him.

The break indicated by the broken quality of Rousseau's own personal life represents, however, the breaking of the absolutist will for form which came to pass in him. This is, first of all, the significance of Rousseau as a phenomenon: here was a man who could not share the general joy which inspired his age, the joy in man's intellectual, technical and moral capacities. A man who could not produce the general unquestioning confidence in all that European society had so far achieved, but who on the contrary dissociated himself from it, so to speak, instead of naïvely taking part in these achievements. A man who measured the whole of these achievements against another Whole, and who from that angle was in a position to regard it with feelings of estrangement, bewilderment, disquiet and revulsion. A man who looking at it from that angle was not only not impressed by this world, who not only had objections to certain of its features, but who regarded this whole world as such as the cause of his suffering, and as such felt compelled to reject it wholly. He felt all this and yet at the same time he felt that he was the advocate, protector and avenger of his fellow-man, this very man who finds cause for triumph in the sum of his achievements and in the possession of the capacities which made them possible, who rejoiced so heartily in them and was so sure that he was on the right path and should go further and further along it.

Rousseau's protest reveals how self-contradictory the attitude of his fellow-man was. Driven by a demoniac or foolish spirit arising out of some depth of his being which was at first completely inexplicable he hurled his impeachment at society—but no, it was not his charge, but society's own, which it had drowned and not heeded. It was that the life of society, ruled as it was by this capacity for civilization and this will for form was no real human life at all, no life in accordance with man's essential quality and nature, but signified rather its complete perversion and destruction; that it was not the heaven it pretended and told itself it was, but a hell. He could see no way of accepting any compromise. His only possible course was radically to deny the spiritual and intellectual, the moral and social forms which, unshaken by the Lisbon earthquake, held sway in Europe from 1750 to 1760. From the world in which Voltaire was a great man Rousseau, shaken to the depths of his being, could only withdraw, depart into the wilderness, into madness, put on fanciful Armenian clothing, marry Thérèse Le Vasseur, copy scores and go plant-gathering. Anyone who was a friend of this world could be no friend of his, even if his name was David Hume, and were he ever so well-disposed, or what passes for well-disposed, towards him. Let all his contemporaries reject him—indeed they must reject him, it cannot be otherwise. The time would come when he would be understood—in his last years Rousseau continually consoled himself with this, his prophecy.

And in considering all this we must always bear in mind that, no matter how often it seemed so to Rousseau himself, he was not fighting against any particular abuses of his time, any particular signs of decadence, folly or vice, not against those aspects of its spirit which were wrong, but against its spirit as a whole, not against the weaknesses of its civilization but against its civilization as such, not against its negative aspects but against the positive ones. That is why it was a struggle which was at once so embittered and so completely hopeless, and precisely why he could not remain hidden from his time, could not be ignored by it as though he were some eccentric of the kind we have always had with us. It was for this reason that his time took such an interest in him—whether this interest took the form of scorn and derision or was manifested as a friendly and sympathetic attention to what he had to say is another question. But his time could not dissociate itself from him, for the simple reason that he belonged to it. He spoke to it from its heart, just because he explained to it its own inner conflict. If Rousseau had been willing and able, he could have brought about a quite different, tranquil, honourable and harmonious end to his life as a respected, nay revered critic and fighter within society with a critical but somehow regulated relationship to the cultural beliefs of his time. It is worth remembering that he did not seek and did not accept any such formal outward kind of truce. He was not drawn by interest in what he was saying, no matter how warmly this interest might be expressed, but treated those who showed friendship towards him like enemies, maintaining his solitariness and therefore his protest not only in substance but also in form. His sense and interpretation of the contrast between himself and his time was as sharp as that. It was in this that his madness consisted. All things considered we cannot help admitting that in its own way it was at least a pertinent madness.

In face of this it might now seem rather remarkable that Rousseau's literary life-work should chiefly consist in the great structures we have mentioned: a political theory in the *Contract*, an educational programme in *Emile*, an interpretation of love and marriage in the *Nouvelle Héloïse*. And I presume we can and must add, a construction of his own life in the *Confessions* and other autobiographical works. In all these undertakings in themselves, and in the most important features of the way in which they were executed, we certainly can and must interpret him from the trends of his time, as being at one with it and as intending and desiring the same things which it wanted and intended. Or was it not the case that also here, in an even bolder and more consequential form than existed at the average cultural level of his time, the contemporary absolutist will for form was at work, whose enemy Rousseau had yet appointed and declared himself to be? Has he not fallen in—and well and truly fallen in—with the Philistines in spite of all things?

There are three primary arguments to discount this:

1. Rousseau betrays the fact that he is a thoroughgoing critic of his age in his literary work as well as in his life by the manifest unity of the anthropological theme running through all his writings. He was obviously never tempted to enter the fields of applied science or historical research. The things which did tempt him were art and natural science. But the thing which really cried out to him was man. The never-ending subject of his meditations was man, and, moreover —in this respect Rousseau is not unlike Socrates—man in relation to the problems he has to face in moulding his own peculiar existence. The results of these meditations he expressed at the very point where his time believed it had already essentially grasped and accordingly could handle everything.

2. Rousseau, in setting his contributions to the human problem beside those of his contemporaries, said things in all three or four spheres which stood out in such a way as to seem, at least relatively, still rather new, strange, Utopian, and indeed revolutionary. While he formally undertook something that could also be and was in fact done by others, he nevertheless drew patterns and created figures—think especially of the figure he presented as his own—which stood out in a sufficiently bizarre way when they were compared with what the others usually intended and achieved. It is true that the *Contract* and *Emile*, and the *Nouvelle Héloïse* too in its way are genuine eighteenth-century

creations, but it is also true that they are infused with an ardour which the rest of contemporary political, educational and erotic literature did not know in this degree, nor in this kind.

3. In contributing with these works to the achievements of his time and sharing through them his time's will to shape and mould, Rousseau made no secret of the fact that he intended even his boldest proposals to be regarded only as suggestions as to how second-best solutions might be reached. The typical man of the eighteenth century, while he was ready to admit that his insight and strength were imperfect, assumed as a matter of principle that he could yet want and achieve the best. He saw in principle only the one dimension of the possible, even when he knew that in practice he could not achieve all that it contains. Rousseau saw the second dimension, composed of the things it is not possible for man to achieve *hic et nunc*, and which therefore could not be taken as part of the programme. The man of whom Rousseau was speaking, whom he wished to help mould his life, was not the man in a state of nature whom he really has in mind, but man in society. Rousseau, as we have shown, was already resigned to this fact before he started to write the *Contract*, *Emile* and the *Nouvelle Héloïse*, but least perhaps in the *Confessions*, without trying to conceal the fact that he was nevertheless not resigned the whole time; that is, ultimately, after all, he has man in a state of nature in mind and only from this standpoint does he speak on the problem of man in society. Truly it is this extraordinary kind of resignation, resting as it does upon a most determined non-resignation, that lends his work the fire and impetus which distinguish it from everything else that was written in his time. It is precisely this kind of writing, where the author consciously refrains from giving of his best, which often has an electrifying effect which is absent from the works of many writers when they are in fact earnestly and passionately trying to write at their best. These then are the arguments against simply ranging Rousseau's works alongside those typical of the eighteenth century.

All the same, it must be maintained here that such a classification is possible. The same Rousseau who raised the anthropological problem in its ethical aspects, as a forerunner of Kant, in a situation when nobody had seen a problem there at all; the same Rousseau whose undertakings were so revolutionary in their effect for the very reason that behind them there is the recognition of a realm to which the only answer can be one of resignation; the same Rousseau said the last word concerning eighteenth-century absolutism. It is precisely in Rousseau that we see that clearly and how this absolutism, to be true, is now being restricted and broken by a new insight, only finally to assume another form in which it would continue to survive and enter the spirit of the new age, the age of Goethe. The two dimensions of Rousseau's anthropology come about only in this way, that he distinguishes between man in nature and man in society. According to Rousseau it was man's transition from this one to the other which constituted what might be called the Fall. And it is because Rousseau was aware of this irrevocable transition, yet declared himself by his suggestion for fallen man, i.e. man in society, and yet on the other hand never lost sight for one moment of the significance of the lost state before the Fall, which he saw as being condemnatory but at the same time indicative of the way we ought to go, that his doctrines of politics and education acquired this fire, this weight and impetus. But the word 'fall' in the biblical sense is not really the right one to describe this transition, however sharply Rousseau felt the contrast it implies, and however sharply this feeling distinguished him from his intellectual environment, whose way of thinking was one-dimensional. Rousseau very seriously takes it to be a transition from a good state to one less good, but not—however severely he may condemn and describe this state—a transition from good to evil.

But where in actual fact do these things have their source and domain, the possibilities of lying, tyranny, injustice, cruelty, intolerance, the effects of which Rousseau had found to be so powerful in human society, as it really is, which made him suffer so, and which caused him to attack society so radically? Wherever they may be, they are not in man, is the answer we must give, to be in agreement with him. They seem rather to be something with which man is faced, mere possibilities existing somewhere outside him. Man's downfall and misfortune consisted in his reaching within and becoming obsessed with them, so to speak, as they became real, at the moment when he went over from the individual, natural state to the social, historical one.

But this reaching within and becoming obsessed in no way alters the fact that man is fundamentally, essentially and naturally good, and has remained so. It is certainly true that his natural goodness does not prevent him from becoming less good. But even while he is deteriorating his natural goodness remains. In common with the whole of the eighteenth century Rousseau was a confirmed Pelagian, a declared opponent of the Church doctrine of original sin and no free will: man can in fact be wicked and is wicked times without number; but he is never essentially wicked and need not be so. He may well do evil but he is not evil. The charge to be brought against man is relevant only in a certain connexion, namely to his existence in society, which brings with it all the evil possibilities we have mentioned. More precisely, it is relevant only to this connexion as such, or more particularly, to society as such. The charge is levelled against the community at large. When applied to the individual the charge loses its force and becomes a warning against the community at large. It does not apply to man himself, man as such. In him it encounters rather a natural goodness, to which an appeal can be made. Thus it must not be taken literally if we describe this transition from man in nature to man in society in Rousseau's sense, as a fall brought about by sin. His man neither sins when he undergoes this transition, nor is he fallen when he has undergone it. He has merely changed in a regrettable way. He has merely acquired a new, lamentable characteristic while remaining substantially unchanged. He does evil, it is true, but he is still free to do good. Rousseau was so energetic in pursuing this idea, so naïve in taking it as his constant premise and in declaiming it, that he drew unwelcome attention to himself even in his own Pelagian century, and became a kind of martyr to Pelagianism, persecuted by a Roman Catholic and Protestant Church both of which, however—they had both been on the slippery slope for some time themselves in this respect—had little enough to show him either as an example or as a defence. Rousseau distinguished himself so much in this respect particularly that it might well seem to us that he, the great opponent of the optimism of his century, was the most optimistic of all its optimists. While he is challenging the customs, institutions, ideals and philosophical dicta of his time, its entire will for form and all its results he yet is all the more consistently able to affirm his belief in man himself, who after all is the subject, the creator and master of all these things.

That is why he is able to construct so boldly, and to make such ruthlessly logical and thoroughly optimistic proposals in the fields of politics and education. It is true that the second-best possibilities to which he devoted himself here were different from the impossible best ones, but even his discussion of the second-best possibilities consistently conveys an underlying faith in man as one who is fundamentally good, to whom one need only appeal, who has only to be provided with the necessary scope, who has only to be freed as far as possible from the temptations and burdens of society, to see appear in him forthwith the natural miracle of virtue, even on his present plane in the midst of society as it actually is.

The tension which is peculiar to Rousseau's teaching, in virtue of his distinction between two dimensions, consists only however of the difference, native to man himself, between the possibility and its particular realization at any time, between man as he is in his heart or hearts and his actual inner life, between what is truly human and man as he is in practice. It was this distinction which Rousseau discovered, and with it the great problem of critical idealism as it was later seen and developed by Kant, less passionately, but on the other hand with far greater precision and insight. And Rousseau's teaching operates with the tension designated by this distinction. But since his teaching recognizes this distinction only in man himself, since man's capacity for doing good is not affected by it, the end-effect of his teaching—and we shall have to say the same of Kant later—is none the less like an augmented and heightened triumph of man, or triumph of man's capacities, which to this extent makes it a solemn repetition and confirmation of the great eighteenth-century thesis. Rousseau believed that in politics we can count upon the *volonté générale* of which he speaks being actually present and active in the consciousness of the individual citizen. He believed that his Emile, having completed his education, will actually have become his own educator. He believed that a conflict such as he described in the *Nouvelle Héloïse* can really be solved in the manner he suggests. Why does he believe that all these things are possible? Because his citizen, his Emile, and his pair of lovers, St Preux and Julie, are fundamentally good human beings, even in the *status corruptionis*, simply because the corruption of this state is only relative corruption.

Rousseau expressed all this in its plainest and most comprehensible form in his autobiographical works. He was in no doubt about his faults and bad habits, and the candour with which he confessed them really leaves nothing to be desired. He made no bones of accusing himself of extreme weakness where his inclinations were concerned, of a laziness to which he again and again succumbed, of frivolity, and even of downright viciousness. As an old man he was still in all seriousness concerned about an act of meanness he had committed in his youth.[1] If it were really the recognition and confession of sin in concrete form which was all-important, then we should have to grant that his *Confessions* are a perfect model. But the other side to the matter is that Rousseau, at the same time as he was confessing his sins, scarcely ever neglected to point out to us that in the midst of and in spite of everything he had a good heart, to enumerate and vaunt the excellent

[1] *Rêv. 4me. promenade*, Basle ed., Vol. 20, pp. 219, 232.

qualities of his true character, the qualities of his inner nature which people did not understand, to emphasize the good intentions which had been behind nearly everything he had done, and either to present his failings as merely negative aspects of his virtues (e.g. his indolence as a manifestation of his great love of freedom, which would have him act always only in response to his very own most deeply personal impulses) or to trace them as regrettable reactions to even more regrettable behaviour prevalent in the world about him. It is scarcely possible to find in these confessions an example of a truly undialectical piece of self-accusation, apart from the memory of his youth we have just mentioned. Another exception may be the fact that he did not tell Madame de Warens the whole truth about his faithfulness to her, at a meeting with her in later years.[1] On the other hand it is quite possible to find more than one passage where he declares that it was always his pride that his misfortune had been undeserved.[2] And there is more than one passage where he quite openly declares that by and large, all his faults, etc., considered, he could not help considering himself the best of all men.[3] Bearing all this in mind, is it not perhaps possible after all to interpret his delusion, his persecution mania, as expressing the only too complete correspondence of his spirit with the spirit of his age? Be that as it may, the church doctrine of original sin has seldom, I believe, been denied with such disconcerting candour and force and in so directly personal a way. The secret that man is good, blurted out so expansively and with such assurance, was bound to appear suspicious even to the many just men of the time who by and large were as hard-boiled as Rousseau himself. But the people who became angry with him in that respect branded themselves by the very fact of their anger as backward, as lacking in understanding of their own time. Anyone who was moving with the times was bound to be thankful to Rousseau, and was thankful to him because he had finally said the last word, because he had so ruthlessly lent such momentum and language to that which they all felt and wanted after all.

Seen from this aspect Rousseau, in the constructions of his main works was not so much a critic and reformer of his time as its leader, its most eloquent tongue, its most perfect culmination. And in so far as the whole new age which made its appearance with him would follow him in this, would not get beyond the distinction between man in his heart of hearts and his actual inner life, between human possibility

---

[1] *Conf.* Basle ed., Vol. 21, p. 198.   [2] *Conf.* 21, 252.
[3] *Conf.* 22, 74; *Rêv.* 20, 265.

and actuality, in so far as the doctrine of original sin would be as a red
rag to it too, in so far as it too would believe that man is good, and
believe it perhaps in a way which was still far more comprehensive, far
more logical and far more suited to genius; thus far this new age too
would only be a culmination of the old one in spite of all the break
with what had gone before. Is there any difference between Rousseau's
Confessions and Goethe's *Dichtung und Wahrheit* except that in Goethe all
the opposition of good and evil, which in Rousseau still seems to be
indicating something like two worlds, is dissolved into the progression
of a single development which is both inwardly and outwardly not
accidental but necessary, so that all the self-justification which still
rings through so naïvely in Rousseau can disappear in Goethe, to be
replaced by a self-representation which is almost, but not quite, self-
satisfied? Is there any difference except that the same good man who in
Rousseau was seeking himself has in Goethe joyfully found himself?
It is the fact that this seeking and finding should become a problem at
all which is the new thing distinguishing the age of Goethe from the
eighteenth century. For the eighteenth century, rejoicing in its command of all things, had *not* asked after this, after man himself, for all
the importance man had assumed for it. But did the new quality of
the age of Goethe signify anything except that man's command was
now regarded as much wider: as including man's command over
himself? Within this new element Rousseau's Pelagianism would then
be to Goethe's as promise is to fulfilment. And we could then certainly
interpret this new spirit as a whole as that of the eighteenth century
reborn, and for the first time assuming classic stature, risen like the
phoenix from the ashes.

But we would be failing to understand Rousseau's—or Goethe's—
Pelagianism if we simply ascribed it, as theologians have so often done,
to a lightness of conscience, and therefore judged it, so to speak, as a
moral deficiency. The decisive factor we must take into account in
considering Rousseau's belief in the goodness of man, held with a
firmness astonishing even to such a time as his, and the wholehearted
support for this view which the age of Goethe then lent him all along,
is the fact that this new age, and Rousseau as one of the first within it,
had made a completely new discovery in the realm of anthropology,
and that it was this same discovery which underlay its contention that
man was good, its rejection of the dogma of original sin, and such self-
appreciations as those of Rousseau, so moving to us now in their *naïveté*;
but which also underlay Goethe's glorified vision of his own existence
and development. From this fact it follows also that what we might

call optimism of the new age was not only incomparably more powerful, but essentially different from what might strike us as being optimism in those belonging to the age which was then drawing to its close.
The natural goodness of man which Rousseau claimed exists is definitely not in any simple or direct sense that which we are in the habit of
calling moral goodness, freedom from evil impulses, freedom from
all kinds of temptation, and freedom to respect the feelings of our
fellow-men. And hence his self-praise is not in any simple or direct
sense moral self-praise. The goodness of which he speaks is of course
moral goodness too: Rousseau imagined that he was good-hearted truly
and particularly also in this respect. But his kind of goodness was not
primarily moral goodness. If Rousseau believed that his heart was good
he did so because he imagined that in the midst of a society whose whole
striving and interest were directed outwards, he had discovered quite
anew that man has a heart, and what the human heart actually is. The
heart is simply the man himself, discounting everything he produces or
which confronts him as an alien existence or as the work of alien hands.
This is what Rousseau has found: himself. And this is what he holds to
be good and even precious: the fact that he exists and does not not-
exist, precisely as the man he is, situated precisely as he is in fact
situated. A whole world revealed itself to him when he gazed into
himself. He did not do this in the manner of the individualism of his
time, which looked within in order to go out again at once into the
outside world, desiring to apprehend, form and conquer. Rousseau
intended to linger there because he had recognized that in it he
possessed his own unique world full of unique forms of truth and beauty.
Existence was not just a predicate, not entirely a matter of how I
conduct myself towards the outerworld. It was definitely not just
acting and suffering. Existence was a beautiful, rich and lively inner
life of its own, so beautiful, rich and lively that anyone who has once
discovered it no longer attributes any worth to any life which differs
from it, and can only have and love anything different from it as it is
connected with this life; but he really could have and love it now in
this connexion. Existence was, so to speak, the realm of the middle, the
mean. It was the paradise of the happy and at the same time the secure
haven of the unhappy. It was the dependable norm for all the distinctions and choices that are necessary in life, and a norm which functioned as it were automatically. Man existing, being himself as Rousseau
more than once said, was in God's presence and like him. If a state
exists where the soul can find a secure place which can contain it whole,
a place secure enough that it can find complete rest in it and can

collect again the forces of its being in it, without needing to recall the
past, nor encroach upon the future, a place where time is as nothing
to the soul and the present lasts for ever, without making its duration
noticeable and without leaving any after-effects, a place where the
soul is without any other feeling, be it privation or pleasure, joy or
pain, fear or desire, except for that of existence, if there is such a state
and if this feeling can fill the soul utterly, while it lasts he who is
enjoying it can call himself happy. It would not be an imperfect, poor
and relative happiness, like that found in the pleasures of life, but a
happiness which is sufficient, perfect and full, leaving no void in the
soul which the soul experiences the need to fill. Such is the state in
which I often found myself on St Peter's Island during my solitary day-
dreams, sitting sometimes in my boat, which I simply let drift as the
waters took it, or sitting sometimes on the shore of the troubled lake, or
beside a river murmuring over the pebbles. What does one enjoy in
such a moment? One enjoys nothing exterior to oneself, nothing except
oneself and one's own existence; while it lasts one is self-sufficient, like
God. The feeling of existing stripped of all other emotions is in itself a
precious feeling of peace and security, which would alone be quite
enough to make one's existence sweet and dear.[1]

This then is the new world which Rousseau discovered, and it was
because he discovered it, unlike the outside world, in *himself*, or rather
discovered it as himself, and found it *good*, once again unlike the outside
world, that he says that man is good naturally, in and in spite of all
things. Nature, which Rousseau so often pointed out as the true source
and eternal law of human life, is very simply man himself, as distinct
from man as he is in his circumstances, as he is in his works, as he is
determined by other people. That is why at the end of his life Rousseau
is able to speak thankfully even of the hard fate which befell him in the
shape of the persecution he imagined was being meted out to him. It
was this fate, he said, which in sundering him violently from the outside world, had forced him to withdraw into himself still more intensively and now even more than ever before.[2] On St Peter's Island
he even felt able to wish he were prisoner,[3] indeed it seemed to him
that a stay in the Bastille, in a dungeon where there were no objects to
catch the eye, might not be at all unpleasant.[4]

But this renunciation of things external particularly, must be interpreted as very dialectic in intention, if we wish to gain a true picture of
the realm of anthropology as discovered by Rousseau. Terms like sub-
jectivism and solipsism would describe badly what Rousseau means.

[1] *Rêv.* 20, 255f.   [2] *Rêv.* 20, 203f.   [3] *Rêv.* 20, 246.   [4] *Rêv.* 20, 257.

He was, as we saw in the confession just quoted, not in a dungeon at all, but surrounded by the delights of nature, and he knows and admits that in effect he cannot do without this partner, the object, at least in this form. No, even the most insignificant object has the power to rouse his imagination and thereby to move him to the depths of his being (*Conf.* 19, 158). He calls himself *une âme expansive*, a soul which simply will and must influence other beings by its feelings and existence.[1] He actually goes so far as to say that it was only in withdrawing into himself and precisely thereby that he first learned to appreciate and absorb external Nature, which previously he had allowed to affect him only in its entirety, in its concrete form, in the diversity of its scents, colours and forms.[2] That is why in old age he took up his botanical studies again after he had for a time given them up because he had tired of them. He started right from the beginning again long after he had given away all his herbaria and sold all his books.[3] It was, to be sure, only botany he took up again. He rejected with horror the suggestion that he should engage also in mineralogy or zoology, explaining that man can approach the study of earth and animals only in such an unpleasant way that this was in itself proof enough that in these sciences man was much too far removed from the will of nature, and therefore from himself. It was only the plant world, he said, which had any immediate contact with man as he truly is. But it is by no means his desire to practise botany systematically and still less with any practical end in view; he just wants to indulge in it as a quietly loving friend of the trees, flowers and grasses, to rejoice without any desire or object in nature's system, of which man cannot become the master because he at once feels himself identical with it, with the whole of Nature, accordingly as he gazes and accordingly as he directly absorbs its reality. To the very attentive, very loyal observer the actual contours of the various single things out there which only just now had been concrete merge into one another again. They cease for him to be single things. Nature becomes a whole again, and man cannot help but feel himself at one with the whole. Thus the single object makes an appearance certainly, but only to disappear again.[4] It is thus that Rousseau can still say that he feels as if he were *brûlant d'amour sans objet*.[5] He yearns for a kind of happiness *sans en savoir démêler l'objet*.[6] He thinks it is again the limitation imposed upon him to the feelings of his own heart which alone enables him to taste the sweetness of existence[7] and believes he can draw nourishment from his personal substance which seems to him inexhaustible.[8] *M'y*

[1] *Rêv.* 20, 287.   [2] 20, 280f.   [3] 20, 277f.   [4] 20, 257, 281, 287.
[5] *Conf.* 20, 75.   [6] *Rêv.* 20, 201.   [7] 20, 300.   [8] 20, 302.

voilà tranquille au fond de l'abyme, pauvre mortel infortuné, mais impassible comme Dieu même.[1]

It would certainly not be right to play off the one group of these remarks about the object against the other. Rousseau needs and does not need the object, he affirms the object and denies it. Both attitudes are equally essential to the 'ecstasy' of his sense of existing. It is a question with this sense of existing of there being a complete cycle, which must on principle be uninterrupted. It is this very cycle from the ego to the object and back again, in which, however, the ego gives to the motion its direction, force and measure, which forms the life of the inner world discovered by Rousseau. We must surely call it ultimately an inner world, an anthropological province: that province in which man, before he takes up any attitude to anything, and before he knows and acts, is immediately aware both of himself and of his relation to an outer world, in such a manner that he is just as able to absorb the second awareness, that of the object, in the awareness of self, as he is to allow the awareness of the object to proceed from the awareness of self in the first place. He is capable here, in his heart, in his sense of existing, of being non-identical with the outside world, and yet again identical with it. It is because the world Rousseau discovered is the world of this human capacity that we must ultimately call it an inner world, an anthropological province.

It is usual in the history of literature and ideas to find this circumstance expressed by means of the assertion that Rousseau, and the age of Goethe which followed him, had looked beyond knowledge and action and discovered their common source, feeling, which they also considered to be the true central organ of the human mind. But he must realize that by 'feeling' is meant the capacity to project consciously, the capacity to assume this dialectical relationship with the outside world, with the object. While feeling, man enjoys himself passively, and rejoices even in an existence which, while different from his own, is yet in contact with it. But in feeling he also has the desire to extend his own existence to include this other existence, and it is thus especially when he is feeling that man becomes and remains truly himself. There is absolutely no question of his perhaps allowing the objects to approach him indiscriminately, allowing himself to be affected and dominated by them without restraint. Nor certainly will he allow himself to fall into that kind of activist individualism, in which man attempts to become the master of the object. With feeling—and it is this which makes for the intoxicating grandeur of the human capacity which has

[1] *Rêv.* 20, 176.

been discovered here, and for the mature wisdom of him who is aware of it—it is always a question of the superior freedom inherent in being able to make contact with objects and yet being able to part from them again, to be separate from them and yet able to make contact with them again and again. The man who is feeling has respect for the object, does not, that is, attempt to interfere with it in its quality as an object. He does not allow it to approach too near, and keeps his distance from it in his turn.

But this respect is nothing but respect for his own existence, which is experienced by the same feeling, the existence which may enrich itself from the object, but may not become submerged in it, and that is why this respect cannot prevent man, in passing from the diastole to the systole, from completely equating the object with himself again. 'To tend nature in oneself, oneself in nature' as Goethe later put it, signifies the revolution of an eccentric wheel, in which the apparent distance of the periphery from the centre is all the more decisively transformed with the next half-turn into the closest proximity.

Goethe was destined to do more honour to the object than Rousseau, engaging not only in botany, but in mineralogy and zoology too, and many other kinds of natural science, without Rousseau's fear, seemingly so childish of offending nature and thereby himself. Goethe would also once again bring historical man into the sphere of the objective world in which he showed interest, the sphere from which he had in the end completely vanished, with Rousseau at least. And Goethe would listen to what the world of objects has to say in a manner incomparably more composed, more earnest and more patient, would be incomparably more receptive and more cautious in the attempt to extend his own existence to include other beings. But for all that Goethe's world would not be different from the inner world discovered by Rousseau, the world containing the simultaneous capacity to take the object completely seriously and not take it seriously at all, the world containing a sovereignty beside which the achievement of the eighteenth century in mastering the object might well seem a lamentably half-hearted attempt, simply because it did not yet have this freedom. It is only when man is capable of controlling his capacity to influence objects, capable of employing or of not employing it, when he is in fact *impassible comme Dieu même*, unaffected by the claims of the object upon him and unaffected by his feelings towards it, that he stands for the first time invested with a true power in the world of things. In this too Rousseau and Goethe were in accord, but whereas Rousseau seems like a novice, agitated, spasmodic and confused, Goethe was calm, superior, composed and lucid. And yet there was a certain selective, reserved and chance quality about Rousseau's attitude to the object which is characteristic of Goethe too: there were certain things in nature even, let alone in history and in life, which Goethe also did not wish to see or know, because they did not accord with his essential being. He did not wish to offend nature either, if only so that nature should not offend him. He also moved through the world of things, not coyly like Rousseau, but *impassible comme Dieu même*, with a supreme refinement, preserving the formalities. And this is how and why he was occasionally free to overlook and forget the non-identity between it and himself. It is not simply in an awareness of identity that Goethe's secret consists; it is just as little true of Goethe as it is of Rousseau— there had been monists long before their lifetime; monism just as much as the dualism of spirit and nature is from the point of view of Rousseau and Goethe a stupidly one-sided view. Their secret is in fact a much greater one, consisting in the freedom to alternate between the awareness of identity and the awareness of non-identity, or in being able to experience both as a unity in their own spirit-nature. There can be no doubt that Rousseau already knew about this spirit-nature. There is already something of the great peace imparted by this Goethean concept in Rousseau's confusion. Thus what Rousseau referred to ambiguously and confusingly enough as 'nature' is really spirit-nature. It was the one positive thing which threw him, as the only one with any knowledge of this matter, into his conflict with his age: twenty or thirty years later he would have been able to find a thousand people who shared his knowledge. He was referring to human spirit-nature when he said that man is good and therefore capable of the fantastic things we have just heard about. The eighteenth century did not understand itself for as long as it failed to understand what a splendid, radiant and at the same time profound Pelagianism Rousseau was offering it. But to a great extent it understood itself and equally Rousseau much better than Rousseau himself imagined in his prophetic solitude. At the points where this happened the new age had already dawned in the middle of the old.

We can now go on to state, in the briefest manner possible, what effect all this was to have upon the theological problem as it existed at this time. Rousseau's attack upon the absolutism of his age could also have signified a protest against his age's peculiar absolutist, i.e. moralizing, intellectualizing, individualizing treatment of the Christian question, and thus against the way theology had developed in his time. The opening up of this second dimension, which is so characteristic of his thinking, could have signified the opening up of a new understanding of sin, grace, revelation and reconciliation. Rousseau opposed his time in a way revolutionary enough to make us wonder whether this solitary fighter and sufferer might not in the last assessment simply have been someone in whose ears the word 'God' rang in quite an unprecedented way. Or are we wrong in being tempted to see in Rousseau, as he was when he made his first public appearance in Paris back in 1749-50, one inspired by a touch of the hem of the mantle of the prophet Amos? Not even the vision which called him was missing, nor persecution, nor the prophet's vicarious suffering. Even at the time of his madness everything had something of the quality of a call being answered, of revelation, inspiration and the inescapable earnestness of the Divine. Even his contemporaries observed this very clearly and he certainly was not lacking in supporters who acknowledged reverently and enthusiastically—quite apart from the fact that this was his own opinion—that he had rediscovered and proclaimed once again the true Christianity.

It is not for us either to confirm or deny that his was the true Christianity. We must however establish that in the very way he understood Christianity he did not deviate from the typical thought of his time, but here also he was merely the man who—putting the famous neologians of his time well and truly in the shade—pursued this thought to its conclusion in a highly radical way. That was what was theologically new about Rousseau: the fact that he broke completely with the doctrine of original sin, which had long been under fire from all sides, and with the conception of revelation also generally threatened for a long time, as an event which was something apart from the inherent development of humanity. Rousseau took both, sin and grace, as being relative movements within human reality, movements in which man, naturally good and persisting in this state of natural goodness, remains assured of his freedom. Rousseau's new gift to theology ultimately consists in this very widening of the concept of reason by means of the discovery of man's spirit-nature, for which objectivity and non-objectivity, non-identity and identity become reciprocal and interchangeable ideas. The theological significance of this discovery was nothing less than the settlement of the conflict between reason and revelation, since by it man was encouraged to look upon himself alternately now as reason and now as revelation. For this it was not first necessary that the word 'God' should take on a new sound. It was enough that the word 'Man' had now for the first time acquired its full, whole tone. Far from contradicting the theological absolutism of its time, Rousseau's doctrine was meant to convey a demand that this theology should at last understand itself rightly, i.e. truly understand man as one who in his true humanity can also command the true God.

Eighteenth-century theology was always thirty years behind the times. This was borne out also in the case of Rousseau. It accounts for the grotesque fact that Rousseau was martyred by an 'orthodoxy' not half so sinister as it seemed to him and to his other secular contemporaries. We must not allow ourselves to be blinded by this spectacle into not realizing that Rousseau did not actually oppose the theology of his time, but only rushed on far ahead of it. He himself prophesied that the theology of his Vicar of Savoy would rise again to a great future. From what we know of the development of the theology of the schools at that time no gift of prophecy was necessary to predict this fact. The theology of the Vicar of Savoy was, of course, like Rousseau's doctrine, still capable of being enriched, deepened and improved in many ways. Simply in the form he first gave it it did not win through. But taking it as it then was we can say in advance that it was indeed bound to have a great future. It is from Rousseau onwards and originating from Rousseau that the thing called theological rationalism, in the full sense of the term, exists: a theology for which the Christian spirit is identical with the truly humane spirit, as it is inalienably and tangibly present to us in that depth of the *ratio* in that inmost anthropological province. Such is the significance of Rousseau for the history of theology—but of Rousseau only as the first harbinger of the age of Goethe: he represented the invitation extended to theology to join forces in determined fashion with this determined rationalism.

III

LESSING

T HE two things we had to say as a preliminary to discussing Rousseau we must also emphasize of Lessing: he was on the one hand a perfect and perfecting man of the eighteenth century and on the other a complete stranger to his age. There are none of the century's peculiarities of interest and desire which we cannot find again in Lessing. So far as theology especially is concerned, we find, just as with Rousseau, only conclusions which are rather forcibly drawn, and insights and attempts at expression which are terminated abruptly, and hang in the air, as it were, just waiting for some completely wise, completely free-minded person to pronounce and formulate them, to rank henceforth as definite achievements in the history of human thought. The philosophy of the Enlightenment, with its unconditional will for form in morality, and resulting respect for the all-embracing power of natural logic, its unquestioning acceptance of the view of life built up on this logic and on natural experience, Lessing effortlessly understood and was able to take as his standpoint without the slightest difficulty, as a self-evident point of departure for every advance. It was right to draw a parallel between the character and achievement of Lessing, and that of Frederick the Great. No one, in Germany in the second half of the eighteenth century, at any rate, afforded so classic an example of the spirit of the age as these two men.

But whilst Lessing represented this age in its most mature form, he also left it behind him. The course of his life, subject to frequent change, outwardly so unrewarding, so often beset by disaster, and no less violent in its way than Rousseau's, already shows that fundamentally he also could not find himself within the limitations imposed by the order, the customs and possibilities of his time. His dealings with Frederick the Great, for instance, in great contrast to what they could and should have been ran their course in the form of a fundamental mutual misunderstanding: Lessing, like so many of his younger contemporaries, honoured and celebrated a fictional, mythical Frederick, not the real one as he lived and had his being at Potsdam;

and thus it was inevitable that in his turn the real Frederick should be completely unable to recognize flesh of his flesh and spirit of his spirit in Lessing. While Lessing was still a young man he had quarrelled with the great Voltaire (we remember Rousseau's relations with the same person) and in later years, in spite of all he undoubtedly owed him as a critic, he became objectively his most bitter opponent. He likewise became the opponent of his compatriot Gottsched, in spite of the fact that the aims they were striving for were related. In theology he came to oppose not only people like Goeze and the orthodox churchmen, but Semler, and those who shared Semler's neological views; further he lent his support to the achievements of Reimarus only because their radicalism interested him from the standpoint of method, and supported them only to reject them eventually dialectically, just as he abandoned the position of the apologists who opposed Reimarus. And even though he did to the last remain the friend of the last great Enlightenment philosopher, Moses Mendelssohn of Berlin, it is nevertheless more than likely that Mendelssohn was fundamentally mistaken in thinking he could command Lessing's services in support of his own harmlessly theistic interpretation of Spinoza against Heinrich Friedrich Jacobi. With or without Spinoza, Lessing had certainly long been on the road which led to Goethe, to interpreting God, in an at any rate quite untheistic way as the immanent principle of the human microcosm and macrocosm. Lessing in fact, although he was everywhere aligned with the front rank of his contemporaries, and functioned as their most eloquent and respected spokesman, had likewise broken away at every point from the positions they characteristically occupied. We must also understand him in relation to the play of the dialectic of tendencies to which this fact gives rise.

In recent years more than one commentator has appraised Gotthold Ephraim Lessing (1729-81) as a specifically masculine genius. There is certainly something illuminating about this remark, especially when we read Lessing after Rousseau. The two have in common the discovery of the second dimension we were talking about, the discovery of human existence as such, as distinct from what man can know and desire. Lessing was more of a scholar than Rousseau. He was, like Rousseau, a moralist. Moreover he had, like Rousseau, the knowledge of something beyond science and morals. He spoke of the heart and of feelings less often and with less emphasis than Rousseau, but he, too, did refer to them, especially at decisive points. The sober Lessing did not advance to that revolution of the heart against science and morals which Rousseau so stormily implemented; therefore he did not come to the self-analytical reveries and constructions, nor, for the same reason, to the educational and political ones, which are so characteristic of Rousseau. Coming from Rousseau to Lessing is like emerging from the twilight into a clear daylight, almost painful in its intensity. But the knowledge of that inner place of existence and of its significance as the source of the whole, the enjoyment of freedom in one's relation to the outside world which springs from this knowledge; these things are also typical of Lessing. For him, too, the ultimate reality is this free, stirring communion of the ego with the object, in which, however, the ego ever retains and regains the mastery. But whereas the use of this freedom which typifies Rousseau consists in a withdrawal from without to within from the object to the ego, Lessing rejoices in this same freedom as the freedom to make contact, the freedom to act. Whereas Rousseau above all always seems to be wanting to draw back from the thing facing him, Lessing rather seemed as if he were constantly wanting to seek it out, without mistaking the tension to which this attitude gives rise, and without relapsing into the naïve individualism of his older contemporaries. Rousseau was the lyric poet, and Lessing the dramatist. This is what might perhaps be meant by the reference to his 'masculinity'. But common to both Rousseau and Lessing was the standpoint of a wider, deeper rationalism, a rationalism deepened in the direction of an independent and permanently independent awareness of one's own existence. It was the same new feeling for life which in the midst of the eighteenth century triumphed both in Rousseau's revulsion, which easily affects us as being childish, and in the maturely tragic quality of Lessing's life.

It is thus not merely by chance that it was the drama and the theory of the drama which outwardly formed the peak of Lessing's life achievement. The drama was for him the highest genre of the poetic art, and therefore of art in general, because, as he intended to show in the continuation of his Laocoön which he never wrote, 'all art should strive to be a direct representation of nature, and poetry, which can depict and represent only indirectly, only by means of words, rises solely in the drama to a true modelling or imitation of life, to developing actions, and to effective speeches, feelings and passions'.[1] What interested Lessing so much about the drama in particular was therefore (as he taught in opposition to the French classical dramatists and together with Sophocles and Shakespeare) that it is to be defined as the poetic representation of an action, whose parts should be formed by their presentation into a unity in such a way that they are bound to appear

[1] Scherer-Walzel, p. 353.

alone and in their relation to one another as a necessary expression of the nature of the human characters taking part; in such a manner, therefore, that what is actually presented is the inner life of these characters, the sight of which must evoke in the spectator feelings of sympathy and of compassion, and compel him to the admission that in the same situation, and at the same stage of such a passion, he would have been bound to act in exactly the same way. Lessing thought that the drama should not arouse mere wonder at this or that sad or merry event, and that it should not therefore present such events to men at all as events but as revelations, and by this method of presentation evoke feelings of sympathy in others, that is, make these others participate in the action which was being presented. For this reason Lessing gave to his own dramas that proximity of the subject to life, that firmness in the construction and execution of his plots, that pregnant quality in the dialogue, which made his contemporaries sense that there was something quite new about them. This was an art which suddenly dared to take as its real object the nature of man himself, which is subject to so many varied influences, as it is seen in the unfolding of human actions. In this conception of art we have before us at the same time the deepest meaning of Lessing's conception of life: his particular problem and theme was man, but man in action, or to put it the other way, action, but action always as human action.

At this point we can very well transfer our gaze directly to Lessing's contribution to the history of Protestant theology, which is of especial interest to us. The son of a pastor in Saxony, he played a part in theology both in his youth and when he was older. It was not only an incidental one but fraught with such passion and with such an extensive knowledge of the subject that it is very much open to question whether it was not here, rather than in the field of art and the theory of art that his true central interest lay. In the last ten years of his life at any rate theological matters claimed his attention, outwardly as well, as nothing else did. We have in our possession a whole series of very characteristic essays and fragments on church history and the philosophy of religion which he wrote when he was still quite young. The decisive step—it has perhaps rather exaggeratedly been called 'one of the most important events in the history of the Protestant church and theology'[1]—came in the years 1774-8. Lessing published a series of fragments which he alleged he had found among the shelves of the Wolfenbüttel library, of which he was in charge, from the *Apologie oder Schutzschrift für die vernünftigen Verehrer Gottes* (Apology or defence for the reasonable worshippers of

[1] Scherer-W., p. 357.

God), written in 1767 by Hermann Samuel Reimarus, Professor of Oriental Languages in Hamburg, who was born in 1694 and died in 1768. He was probably given this manuscript, which its author did not intend to have published, by the dead man's sister, Elise Reimarus, a gifted woman who also numbered Mendelssohn and Jacobi among her friends. The fragments published by Lessing developed in an intensity which until then, in Germany at least, had been absent from public discussion of the matter, a fundamental denial of the necessity and possibility of all revelation and especially of the biblical Christian revelation when seen against the background of the implemented conception of a purely natural religion, a religion, that is, representing a universal, timelessly valid human possibility, such as forms the basis of every historical, positive and allegedly revealed religion and which is more or less decayed in all of them and to which, therefore, a reasonable worship of God must now go back whatever its present position may be. It was essentially the same reduction which we know from Rousseau's confession of the Vicar of Savoy, written a short time before.

Lessing provided this publication with a continuous commentary in which, as its title, *Contrasts*, states, he expressed his material denial of much that Reimarus presented, but also his partial agreement with it, and above all his belief that the problem which Reimarus had raised was highly important from a fundamental and methodological point of view. The violent polemical repercussions which the publication immediately called forth provided him with a favourable opportunity, in the famous series of polemics in which he gave his further views on the subject, *Über den Beweis des Geistes und der Kraft* (Concerning the proof of the spirit and the power), *Das Testament Johannis* (St John's Gospel), *Eine Duplik* (A Rejoinder), *Eine Parabel* (A Parable), *Axiomata, Anti-Goeze*, etc., of engaging less in a defence of Reimarus than in an attack upon and exposure of Reimarus' opponents. It was the censor's office at Brunswick which put a stop to the continuation of the fragments and to the further development of the dispute in 1778. This could not, however, prevent Lessing in 1779 from giving classic expression, in *Nathan der Weise* (Nathan the Wise), his most mature dramatic work, to his notions concerning the relationship between natural and positive religion which had matured in the course of the struggle he had been engaged in. The series of theses, *Die Erziehung des Menschengeschlechts* (The Education of the Human Race), published in 1780, which belong with *Nathan*, are a last systematic exposition of the same ideas. Their genuineness as Lessing's work is in dispute. Their content, however, coincides so exactly with the views

Lessing expressed elsewhere that the question as to whether and to what extent he perhaps allowed someone else to speak as a witness, as he in fact loved to do, is for all practical purposes an idle one. (It is considered that his collaborator was most likely the young farmer Albrecht Thaer.)

If we wish to understand Lessing's aims as a theologian we must proceed from the fact that every one of the positions of the theological neologians of that time, up to and including the thoroughgoing neologism of a man like Reimarus, which tended to turn into rationalism, were also contained and preserved in Lessing's own position. His early theological works testify that here he had his origins. But *Nathan* and the *Education* still show this very plainly. It would be possible to put a construction upon Lessing's theology which would show him to have been simply a particularly bold and advanced but ultimately typical neologian. Lessing was one when already in his younger days he was of the opinion that the Christian religion was not something 'that should be taken on trust and belief from one's parents'.[1]

> A man like you does not
> Stay in the station birth by chance
> Accords him: or if he stays, he stays
> From choice, by reason of his insight[2]

is still the view expressed by Saladin to Nathan (Act III, Scene 5). Just as Lessing in 1751 already thought it a great thing 'to think for oneself and challenge accepted prejudice', 'to convince oneself of one's belief', and indeed by the method of a comparative testing of the various religions in the form of a religious discussion, the form in which, twenty-five years later, he actually presented it in *Nathan*[3]—so in 1760 he exhorted himself with the words: 'I say to myself, submit to this investigation like an honest man! Look everywhere with your own eyes! Distort nothing! Embellish nothing! Let your conclusions flow as they will! Do not impede, do not attempt to guide their course!'[4] and so in 1778 still he declares it his duty 'to test with his own eyes, *quid liquidum sit in causa Christianorum.*[5]

We hear the typical moralistic refrain of the entire theology of the eighteenth century in the young Lessing's angry growl at the supposed believer, 'who has memorized and who utters, often without understanding them, the principles of Christian doctrine, who goes to church

---

[1] *Letter to his father*, 1749, quoted from: *Lessing's Theologische Schriften*, ed. C. Gross, I, p. 8.
[2] For original, see Appendix, p. 400.
[3] *Theologische Schriften*, I, 25.33 (Theological Writings).
[4] Ibid., I, 222.
[5] Ibid., IV, 166.

and takes part in every ceremony because it is customary', at that 'majority of people' who show by their 'comportment' 'what proper Christians they are'.[1] And we hear this refrain again when Nathan (Act I, 2) breaks into the famous words:

> But do you comprehend
> That it's far easier to be in ecstasies
> Than to act well? How willingly the feeblest
> Welcome ecstasy, but to escape—
> And be they of their object unaware—
> The task of being virtuous in life?[2]

We hear the well-known neological rejection and re-interpretation of the dogma of original sin in hearing[3] that its truth consists in the fact that man at the first and lowest stage of his humanity was simply not sufficiently master of his actions to be able to act in accordance with moral laws, or in hearing[4] of original sin that it consists in the 'superior power of our sensual desires, our dark imagination over all knowledge be it ever so clear', a power which 'we have it in us' to weaken and which we can even 'use just as much for the doing of good as for the doing of evil'. The characters in *Nathan* are thus accordingly (with the exception perhaps of the odious patriarch) all splendid, lovable people,[5] well able to take comfort even after their less glorious deeds:

> Why should I be ashamed of a mistake?
> For is it not my firm resolve to right it?[6]

For the same reason the truth of the doctrine of the atonement through the Son of God is therefore held to consist simply in God's giving moral laws to man, in spite of man's original incapacity for them, out of consideration for his Son; but this, according to Lessing, means out of consideration for his own perfection, the perfection which annuls individual man's imperfection, and thus in his not excluding man from the prospect of moral blessedness. For the doctrine of justification by faith Lessing can altogether find only the angrily derisive cry: to faith 'you give the keys of heaven and hell, and sufficient good fortune to make for virtue, so that by the skin of your teeth you can make virtue into some sort of companion to faith! With you the worship of sacred chimeras makes blessed without righteousness, but not righteousness without the worship. What a delusion!'[7]

---

[1] *Letters to his father*, 1749, I, 8.   [2] For original, see Appendix, p. 401.
[3] In the *Erziehung des Menschengeschlechts* (Education of the Human Race), para. 74.
[4] In the *Theologische Schriften* (Theological Writings), II, 265f.
[5] Scherer-W., p. 363.   [6] *Nathan*, V, 5; cf. Appendix, p. 401.
[7] *Theological Writings*, I, 39f.

The Christology to go with this has as its main tenet the affirmation of a 'Religion of Christ' most clearly and plainly contained in the Gospels: 'The religion of Christ is the religion which Christ himself knew and practised as a man; which every man can have in common with him; which every man must wish more and more to have in common with him, the more sublime and lovable he conceives the character of Christ as a mere human being to have been.' The 'Christian religion', on the other hand, is something quite different, consisting essentially in the acceptance of the belief that Christ was more than a mere human being. It is inconceivable, says Lessing in this fragment, that anyone could hold these two religions simultaneously.[1]

Also most genuinely in the style of the eighteenth century, having become typical since Gottfried Arnold, are the young Lessing's ventures upon all sorts of 'saving' actions, i.e. his defence of certain historical figures which the writers of official Protestant church history were alleged to have treated badly: the Renaissance philosopher Cardanus, Cochleus, the Roman Catholic writer of polemics, the anti-Trinitarian Adam Neuser, who embraced the Islamic faith in the second half of the sixteenth century, and other similar figures. In a piece of 1750, about the Moravian brethren, which he unfortunately only managed to begin, Lessing glowingly compared this community with Socrates, as opposed to his pupils Plato and Aristotle, who had already fallen short of the simplicity of their master; with Descartes, as opposed to Newton and Leibnitz, philosophers who simply filled the head but left the heart empty, with the 'simple, light and lively religion of Adam as opposed to the religion of Judaism, with the Christianity of Christ and of the first century as opposed to that of the Middle Ages, with the beginning of the Reformation as opposed to everything which had followed the dispute about the Eucharist'.[2] And the historical phenomena which traditional church history usually accords a positive value, he treats with sound neological scepticism and malice in just the opposite manner.

> When was I not all ear as often as
> It pleased you to recount the story of
> The heroes of your faith? Have I not ever
> Gladly paid their deeds the constant tribute
> Of my wonder, their sufferings the tribute
> Of my tears? Their faith, I must confess,
> I never found their most heroic part[3]

we hear Nathan's ward Recha, who, as we know, has been brought up in two faiths, saying to Daja, her nurse. And the young Lessing does not

[1] *Theological Writings*, IV, 248f.   [2] Ibid., I, 204f.
[3] *Nathan*, III, i. For original, see Appendix, p. 401.

shrink from stating that he has noticed that amongst the much praised early Christian heroes there had been some who deserved the name of fools or madmen rather than that of martyrs and he makes no secret of his belief that a bee in somebody's bonnet can achieve as much as the truth in all its glory.[1] Concerning the persecutions of the early Christians he remarks that they were never so general or official as they have often been represented and, moreover, he thinks he is right to ask whether the Christians were really quite without blame in the matter. Did they not deserve to be punished for their nocturnal gatherings, which gave offence and were after all forbidden in Rome? 'Since their religion did not in the least demand such meetings, why were they always running to meet each other? Why these night-gatherings of whole hordes of people of every age and sex? They were bound to be suspect to any good police force.' And their love-feasts! 'What was the point of these sacred revels?'[2] And then again, in his *Rettung des Cochleus* (Deliverance of Cochleus) in 1754 Lessing makes it quite apparent that in his opinion the sixteenth-century Reformation too, for all the infinite good it may have done, rests historically on a 'monks' quarrel', the one between the Augustinian and the Dominican orders.[3] Relevant here is the caricature of the Patriarch in *Nathan*, and also the other caricature on which it is based, that of his enemy Melchior Goeze, a figure which in Lessing's polemics belongs as much to fiction as to truth.

But behind this criticism of dogma and of church history there stands, however, a criticism of the concept of revelation as such no less definitely than with a man like Reimarus. Lessing holds that man's only duty that can in any real sense be called a duty, is to practise 'natural religion', i.e. to recognize God, to form only the noblest conceptions of him, and to bear these in mind in all his thoughts and deeds. It then became necessary, purely sociologically, 'conventionally', for people within this one natural religion to come to some agreement concerning certain things and concepts, and to attribute to the concepts and things thus singled out the same force and necessity which the naturally perceived religious truths had of themselves. 'From the religion of nature a positive religion had to be constructed, just as a positive law had been made out of the natural one.' 'This positive religion acquired its sanction by the respect accorded to its founder, who alleged that the conventional element in this religion came just as certainly from God, only indirectly through himself, as its essentials came directly through the reasoning powers in each one of us.' The inner truth of a positive

---

[1] *Theological Writings*, I, 35.   [2] Ibid., I, 231f.   [3] Ibid., I, 82f.

religion as such cannot consist of anything but its practical indispensability. 'All positive and revealed religions are thus equally true and equally false': equally true to the extent that an agreement concerning non-essentials was everywhere necessary, and equally false as far as every such convention signified a weakening and suppression of the essentials. 'The best positive or revealed religion is the one containing the fewest conventional additions to natural religion and least limits the good effects of natural religion.'[1] His tone in 1760 is much more malicious still, and reminiscent of the Voltairean style in religious criticism: 'This is the real artifice of a founder of a religion. He must not say: "Come, I want to teach you a new religion!" Such a speech evokes dread in his audience. He begins by instilling scruples against the accepted religion, and instilling them in confidence, like a man who has his friend's welfare at heart. This cavilling gives rise to assertions. The assertions give rise to voluntary dissociations, first in trifles and then ultimately embracing the whole. The religious founder's most difficult task is to procure his first dozen followers, really blind, obedient, enthusiastic followers. But once he has them, his work begins to go much better. . . . Who is there, believing himself inspired, who will not gladly in his turn inspire? It is always the most ignorant, the most simple who are most busy at it . . . Especially the women! It is too well known how surpassingly well all the heads of new religions and sects, like the first founder . . . in paradise, have understood how to make use of them.'[2] Corresponding to this historical denigration of revelation there is the factual one Lessing presented in 1754: 'They all refer to higher revelations which have not even been proved possible. They want truths to have been received through these which might be truths perhaps in another possible world, but not in ours. This they recognize themselves, so they call them mysteries, a word which refutes itself. I will not name these mysteries to you, but simply say that they are like the ones which give rise to the most sweeping and material notions of everything that is divine. They are the ones which never allow the common people to think of their Creator in a becoming fashion. They are the ones which tempt the mind away to all sorts of barren reflections and create for it a monster, which you call faith.'[3]

That is why Lessing's judgment of miracles is exactly the same as the one we can find in his edition of Reimarus' works.[4] It is that: 'Only those men need to perform miracles, who wish to convince us of inconceivable things, in order to make inconceivable things conceivable

[1] *Über die Entstehung der geoffenbarten Religion* (Concerning the origin of revealed religion), 1755-60; *Theological Writings*, I, 219f.
[2] Ibid., I, 234f.   [3] Ibid., I, 39.   [4] Cf. ibid., II, 387.

by means of miracles. But those who have nothing to present but teachings, whose touchstone every man carries with him do not need them.[1] And that is why the foolish Christian woman Daja, when she asks what harm there is in attributing an unexpected deliverance to an angel rather than to a man and thereby feeling all the nearer to God, the first inconceivable cause of such an event, receives from the wise Nathan the answer:

> Pride! and nought but pride! The pot
> Of iron would fain be lifted from the fire
> With silver tongs, to think itself more precious.—
> Bah!—And what's the harm, you ask, the harm?
> —What good is it, I might but ask in turn—
> For your 'To feel oneself the nearer yet
> To God' is folly or a blasphemy.—
> It only harms—it's harmful utterly.[2]

It is harmful in fact—and at this we have arrived once again at the beginning of this line of Lessing's thought—because it leads man to ecstasize where he should quite simply do good.

The existence of this line of thought, and the entirely unequivocal and decided way in which Lessing expresses it, must be borne in mind. One must, however, note simply that it was precisely the most pungent of the passages written by the young Lessing and quoted beforehand which was published from the papers found after his death, and the ones, therefore, which strictly speaking, while he thought them and committed them to paper, were never actually uttered by him. And we must above all be clear that here it is a question of only one line of Lessing's theological thought. Anyone wishing to attribute to him only this one line of thought would be misunderstanding him just as much as anyone who overlooked it altogether. Lessing could speak quite differently —and did speak quite differently. Friedrich Nicolai, his Enlightened friend, once wrote of him, as one who knew him well: 'Lessing could not tolerate anything which was all too clear-cut, and was in the habit, in polite or learned discussion, of espousing the weaker cause or the one whose opposite someone was trying to assert' and he adds the lovely illustration: 'Many of Lessing's friends will still recall that during the Seven Years War he always supported Prussia at social gatherings in Leipzig, and in Berlin the cause of Saxony. He was thus an object of heartfelt hatred to the true patriots in both places, who, as is well-known, were a trifle fierce while the war lasted.'[3] Lessing the dramatist was doubtless glad to keep this attitude, not only in society, but also

---

[1] *Theological Writings*, I, 40.   [2] *Nathan*, I, 2. For original, see Appendix, p. 401.
[3] *Theological Writings*, IV, 267.

as a writer, and indeed as a theological writer particularly. The impression which this attitude made must, in his lifetime at least and especially among free thinkers, have been that of a conservative thinker rather than that of a free thinker. No, we hear him declaring just as definitely, although after what has gone before something different might have been expected, that what he means and intends is precisely not the 'reasonable Christianity' of his time. 'What a pity nobody really quite knows where his reason or where his Christianity are'[1] we hear him mocking. No, he has no love at all for the people whose leader we were just thinking we should have to take him to be, the 'new-fangled clergy, who are far too little theologians and not nearly philosophers enough'.[2] But certainly he wished to be a disciple of the Enlightenment, also, and especially, in matters affecting religion, 'I should despise myself if my scribblings were devoted to any end but that of helping to further these great intentions. But do leave me my own way in which I think I can do this.'[3]

What is there then about his own way, in opposition to that of the neologians—now so abruptly dismissed? Why do they please him neither as theologians nor as philosophers? What can he mean when he protests, over against Goeze, that he is no less well-intentioned towards the Lutheran Church than Goeze—when he, too, thinks he can appeal to the 'great misjudged man' Luther? 'The more insistently one man wanted to prove Christianity to me, the more doubtful I became. The more wilfully and triumphantly another sought to trample it completely underfoot the more inclined I felt like upholding it, in my heart at least.'[4] What is the meaning of this defiance of Lessing's towards that standpoint too, and in particular the point where we thought we saw him stand himself, without any qualification whatsoever? The answer sounds enigmatic enough, but is highly typical of Lessing: 'The freemason quietly waits for the sun to begin to shine and lets the lamps burn as long as they are willing and able to burn—to put out the lamps and take note, when they are put out, that the candle-ends must be relit, or even be replaced by others—this is not the freemason's concern.'[5] 'Take care, more capable individual, you who paw the ground and are aglow on reaching the last page of the first primer (the Jewish-Christian revelation!), take care not to let your weaker school-fellows feel what you are sensing or already beginning to see. Until these weaker school-fellows have caught up with

---

[1] *Theological Writings*, II, 103. [2] *Letters to Nicolai*, 1777, II, 11.
[3] *Letters to his brother*, 1774, II, 11. [4] *Theological Writings*, IV, 169.
[5] *Ernst and Falk*, 5.

E

you, turn back the pages of this primer again, and find out whether
what you take to be the result of mere expressions of method, make-
shifts of the teaching system, is not perhaps something more.'[1] Or
concretely, about the relation between orthodoxy and neology: 'I
should not wish the impure water, which has long been unusable,
to be kept; it is only that I should not wish it to be poured away before
we know where we can get purer; I simply do not want it poured away
unthinkingly, and the child to be bathed thereafter in manure. And
what else is the new-fashioned theology, as compared with orthodoxy,
but manure as compared with dirty water? . . . I beg of you, dear
brother, enquire just a little more closely into this point, and look
rather less at what our new theologians reject than at what they want
to put in its place! I agree with you that our old system of religion is
false, but cannot agree with you in saying that it is a makeshift contrived by bunglers and pseudo-philosophers. I know of nothing else
in the world where men have shown and practised their judgment more
than in this. It is the new system of religion which is intended to replace
it which is a bunglers' and pseudo-philosophers' makeshift and it has
at the same time far more influence over reason and philosophy than
the old one presumes to exercise. And yet you take it amiss that I defend
the old system? My neighbour's house is on the point of collapsing.
If he wants to pull it down I will willingly help him. But he wants to
prop it up and support it . . . by means entailing the complete ruin of
my house. He must stop this or I shall take care of his collapsing house
as if it were my own.'[2]

These were Lessing's reasons for remaining largely silent, after the
manner of the freemason, about his objections to orthodoxy—'The
wise man cannot speak about the things it is better he should keep
to himself'.[3] They were also his reasons for actually taking up from
time to time the cause of the orthodoxy which was under attack, or
of the old system of dogma, to the horror of his Enlightenment friends.
There can be no doubt: Lessing considered the orthodox position, he
considered the whole Jewish-Christian revelation upon which this
position rests, not to be something that is absolute but something we
can in principle rise above. It is not the rising sun, but a man-made
lamp, burning for the time being, which will later be extinguished;
it is to be likened to impure water, to a house in need of reconstruction.
It is not the final terrible truth that mankind must and indeed shall
know for his salvation, but only a first primer intended to prepare

[1] *The Education of the Human Race*, paras. 68-9.   [2] *Theological Writings*, II, 11f.
[3] *Ernst and Falk*, 2.

man for the final truth. Lessing is aware that in this critical insight
he is at one with the neologians. He thinks that he too knows everything
there is to be known in this respect. But that the sun might already
be risen, and clean water at hand, that the tottering house could be
transformed into a new one by the addition of a supporting wall—
these things he denied. In other words he denied that the Jewish-
Christian revelation had in fact already been superseded and relieved
of its task by something better. It is still better and stronger than the
reasonable Christianity of the neologians, provided it is properly
represented. This Christianity of reason, which is no longer Christian
and not yet reasonable, is a hybrid. Thus there is no point in putting
this critical insight already into practice and in wanting already to
dispense with the first primer. There would only be sense in this if
something better had already come, if the sun had already risen, if
pure water were already at hand, if the old house could really be de-
molished. The poverty of what is offered in place of revelation proves
that this is not the case; that revelation is not yet finished with. The
wise man, the freemason, in Lessing's sense, will therefore not join in
the neologians' direct attack on the Church and on dogma, although he
knows all that they know. He hopes. He is quite sure of himself and his
cause: 'The development of revealed truths into truths of reason is
necessary at all costs.'[1] 'Or could it be that the human race is destined
never to arrive at these highest stages of enlightenment and purity?
Never? Never?—Let me not think such blasphemy, all-bountiful
Lord!—Education has its aim, with the race no less than with the
individual. That which is educated is educated for something.'[2] 'The
time will certainly come, the time of a new, eternal gospel, which is
promised to us even in the primers of the New Covenant.'[3] It is however
precisely the wise man, who knows and hopes for this, who can wait.
'Go your imperceptible way, eternal Providence! Just do not let me
despair of you because of this imperceptibility!—Do not let me
despair of you even if it should seem to me that your steps are leading
backwards!—It is not true that the shortest line is always the straight
one. You have so much to carry with you upon your everlasting way, so
many digressions to make from the path!—And what if it were as good
as arranged that the big, slow-turning wheel which is bringing the race
nearer to perfection, could only be set in motion by smaller, faster wheels,
each one of which contributes its own individual effort to this cause?'[4]

From this it almost necessarily follows that Lessing was bound to
have a positive interest in revelation, for all that he completely saw,

---

[1] *Ed.*, para. 76.   [2] Ibid., paras. 81-2.   [3] Ibid., para. 86.   [4] Ibid., paras. 91-2.

admitted and stated that the nature of that interest was relative. From this standpoint Lessing quite honestly found himself placed in a position where he not only could tolerate the belief in revelation and accept it as fact, but was able to ponder on it and express himself on how, *rebus sic stantibus*, it might most properly be represented.

This firstly makes plain the concern which prompted Lessing in the dispute of the Fragments. In it he was in his way really well-intentioned towards the Lutheran Church, without, for all that, being less well-intentioned towards the Enlightenment. As a wise disciple of the Enlightenment, who paradoxically but very subtly does not consider the straight line to be the shortest line, who knows of those digressions eternal Providence must make, in order to set in motion for its own part the smaller, faster wheels which move the big, slow one, he can, no, must in fact have the interests of the Lutheran Church at heart. It was Lessing and nobody else who honestly knew himself to be qualified and called to offer it some good advice. This was Lessing's desire in the dispute of the Fragments: he wanted, from the lofty watchtower of the wise man of the Enlightenment, of the true freemason, to give the Church, Christianity and Christian theology some good advice. He thought it could certainly be surpassed and he thought it was certain to be surpassed in the future, but he wanted to advise it on how it should conduct itself as something which was for the moment not surpassed, so that by its behaviour it should prove that it was not yet surpassed.

Lessing was interested in Reimarus' critique of all revelation including the Christian revelation. It interested him as a sign of the times. His dramatic conception of history perhaps contained certain traces of chiliasm, for a certain passage in Cardanus seems to have made a great impression upon him. It said: *Necesse est anno Christi millesimo octingentesimo magnam mutationem futuram esse in Christi lege*, 'that in the year 1800 a great change will come about in the Christian religion'.[1] It is not impossible that in view of this prophecy Lessing held that the coming of the last things was near, as far as the completion he mentions of the education of the human race and the actual surpassing of revelation were concerned. Be that as it may: Lessing was not interested in Reimarus in the way that Reimarus was bound to interest the common run of men of the Enlightenment. He was not interested in him as the implementer of a simple advance along the way to overtaking the belief in revelation—it was precisely the idea that such an advance could come about simply by means of criticism that Lessing denied. But Lessing was certainly interested in Reimarus as the provider of an

[1] *Theological Writings*, IV, 250f.

opportunity in the face of which the belief in revelation, in so far as it was not yet surpassed, must prove itself in its temporary truth and validity; as a chemical test, so to speak, to which the belief in revelation, the Church and theology must react in a certain way, inasmuch as their last hour had not yet struck. It was to this extent that Reimarus really interested Lessing for the Church's sake. It was to this end that he addressed the theologians in the dispute of the Fragments. And what excited and angered him to the astonishing extent to which he *was* angered and excited in the course of this dispute was the fact that he thought that they were not reacting in the only way possible; they were failing to grasp what was being asked of them and what their answer should be, failing to understand themselves and their own cause, neglecting the favourable time, the great opportunity that was offered them to prove themselves. And now he, the man of the Enlightenment, the one who is convinced that all revealed truth will hereafter be transformed and merged into the truth of reason—he has to tell the theologians how they must behave if in actual fact things have not progressed so far! That, in Lessing's eyes, was the problem, the fierce humour and bitter tragedy of the dispute of the Fragments.

What then was essential about the Fragments of Reimarus? For Lessing it was the fact that they represented a historian's historical attack upon the historical reality and possibility of revelation. Does this historian know, Lessing asks, that revelation—assuming that such a thing exists—cannot in any circumstance be denied historically as a historical quantity? But in this matter Lessing has to do not with Reimarus but with the Lutheran theologians. That is why he is immeasurably more concerned with the other question: Do these theologians know that revelation cannot ever be affirmed, justified and defended historically as a historical quantity? Lessing was the man who held that revelation can be surpassed in principle, who knew the objections against its historical reality and possibility as well as Reimarus did, and who was not at a loss, as we have seen, to produce all kinds of natural explanations for the things the Church declared were phenomena of revelation. But he thought he knew enough about the matter to say that revelation should at all events be interpreted as a fact proved in itself, i.e. not as one which can be either proved or attacked historically, but as one which is certain in itself. He thought that in this he was in agreement with the older theology, i.e. the orthodoxy of the sixteenth and seventeenth centuries, which was in the habit of presenting the historical proof only incidentally and without emphasis, and was not of the opinion that it could and should prove revelation as such by these means.

Lessing, however, did not find himself in agreement with the theology of his own time, not even, especially not, with the allegedly orthodox theology.[1] This theology replied to the historical criticism of revelation with a historical defence. This, Lessing maintained, was to the detriment and obviously in misunderstanding of its own cause; Lessing called it a 'theological innovation', and it was the essence of his complaint against Melchior Goeze that the latter made himself guilty of that innovation! It was against this, and ultimately only against this, that Lessing directed his polemic in this fight. 'They should be ashamed, these men who have the promise of their divine Teacher, that his Church shall not be overcome by the gates of hell, and are foolish enough to believe that this cannot otherwise come about than by their overcoming the gates of hell themselves!'[2] 'When will they cease to want to hang nothing less than the whole of eternity on a spider's thread!—No, scholastic dogmatics have never inflicted such grievous wounds upon religion, as that which the historical exposition of the Scriptures is now daily inflicting.'[3] 'Great God, it is to this mire, to this mire, even if there are perhaps some few specks of gold beneath it, that my neighbour in boldness and defiance transfers the completed edifice of his faith! . . . God! my God! what things men can found a faith upon, by which they hope to achieve eternal happiness!'[4]

Lessing likens the theological apologists to the inhabitants of a palace, oddly constructed to be sure but quite habitable, who each possess different plans of the building, which, they claim, derive from the first architect, which they do not understand and which seem to contradict each other. They are continually quarrelling about which is the right one. Some few, laughingly, and to the annoyance of the others, do not take part in this quarrel, but content themselves with rejoicing at the fact that they are actually allowed to live in this palace, whatever its plan may be. 'Once, when the quarrel about the plans was not so much settled as dormant, once upon a time at the midnight hour the voice of the watchmen suddenly rang out: "Fire! Fire in the palace!" And what took place? Everyone started up from his bed, and everyone —as if the fire were not in the palace but in his own home—ran to get what he believed to be his most precious possession—his plan. "If we can only save that!" each one thought; "the palace can burn nowhere more truly than as it stands described here!" So each one ran with his plan into the street, where he first of all wanted to show the others on

[1] *Theological Writings*, III, 107.   [2] Ibid., II, 287.   [3] Ibid., III, 34.   [4] Ibid., III, 89f.

his plan where the palace was supposed to be burning instead of hastening to save the palace. "Look, neighbour! Here's where it's burning!
Here's where we can best get at the fire!" "Or here rather, neighbour,
here!"—"What are you two talking about? It's burning here!" "What
would it matter if it was burning there? But the fire is certainly here!"
"You can put it out here if you like, I'm not going to!"—"Nor am I
going to put it out there!"—"And nor am I going to put it out there!"
And while they were busily arguing the palace, if it had been on fire, might
very well have been burned to the ground. But the startled watchmen
had mistaken the northern lights for a conflagration.'[1] Let the historical
proofs of revelation rest where they will! 'Would it be a great misfortune if they were put back again into the corner of the arsenal they
occupied fifty years ago?'[2] Why are they superfluous, even harmful?
Why are the reasons with which the theological apologists work like
spiders' webs, mire, a paper plan, and ultimately downright dangerous
to religion? Because they divert the question of the truth and reality
of revelation on to a track which is the very one where it cannot with
certainty be answered. Historical proof of revelation means the
historical proof of prophecies fulfilled and miracles which actually
came to pass. But this proof cannot serve as proof of revelation. For the
certainty which would have to be contained in a proof of revelation
would necessarily be lacking in such a historical proof. 'Fulfilled
prophecies which I myself experience are one thing, and fulfilled
prophecies of which I know from history only that others claim to have
experienced them, are another. Miracles which I see with my own eyes
and have the opportunity to test are one thing, and miracles, of which I
know from history only that others claim that they have seen and tested
are another.'[3] The most reliable information about the latter does not
therefore make my knowledge of it more reliable than it is possible for
knowledge based on historical data to be; it is not possible to place
more confidence in it than we are generally entitled to place in any
truth shown by history. For no historical truth, even when it is supplied
with the best evidence, can be demonstrated. But if 'no historical truth
can be demonstrated, then neither can it in turn be used to demonstrate anything'.[4] 'To jump over' with this historical truth—assuming
and granting that it is such—'into a completely different class of truths,
and to demand of me that I should adapt all my metaphysical and
moral notions accordingly . . . if that is not a μετάβασις εἰς ἄλλο γένος,
then I do not know what else Aristotle can have meant by the term'.[5]

[1] *Theological Writings*, III, 95f.   [2] Ibid., III, 34.   [3] Ibid., III, 9f.
[4] Ibid., III, 11f.   [5] Ibid., III, 13.

'That, that, I say, is the nasty big ditch I cannot get over, often and earnestly as I have tried the jump. If anyone can help me over, let him do so; I beg him, beseech him to do so. By me he can reap a reward in heaven.'[1]

And now for Lessing's positive thesis, the better suggestion he thinks he can make to theology. This lament about the impossibility of passing over from the historical proof to the faith of revelation is in fact not genuine. Lessing could perfectly well do without what he represented in those sentences as being inaccessible to him, and he wished to make it clear to the theologians that it is not only inaccessible but also superfluous for them, and that for the sake of their own cause they should give it up. Is the situation such that 'I should hold a geometrical theorem to be true not because it can be demonstrated, but because it can be found in Euclid?' 'The fact that it is to be found in Euclid can prejudice us in favour of its truth as much as it will. But it is one thing to believe a truth on the strength of a prejudice, and another to believe a truth for its own sake.'[2] The learned theologian may finally be left in a state of embarrassment as a historian by an attack like that of Reimarus. 'But the Christian too? Most certainly not! Only possibly to the theologian might it be a cause for confusion to see the supports with which he wanted to shore up religion shaken, the buttresses cast down with which, God willing, he had so beautifully secured it. But of what concern to the Christian are the hypotheses and accounts and proofs of this man? For the Christian it is simply there, the Christianity he feels to be so true, in which he feels himself so blessed.—When the paralytic is undergoing the beneficent shock of the electric current, what does he care whether Franklin or Nollet is right, or neither of them?'[3] 'If I see these fruits ripening and ripened before me, should I not eat my fill of them, not perhaps because I deny, or doubt the pious old legend that the hand which scattered the seed for this fruit must be washed seven times in snails' blood at every throw; but have merely left it consigned to its proper place?—What do I care, whether the tale is true or not: the fruit is delicious. Supposing there were a great, useful mathematical truth, arrived at by its author by a palpably false conclusion. (If there are no such truths they might well exist.) Would I be denying this truth, would I be refusing to make use of it: would I be an ungrateful blasphemer against the author, if I did not wish to use his acuteness elsewhere, and did not think that his acuteness elsewhere could be used to prove that the false conclusion by which he had stumbled on the truth could not be a false conclusion

[1] *Theological Writings*, III, 13f.   [2] Ibid., III, 127.   [3] Ibid., II, 261.

at all?'[1] One should 'not act as if someone who doubts certain proofs of
a matter doubts the matter itself. Anyone who as much as points his
finger in this direction is as guilty as an assassin.'[2] 'He who has a more
Christian heart than head' is not deterred in the slightest by these
objections, because he *feels* 'what others are content only to think,
because he at all events could dispense with all the Bible. He is the
confident victor who leaves the fortresses alone and captures the land.
The theologian is the anxious soldier who runs his head against the
strongpoints on the border and in so doing sees hardly anything of the
country.'[3]

We must now try to find out more precisely what Lessing means
when he speaks of this 'victor'. We have not yet quoted the best-
known of the various formulations in which Lessing has expressed his
belief in the superiority of Christianity over all historical polemics,
or alternatively in the fact that it cannot be proved by any historical
apologetics. It runs: 'Accidental historical truths can never become
proofs for necessary truths of reason.'[4] This sentence does not say—in
Lessing's context it cannot say—what Fichte later said: 'It is only the
Metaphysical and on no account the Historical, which makes blessed.'
Lessing does not maintain that the 'necessary truths of reason' are
self-evident, certain without regard to time and space, and that history
has no significance in their knowledge. In the dispute of the Fragments
he most definitely took it as his premise that the education of the human
race was not yet complete, and that revelation, a historical way of
knowledge (as distinct from the continual present—without regard to
time and space—of the necessary truths of reason) was therefore still
possible, indeed necessary.

Lessing it is true, is aware of one proof of Christianity, i.e. a growth
of a knowledge of God through Christ, through present-day man's
encounter with the Christian tradition. But this proof must be 'the
proof of the spirit and the power' as the title of the famous writing of
1777 runs, from which comes the famous sentence just quoted.
'Accidental truths of history', which as such cannot become proofs of
necessary truths of reason, are, in the context of this writing, to be
understood as such particular, concretely unique historical truths,
about which I am merely informed by others, which are merely handed
down to me as true. I have not myself encountered them, I have not
myself experienced them as true. Truths of history can indeed become
proof for me of necessary truths of reason, but only when they are
not merely 'accidental' historical truths, but have become convincing

[1] *Theological Writings,* III, 14.   [2] Ibid., III, 107.   [3] Ibid., III, 122.   [4] Ibid., III, 12.

to me as historical truths, have become necessary, and indeed directly necessary to me. The historical truths which are merely handed down and attested have as such not this power of proof, no matter how well they have been handed down and how definitely attested they are. Historical (from ἱστορέω) is, that which I must first make part of my own experience by investigation, and which is therefore in the first place not experienced by me. Historical truth as such, the truth which is in need of such investigation and is not yet part of my own experience, cannot be the legitimate and fully-authorized messenger of the truth of revelation, i.e. the truth which necessarily imposes itself upon my reason, which is ultimately certain. Historical truth, if it were to have this significance for me, would have to come to me by other means, not as 'historical' and not as 'accidental truth', not as requiring my investigation, and thus not at all merely as truth which has been handed down, and further by no means in such a way, that there should be any question at all of the problem of the 'nasty big ditch'. 'It is impossible for a revealed religion which rests upon human testimony, to afford an undoubted assurance in anything.'[1] There is, according to Lessing, another way.

With Lessing we have seen how at the decisive point the concepts 'feeling', 'experience', 'heart', and the image of the 'beneficent shock of the electric current' occur. This is what he would have us understand as the 'proof of the spirit and the power'. It is not as historical truth but through *experience*, that the historical element in Christianity assumes the power of proof for Christianity itself, and that, by way of historical truth, necessary truths of reason are proved. The way of Lessing's victor is the direct way from historical truth to the *heart* of present-day man. The fact that this way exists is the positive side of the negative sentence we quoted. Lessing knows very well about historical truths which can become proof of necessary truths of reason in this manner. From Luther's writings he appealed to the spirit of Luther;[2] likewise from the letter of the Bible to the spirit of the Bible, and from the Bible as such to religion, which was in existence before the Bible,[3] from the facts narrated in the Books of the Bible to the principles of the Christian teaching, which do not all rest upon facts,[4] from the miracles worked by Christ and his disciples to 'the miracle of religion itself, which is still continuing in its effects',[5] and finally from the Gospel of St John to St John's testimony: 'Little children, love one another!'[6] and, as we have already seen, from the Christian religion to the

---

[1] *Theological Writings*, IV, 253.   [2] Ibid., III, 140.   [3] Ibid., II, 271f.; III, 113f.
            [4] Ibid., III, 118.   [5] Ibid., III, 33f.   [6] Ibid., III, 14.

religion of Christ himself.[1] 'Surely in Hamburg nobody will any longer wish to dispute with me the whole difference between gross and net?'[2] No: 'the historical words are the vehicle of the prophetic words'.[3] 'It must be possible for everything the Evangelists and Apostles have written to be lost again, and for the religion they taught to remain notwithstanding. Religion is not true because the Evangelists and Apostles taught it, but they taught it because it is true. The tradition handed down to us in writing must be explicable by its inner truth, and no written tradition can give it inner truth if it does not contain any.'[4] 'Within the last seventeen hundred years has the first, the only spring never flowed, has it never found its way into other writings? Has it never and nowhere found its way into other writings in its original purity and healing quality? Must every Christian without exception draw from this spring and this spring alone?'[5] Goeze had asked Lessing whether he thought that without the presence and tradition of the books of the New Testament there would be any trace left in the world of what Christ had done and taught. Lessing answers: 'God preserve me from ever holding the teachings of Christ in such little esteem, that I should dare to answer this question quite directly with no! No, I should not say this "no" you want me to say,—even if an angel from heaven were prompting me to do so, let alone when it is only a Lutheran pastor who is trying to put the word in my mouth.'[6] We are not worse, but better off than the Christians of the second generation, in whose time the eye-witnesses were still present. 'We are abundantly compensated for the passing of the eye-witnesses by something which it was impossible for the eye-witnesses to have. They had only the ground before them, upon which, convinced of its firmness, they dared to erect a great edifice. And we, we have before us this great edifice itself, complete.'[7] The inner truth which no written tradition can give to Christianity and which Christianity therefore cannot derive from it[8]—the inner truth, on the one hand, comes from before the written tradition and, on the other hand, has its place behind it, in the 'edifice' of the whole of Christian history, which we see standing before our eyes. This inner truth 'is not a kind of wax nose that every knave can mould as he likes to fit his own face; it is the fact of revelation which speaks directly and with certainty to us ourselves, to our hearts. It is something, that is, which is capable of being felt and experienced. Because there is such a foundation for Christianity before and after the Bible, and because the Christianity resting

[1] *Theological Writings*, IV, 248f. [2] Ibid., III, 108. [3] Ibid., III, 112.
[4] Ibid., II, 262, III, 120, 125f. [5] Ibid., III, 128. [6] Ibid., III, 118.
[7] Ibid., III, 32. [8] Ibid., III, 129.

on this foundation is the essential, the true one, objections raised against the historical element in religion as for instance indications of contradictory passages in the various Gospels, and doubts cast as to this or that report of a miracle are on principle irrelevant.[1] And for this reason the theologian should not try to impose his learned study of the Bible, with the pros and cons of his conclusions, upon the Christian as something which is of decisive importance for his religion.[2]

With this theological view in mind Lessing among other things also upheld two historical hypotheses which very significantly explain what he wanted. First, he assumed that there must have been an original Gospel, written in Hebrew, older than that of St Matthew, as the earliest of the Synoptic Gospel Writers[3]—the historical truth with the power of proof *before* the Bible! Secondly, he held that the *regula fidei*, the confession of faith (also in itself, incidentally, older than the New Testament) was the rock upon which the Church of Christ was afterwards built and not upon the Scriptures[4]—the historical truth with the power of proof *after* the Bible!

This teaching of the proof of the truth of Christianity, which must be brought as a 'proof of the spirit and the power', Lessing would no doubt also have us recognize as the meaning of the famous fable of the three rings in *Nathan*.[5] Here also it is a matter of the proof of the truth of Christianity, but not now as regards the problems presented by Christian history itself studied for its own sake, as in the polemics against Goeze. Now it is studied in relation to the fact that the history of Christianity, as a relative phenomenon, is a part of the universal history of religion, together with several other religions. Is Christianity, when ranked with the other religions, really the true religion, or, as was to be said later, the absolute religion? And how should the justification for his claim show itself, if and in so far as it is justified? That is the theological question which is discussed in *Nathan*.

The fable of the three rings is as follows: In an ancient family it is the custom for the father to give his favourite son a ring for his inheritance, a ring possessing the miraculous power of making whoever owns it beloved in the sight of God and man. One father, in this family, has three sons whom he loves equally. In order to hurt none of them he has two perfect imitations of the true ring made, which even he cannot detect and gives each of the three sons his blessing, and one of the rings, and dies. What happens then is obvious, of course. Each of the three sons considers that the other two are deceivers.

[1] *Theological Writings*, II, 282; III, 24, 132.   [2] Ibid., III, 129.
[3] Ibid., IV, 119f.   [4] Ibid., III, 215.   [5] *Nathan*, III, 7.

> They search, dispute, lament.
> In vain; the proper ring could not
> Be found; 'twas hid as well almost
> As—the true faith from us today.[1]

The three sons hasten to the magistrate:

> And each swore to the judge
> He had the ring directly from his father's hand—
> And this, of course, was true![2]

The judge then has a timely recollection of the miraculous power the true ring is said to have:

> This must
> Decide! The rings, if false, will surely not
> Possess this gift! Say, two of you, forthwith
> Whom you do love the most. No word? The rings'
> Effect is just within, does not project?
> Each loves himself the most—all three of you
> Are then deceived deceivers! All the rings
> Are false—the real one was doubtless lost.
> Your father had the three rings made
> To hide the loss and make it good.[3]

The judge, however, like Lessing himself, is not disposed to make practical use of this critical opinion, which simply deprives the question of which is the real ring of its object. Apart from this judgment of his (which was, if it had been simply a question of judgment, the only one he could give), or rather instead of it he had a 'piece of advice' to offer:

> My counsel is, you should accept
> The matter simply as it stands. If each
> Received his ring from his father's hand
> Then let him think his own is without doubt
> The real one.[4]

It might also be the case, the judge now reflects—and in so reflecting hits upon the cause of the whole problem, which the fable pre-supposes as true—that the true ring has *not* been lost, but is there, unrecognizable together with two false ones by the father's own will. How then could judgment be passed? The counsel just mentioned can, however, very well be given, and explained in the following manner:

> So be it then!
> Let each one seek the unbought love that's free
> From prejudice, as promised by the ring!

[1] For original, cf. Appendix, p. 401. [2] For original, cf. Appendix, p. 401.
[3] For original, cf. Appendix., p. 402. [4] For original, cf. Appendix, p. 402.

> Each strive in contest to reveal the jewel's
> Strength! And aid this force by gentleness,
> A heart-felt tolerance, good works and deep
> Submission to God's will! And should the powers
> Dwelling in the stones then come to light among
> Your childrens' childrens' heirs, I then, when
> Thousand thousand years are past, invite them
> Once again before this judgment-seat.
> A wiser man will then sit here and speak.
> Now go your ways! Thus quoth the modest judge.[1]

According to this second opinion of the judge, be it noted, one of the rings is in fact genuine, and the decision about which is the genuine one will be made at some future time—in a thousand thousand years, to be sure, in a time completely inaccessible to us—by a wiser judge, when in fact the power of this genuine ring has in the meantime 'come to light'. In other words: a true faith does exist, and this faith will bring the proof of the spirit and the power, and it is then that the judgment, upon what is really the truth in religious history which is at present impossible will be passed. At the present time, however, this cannot come about. The contemporary student of religious history must declare, with Saladin in the play:

> Nathan, cherished Nathan!—
> The thousand thousand years of this your judge
> Are not yet past. His judgment-seat is not
> My own.[2]

For the present it is only possible to advise the devotees of every religion, the Christian religion included, that they should assume the alleged miraculous power of their faith to be real, and act in a way that will foster it. That is, they must be what people who have this miraculous power must be, with 'gentleness, a heart-felt tolerance, good works and deep submission to God's will', without themselves doing injury to the prejudice inherent in their faith, but also without consideration for it. It will not be this contest of virtue which will decide the argument but the miraculous power of true faith, which is not now discoverable as such. But this contest of virtue is the only possibility which can at present be recommended to all participants, for the miraculous power will certainly be revealed as a fostering of virtue which makes men beloved in the sight of God and man.

There are two elements in the thought of the play which seem to be new. The first that strikes us is just this indication of right, that is, virtuous conduct which is in accordance with the miraculous power of the

[1] For original, cf. Appendix, p. 402.   [2] For original, cf. Appendix, p. 402-3.

true faith, which encourages, and even aids it. In the dispute of the Fragments, in the passages most relevant to this question, Lessing always spoke of the experience which had to be acquired. Now we are expressly told, that whichever faith presents itself by experience as the true one, this experience will in all circumstances be an experience of a moral kind. The man who is beloved in the sight of God and man, as is promised to the true believer, will in all circumstances be a man who is graced by definite specifiable virtues, who is triumphant in the spheres where they are exercised.

Another striking element is the expressly stated assumption in the parable of the rings that *one* of the positive historical religions, unidentifiable as it now is among them all, will show itself, by means of the proof of the spirit and the power, to be the true one, and can and must ultimately come to be judged as such. The judge's decision, in the fable, was to give his advice, instead of his judgment, which would inevitably have amounted to a *non liquet* and stamped all three of the brothers as 'deceived deceivers'. In giving preference therefore to the second possible view of the matter over the first, which was also possible in principle, he opts—without knowing it, only sensing it, although the author knows—for the true view in opposition to the false one: the true ring was in fact *not* lost. His counsel rests upon this second view which he prefers and is in accordance with the facts. And that is precisely why no proclamation of a universal religion comes about in *Nathan*. It is true we hear Nathan sighing at the beginning:

> Are Jew and Christian Jew and Christian first
> And not first men? Oh! if only from among
> Your kind I'd found one more who is content
> To bear the simple name of man![1]

We hear the same Nathan soliloquizing, however, just before the scene of the rings:

> It does not do to be an arrant Jew,
> But even less to be no Jew at all.[2]

But Saladin too declares later on:

> I have never wished to find
> The same bark growing upon every tree.[3]

And the Templar likewise knows that he who is thought to stand—and declares he stands—above all parties, in fact supports a party too:

> Since this fact is simply so,
> It's rightly so, I trow.[4]

---

[1] *Nathan*, II, 5; cf. Appendix, p. 403.   [2] Ibid., III, 6; cf. Appendix, p. 403.
[3] Ibid., IV, 4; cf. Appendix, p. 403.   [4] Ibid., IV, 1; cf. Appendix, p. 403.

The meaning of this conservative aspect of the conclusions presented in the play is of course to be found in the assumption that *one* of the positive historical religions—we do not, admittedly, know which—is the true one and will show itself as such. Because this is so, there would be no sense in changing one's own religion to which one belongs after all for one of the others, and even less in changing it for some kind of universal religion.

These two seeming innovations in *Nathan* can, however, be taken only as elucidating Lessing's basic position, which we know already. The really significant thing is that we find Lessing the theologian in *Nathan* too, and in *Nathan* particularly, in the benignly superior *rôle* of the counsellor—poised upon the lofty watch-tower of the man who he is not so completely tied to any one of the positive religions that he is bound to consider it to be the only true one. On the other hand, he is not so completely inimical to any of them that he would think it out of the question for it to be the true religion. He considers the whole formed by the concrete historical plan or succession of these religions to be so meaningful, and reckons so completely with the inner teleology of this whole, that it is for him certain that one of these religions will prove to be the true one and in doing so justify the whole of which it was a part. But the circle is complete—he feels himself bound to maintain in the face of all opposition, that the superiority of this one religion —'the thousand thousand years of this your judge are not yet past'— has not yet emerged in a manner making it ripe for judgment, and it can therefore for the time being not be made valid in practice. He points out, with this proviso, that the experience of the true religion will manifest itself, come what may, in the practice of the quite definite moral virtues he mentions and thus he points to this practice of virtue as the most promising path, *rebus sic stantibus*, which every religion can and should tread.

We must be clear in our minds that this is Lessing's standpoint (it is simply more clearly recognizable in *Nathan*) when giving counsel to the Lutheran Church in the dispute of the Fragments. He who gives counsel here, does not stand on the ground of the Lutheran faith in revelation but adopts this ground for a certain accidental reason and a higher insight. He is given the certain accidental reason for acting in this way by the fact that he happened to be born on the ground of Lutheran Christianity. The higher insight which leads him to take this fact seriously is not by any means the truth of the Lutheran faith in revelation itself. It is his comprehensive knowledge of the great connexion between the parts of the whole of history, which is moving towards a final decision, and within which there happen to be after all stages and stopping places, i.e. such provisional decisions as that for the truth of the Lutheran faith in revelation, within which, since it is so, everyone must make some such kind of preliminary decision, in accordance with the occasion of his birth and education. 'Let each think his own is without doubt the real ring.'

In this sense Lessing 'believes'. Nothing but this provisional decision, and not, for instance, the necessity for the final decision upon the whole of religious history, does bind him to this particular faith of this particular Church. He knows that we cannot know of the true faith, but that we can only simply assume that some one faith is the true one. This, in fact, he does. And, of course, he knows that his choice may not be without good cause; that his ring may perhaps really be the genuine one. It certainly does not seem out of the question to him that the Lutheran Church itself might at some time show itself to be the true Church and religion. It is because this chance exists that he is concerned about the Lutheran Church and thinks it worth the trouble to give it good counsel, to put its theologians to the test. For the same reason he can become quite angry with them when they fail in this test, and do not accept or understand his advice. He does this, be it well understood, because of that chance! He knows for certain that such a chance exists, for he knows for certain of the related meaning which exists between all such preliminary decisions. Because he knows this he knows for certain that history has a purpose and that one of these preliminary decisions will approximate most closely to history's purpose; that it will be directly responsible for the transition to the age of the new, everlasting gospel and thus prove itself in the sight of the other preliminary decisions to be the true one.

Lessing gave the Lutheran Church advice from this watch-tower of the philosophy of history. Does his advice differ in content and in purport from that of the philosopher of history, from that of the wise judge in the parable of the rings? We have seen that this advice consisted in the indication of experience, the lessons of life, the feelings and the heart: it is as something which reaches and touches us directly, as something which immediately enlightens and enters into us, that historical truth becomes revelation and proves that it has the force of the necessary truth of reason. The advice of the judge in the parable of the rings also consisted in the pointing out of the self-proving miraculous power of the genuine ring. One thing is certain: Lessing was here not pointing out to the Lutheran Church that which, at any rate in its origins and confessional writings, it had understood as

revelation; he was not pointing to the 'miraculous power' with which
God, as the Lord of history, espouses the cause of historical man in a
historical encounter which man comes to share directly. This interpretation of Lessing's *Proof of the Spirit and the Power* from the dispute
of the Fragments, which in certain passages is not an impossible
one (just as with Rousseau), is shown to be completely out of the
question when the *Proof* is seen beside *Nathan the Wise* and beside
the *Education of the Human Race*. Within history, in which there are the
various religions, and in which there is also a Lutheran Church, there
are only human pre-decisions, and human affirmation of this or that
historical possibility. But there is no encounter with God decisively
intervening from outside or above, and demanding faith as man's final
decision to obey; no revelation in the sense in which the Lutheran
Church had understood it before the eighteenth century. According to
Lessing no Church and no religion can or may call revelation in this
sense to witness. It is precisely revelation in this sense which, in Lessing's view of history, is utterly precluded. Now this means that the
polemics of the dispute of the Fragments, occasionally so instructive
and amusing to read, are in their essential passages without doubt
arguments against just this conception of revelation. For in their
essential principles they are not relevant, as according to the programme they should be, to the historical apologists who desire to prove
historically the revealed character of certain historical truths, but they
are relevant to the notion that the Holy Scriptures are the authoritative document for the historical truth which to the Church is identical
with revelation. This, however, means that the polemics are relevant to
the authoritarian character, upheld by this notion, of what the Church
calls revelation, its character as historical truth which descends from
above, a particular truth stepping in from outside in distinction from
all other historical truth; a truth which is, indeed, uniquely qualified.
For that is the character which the Protestant doctrine of Scripture
concretely ascribes to revelation.

And it is precisely the Protestant doctrine of Scripture that
Lessing is trying to juggle away, with all the means at his disposal, in
favour of this historical truth with the power of proof which exists
before and after the Bible, in favour of the prophetic word which is not
bound up with the vehicle of the historical word, in favour of the
original gospel and of the *regula fidei*, in favour of the spirit and the
inner truth and the 'ever-continuing miracle of religion itself', in
favour of the whole 'edifice' of the Christian Church. In short he
seeks to achieve this end in unison with Roman Catholicism and the

whole of Protestant modernism (and as one of the first quite obvious heralds of the programme of Protestant modernism) in favour of history itself as distinct from and as against the Lord of history, who is indelibly denoted precisely by the Protestant doctrine of the Scriptures.

With Lessing there is no such thing as a Lord of history within history. Indeed he discusses miraculous powers and events experienced or recounted in history, the 'grateful shock of the electric current' and the like, he believes it possible of the positive religions that such things could actually come to pass, in their sphere, and come to pass so genuinely even, that one of them might finally and at last show itself to be the genuine, the true religion, he shows enough trust in Lutheranism in spite of everything to urge its believers to let the empirical nature of the historical fact which gives the Church its foundation be the decisive factor. But in discussing these things he is thinking simply of possibilities within history, which can and may be reckoned with and pointed out, but which are all subject to the proviso that it is ultimately impossible to pass any judgment upon their truth or genuineness. *History in revelation;* this is the principle denied by the Protestant doctrine of Scripture, but upheld by Lessing, the counsellor of the Lutheran Church. The meaning of revelation in Lessing's sense was the successive or simultaneous working-out of the possibilities proper to and inherent in historical humanity. Revelation is the 'education which the human race has undergone and is undergoing still'.[1] Education, however, 'does not give man anything he might not also take from within himself; it is just that it gives him more quickly and easily what he might have from within himself. Revelation too therefore does not give man anything which human reason left to itself would not also discover; it is just that it gave and is giving him the most important of these things sooner'.[2] The concise parallel to these sentences, in themselves already concise, is quite simply the fact that the judge in the fable of the rings knows as a matter of course wherein the quality of being beloved of God and man, promised to the owner of the genuine ring, will at all events consist: it will consist in a moral virtuousness which can be most directly specified. If this is so, what then is the 'proof of the spirit and the power'—whether it is triumphantly brought by the one religion or by the other—but the event, in which humanity in fact arrives at that which is the goal required by its own nature, the realization of its possibilities.

Can a Lord of history exist in these circumstances, even solely as a Lord over history? Lessing speaks of 'God' as the educator of the

[1] *Ed.*, para. 2.   [2] Ibid., para. 4.

human race. He speaks of the steps of 'eternal Providence' which are accomplished in this education. But he can also (as in the foreword to the *Education*) simply speak of the course visible in the history of the religions, 'which is the one and only thing by which human understanding everywhere can develop itself, and is meant to develop itself, even further'. This is new in Lessing as opposed to the other neologians: the fact that for him such a 'course' of history does exist, and it was in all probability this discovery, the discovery of the dramatic quality active in history, which gave him the courage to utter the old word 'revelation' with a new solemnity as a description of this course. But does it make any difference to his interpretation of this 'course' whether we say 'God' or whether we say 'human understanding' in the significant places, and whether we interpret revelation as being education by an educator or self-education or even more simply development, and thus allow the Lord of history to coincide with history itself, or alternatively with its subject, with the humanity educating, or alternatively, developing itself? It is difficult to say in what respect there is meant to be a distinction, and perhaps it is only a part of Lessing's freemason's wisdom that he did not go so far as to say openly that it really does not make any difference. As Lessing, in *Minna von Barnhelm*, presented the noble Tellheim, the surly Just, the faithful Werner and the thankful 'Lady in mourning', and in *Nathan* the Christian Templar, the Mohammedan Sultan and the Jewish merchant, the highest law to which all these figures are subject, in the one play just as much as in the other, is apparently: 'Act in accordance with your individual perfections!' (as Lessing put it in formulating the categorical imperative in a strange early work of his[1]), and in each of them it is a 'course' which welds these figures into a dramatic unity. Is it actually a God which is necessary in *Minna* and in *Nathan* to set these characters in motion either in isolation or in their relationship one to another? Is not the thought of a God in both of them bound to appear like that of a fifth wheel on a carriage? Is not all that is necessary in both of them a poet and thinker, perhaps, a playwright of genius? To put it differently: is man not, in the one play just as much as in the other, best understood when he is understood as being sufficient unto himself? Did Lessing really even count upon God's final word concerning the dramas and drama of human history, after having in principle cut God off from every word previous to the last word spoken, or to be spoken, within this history? Is it not a fact that Lessing's man is self-sufficient, and has no need of God in any event?

[1] *Th. Wr.*, I, 217.

And now in conclusion let us quote the most famous words which Lessing wrote, without comment, since they of themselves best bring the proof of Lessing's spirit and of his power. They are to be found in the polemic *A Rejoinder*, written in 1778.[1]

'A man's worth does not consist in the truth any one man may happen to have in his possession, or thinks he has in his possession, but in the honest endeavour he has brought to bear in his attempt to discover the truth. For it is not by the possession of truth but by the search for the truth that his powers are enlarged, which alone go to make for his ever-increasing perfection. Possession makes men placid, indolent and proud.

'If God were holding all the truth that exists in his right hand, and in his left just the one ever-active urge to find the truth, even if attached to it were the condition that I should always and forever be going astray, and said to me, "Choose!" I should humbly fall upon his left hand and say: "Father, give! Pure truth is surely only for thee alone!"'

[1] *Th. Wr.*, III, 26.

IV

KANT

I. It was in the year of Lessing's death, 1781, that Kant's *Critique of Pure Reason* appeared. What was the significance of this man and of this work? In connexion with our observations in this book our answer must simply be that it was in this man and in this work that the eighteenth century saw, understood and affirmed itself in its own limitations. Itself—in its limitations! In saying this we are saying that Kant, like Rousseau and Lessing, stands at the turning-point of his age. We must, however, immediately add that he does this because in him just this one simple thing happens. There is no disclosure of a new dimension, no discovery of new provinces and powers, as with Rousseau and Lessing—if that were the point, we might very well find that Kant after Rousseau and Lessing might appear to us to be a reactionary—but just this one simple thing: the century's coming to an understanding of itself—but of itself in its limitations. With Kant only this one simple thing happened and for this reason he stands, in effect, much more basically, much more comprehensively and more radically, and, in historical terms, much more interestingly and more significantly at the turning-point of his age.

The singularity of Kant's position can be seen already by the fact that, comprehensive and typical in both directions as it is, it is a solitary one. Just as on the one hand he lent the eighteenth-century spirit a pregnancy of expression which, for all the connexions he has here, makes of him an incomparable figure, so on the other hand in spite of every connexion, as a surmounter of this spirit he does not align himself with the companion figures of the new age—the line of succession leading from Rousseau by way of Lessing and Herder to Romanticism. He stands by himself—in this respect he can only be compared to Goethe after him—a stumbling-block and rock of offence also in the new age, someone determinedly pursuing his own course, more feared than loved, a prophet whom almost everyone even among those who wanted to go forward with him had first to re-interpret before they could do anything with him.

The singularity of Kant's position can also be seen, particularly in his special position in relation to the theological problem: he and only he was in fact the man, also here, and here in particular, in whom the the century saw 'itself in its own limitations'. Nobody from China to Peru brought into the open the theological viewpoint, thought and intent of the eighteenth century with so much determination, in such concrete and logical terms with so unemotional a clarity (in contrast to Rousseau), and with such an unfreemasonly candour (in contrast to Lessing) as he did. There was moreover nobody at all who saw so clearly that this theological thought and intent were one, given their limits by a theological possibility not only relatively but absolutely different. Kant personally never considered passing these limits for one moment. He did really stand with both feet within them. And yet he saw them, no matter how deprecatingly, how polemically. Rousseau and Lessing and later Herder, Schleiermacher and Hegel did not see them. Of Goethe too we must probably say that he did not see them. It is fundamentally impossible to conduct a conversation with them from the point of view of this altogether different theological possibility, because they simply did not recognize it as a distinct opposite of their own possibility, because it simply did not exist for them as an opposite. Kant, however, recognized this other possibility, even though it was at a distant periphery of his thought. He recognized it as an opposing force which he rejected, but still as an opposing force, as an instance which he dismissed in practice but not in principle, as an instance, that is, which he was not capable of including in his own position. Kant did not, like Rousseau, go to Holy Communion, did not, like Lessing, call Luther to witness. Instead, when the university of Königsberg was proceeding in solemn procession from the Great Hall to the church for the university service on the *dies academicus* Kant used ostentatiously to step away from the procession just as it was entering the church, make his way round the church instead, and go home. We have before us in all his writings the same refreshingly unequivocal attitude. With such a man a conversation from the other point of view, from the point of view of a completely different theology, is possible, because it is precisely when it is seen from there that it has quite definite outlines. The confusion of both worlds, which is more or less likely to lead one astray with everybody else, is almost impossible with Kant. Particularly in our field he points beyond the relative distinction between the old and the new time which concerns us here. And he points beyond what is common to them both.

In a little essay he wrote in the year 1784, Kant gives the following answer in the first few decisive sentences to the question of the title, 'What is Enlightenment?': 'The Enlightenment represents man's emergence from a self-inflicted state of minority. A minor is one who is incapable of making use of his understanding without guidance from someone else. This minority is self-inflicted whenever its cause lies not in lack of understanding, but in a lack of the determination and courage to make use of it without the guidance of another. *Sapere aude!* Have the courage to make use of your own understanding, is therefore the watchword of the Enlightenment.' Nobody saw, knew or said in the way that Kant did what this mature, courageous man who makes use of his own understanding looks like, what his position is and how he conducts himself. Nobody strikes us as so worthy of belief and so honourable as he does when he baldly announces the advent of this kind of man, and when he naïvely expresses the conviction that his own present, as the time of this man, is without doubt the best of all the ages which have gone before.[1] Perhaps the reason for this is simply that nobody really lived the life of the man Kant had in mind as economically and as existentially as it was possible for Kant himself to live it, as he lived it in his study and during the measured walks he took in the town he never left in all his days. It was the life of one who vigorously, indefatigably, and in every respect made use of all his human capacities. But the deeper and more significant reason why he strikes us in this way is the fact that the naïveté with which he praised his time and the man of his time, and the complete and unquestioning way in which he embodied this man in his own person were based upon a most scrupulous and calculated testing of these capacities, upon a most logical carrying to its conclusion of the 'emergence from minority', upon a complete understanding of the problems with which—as well and particularly—the man who makes use of his own understanding is faced.

Kant inspires our awe as a representative of the spirit of the eighteenth century. We cannot help feeling that in him this spirit has not only reached maturity and beyond. In him, we feel, this spirit is not merely at loggerheads with itself in a riotous way; it does not merely strive beyond itself in enthusiastic or poetic fervour and it does not become a prey to Mephistophelean self-mockery. It has quite simply come to terms with itself; it therefore knows where it stands and it has thus acquired humility. With Kant we do not find any narrow-minded, ignorant self-satisfaction within the confines of this spirit,

[1] *Die Religion innerhalb der Grenzen der blossen Vernunft* (Religion within the Bounds of Reason Alone), p. 197, quot. from 2nd ed., 1794.

neither do we find any exuberant, lawless unrest in the face of these confines, according to the prescription:—
Any fence we find we'll crash

> What else are fences for, now?

Any lamps we find we'll smash—

> Our lights are lit, we trow!

In Kant we find this spirit at a point beyond self-satisfaction and rebellion in being what it is, namely, distinct, existing in history as it does, keeping within its confines, being completely itself and completely self-conscious, and in its limits. In its limits, as they are understood by Kant, something of humanity's limits in general, and at this something of wisdom seems to become visible. In Kant's philosophy, as in the music of Mozart, there is something of the calm and majesty of death which seems suddenly to loom up from afar to oppose the eighteenth-century spirit. That is why, in Kant, thrown completely back upon humility, it shines forth once again in its full splendour. That is why it here commands our respect.

In a more important passage than the one previously quoted[1] Kant gave another answer to the question about the meaning of his time or rather he gave the same answer in more fundamental and significant terms: 'Our age is the true age of criticism, to which all things must be subjected.' In the way Kant meant it this was an interpretation or characterization of the age completely new to his contemporaries, and was, strictly speaking, only applicable to one single man of the age, namely to Kant himself. In Kant's sense 'criticism' does not mean a kind of knowledge fundamentally consisting in the total or partial negation of another merely alleged or at any rate disputable piece of knowledge. Criticism in Kant's sense does not consist in casting doubt upon or denying certain propositions, or alternatively certain things contained in these propositions, which are declared to be objects of knowledge. He could not, it is true, embark upon or set forth his own kind of criticism without using the usual kind of criticism as well. But his own criticism is essentially quite different from it: it is criticism of knowledge itself and of knowledge as such. This does not mean that it is a complete or partial denial of the possibility, validity and worth of the human method of forming knowledge. Even if it was David Hume, the 'sceptic', who by Kant's own admission first roused him from his 'dogmatic slumbers', i.e. first shook him in his untested

---

[1] *Critique of Pure Reason*, 1st ed., Preface V.

assumption that human knowledge was possible and valid, this does not mean that Kant intended to pursue the same road as Hume, i.e. that he intended to make the challenging of this assumption his actual goal. Those have truly been guilty of misunderstanding him who have taken him to be a kind of super-sceptic, who have looked upon him as the 'all-annihilating one', as far as the reality of knowledge, the reality of science and morality, art and religion are concerned: and have regarded him as the man who contemplates civilization from outside, and challenges its values, so to speak, in order to provide it, on his own initiative, with a new basis, or in order to refrain resignedly from the possibility of giving it a basis.

Kant himself, although he compared his enterprise with that of Copernicus, or rather precisely because he made this comparison, looked upon it as anything but a venture in criticism in this sense. Kant was not Rousseau, and Rousseau himself cannot be understood only in this sense. In Kant's eyes civilization has its basis. For him civilization, the achievement of his age, the achievement which is also and in particular the achievement of human knowledge in all these fields, is an event beyond question. It is this event that provides him with the ground upon which he stands. His investigation does not seek to answer the question of whether this achievement has any basis, but the question as to what its basis is. It seeks to establish the method of this civilization: it seeks, in so far as this civilization is firstly and lastly that of the Enlightenment, to bring about an enlightenment of the Enlightenment about itself, so that, safe from all misunderstanding of itself, it might thenceforward adopt a certain, sure and tranquil course. Kant intends to see to it that the man who has come of age, whom he believes he can recognize and may praise in Enlightenment man, does not use his understanding wilfully and as he thinks fit, now that he has mustered the courage to use it at all. This does not mean that he should make his understanding the object of a sceptical mistrust. It means that he should understand it and thus, knowing about it, for this reason use it calmly and surely and constantly. And the courage (*Mut*) demanded here from him is not meant to be arrogance (*Hochmut*), let alone faintheartedness (*Schwachmut*), but—lying midway between the two—humility (*Demut*), enabling man to subject himself to a searching criticism of his capacities which will show him the right course and which, precisely because it is searching and showing the right course, will clarify and confirm his ability to subject himself to, and, once he has done this, to be guided by the results of this self-criticism. The critique of reason is reason arriving at an understanding of itself. Its pathos is not by any means that of a denial; it is rather, in the most explicit manner possible, that of an affirmation of reason. Kant is not Jacobi. Kant is not Hamann or Claudius or Lavater. Kant is Kant and his critique of reason has nothing at all to do with a weariness of civilization or a weariness of the Enlightenment. Kant both has and demands an almost unconditional faith in reason. But the only kind of reason he considers worthy of his trust is the reason which has first of all come to be reasonable as regards itself. The meaning of his critique of reason consists in the attempt to bring this kind of reason into prominence.

The essential quality of eighteenth-century man before Kant was a joyful affirmation of the actual capacity of human reason, which stood, so it seemed, as an incontrovertible fact visible to all in the irresistible forward march of natural and technical science, of historical knowledge, and surely also of moral feeling. As a true child of his age Kant is also to be found among the joyfully participating admirers of this process. He conceives and announces his teaching as one who is engaged in furthering this process, as one who is to a great extent himself actively concerned with it. It is well known that with the astronomical theory which shares his name and that of Laplace he intervened significantly in the sphere of natural science, and with his shrewd and lively spectator's eye he was, so to speak, always present whenever there was something to be seen. He never stood apart but always faced, was always in the middle of the real intellectual movement of his age. 'Such a phenomenon in human history will never again be forgotten, because it has revealed a disposition and capacity for betterment in human nature.'[1] This he said of the French Revolution, the outbreak and development of which he followed with the closest attention and with an almost boyish sympathy and expectancy, in this resembling only too closely a contemporary like Lavater, from whom he was in every other respect totally dissimilar. But we must note that only because and in so far as it reveals a disposition and capacity in human nature does Kant affirm the tendency of his time. 'It is already a beginning of the reign of the good principle and a sign "that the kingdom of heaven is at hand", even if only the fundamentals of its constitution come to be commonly known. For something is already present in the world of the understanding, and the roots, from which alone it can spring, have already established themselves everywhere, although the complete development of its appearance in the world of

[1] *Streit der Fakultäten* (Dispute of the Faculties) Vol. 46D of the Phil. Libr., 2nd ed., p. 135.

the senses still lies in the unforeseeable future.'[1] Kant, faced by the
actual capacity for human reason as manifested in the trends of science
and morality, of art and religion in his time, is not interested in this
actual capacity in itself and as such, but in the deeper actuality of this
capacity in principle. Faced with what reason has brought into being
he is interested only in its *a priori* capacity for achieving these things;
faced with the accidental historical aspect of civilization he seeks
instead what is essential and necessary about it, the quality which
makes it into an unforgettable phenomenon.

And now the question he asks is about the nature of this basic
capacity, about the definite order and structure of this necessity, about
the laws governing its essential quality, without perception of which
the actual capacity could not in the long run remain certain of its
objectives and its course. Thus he himself called his great main work a
Treatise on Method.[2] He might also have said the same of his other
three main works and of the lesser works which accompanied them.
Man has come of age. But in what does man's majority consist? Only
Kant, the perfect man of the eighteenth century, could dare to accept
the assumption which underlay this question: the assumption that
reason is right in its activity, as an actual capacity, as and in so far as,
a priori, preceding its activity, it necessarily rests upon itself. But the
question which was put on the basis of this assumption, the question
about this 'as and in so far as', in bringing the spirit of the age to its
culmination, also overcomes it.

The Enlightenment before Kant was the absolute and boundless self-
affirmation of reason, which, as such an affirmation, was ultimately
bound to be uncertain of itself. Even if we wish to characterize Kant's
intellectual quality and that of the time after him as part of the Enlightenment—as in a certain sense we not only can but must—it is now
at all events a relative and bounded self-affirmation of reason, critical
and now for the first time sure of itself, to the extent that it possesses
these qualities. That is what is new in Kant. And it is also a new side of
the intellectuality of the nineteenth century, as opposed to that of the
eighteenth. The actual capacity of human reason was destined to
march onward in this new century, in which Kant himself, grown tired,
and the balance of his mind somewhat disturbed, was to live only for a
few years. It was destined to assume quite different dimensions from
those of which Kant could have any idea; there would be quite
different and ever-increasing occasion for the self-consciousness which

[1] *Rel.*, 225.
[2] *Critique of Pure Reason*, 2nd ed., Pref. XXII.

distinguished the old Enlightenment and which was also alive in
Kant. But from now onwards, from Kant onwards, all self-affirmation
of human reason would be asked, and would continually have to bear
with 'being' asked, whether it in fact rests upon a true maturity. And
everyone who used this reason would be asked from now on whether
his use of it might not perhaps just be sophistry masquerading as
reason, an uncritical adventure of the understanding prompted by
obscure feelings. With Kant and from Kant onwards the human use
of reason has left the broad way and finds itself within the 'strait gate'.[1]
This was also, and particularly, true of theology. From now on theology
would no longer be able to formulate its tenets, no matter on what
foundation it might base them, without having acquired a clear conception of the method of reason, which it also uses in the construction
of its tenets. Any theology which had not at least faced this question
and presented its credentials was backward, from now on, superseded
in its relation to the age, no matter how valuable or worthless it might
otherwise be; it would not be the theology of the new century which
was just coming into being. Further, it would in any case be typical of
the theology of the new century to absorb the idea of the critique of
reason, in a vastly different form perhaps from that of Kant himself,
but in consideration, nevertheless, of the problem which Kant raised.

It cannot be our concern here to develop even at moderate length
Kant's critique of reason in its historical course and philosophical
content. We shall content ourselves with establishing what its result
was and with establishing its two basic trends, which have an especially
important bearing upon theology.

The one has its goal in the insight into the ideal character of all
knowledge achieved by pure reason. (From it the way of thought
Kant founded and which was developed directly after him acquired
the ambiguous title of 'Idealism'; 'Criticism' or 'Rationalism' are
terms which would have typified much more clearly and comprehensively all that Kant, at any rate, wanted.) By pure rational knowledge Kant means that necessary knowledge which refers not to what
is, but to an object that transcends all experience, to what must be
and only in this sense 'is'. This pure rational knowledge which is
necessary since it accompanies and directs all empirical knowledge—in
substance Kant here simply follows the metaphysics of his time—is the
knowledge of the ideas of God, freedom and immortality. It is clearly
in the realm of this knowledge of ideas, the realm of metaphysics, that
there take place all the reason's misconceptions and deceptions about

[1] *Critique of Practical Reason*, 1st ed., p. 163.

itself. To clarify and lay foundations for this knowledge of ideas, and to provide in this sense a criticism of it, is the task of the *Critique of Pure Reason*. That is why Kant gave its distinctive title to the, as he intended, popular compendium with which he at once followed up the longer work: *Prolegomena to any future metaphysics which can possibly pretend to be a science*. Empirical knowledge is not knowledge of ideas and knowledge of ideas is not empirical knowledge, indissolubly interconnected as they are—that is what, above all, human reason must make clear to itself, in order to understand itself.

Empirical knowledge is constituted by intuition (*Anschauung*— immediate perception) and the Understanding, the two forms of knowledge peculiar to human reason. Their object cannot be the 'thing-in-itself', that is a thing manifest to us in its essential nature; but is the thing as it is given and comprehended by virtue of these two forms of knowledge. Their object is *given* to us under the forms of space and time, so that its existence and characteristics become to us intuitively evident. We *comprehend* however its existence and characteristics by means of the Categories or forms of the *Understanding* which correspond to the forms of intuition (the forms of space and time). By means of the Categories of the Understanding we attempt to think what we have intuited. Genuine empirical knowledge is achieved when there is a concrete unity of intuition and concepts. This is what corresponds to the transcendental act of apperception, that is to what underlies this achievement, the synthetic *a priori* determining principle of our reason. Only empirical knowledge is genuine theoretical, rational knowledge, that is, knowledge of what exists. For only in the *unity* of intuition and concepts is there knowledge of what exists.

As intuition without concepts would be blind, so—and this is the aspect of the matter emphasized by the Kantian teaching—concepts without intuition are empty, that is, they cannot be made to yield any knowledge of what exists. When assertions or denials about what exists are made by means of forming concepts which lack any actual or at least possible intuition, the illusion of genuine theoretical knowledge and not the reality is achieved. For there is wanting any basis in transcendental apperception and thus any test of pure rationality. This illusion will very soon produce difficulties in its train by developing antinomies, necessary self-contradictions in which at once such a desire for ideal knowledge of a merely conceptual kind will be entangled. Examples are the contradiction between the assumption of a First Cause and that of a *regressus in infinitum*; or that between the assumption of human free-will and the assumption that there is no such thing. So far as the objects of intuition and the Understanding, of empirical knowledge, are concerned, God, Freedom and Immortality are not objects of our knowledge. That means: they are not objects of our theoretical knowledge. They are not to be comprehended simply as existent reality. Only sophistry can present them and treat of them as such. Metaphysics—metaphysical cosmology, psychology and theology—is impossible, if one understands by it a theoretical knowledge of objects, the concepts of which must be devoid of corresponding intuitions. They are impossible 'since for determining our ideas of the supersensible we have no material whatever, and we must derive this latter from things in the world of sense, which is absolutely inadequate for such an Object'.[1] All theoretical proofs and disproofs of God's existence, for example, fail equally, since the propositions, 'God exists' and 'God does not exist', can express in their theoretical meaning only the illusion of knowledge and not knowledge. For they apply the Category of being, positively and negatively, to an object which lacks intuition. God is a limiting concept, a regulative idea, a pure thing of thought. We imagine that when we assert or deny God's existence we have said something about God. In fact to speak of existence or non-existence is *per se* not to speak of God.

Be it well understood: the significance of this, the negative aspect, of Kant's endeavour to bring reason to an understanding of itself, does not consist in an attempt to dispute or even only cast doubt upon the metaphysical reality or unreality of God, freedom and immortality. It certainly does consist in criticism of the means by which they are known, in the attempt to demonstrate that this knowledge is that of pure reason, that its nature is strictly ideal; and in the making of the proviso, that it may on no account claim to be theoretical knowledge.

There is, however, a second aspect, a positive aspect to Kant's undertaking. According to Kant knowledge by pure reason is also and in particular true knowledge by reason, however necessary it is to all empirical knowledge. Reason must, however, learn to understand itself as pure reason. It will not have come to an understanding of itself so long as it imagines itself merely to be theoretical reason and not active, practical reason. In Kant's teaching 'practical reason' is not a second kind of reason existing beside the theoretical form; it is rather that the one kind of reason, which is also theoretical, is also and, it must actually be said, primarily, practical reason. Surely the union of intuition and concept, whence empirical knowledge derives its

---

[1] *Critique of Judgment*, 3rd German ed., p. 453; transl. by J. H. Bernard, 2nd ed., p. 403.

reality, is in fact action, practice, having its basis in transcendental apperception. It is in this act as such that man is laid hold of not only by the being of things, i.e. by nature in its reality in time and space, but beyond this and above all by the thing that must be, hidden from us as a 'thing in itself' which is, as a thing, undiscoverable; by the world of freedom which limits time and space and resolves them in itself. I am laid hold of, to use the words of Kant's famous passage,[1] not only by the star-strewn heavens above me, but also, at the same time, and chiefly, by the moral law within me. Abstract man, the man who is held to be a creature of theoretical reason, is not the real man. I am not a real man, a real creature of reason, simply by virtue of this capacity I have for perceiving things in time and space, but this capacity for perceiving things in time and space is itself based upon the true and essential reasoning capacity, namely that by which I perceive necessity and law, in such a way that law and necessity are imposed upon me as a person who acts. God, freedom and immortality—these ideas which in their regulative use are indispensable also in empirical knowledge—cannot be perceived *in abstracto*, i.e. by contemplation in isolation, but they can be perceived *in concreto*, i.e. in actual fact. It is in and with the *fact* that their true contemplation is accomplished; it is in practice that the true thing is accomplished, the theory which accompanies, provides the basis for and contains within itself all empirical knowledge but which now also rises truly and legitimately above it. They have no truth in a theory by itself.

Their truth is contained in the truth of the will for good, beside which 'it is not possible to conceive of anything anywhere in the world, or, indeed, outside it which could be taken as good without restriction'.[2] The will for good is a will not governed by any object, nor significantly guided by any desire or end or authority, but subject by its own decision to the categorical imperative of duty, in its quality as the rule for that which is universally valid, as the quintessence of the law, as the voice from the world of freedom Kant alludes to. Pure reason, reason as the capacity for knowing ideas, is practical reason. Knowledge by pure reason too, the true knowledge of God, freedom and immortality, is knowledge by practical reason, as it is implicitly accomplished in the deed performed in accordance with duty, and knowledge by practical reason is knowledge by pure reason. The act performed in accordance with the will for good, the moral act, is not

---

[1] *Critique of Practical Reason*, V, 161.
[2] *Grundlegung zur Metaphysik der Sitten* (Background for a Metaphysi cs of Morals), Phil. Libr., vol. 41, p. 10.

possible without, but comprises, not the establishment but certainly the *pre-supposition*—Kant's word for these, not a very happy choice linguistically, was 'postulates'—that all these ideas which transcend every experience and yet for their own part comprise all empirical knowledge are *true*: There are:

1. The pre-supposition of the truth of the idea of *God*, of the truth, that is, of an ultimate unity of nature and freedom, of that which is with that which must be, and thus of duty and desire.

2. The pre-supposition of the truth of the idea of *freedom*, of the idea, that is, that our moral existence is superior in its origins to our natural one.

3. The pre-supposition of the truth of the idea of *immortality*, of the idea, that is, of the infinite convergence of the two lines upon which our existence runs.

The truth of ideas (this, however, means truth in general, in so far as the truth of things is comprised in the truth of ideas) is practical truth, truth, that is, which is perceived in the form of such pre-suppositions (Kant says, in the form of 'postulates') which are accomplished in the moral act. As theoretical knowledge (whose objects can only be objects of experience), knowledge by pure reason is impossible, having its inevitable, true and sure basis in the knowledge of ideas, a knowledge which cannot be affirmed or denied, but which can certainly be believed, and believed, furthermore, as something jointly based with the moral demands on reason, as something, therefore, which is to be believed to be reasonable. It is impossible to bring forward the proof of God as an ontological, cosmological or teleological proof, as ultimately the school of Wolff still wanted to bring it. The proof of God is ever to be adduced as a demonstration of the presupposition that is assumed in deciding to accept the commandment of the inscrutable Law-giver, in subjecting oneself to the judgment of the inscrutable Judge. It must be brought forward as a moral proof of God.

There is, therefore, according to Kant, one knowledge of God, namely that one which lay a practical basis and meaning: 'After the analogy with an understanding I can very well . . . conceive of a super-sensory Being, without however wishing to perceive him thereby theoretically; if, namely, this definition of his causality concerns an effect in the world containing an intention which is morally necessary but which sensory beings are incapable of implementing; since then a knowledge of God and of God's existence (theology) is possible by means of qualities, and definitions of his causality, attributed to him simply by analogy, the which (*sc.* existence) in its practical aspect, but then again only in

F

respect to its practical (i.e. moral) aspect, has all the reality anyone might wish for.'[1] The critique is therefore meant to have brought honour, and not discredit, to knowledge by pure reason in particular: Kant does not think that in clarifying the relationship of knowledge by pure reason to empirical perception he has destroyed metaphysics, but rather that he has first and foremost made it possible as a science: metaphysics as knowledge by means of practical reason.—That then is the true use of pure reason as it at last and finally emerged from the fire of Kant's critique of reason.

As a result of this teaching theology, at least as much as philosophy and every other branch of learning at that time, found itself faced with the problem of determining its future attitude to Kant's critique of reason in the formation of its peculiar and necessary propositions. Kant, however, did not first wait for the theologians to declare their attitude to his philosophy, but immediately advanced to meet them—in accordance with the careful thought and precision he devoted to all his work—by dictating his own terms for peace, i.e. by giving an explicit and exhaustive explanation of the way he thought this attitude should be formed. These terms for peace are contained in his philosophy of religion, set down in his fourth main work, *Religion Within the Limits of Reason Alone* (1793), to which in 1798, with the *Dispute of the Faculties* (which, significantly, concerns only the dispute between the philosophical and theological faculties!), he added a rider which was meant to emphasize and enjoin upon them what he had said in the previous work. It is to these works and to the very categorical proposal made to theology in them that we have now to devote our attention.

It is possible to distinguish in Kant's dictation of peace terms—just as with every such dictated peace, however severe—between what the dictator definitely wants, and what he does not necessarily require, according to his explicit or tacit explanation of his terms—but leaves to the discretion and decision of the second party to the contract, until he has seen how things are going, at any rate. We cannot therefore explore all the possibilities of characterizing Kant's theology and describing its historical significance simply by explaining and assessing the content of his teaching, or alternatively of his terms for peace as they stand. We shall have to pay strict attention also to the passages where the philosopher has not expressed his own opinion, or has not stated any conclusion, but has merely left the question open. It is fitting to set out first in pursuit of what Kant in his works expressly stated and definitely wanted in his discussion of the theological problem. We shall then in

---

[1] *Critique of Judg.*, 482, cf. 424, footnote, 434, 472.

conclusion examine the other things, those upon which he was strikingly unwilling to express himself either explicitly or tacitly, and in which, therefore, he did not wish to act as a dictator towards theology.

What are Kant's aims as a philosopher of religion? The answer we must give is a double one: he wants on the one hand, as a philosopher, i.e. as the advocate of human reason in the general sense—which is seeking to understand itself and is thus self-critical—to remind religion too and theology as religion's mouth-piece of the significance of the fact that it too is a matter in which reason plays its part, an additional part, at all events, just as certainly as it too at least *makes use* of reason in the establishment of its propositions. And on the other hand, once again as a philosopher, he wants to assess religion as a phenomenon of reason, as a cultural manifestation, in so far at least as it is these things; he wants to make it intelligible within the frame-work of all the other phenomena of reason, to construct it by applying the general principles pertaining to all civilization. The theological propositions are at all events also, those of reason. And reason for its part has the 'idea of a religion'[1] as something which is, at all events, also peculiar to it.

In respect to theology philosophy therefore has on the one hand the task of critically examining in principle theology's 'interpretations', i.e. the tenets calling revelation to witness.[2] This at all events theology cannot disallow: 'The theological faculty's proud claim that the philosophical faculty is its handmaid (which still leaves open the question as to whether the latter carries her mistresses' torch before her or her train after her) can be conceded only so long as the maid is not driven out or gagged.'[3] Kant is bold enough to make the suggestion that candidates for theology should be compelled upon completion of their instruction in theology proper, biblical theology, to hear a special lecture upon purely philosophical religious teaching, as something necessary to their complete preparation.[4] 'It doesn't matter whether this makes the theologian agree with the philosopher or makes him feel that he must defeat his arguments, so long as he only hears him.' We shall hear what there is to hear for the theologian on this subject.

On the other hand, however, the philosopher is bound to feel it important for his own sake 'to form some coherent idea of those things in the Bible, the text of a religion which is held to have been revealed, which can also be perceived by reason alone',[5] and 'to seek that meaning in the Scripture which is in harmony with the holiest of reason's

---

[1] First draft of the Foreword to the *Rel.*   [2] Loc. cit.   [3] *Disp. of the Facs.*, 67.
[4] Foreword to the 1st ed. of the *Rel.* XIX.   [5] *Disp. of the Facs.*, 44.

teachings'.[1] The revealed or church faith, the positive religion, contains the inner, smaller circle,[2] Kant says (but he means to say: as the shell contains the kernel). It is this religion of reason as such, or the inner circle of positive religion, where it too is comprehensible as a religion of reason, and only in so far as it is here comprehensible as a religion of reason too, which interests the philosopher. It is in this respect that the philosopher is interested in positive religion as such too. It and it alone (*sc.* the religion of reason) is the object of the philosophy of religion. Only seemingly does the latter trespass upon theology's ground, in for its own part, for instance, basing its arguments upon quotations from the Bible; only seemingly because it does this simply to explain, and at most to affirm its own tenets relevant to this inner circle. It is on principle concerned with Christianity in particular and the documents of Christianity only as an example, in order to reveal by it the sole conditions 'whereby the idea of a religion can be realized',[3] i.e. in order to demonstrate by such examples the universal truth of religion.

Such then, in very general terms, are the two aims expressed in the title 'Religion within the limits of reason alone'. This title does not at all imply that religion exists solely within the limits of reason. It does, however, state that religion at all events is to be contemplated also within the limits of *reason* alone, and secondly that within the limits of reason alone *religion* too is to be contemplated. In this it must be borne in mind that 'reason alone' must in no circumstances be confused with 'pure' reason, the capacity for the knowledge of ideas, but stands in contrast to the reason illuminated by revelation, the reason which believes positively and concretely. Kant's undertaking in the philosophy of religion is not concerned with this last kind of reason as such and in itself. The contemplation of revelation, or alternatively of the reason which believes positively and concretely as such and in itself, has for the philosopher the significance of contemplating the border beyond which he feels, declares and conducts himself as one not competent, as a spectator, as a member of another faculty which is not qualified to judge of the matter, giving way respectfully and a little maliciously to the theologian, not contesting what he says, but not expressing agreement either, interested, but disclaiming all responsibility, waiting to see whether the other, the theologian, will find the desire and the courage really to take up the position which is his due as the proclaimer of revelation, of religion, that is, within and without

[1] *Rel.*, 115f.   [2] Foreword to the 2nd ed. *Rel.*, XXIf.
[3] Second draft of the Foreword to the *Rel.*

the limits of reason alone. Such is the strange restriction of the problems dealt with in Kant's philosophy of religion, concerning which we shall have several things to say later. Let us turn first of all to the details of the Kantian teaching of religion *within* the limits of reason alone, within the reason, that is, which in respect of any kind of positive faith based on revelation is, so to speak, merely a void, but which, precisely because of this, is the necessary form in all reason too which is filled by faith based on revelation.

Kant himself described his standpoint in the philosophy of religion as being that of 'pure rationalism'.[1] In order not to misunderstand him, being misled by the narrower sense which this word normally has when we use it, we must once again reflect that with Kant *ratio*, reason, does not refer to the isolated theoretical, intellectual human capacity but to that human capacity which is, decisively even, determined by practice. It is precisely Kant's 'rationalism' which remains untouched by the arguments it is customary to raise against 'intellectualism'. Taking Herder or Rousseau as one's guide it is possible to attack Kant's rationalism for its narrowness, as the Romantics who followed them did in fact attack it. But it is precisely as intellectualism that it is impossible to condemn it. Kant is only carrying out an analysis of the problematical notion of 'religion within the limits of reason alone' when he explains his 'purely rationalistic' standpoint by saying that as far as the latter is concerned the reality of a divine revelation is indeed 'admitted', left undecided, that is, as a possible answer to a question which is deliberately not put but which is merely alluded to, but that it must also be affirmed that it is not necessary to religion (within the limits . . .) that such a revelation should be known and assumed to be real.[2] Religion (within . . .) is 'knowledge of all our *duties* as a *divine* commandment'[3] or, conversely, it is 'that faith which sees man's *morality* as the essential part of all worship of the *Divine*'.[4] Religion, the religion of reason as we shall now always call it, using Kant's own abbreviation, is distinguished from morals as the primary use of reason not in its content but merely in its form, inasmuch as it represents morals in a certain connexion, inasmuch, namely, as it gives to the idea of God which is evolved from morality itself an influence upon the human will for the fulfilment of every human duty.[5] 'When morality knows in the holiness of its law an object worthy of the greatest esteem, it (morality) represents the cause of that law's fulfilment on the level of religion at its highest as an object of adoration and it appears in its majesty.'[6] This then, the

---

[1] *Rel.*, 231f.   [2] Loc. cit.   [3] *Crit. of Judg.*, 477; *Rel.*, 229.   [4] *Disp. of the Facs.*, 93.
[5] Ibid., 77.   [6] Foreword to the 1st ed. of the *Rel.*, Xf.

fact that morality in religion appears 'in its majesty', is the formal distinction, i.e. the sole possible distinction, between religion and morals as such. 'Morality inevitably leads to religion, and in so doing extends itself into the idea of a moral legislator possessed of power and existing outside man.'[1]

Revelation is not in itself necessary to this extension of morality, to this emergence upon the higher plane. The movement from morality to religion consists in fact in the moral mode of thought of reason itself, namely 'in the belief that those things are true which are inaccessible to theoretical knowledge, in the belief that the ideas, and especially and most decisively the idea of God, are true, the belief which comes about implicitly, which is pre-supposed, in every act performed in accordance with a genuine will for good. And just as it is not an object that can be proved theoretically which we accord this supposition of truth, we are not bound either by any external authority to that supposition, but accomplish it spontaneously, in accordance with the laws of freedom.'[2] Kant expressly declared that while indeed it had a dubious sound it was 'by no means reprehensible to say that every man makes a God for himself, and indeed, according to moral concepts, . . . must make a God for himself, in order to worship in him the One who made him'. He has to be in a position to measure the God who is, perhaps, proclaimed to him or who, perhaps, even reveals himself to him, against an ideal conception of God which he has set up for himself, in order (it is surely only thus that it is possible!) to recognize the former as God.[3] He must therefore have already perceived God directly and in himself before any act of revelation has taken place. Kant finds himself in agreement with Augustine's teaching that the knowledge of God is a recollection of a notion of God which has already dwelt within our reason beforehand, because it has always been within us from the very beginning. And that is why he is not afraid to speak expressly—a thing impossible even on the basis of the teaching of Augustine—of the 'God within ourselves', who must be the authentic interpreter of all revelation, 'because we do not understand anyone but the one who speaks with us through . . . our own reason'.[4]

We shall certainly not find any criterion in the sphere of our experience by means of which a revelation which is thus encountered, as experience, might be distinguished from other experiences, and which might be perceived as revelation as distinct from these. 'For if God really spoke to man, he would never be able to know that it was in

[1] Loc. cit., IX.   [2] Crit. of Judg., 462.
[3] Rel., 257.   [4] Disp. of the Facs., 91.

fact God who was speaking to him. It is an utterly impossible demand that man should grasp the Infinite One by means of his senses, distinguish him from sensory beings, and perceive him thereby.'[1] But neither is it permissible to characterize such experience, difficult and impossible as it seems to us to exalt it to the level of empirical knowledge on account of its incomprehensibility, as divine revelation, since in order to do this we should already have to have some prior knowledge of what revelation is, and of what God is. 'It might at most be allowed, that man had had some inner experience of a change which he was at a loss to account for other than by a miracle, an experience, therefore, of something supernatural. But an experience concerning which he cannot even be certain whether it was in fact an experience, because (being supernatural) it cannot be reduced to any rule partaking of the nature of our understanding, and thus substantiated, is an interpretation of certain sensations we do not know what to make of, and concerning which we do not know whether, as something belonging to knowledge, they have a real object, or whether they are mere fantasy. The wish to feel the direct influence of the Deity as such is a self-contradictory piece of presumption, since the idea of the Deity has its seat in reason alone.'[2]

If then there is no empirical criterion, and therefore no empirical knowledge either, of true revelation of the true God, this criterion can only ever be perceived by its 'correspondence with that which reason declares to be proper for God',[3] and it should now be clear where in fact we must look—judging always from the standpoint of the religion of reason—for the true, original revelation, if we might speak of such a thing. The true miracle of revelation, or, at least, what is the highest degree to be wondered at in the founding of the religion of reason is— reason itself in its own eyes, as moral reason, namely—'There is in fact something within us which we can never cease from wondering at, once we have looked well upon it, and this is the thing which at the same time exalts mankind ideally to a dignity which one would not expect in man as comprising objects of experience', 'the superiority', namely, 'of the super-sensory man in us over the sensory', the moral disposition in us which is inseparable from humanity.[4] 'The incomprehensibility of this disposition which proclaims our divine origin must affect the mind with the force of an inspiration.'[5] It is the object of our highest wonder, 'which can only ever increase, the longer one gazes upon this true (and not invented) ideal; so that those men can well be

---

[1] *Disp. of the Facs.*, 109f. [2] Ibid., 102f. [3] Ibid., 89.
[4] Ibid., 103f.; cf. *Rel.*, 57. [5] *Rel.*, 58f.

pardoned who, misled by its incomprehensibility, consider this super-
sensory quality in man, because it is practical, to be supernatural,
something, that is, which does not lie in our power at all and belong to
us as our own, but which is rather to be ascribed to the influence of
another and higher spirit; in which belief they are, however, very much
at fault'.[1]

We see, then, upon the one hand the inspiration, whose object
resides within ourselves, in so far as the idea of humanity and therefore
this moral disposition reside within us too; and, upon the other, the
'influence of another, higher spirit'. It is between these two, between
the notions of a 'disposition' proclaiming a divine origin on the one
hand, and 'revelation' on the other, between the 'supersensory' and the
'supernatural', that the exact border between the things which can be
supposed and the things which may not be supposed, runs, in matters
concerning the religion of reason. Anyone who speaks of revelation is
bursting the religion of reason asunder, for he is bursting asunder
'mere' reason, he is speaking of something which cannot be an object
of empirical knowledge. The critical philosophy of religion cannot
therefore speak of revelation. This, then, is Kant's 'pure rationalism'
in this matter.

From the point of view of religion which has its foundation in reason
itself, i.e. the religion which refers to this disposition to be discovered
in ourselves, the following may be said concerning positive, allegedly
revealed, statutory religion, in so far as it, also at any rate, presents
itself as a phenomenon of reason, and is to be judged as such: it rests, as
distinct from the religion of reason, upon 'a teaching which has been
passed on to us'.[2] It is 'based upon facts'.[3] It is a 'historical faith'.[4]
It has need, in so far as it has its basis in books, of the control of historical science.[5] In consequence 'its validity is always only of a particular kind'—it is valid, that is to say, only for those who have been
reached by the history upon which it rests. Its knowledge is not necessary and uniform, but accidental and diverse, it is not *per se* the one,
pure religious faith which should distinguish the one true Church.[6]
Such a historical faith is, however, as such not a living, not a salutary
faith, and is therefore not necessary either. It is 'dead in itself'.[7] The
idea that 'it is our duty and essential to salvation, is superstition'.[8]
Those who represent it are in error in attempting to take 'its statutes
(even if they were divine revelations) to be essential parts of religion,

---

[1] *Disp. of the Facs.*, 104.   [2] Ibid., 91.   [3] *Rel.*, 145.   [4] Ibid., 161.
[5] Ibid., 194.   [6] Ibid., 167; cf. 154; *Disp. of the Facs.*, 91.
[7] *Rel.*, 161; cf. *Disp. of the Facs.*, 113.   [8] *Disp. of the Facs.*, 112.

thereby foisting rationalism upon empiricism in matters of faith [Kant means foisting the necessary quality of reason itself upon the empirically determined nature of the reason which positively believes], and thus representing that which is merely accidental as something necessary in itself'.[1] For 'in itself, looked upon as a confession, it contains nothing which might have moral value for us'.[2] Historical knowledge, which bears no inner relationship valid for all to the betterment of mankind, 'has its place among the things (*adiaphora*) which may or may not be believed, which each one may treat in the manner he finds most edifying to himself'.[3]

Kant does not, however, wish to say outright that revelation is therefore completely unnecessary and superfluous.[4] He does, admittedly, say quite openly that it is a consequence of a special weakness in human nature, that the religion of reason 'can never be relied upon to the extent it certainly deserves, namely to the extent of the foundation of a Church upon it alone'.[5] But since this is once and for all so, the faith of a Church must be determined, in contrast to this religion *a priori*, as religion *a posteriori* or as religion *in concreto*, as a 'working-out' of the former's demands,[6] as a 'means to its furtherance',[7] as its 'vehicle' as Kant was especially fond of saying.[8] Dogma might, for instance, be honoured as the 'shell' which has served to set the religion of reason publicly in motion.[9] Taking the ideal case it might so be that the revealed and the natural religion were one and the same, in the case, namely, 'when the positive religion is so constituted, that men might and should have been able to discover it for themselves by the sole use of their reason, albeit they would not have discovered it so early or in such large numbers as is expected of them, so that at a certain time and in a certain place a revelation of the same might be wise and very advantageous to the human race; a revelation made, however, in such wise that all men thenceforth, once the religion thus introduced is there, and has been made publicly known, can convince themselves of its truth by their own inner resources and by their own reason. In this case the religion is objectively a natural one, although subjectively it is a revealed religion, for which reason also it is the former name which truly befits it.'[10] Thus pure rationalism prevails in this case too. This supposition that the revealed and the natural

---

[1] *Disp. of the Facs.*, 93.   [2] *Rel.*, 161.   [3] Ibid., 47; *Disp. of the Facs.*, 82.
[4] *Disp. of the Facs.*, 50.   [5] *Rel.*, 145.   [6] First draft of the Foreword to the *Rel.*
[7] *Rel.*, 148, 250.
[8] Ibid., 152, 153; *Disp. of the Facs.*, 78, 91, 95—'vehicle' means a 'conducting substance', and is a technical term which was used in pharmaceutics at Kant's time.
[9] *Rel.*, 118.   [10] Ibid., 233.

religion might be one and the same, is, in Kant's opinion, true of Christianity. And thus the Christian preaching has also at any rate the task of presenting the biblical teaching of the faith in the form in which we can develop it from within ourselves by means of reason.[1]

What there is to be said, from the point of view of Kant's conception of the problem of a 'religion of reason', concerning the significance of the Bible can now to a certain extent already be foreseen. There is above all this to be said that the Bible too, like religion itself, 'is made up of two unequal parts; the "canon", which contains the pure religious faith, and the "organon" or "vehicle", containing the church faith which allegedly rests upon revelation'.[2] The thing which affirms its truth (judged always from the standpoint of the religion of reason) is not the especial 'learnedness in divinity' of those who wrote it, but the popular effect of its popular content, and it is precisely thereby that it betrays itself as an affirmation 'from the pure spring of the universal religion of reason, which dwells with every common man'.[3] This acknowledged effect which it has of 'giving rise to religion in human hearts' surely has its quite simple explanation as the 'effect of nature and result of progressive moral civilization in the general course of Providence'. And it is precisely because this effect is ultimately the effect of the religion of reason itself that it is independent of all historical and critical investigation of the Bible. May the latter even be 'greatly or little lacking in items of so-called historical proof', the divine nature of its moral content yet justifies the pronouncement, 'that the Bible just as if it were a divine revelation deserves to be preserved, used in moral questions and employed as a manual for religion'.[4]

Since this is the position in respect of the authority of the Bible, its exegesis must consist in a thorough 'interpretation' of the Bible 'into a meaning which concords with the general practical rule of a religion of reason. For the theoretical element in the church faith cannot hold any interest for us from a moral point of view, if its effects do not tend to the fulfilment of every human duty as a divine commandment'. Even if this exegesis then 'often seems forced, and often really is so too', it is nevertheless resolutely to be preferred to a literal but morally insignificant one.[5] The learned man of Scripture is subordinate to the interpreter of Scripture.[6] And the interpreter of the Scripture, should the occasion arise, is quite entitled to 'convey' the true teaching of the religion of reason into the Bible, if by any chance he does not find it

<hr />

[1] *Disp. of the Facs.*, 105.   [2] Ibid., 78.   [3] Ibid., 110.
[4] Ibid., 111.   [5] *Rel.*, 158.   [6] Ibid., 162.

there.[1] 'Passages in the Scripture containing teachings which, while they are theoretical and proclaimed sacred, yet transcend every concept of reason (even the moral one), *may* be interpreted to practical reason's advantage, but those containing tenets which contradict practical reason *must* be thus interpreted.'[2] The words 'He that believeth and is baptized shall be saved' (Mark 16.16), for example, must not be interpreted literally and historically.[3] 'It is therefore only the doctrinal exegesis, which does not seek (empirically) to know what sort of meaning the holy author might have attached to his words, but to know with what sort of teaching reason (*a priori*) can support the Bible, in regard to morals, with a scriptural saying giving occasion for its text, which is the sole evangelical-biblical method of instruction for the people.' And it is precisely this interpretation, Kant thinks, which is in fact the authentic one, i.e. 'it is thus that God would have his will as revealed in the Bible understood'. 'The God who speaks to us through our own reason (reason practical in what concerns morals) is an infallible and universally comprehensible interpreter of this his word.'[4] 'The God who is within us is the interpreter.'[5] Such therefore is the doctrine of the Scriptures and such is the interpretative method (Hermeneutics) of pure rationalism.

What form will the Christology of this teaching take? It is typical of Kant (and indeed typical of him in a way which is also entirely to his credit) that the name Jesus or Christ never, so far as I can see, flowed from his pen in any of his writings, and that he even found a way of avoiding it in the numerous quotations from the Bible which he used in the 'Religion within'. He allows him to appear only as the 'teacher of the Gospel', as the 'founder of the Church', as Son or Ambassador of God, and of course as the preacher too who is legitimized by the content (in accordance with reason) of his preaching, and who is therefore on principle subordinate to it. He grants him that, seen historically, he brought about 'a complete revolution' among the race of men, in respect of religion, at least.[6] But Kant's interest did not stop here. He was also interested in the Christological dogma and tried to derive a meaning, his own meaning, of course, from it. There is even a Kantian doctrine of the Trinity, held together by the idea of love, in so far as one 'can' (!) worship in God: firstly, the loving one, who loves with the love inspired by his being well-pleased morally with mankind (in so far as man lives up to his holy law), as the Father; secondly, representation in the idea of humanity which is begotten

[1] *Disp. of the Facs.*, 116.   [2] Ibid., 80.   [3] Ibid., 84.
[4] Ibid., 114.   [5] Ibid., 91.   [6] *Rel.*, 79.

and loved by him himself, as the Son; thirdly, his wisdom, in which he bestows his favour upon those who fulfil this condition, as the Holy Ghost.[1]

The specifically Christological doctrine of Kant takes a form in which the incarnate Son of God is interpreted as 'the idea set before us for our emulation' of moral perfection, an idea which as such cannot be any created thing, but only God's only begotten son.[2] We cannot conceive of the 'ideal of the humanity in whom God is well-pleased' other than as it is contained 'in the idea of a man who is prepared not only himself, to exercise every human duty . . . but also, although . . . tempted, to take upon himself every suffering, even a shameful death for the best good of the world and for the sake, even, of his enemies'.[3] On principle, however, this ideal does not require any historical realization, either, in order to be an example, but it, too, as such resides already in our reason, and even if its historical realization must on principle be possible, its true and original source is still to be found in reason itself. 'Even the Saint of the Gospel must first be compared with our ideal of moral perfection, before he can be perceived as such; he too says of himself: Wherefore do ye call me (whom you see) good? No one is good (is the archetype of goodness) but the one God (whom you do not see). But whence do we derive the notion that God represents the highest good? Solely from the idea, which reason *a priori* traces of moral perfection and inseparably links with the notion of a free will'.[4] This 'archetype residing in our reason' which we use to 'attribute' to the phenomenon Jesus, is 'the true object of the faith which saves',[5] so that we have no reason to suppose in Jesus anything but the example of a life well pleasing to God, i.e., however, 'a man of natural origin'. An exaltation over our frailty, such as would be postulated by a different kind of pronouncement concerning him, would even actually impede the practical application of the idea which he preached.[6]

Thus if, according to Kant, something corresponding to what is called the 'Word' in the prologue to St John's Gospel exists, there is certainly, according to him, no suggestion that this Word might by any chance have become flesh. To the religion of reason the Son of God is not a man, but 'the abstraction of humanity'.[7] Thus the belief in him should not rest upon miracles either, the demand for which is rather to be characterized as 'moral disbelief',[8] which the man guided by reason does not consider as a possible factor in the present at all,

[1] *Rel.*, 220   [2] Ibid., 73.   [3] Ibid., 75.   [4] *Basis for a Metaph. of Morals*, 29.
[5] *Rel.*, 175.   [6] Ibid., 79.   [7] *Disp. of the Facs.*, 81.   [8] *Rel.*, 77, 116.

but only at best as something belonging to the distant past[1] and which at all events cannot have any other significance but that of 'effects of nature', and not that, therefore, of objects of belief.[2] The *work* of the Son of God, however, in so far as it exceeds his teaching—his vicarious suffering above all—is, according to the one passage in Kant, to be interpreted as meaning that from a moral point of view *intelligible* man is in God's eyes different from empirical man; that as the latter's vicar he carries empirical man's guilt incurred by sin, meets the demands of the highest justice through suffering and death and is therefore his Saviour, so that empirical man, in so far as he is yet identical with intelligible man, can hope to appear before his Judge as one vindicated by him.[3] According to the other, less profound, passage the vicarious suffering is interpreted as meaning that Jesus by his death 'represented the good principle, mankind, namely, in its moral perfection, as an example to be imitated by everyone' and thus made visible 'the freedom of the children of heaven and the slavery of a mere son of earth in the most striking contrast'.[4] The belief in Christ, the Christian belief, whereby a person becomes well pleasing to God, must therefore, according to Kant, consist in placing in oneself the well-founded confidence that one will, 'while subject to similar temptations and sufferings . . . unwaveringly cling to the archetype of humanity and remain true to his example in faithful imitation'.[5]

It has to do with the primacy Kant bestows upon practical reason that, as compared for instance with Lessing, he takes a quite strikingly systematic interest in the notion of the Church. It is here for the first time that something becomes visible of the borders of the conception of the problem peculiar to him. The reign of the good principle of humanity demands and makes necessary—as he puts in at this point—the setting-up and spreading of a 'society in accordance with the laws of virtue and for the purpose of the same'.[6] This demand, however, presupposes a higher moral being beyond the insufficiency of the individuals, upon which this demand is made[7] a supreme law-giver and universal searcher of hearts, a moral world-ruler.[8] It would be 'against all reason to say that the kingdom of God should be instituted by men. . . . God himself must be the originator of his kingdom'.[9] 'The creation of a moral people of God is therefore a work the execution of which cannot be expected of men, but only of God himself.' Kant hastens to add that this still does not permit man 'to be inactive in the expectation of this work and to allow Providence to reign'. 'He must

---

[1] *Rel.*, 118.   [2] Ibid., 124.   [3] Ibid., 98f.   [4] Ibid., 112f.   [5] Ibid., 76.
[6] Ibid., 129.   [7] Ibid., 136.   [8] Ibid., 138f.   [9] Ibid., 227.

rather proceed as if everything depended on him, and it is only upon this condition that he dare hope that a higher wisdom will allow his well-meaning efforts to blossom into fulfilment'.[1] As God, as the founder, is the creator of the constitution of this kingdom, thus men as its members and free citizens are at all events the creators of its organization.[2]

Ideally this kingdom coincides with the Church;[3] empirically, as the visible Church, 'it is diminished at the hands of men into an institution, which, . . . so far as the means for the setting-up of such an entity are concerned, is very restricted, according to the limits imposed upon a sentient human nature'.[4] But from its identity with the invisible Church, there yet result certain demands upon the visible Church, the entire meaning of which is to make the invisible Church as visible as possible in it. These are unmistakably the well-known predicates of the old Christian conception of the Church: *ecclesia una sancta catholica et apostolica;* which Kant has in mind when he says: (1) that only those elements in the Church should be considered essential, which must necessarily lead to a universal union into one single Church;[5] (2) that only morality, but not superstition and enthusiasm, might be the principle of ecclesiastical union;[6] (3) that this Church must distinguish itself from a political entity by its tendency to achieve unanimity in all men, by its tendency to be an ethical entity in which only the pure religious faith, the *catholicismus rationalis,* and not the *catholicismus hierarchicus,* whose aim is to establish one particular church faith as the universal one, may hold the reins of government;[7] and (4) that its constitution must be inalterable, and only its administration alterable, the accidental order which adapts itself in accordance with the demands of time and place.[8] This inalterable constitution of the Church is the work of God and of God alone. But Kant saw clearly enough and he thought practically enough, that 'if there is simply no means of arranging things otherwise' regarding the fact that the pure religious faith has need of a statutory church faith as its vehicle, that there must be, as against this divine constitution, a statute on the human side, which, even if it is not to be considered as divinely statutory, is yet an equivalent raised publicly to the status of a basic law; a humanly inalterable, humanly qualified statute, as it were: the Scripture, beside which, however, no tradition and no symbols must then be set up as equal to it in value.[9]

---

[1] *Rel.*, 141.   [2] Ibid., 227.   [3] Ibid., 142.   [4] Ibid., 141.
[5] Ibid., 143; *Disp. of the Facs.*, 91, 96.   [6] *Rel.*, 143.
[7] Ibid., 143; *Disp. of the Facs.*, 93.   [8] *Rel.*, 143f.   [9] Ibid., 143f., 150, 152.

I say that something of the borders of Kant's conception of the problem become visible here. This it is possible to say, but more cannot be said. Kant, in wishing to show that the conception of the Church is rationally necessary, and in passing swiftly (a thing we are already accustomed to in him) from the proposition that God alone can be the founder of the Church to the other, that man must therefore proceed in the Church as if everything depended upon him alone—suddenly speaks of the Church in its visible form in quite different tones and with a quite different emphasis, surely, from that with which we heard him speak of the parallel notions of positive religion, the Bible and the historical Christ. It is here precisely not the divine constitution alone which is rationally necessary, but, on principle, the human organization of the kingdom of God also, even if Kant does establish here, too, the fact that this kingdom dwindles in the process into an institution and becomes subject to the limitations of sentient human nature. For the first time unequivocally in this philosophy of religion he says that the concretion, the thing which he otherwise treats above all with suspicion or at least as a mere *adiaphoron*, is on principle necessary, and that it is worth the trouble to devote serious thought to it in itself.

The fact that Kant did in fact do this, to a certain extent at least, is evidenced by the qualified significance he yet attributed in particular to the Bible within this concretion. And what are we to think when we hear him declare in respect to the constitution, not of the invisible *civitas Dei*, but of the concrete, visible Church, that it must not, according to its principles, be similar to a political constitution, must not, therefore, be either monarchical (papal) or aristocratic (episcopal), or democratic (after the fashion of the 'sectarian *Illuminati*'), but 'might best be compared with that of a household (family) under a common, albeit invisible moral Father, inasmuch as his holy Son, who knows his will, and at the same time stands in blood-relationship to all its members, represents him by making his father's will more clearly known to them, who therefore honour the Father in him, and thus enter into a voluntary, universal and perpetual union of the heart one with another'.[1] Is this still the Church of the religion of mere reason? If it is, it is certainly at the same time a picture of the Christian conception of the Church showing no lack of careful study. And if the philosopher should answer that it is precisely in this that the occasional happy coincidence of the Christian with the reasonable element comes to light, we could then ask in return whether it was in fact the reasonable element which served as the archetype in this construction, the Christian element

[1] *Rel.*, 144.

serving only as an example or vehicle, or whether perhaps things turned out differently from what Kant planned and intended, whether he might have used the text of a religion other than that of his religion within. . . . And even if all these questions could be controverted, it might still be affirmed that it was precisely at this point, where the gaze of the philosopher turned to the phenomenon of the Church, that this coincidence of the Christian and the reasonable must have met him in a quite particularly pregnant fashion.

The observation that the conception of the problem contained in Kant's philosophy of religion in fact has its frontiers, and the supposition this implies, that he could or would not say more, with this conception of the problem, in his philosophy of religion than it was, quite simply, possible for him to say, once he had chosen it as the instrument for his work—this observation and supposition are confirmed when we turn finally to the decisive part of his teaching of the religion of reason: to his reflections on the complex of questions which directly concern the *reality* of religion in the individual man, and which therefore directly concern the reality of practical reason in the human will for good, the will, that is, which is in accordance with the law, and which thus contains the knowledge of God and the hope in him. Kant did not try to evade this question. He makes its discussion the starting-point for his philosophy of religion, even, and thus it comes about that the reader of the 'Religion within . . .'—his first contemporary readers found it so, too—finds himself at once confronted in the very first pages by the most difficult questions of interpretation. One certainly does not expect, having a knowledge of Kant's ethics from his earlier writings, and looking at the rest of the contents of his teaching of religion after this beginning, to be met here immediately on the doorstep with a detailed doctrine of the problem of evil, and above all with that kind of doctrine. It is in fact the last thing one would expect.

'The lament that the world is wicked is as old as history', Kant begins. He develops the biblical form of this 'lament', without, surprisingly, attempting to criticize or dissociate himself from it in any way, and then goes on to oppose it to the 'heroic' belief—'held, perhaps, only by philosophers and, in our time, especially by educationalists', 'that the world is constantly (albeit almost imperceptibly) advancing from worse to better', and that there is a corresponding disposition in human nature, and therefore a kind of *a priori* necessary superiority of good in us. Kant, however, objects that this belief is certainly not drawn from experience. The history of every age speaks strongly against it and it is 'presumably merely a benevolent pre-supposition of the moralists, from Seneca to Rousseau, made in an effort to encourage the cultivation of the germ of good which perhaps resides within us'.[1] To anyone who knows Kant this is indeed a legitimate cause for surprise. We saw that he held the view that his time was the best there had ever been, and saw his joyful appreciation of the historical advance of the human life of the spirit. Even in the *Dispute of the Faculties* we find in that request still the remark that it is 'no merely well-meaning and for practical purposes expedient proposition, but one which is tenable also, having regard to the strictest theory, in face of all unbelievers, that the human race has always been advancing to a better state and will continue to do so . . . a fact which reveals a prospect into an unforeseeable time; always provided that the first revolutionary epoch of nature, which buried only the animals and plants, is not followed by a second which will also include the human race, so that other creatures may walk upon this stage'.[2] But in this passage too Kant means something quite different from the 'heroic' or even 'well-meaning' conviction held by all moralists from Seneca to Rousseau; he is in fact simply thinking of the actual decrease of merely outward violence, the increase of lawfulness, of beneficence, etc., of the trend in politics, even, towards a 'society of world-citizens', of the victory of democratic principle, and the gradual elimination of war (against which he always expressed himself in the strongest terms);[3] as— optimistically enough, we are now tempted to say—he imagined all these things to be coming.

He is, however, explicitly *not* thinking of a progress 'consisting in an extension of man's moral basis, . . . for which a kind of re-creation (supernatural influence) would be required'.[4] He expects this progress to be achieved 'not by what happens from below to above, but by what happens from above to below'. To bring this progress about by the education of youth, for instance, namely to an intellectual and moral civilization, 'strengthened by the teaching of religion', is a plan which Kant considers 'has very little hope of meeting with the desired success'.[5] Instead he sees this progress—we have met, by the way, with a similar train of ideas in Rousseau—quite dispassionately, as being founded primarily in part upon the love of honour, and in part upon the enlightened self-interest of men and peoples. Such is the foreground. The background, however, has as its basis not an advance in reason, but 'a wisdom descending from above (which, when it is invisible to us, is called Providence)'.[6] This flat denial of an actual moral progress in

---

[1] *Rel.*, 3f. [2] *Disp. of the Facs.*, 135f. [3] *Rel.*, 30; *Disp. of the Facs.*, 132, 141
[4] *Disp. of the Facs.*, 139. [5] Ibid., 140. [6] Ibid., 141.

history, of a progress 'within the limits of reason alone', a denial made in face of the importance which Kant yet certainly attached to this very idea of progress; this and his act of founding what he recognizes as progress upon eudemonism on the one hand and providence on the other—both of them motives which clearly have no indigenous claim to belong to the teaching of the religion of reason as such—these things present us with the first riddle we have to face here.

It is indeed not at all Kant's wish in this beginning to the 'Religion within . . .' to place himself on the side of the moral pessimists whose views he had first of all presented. His intention is stated rather in the title to the first part of the work, which runs: 'Concerning the inherence of the evil *principle* together with the good.' It is, however, precisely this inherence—let us reflect: the inherence of an evil principle *together with* the good!—which evidently prevents him from affirming the existence of moral progress in its true sense (because he sees, in the very moral foundation itself, whose 'extension' would be in question if such a progress were to come about, an evil principle firmly rooted together with the good)—it is precisely this inherence, which Kant believes he must assert here, which presents us with a second and greater riddle. 'The inherence of the evil principle together with the good' surely means—and it is thus that Kant did in fact mean it—that in the same incomprehensible freedom of reason in which the good, lawful will can be made actual, its great opposite, a will for evil, can be made manifest too.

This was, perhaps, implied in the philosophy of practical reason as Kant had represented it prior to 1793, but not, at all events, expressly stated. How startling were the effects of his statement of it now upon his contemporaries can be seen by Goethe's outburst in a letter to Herder (7th June 1793, from the camp near Mainz) in which he said that Kant, 'had criminally smeared his philosopher's cloak with the shameful stain of radical evil, after it had taken him a long human life to cleanse it from many a dirty prejudice, so that Christians too might yet be enticed to kiss its hem'. It is not the fact *that* the philosopher takes evil into account at all, or the fact that he does this earnestly and emphatically, which was and is astonishing here—what moral philosopher could do otherwise?—but certainly the *manner* in which he takes it into account, i.e. that he speaks of an evil *principle* and therefore of a source of evil within reason, and of a *radical* form of evil in this sense. It might once again well be asked whether Kant has here not, willy-nilly, incurred the guilt of falling in with the scandal and folly of the Christian-dogmatic teaching. Surely, he could have

remained on the broad highway of the usual philosophical interpretation of the notion of evil, which was also largely usual for theology too,
and therefore he could have allowed evil to appear as the opposite of
good just as sensuality appears as the opposite of reason, and folly as
the opposite of wisdom, proceeding then to explain evil in the way of the
Augustinian teaching, from which in other respects, he is not quite
removed, as a *privatio boni*. It may seriously be asked whether it might
not have been more befitting to Kant's whole starting-point, and, at
all events, to the conception of the problem underlying his philosophy
of religion if he had in fact so treated it. Instead of this he now embarks
upon a polemic against the Stoics, of all people, because they had
sought to find the foe in the natural *inclinations*, which after all, considered in themselves and for themselves, were yet good, and by no
means were to be stamped out. They had summoned up wisdom against
folly, instead of calling it to aid against the *malice* of the human heart,
against the much more dangerous, because, as it were, invisible foe,
concealing itself behind reason.[1] In opposition to the Stoics Kant
declares himself in due form for the words of St Paul in Ephesians 6.12:
'For we wrestle not against flesh and blood (the natural inclination),
but against principalities and powers—against spiritual wickedness.'[2]
The essence of wickedness, Kant tells us in interpreting the biblical
story of the Fall, consists firstly in doubting the strictness of the commandment itself, then in giving it the new meaning of a commandment
to self-love, and finally in the subsequent over-emphasis of the sensual
impulses in the maxims, i.e. the fundamental orientation to which
man's conduct, governed by this undue emphasis, is for ever subject.[3]
Kant describes wickedness elsewhere as being primarily the weakness
of the human heart, the frailty of human nature in respect to the
decision to perform the act which is in accordance with the law—he
quotes here Romans 7.18: 'For to will is present with me; but how to
perform that which is good I find not'; then as the self-interest in
which man is able to link moral and amoral motives, and thus deceive
himself, and finally as the malevolence in which he is able to acquiesce
to the amoral motives made tangible in this manner.[4] 'Man is wicked,
i.e. he is aware of the moral law and has yet incorporated the (occasional) deviation from it in his maxims.'[5]

On the basis of this primary frailty or self-interest or malevolence,
which Kant himself describes as the *peccatum originarium* and concerning
which he declares himself in agreement with another saying of St Paul,
Romans 5.12: 'In Adam we have all sinned'[6]—on the basis of this

---

[1] *Rel.*, 67f.   [2] Ibid., 72.   [3] Ibid., 44f.   [4] Ibid., 21f.   [5] Ibid., 26f.   [6] Ibid., 45.

pre-supposition all man's actions (in so far as the freedom to do good
has not snatched some place for itself) are to be described as wicked.
For 'the first incurring of guilt remains, even if the second (the wicked
deed) be very often avoided'.[1] Yet another quotation from St Paul
makes its appearance here—Romans 14.23: 'For whatsoever is not of
faith (of the moral law as the sole motive-force) is sin.' Man can and
must then, even if he only does good deeds—the accidental coincidence
with the law helps him then not at all—nevertheless be wicked.[2] It is a
question of a 'bent for wickedness',[3] of a guilt which is inborn because
it can be shown to have been in man just as early as the use of freedom
in any form was in him,[4] of an 'attitude which is part of his nature'
that was not merely acquired with the passage of time,[5] of 'an inscrutable reason for the acceptance of maxims which are counter to the
law', which typifies man as such and the human species.[6] That the
manifestation, the actualization of this evil principle concerns human
freedom just as much as does obedience to the law, that we are account-
able and responsible for it, as Kant emphatically points out,[7] and
that it must be thought of as something which it is possible to overcome, all this only serves to confirm the original and inscrutable
quality of this evil principle, a quality comparable to and vying with
that of the freedom to do good. It is called '*radical* evil', however,
because it is a corruption at the very source, a corruption of the chief
subjective basis for all maxims. It cannot actually be rooted out by
any human endeavour, since this could only be achieved by means of
good maxims, by means of a betterment at source—precisely by means
of the good maxims which are threatened and annulled by this
principle![8]

To say that this doctrine of radical evil is in the nature of a 'foreign
body' in the Kantian teaching is a possibility so obvious in interpreting
his work, and one which has been presented so often, that simply for
this reason one is unwilling to concur in it. It would perhaps not be a
foreign body at all if it were part of a total survey given from the
Kantian point of view, a survey which we must say Kant neglected
to give, both to his own time and to us, and which, considering his
position, he was bound to refrain from giving; a total survey embracing
not only the truly wide horizon of the field he in fact chose as presenting
his problem, but also the horizon of the neighbouring fields upon its
borders, and not merely regarding these as marking its limits. It cannot,
however, well be denied—and to this extent we cannot dissociate

[1] *Rel.*, 25.   [2] Ibid., 24.   [3] Ibid., 27.   [4] Ibid., 36f.
[5] Ibid., 14.   [6] Ibid., 7.   [7] Ibid., 46f., 42.   [8] Ibid., 35.

ourselves from the general judgment just mentioned—that the closed and rounded quality of the Kantian system as it stands, i.e. the rounded quality of the Kantian conception of reason and of the religion of reason as postulated in his philosophy of religion, is disturbed by the doctrine of radical evil. That this is so is shown in the developments which this teaching brought about in the further course of the Kantian philosophy of religion.

If it should be so that the notion of evil must in all seriousness be accepted as a concept of reason, which, even if it greatly conflicts with the general plan, must yet be considered as necessary; if there is really an *evil* of reason, an *a priori* evil, an evil principle, opposing the *law* of reason; and if, as the title of the second part of Kant's book says, a 'Conflict between the good and the evil principle for the mastery of mankind' must take place, then we are at liberty to ask whether Kant's doctrine of this conflict, of religious reality being the reality of this conflict, and his doctrine of man's *redemption*, might not, at least, and perhaps should, have been cast in a mould entirely different from the one which they did in fact receive. Is it possible with impunity to be so far in agreement with St Paul as Kant after all was in his doctrine of sin? Indeed the fact that he did go so far in this respect, as we have just discovered, also affects his doctrine of salvation. In this conceptions like those of vicarious atonement, justification, forgiveness, re-birth and even predestination, make their appearance here, like strange visitors from another world, upon the horizon of a philosophy of religion, without there being any attempt to disguise the mystery that is implied in them. They are greeted with a mixture of understanding and surprise, of request and a respectful shaking of heads, and they are acknowledged somehow as conceptions which are at any rate possible, as indicative of open questions, at the least.

One is apt to wonder, arriving at this point by way of Kant's doctrine of radical evil, why Kant does not seize upon this subject even more forcefully. But then again we should not really feel any surprise at all —in view of the rest of the general purport of this doctrine of religion and of the philosophical frame within which it is set—that this does not happen, and that these concepts, for all the reverence with which they are treated, are in effect eliminated in so far as Kant finds that their mystery cannot subsequently be resolved in terms of practical reason, or, wherever Kant thinks this possible, they are simply given a new meaning as concepts of reason, in accordance with the method of interpretation (hermeneutics) already referred to. The end-effect of all this is doubtless to show that here, too, the problem-concept which was postulated is victorious at the last; only the difficulty of carrying it through to victory in this field too has been plainly revealed, and its limited nature has once again, and here most palpably, been made visible—the limitation imposed by problems in other fields which Kant avoided, but which *were* only avoided by him, and not refuted.

Let us once again go into detail. Kant felt himself able to repeat also in the later parts of his book the proposition that 'Man as we know him is corrupt and not by any means in himself a fit subject for this holy law'.[1] He goes on to state what may be inferred from this, too: 'How it is possible for a man who is by nature wicked to make himself good is something which passes all our comprehension; for how can a corrupt tree bear good fruit?'[2] Passes all our comprehension! It is with this statement that these conceptions of the biblical and church doctrine of salvation come within the sphere of Kant's observation, commanding, as it were, consideration of themselves. 'That someone, however, . . . should become . . . a morally good man (one well-pleasing to God) . . . is something which cannot be accomplished by gradual reform so long as the basis of man's maxims remains impure, but which must rather be brought about by a revolution in his mind; and a new man can come into being only by means of a kind of rebirth, like that achievable by a new creation (John 3.5; cf. Gen. 1.2) and by a change of heart.'[3] Kant knows that 'it is possible to conceive of guilt-laden humanity being granted absolution by divine justice only provided that humanity undergoes a complete change of heart,[4] and that the revolutionary change in man's way of thinking must not only correspond to the reform of his disposition which is to be demanded of man but must precede it on principle—that man would have 'to put on a new man'.[5] Kant also knows, however, that observation of his previous course of life can never provide man with the conviction that such a change has taken place, and that he could never have an immediate awareness of it either, since 'the depth of the human heart (the subjective first basis for his maxims) is unfathomable to man himself'.[6]

Kant goes on to say that we can only hope at least to arrive on the way which leads there (to righteousness in God's sight, that is) by the employment of our own powers: for only that can be morally good which can be attributed to us as performed by ourselves; we can, however, only *hope* for even such a 'being on the way' since, and in so far as, this way has already been 'pointed out' to us 'by a disposition

---

[1] *Rel.*, 216.   [2] Ibid., 49.   [3] Ibid., 54.
[4] Ibid., 102.   [5] Ibid., 55.   [6] Ibid., 61.

that is fundamentally improved'.[1] The quality our deeds have of being well-pleasing to God can 'with us in our earthly life'—but also perhaps in all future ages and in all possible worlds—only ever be something that is coming into being, and we cannot base any claim that we are right upon what we ourselves know of our deeds. From what we know of ourselves the prosecutor in us must rather always demand the sentence of damnation. 'It is therefore always only a sentence of judgment prompted by mercy, albeit one . . . completely in accordance with everlasting righteousness, if we are relieved of all responsibility for the sake of the goodness contained in our faith.'[2] It is solely in the *idea*, known only to God, of the improved disposition, that justice can be done to eternal righteousness. It is this ideal righteousness which is thus our righteousness, and not the righteousness of a disposition which we might actually find present within us! It will therefore 'always remain a righteousness which is not our own'.[3]

Does Kant after all perhaps know what justification is, in the sense of the Reformation? This question at least one cannot possibly escape, after carefully analysing the multifariously involved utterances of this, the work of his old age—and it is inescapable at this point in particular. It is, of course, impossible, in face of the Kantian re-interpretation, of the Christological dogma, to answer this question in the affirmative. But how can it be denied, when it is so plain that it was none the less precisely the Christological dogma by means of which he has here interpreted the text, that text, he alleges, which was the only one which interested him of practical reason? Kant, it is true, very strongly denies the validity of all 'expiations' which seek to replace this 'change of heart' as the true and decisive, but also at the same time non-intuitive human deed, be they of the atoning or of the sacramental kind; he rejects all invocations and promises of adoration, even that of the vicarious ideal of the Son of God, because this ideal must be taken up into our disposition in order to intercede for us in place of the failure to act. In Königsberg, for example, where he lived near the castle, which also served as a prison, Kant was angered by the loud and persistent hymn-singing of the prisoners, which was particularly irksome to him in the summer, when he liked to philosophize with his window open, and complained to the town-president about the 'stentorian devotions of those hypocrites in the gaol', the salvation of whose souls would certainly not be imperilled even if 'they listened to themselves behind shuttered windows and then even without shouting at

[1] *Rel.*, 61.   [2] Ibid., 101.   [3] Ibid., 83.

the tops of their voices'.[1] 'Everything that man imagines he can do to win favour in God's sight over and above living the good life is mere religious illusion and mock-service of God.'

But note how the continuation of this very sentence, for all its sharpness: 'I say: What *man* thinks he can do; for whether there is not something more, beyond everything *we* can do, something residing in the mystery of the highest wisdom, which only *God* can do, to make men well-pleasing in his sight, is not negatived thereby.'[2] For 'one cannot prove either that this is impossible, since freedom itself, although it contains no supernatural element as a concept, yet remains just as incomprehensible to us, in what concerns its possibility, as the supernatural, which one is tempted to embrace as a substitute for the self-active but defective determination of the same'.[3] In 1789 Kant wrote the following to Jung-Stilling: 'You also do very well to seek the final satisfaction for that mind of yours which is striving for a sure basis for hope and doctrine in the Gospel, that immortal guide of true wisdom, which is not only met by a reason which has brought its speculation to a completion, but whence reason also acquires a new light in respect to that which, even when it has marked out its entire field, still remains hidden from it, and from which it is still in need of instruction.'[4]

Kant, it is true, takes as it were a step backwards at this point with truly remarkable alarm, with alarm, one is tempted to say, which is worthy of imitation: in the conflict between his duty and his incapacity man finds himself drawn to the belief in a moral world-ruler's helping or shaping hand, 'and now the *abyss* opens before him of a secret, the secret of what part God plays in this respect: of whether anything at all is to be attributed to him, and if so, *what* in particular'.[5] 'This idea is one that knows no bounds, and it is moreover salutary that we should keep at a reverent distance from it as from a thing which is sacred.' What cause is there for alarm here? Kant, of course, feared above all, from an actual vindication of the 'idea' of God's autonomous action, the result that it might 'make us all incapable of any use of our reason, or encourage the indolent habit of expecting in passive ease from above that which we should seek in ourselves'.[6] But he also further saw and above all did so with great clearness, that that 'which God alone can do to make us into men well-pleasing in his sight', must be to *forgive*; it is forgiveness which must be the decisive justification of man who, as we know him, is corrupt. But it is precisely

[1] Vorländer, *Life of Immanuel Kant*, p. 138.   [2] *Rel.*, 261.   [3] Ibid., 297.
[4] *Corres.*, XI, 10,   [5] *Rel.*, 210,   [6] Ibid., 298.

of divine forgiveness that Kant says that 'an immediate divine revelation in the comforting utterance: "thy sins are forgiven thee", would be a super-sensory experience, because it is impossible'.[1] And he saw moreover with an equal clarity that the notion of a historical faith that justifies, i.e. one achieving this unfathomable improvement of mankind fundamentally, just as much as the notion of vicarious atonement as the object of this faith 'ultimately leads to the conception of an absolute divine decree: God "hath mercy on whom he will have mercy, and whom he will he hardeneth"', which, as Kant at one point says, 'represents, if taken literally, the *salto mortale* of reason', whereas elsewhere he says: 'It must at all events refer to a wisdom the rule for which is utterly and completely hidden from us.'[2]

It is at this point that Kant resolutely turns back. 'God has revealed nothing to us concerning these secrets, and cannot reveal anything either, simply because we should not understand it.' We certainly understand the individual words, but not what the words are saying. And even a supernatural prompting could not at all alter the fact that it 'cannot inhere in us at all, since the nature of our understanding is incapable of it'.[3] Grace, miracle, the mysteries of the call to faith, of atonement and of election, and the possibility of means of grace, are '*Parerga* of religion within the limits of reason alone' as the methodically very illuminating expression runs; 'they do not belong within it, but are yet adjacent to it. Reason, in the knowledge of its incapacity to satisfy its moral requirements, extends itself to extravagant ideas, which could supply this need, without, however, appropriating them as its own extended possession. Reason does not dispute the possibility or reality of the objects of these ideas; it is just that it cannot include them in its maxims for thought and action.'[4]

It should be clear from the foregoing that Kant, whenever and wherever he did not tend to characterize these *parerga* simply by remaining silent, was forced to have recourse to the method of re-interpreting them in order to point them out. He adopts two ways of re-interpreting justification. The first is the way which has over and over again been trodden through the ages, by Augustine first and latterly by Holl and his disciples: the indirect equation of divine justification with the event of the good human will, the interpretation of the imperfectly good human deed as a *larva* of the perfectly good reality of the divine grace. 'If by nature (in its practical significance) we understand the capacity to achieve any certain aims by our own strength, then grace

[1] *Disp. of the Facs.*, 90.   [2] *Rel.*, 177f., 217; *Disp. of the Facs.*, 83.
[3] *Rel.*, 217.   [4] Ibid., 63.

is nothing else but human nature, in so far as man is determined to actions by his own inner, but super-sensory principle (his conception of his duty), which we imagine to be the impulse to do good imparted to us by the Godhead, the basis for which we have not ourselves laid down in us, and which therefore we imagine to be grace.'[1] ' "A yearning for the kingdom of God"—if only one were assured of the immutability of such a feeling(!)—will be tantamount to knowing that one is already in possession of this kingdom.'[2] 'The Comforter (paraclete), whenever our transgressions trouble us by reason of their persistence', is 'the good and pure disposition (which may be called a good spirit which governs us) of which we are aware'.[3] And rebirth is the 'revolution of the mode of thought', the 'foundation of a character', in which man 'reverses the supreme basis for his maxims, on account of which he was a wicked man, by one single immutable decision', so that 'he puts on a new man', and becomes 'a subject receptive to good'. A 'reform of the disposition' must then correspond to this revolution, a reform, that is, which consists in a gradual but constant advance from worse to better, which is taken by God to have been completed in consideration of the revolution which has supplied the basis for it.[4] We have only to think of Kant's aforementioned explanation, that it is rather the idea of the disposition which shall justify us, and precisely not a disposition of which we are *aware*, precisely not the 'foundation of a character' which is conceivable as something which we can achieve ourselves, in order to see the seam hiding a tear which is palpably ill-mended here. 'If only one were assured of the immutability of such a feeling!' But how then is man to be able to recognize in his empirical goodness any analogy even, and thus any guarantee, for his intelligible goodness, his quality of being well-pleasing to God? What the belief in divine justification should achieve in view of the radical evil, according to Kant's own premises, it manifestly cannot achieve in this interpretation (an interpretation, that is, which is bound to a good disposition that is to be empirically established).

Kant's other re-interpretation of justification is in its groundwork identical with that known to us from the old Catholic Church of the second and third centuries, from the Greek fathers, and especially from the Franciscan scholasticism of the late Middle Ages: each one of us must *do as much as is in his power (facere quod in se est)* to become a better man. He may then hope that what lies beyond his capacity will be supplied by a higher power which is aiding him. This can come about, according to Kant, without it being necessary for us to know in

[1] *Disp. of the Facs.*, 85.   [2] *Rel.*, 86f.   [3] Ibid., 91f.   [4] Ibid., 54f., 85.

what this extra help consists and how it takes effect.[1] Whether it consists in a diminution of the obstacles standing in the way of the will for
good, or in positive aid for this will, man must previously make himself
worthy of it and he must also, which is, after all, no mean thing either,
be prepared at all events to accept this aid of his own accord.[2] Of the
two conditions for salvation, the belief in the atonement which inter-
cedes for the transgressions we ourselves cannot make amends for, and
the belief that we can in future become well-pleasing to God by living
the good life, the second must in all circumstances be placed in the forefront and the first, as a reinforcement of our determination to stand on
our own feet, in the background.[3] 'The right course, is not to proceed
from the receiving of grace to virtue, but rather from virtue to the
receiving of grace.'[4]

It is clear that it is this doctrine of grace or the Augustinian one or a
combination of the two (with Kant they frequently merge with one
another), or, in short, the Roman Catholic, the decidedly non-refor-
matory doctrine of grace which emerges as the result of these re-
interpretations, and which also doubtless accords with the true line of
Kant's undertaking, or, to put it more cautiously, with that of Kant's
philosophy of religion. Where else is a doctrine of salvation to end,
which is intended to be anthropology and nothing but anthropology,
even if it does have as its background a metaphysics with an ethical
foundation—where else could it end, but in the twofold possibility
of the Roman Catholic doctrine of salvation? Kant's emergence
into the Augustinian mystic teaching of the dual picture of reality
and into the vulgar Pelagian doctrine of justification by words is no
less necessary after its fashion than the emergence of Lessing's theology
of history into the Roman Catholic principle of tradition. These roads
must all lead to Rome! Those features in Kant's philosophy of religion,
then, and those especially which are relevant to this last point, which
have struck us as being upsetting to the general plan, can certainly
only be adjudged deviations which have their origin in another field
of magnetic force, and not peculiarities of Kant's own system, as
Kant himself wished it to be understood. We must be well on our
guard against the desire to re-interpret Kant, according to the rules
of his own hermeneutics, as if what he said and meant were at bottom
the same as what Luther and Calvin said and meant. It is, however,
no re-interpretation for us to note the presence of these deviations,
the deviations which occur precisely at the most significant point:

[1] *Rel.*, 62, 262; *Disp. of the Facs.*, 86   [2] *Rel.*, 47f.
[3] Ibid., 168, 173, 284.   [4] Ibid., 314.

are *'parerga* of religion' which, according to Kant's own explanation, *abut* upon the 'religion within the limits of reason alone'. And in this, incidentally, we are certainly at liberty to take this 'abutting' as implying not only adjacency but a clash.

To summarize: Kant's philosophy of religion has the significance of an attempt to interpret religion, too, as a necessary phenomenon of reason, in pursuance of his general undertaking of the critique of reason; an attempt, that is to say, to reduce it to a capacity *a priori* and measure its concretely empirical content against this capacity as if this were its inner law. Kant interprets religion by means of the two most significant results of his general critique of reason: the ideal and practical nature of all knowledge by pure reason. Since it is reason itself which has alone been able to perform the critique of reason and has thus supplied those results of the critique of reason which have now become criteria, it is already taken for granted by the very starting-point of this philosophy of religion, and by the conception of the problem it is supposed to involve, that it is the agent of reason, man, that is, who, just as he is the measure of all things, is here thought of and provided for as the measure of religion, too: of its practical and theoretical possibilities, and also, and in particular, as God's measure. This conception of the problem proves itself faultlessly in execution for precisely as long as it is merely a matter of its own development, of drawing the limits, that is, between it and the notion of a revealed positive religion, between it and the authority of the Bible when this authority is conceived as a merely historical one, and between it and the merely historically conceived instance of a Word of God made flesh confronting man. Kant's programme is unfolded over against these notions in such a way that he shows, or alternatively affirms, in each case that the allegedly revealed knowledge of God which is claimed along these lines bears a relation to the ideally practical knowledge of God by pure reason akin to that of a vehicle to the actual remedial substance; it is to be understood, that is, in comparison with the other, as something only relatively necessary, as something which in case of conflict is always to be understood from the standpoint of and to be measured by the ideally practical knowledge of God by pure reason, and not the other way round.

It first struck us, however, in the discussion of the notion of the Church that Kant himself feels he has occasion to place a positively historical factor, in the form of the notion of the organization of the kingdom of God, or alternatively, of the visibility of the Church, in close proximity anyway to the timelessly reasonable necessity of his conception of religion. It struck us that the necessity of this conception of religion seemed to show, in this context even, at least a strong relationship to the 'statute' of the positively historical, the Christian religion.

We were secondly surprised to find that Kant is unable to speak of the reality of religion in the individual without at once introducing a principle which in the rest of his analysis of what generally appertains to reason is not, at all events explicitly, held up to view, a principle which is against reason, but which yet, surprisingly, precisely as such belongs to the order of reasonable things, the principle of *radical evil*.

And thirdly it struck us in Kant's teaching of atonement, that he, the philosopher, cannot help but acknowledge the presence, at the back at least of the atonement by one's own good deed, which, according to his teaching, is apparently the only possible kind, of certain problems of another order; these problems are concentrated in the notion of *grace*, mysteries which he leaves undiscussed, as *parerga* of the religion of reason, or attempts to make accessible to a degree by re-interpretation; but whatever his treatment, Kant still acknowledges that they 'abut' upon the religion of reason.

With this we return to the introductory sentence, in which we said that the dictation of peace terms with which Kant, commandingly enough, advanced upon theology, does at least contain a certain gap. Seen in relation to the entire Kantian plan this gap doubtless signifies the presence of a certain inconsistency. The inconsistency becomes visible in the execution of the Kantian enterprise: the conception of the problem which Kant takes as his instrument cannot be equally triumphant all along the line. For the Kantian enterprise consists in a great 'if . . . then' sentence: *if* the reality of religion is confined to that which, as religion within the limits of reason alone, is subjected to the self-critique of reason, *then* religion is that which is fitting to the ideally practical nature of pure reason, and that only. It is in the execution of the 'then' part of the sentence that the inconsistency shows itself. I say, shows itself, and the question now is, whether it could show itself if it was not somehow contained in the 'if' part too, in the premise. This once again might have two meanings: it can mean, firstly that the premise Kant made is, in the way in which he fashioned it, perhaps not complete, but in need of improvement. It could, however, also mean that there is an entirely different premise apart from and opposing the one made by Kant, which he has not made at all, and which yet should have been made. According to the place at which the source of the error is sought three possibilities arise, then as now, for the understanding of the theological relevance of Kant's teaching:

First theology can take the Kantian premise just as it is as its standpoint; the premise that the criteria Kant took from his philosophy are correct, complete, and that they really set the standard, in order then, with this as its basis, to execute the Kantian programme in a way which is somewhat different after all from that of Kant himself, be it in an even more compact way, or in an even freer way, moving in the latter case in the direction of the gaps existing in Kant's own work. We find following this line of development, firstly the so-called rationalistic theologians, at the end of the eighteenth century and in the first half of the nineteenth, whose only completely thorough-going representative of note was in fact Wegscheider of Halle; and then much later and of a quite different stamp, as a result of the great Kant-revival of the second half of the nineteenth century, A. Ritschl, and particularly distinct among his pupils W. Herrmann.

Secondly, theology—now convinced that the Kantian premise should not be accepted just as it is—can, while it indeed affirms it in what concerns method, subject it to an immanent critique. For it can undertake to broaden and enrich the conception of reason which forms the premise by pointing out that there is yet another capacity *a priori* which is part of the necessities of human reason, apart from the theoretical and practical ones: the capacity of feeling, as Schleiermacher put it, or that of 'presentiment', as de Wette preferred to express it, linking up with the philosophers Jacobi and Fries. It is this second possibility, that of correcting Kant's conception of the problem— a correction which was then of course bound to bring about also a change in the execution of the programme—which became characteristic of the stamp of theology in the nineteenth century, and in particular, of the so-called conservative or positive theology, just as much as of the so-called liberal theology of this century. Both these first possibilities have it in common that theology desires in principle to keep to the Kantian terms for peace, and to enter into negotiations, merely, with their dictator, whether it be upon the conditions he has laid down for their execution, or upon the actual terms for peace themselves. It is in pursuing these two lines of development that nineteenth-century theology is destined to be the direct continuation of the theology of the Enlightenment.

The third possibility, which also clearly exists, was not taken seriously into account throughout the whole of the nineteenth century, the possibility, namely, of at least questioning not only the application of the Kantian conception of the problem, but that conception itself, and therefore the autocracy and its competence to judge human reason in relation to the religious problem. It might perhaps well be possible to concur with an untroubled mind in the premise of Kant's undertaking, be it in the form set down by Kant, or in its corrected form, but at the same time have it emphatically understood that this premise is not the only one to be made in an objective treatment of the religious problem. It might be possible to object that with the problem conceived as 'religion within the limits of reason alone' only the one side of the problem, namely religion as a human function, is seen, and not the other side, the significant point to which this function is related and whence it springs, the dealings, namely, of a God who is not identical with the quintessence of human reason, with the 'God in ourselves' —thus restricting the validity of the enquiry in a manner which must also of necessity adversely affect the presentation of the first side, the interpretation of this human function. This third possibility would, in a word, consist in theology resigning itself to stand on its own feet in relation to philosophy, in theology recognizing the point of departure for its method in revelation, just as decidedly as philosophy sees its point of departure in reason, and in theology conducting, therefore, a dialogue with philosophy, and not, wrapping itself up in the mantle of philosophy, a quasi-philosophical monologue. It can only be said of this third possibility, which becomes visible on the borders of the Kantian philosophy of religion, that it is at all events observed by Hegel and by several of his pupils in theology—I am thinking of Marheineke in the first half of the nineteenth century and of I. A. Dorner in the second—further that it was tackled by certain outsiders (often, unfortunately, without taking sufficiently into account the problems as raised by the Kantian enquiry), again, that it was more or less clearly aimed at by the conservative schools (which for the rest were under the influence of Schleiermacher) as part of their teaching, but that right up to our own time it could not get the better of the actual trend of the time, which at first took its course from Schleiermacher (with the detour via Ritschl) to Troeltsch.

There remains for us, in our study of Kant, the task of ascertaining whether, and if so, in what respect the prospect of this third possibility might really present itself even from Kant's own standpoint. We shall now make no further reference to the inconsistencies we have been discussing in his philosophy of religion. They speak for themselves in this respect, in their unmistakable equivocality, at least. It would also be better for us to renounce the bold attempt to try to understand

Kant better than he understood himself, to renounce the wish, that is, to deduce and construct a philosophy of religion from the philosophy of Kant, other than that with which he himself thought he should and could crown his work in the field of theology. The question as to whether this might not be possible is a permissible one, but even assuming that the question of the theological significance of such an improved philosophy of religion based on Kant were clarified, the task of developing it would at all events be one of a purely philosophical kind. Philosophy, however, is in itself a strict study covering a vast field, and it is not for the theologian to conduct himself as if he were in a position to propound a philosophy, as if this were some subsidiary part of his office, and to pull a philosopher's work to pieces, especially if that philosopher happens to be Kant. We shall remain, therefore, within the framework of an immanent interpretation of Kant, of the Kant who, upon the border between philosophy and theology and in that he was not able to avoid taking half a step over this border, did in effect intrude upon theological matters as a philosopher. In remaining true to this Kant, and in taking him as he presented himself, we are enabled to establish the fact that he yet said several things upon this border which might at least have led theology to take this third way into consideration too, together with that leading from Wegscheider to Ritschl and Herrmann and that leading from Schleiermacher to Troeltsch.

Kant, as we have seen, with the notion of the Church as his starting-point, pondered the possibility of the Bible having a position and significance, which, even if it were not 'divinely statutory' would yet be extraordinary and qualified, and he went on from this to ponder also the possibility of a theology which would be *different* from the philosophical theology he himself was propounding. He explicitly calls this other theology, which limits philosophical theology, '*biblical* theology', and it is his wish that the affairs of this biblical theology should not 'be allowed to mingle' with those of philosophy. He wants rather to form for it a definite distinct idea as befits its own peculiar nature.[1] For Kant the possibility for such a discipline or faculty, which is theological in the narrower and specific sense, is given, first of all formally, simply with the existence of the Church which has its foundation in the Bible. Philosophy would be exceeding its rights if it were by any chance to proceed to the formation of a Church, to a special philosophical preaching, on the basis of its own understanding of religion.[2] Philosophy does not offer itself as a rival to theology, but as a

[1] *Disp. of the Facs.*, 63.   [2] First draft of the Foreword to the *Rel.*

'friend and companion'.[1] 'A minister of a Church is bound to convey his message, to those he is teaching the catechism, and to his congregation, according to the symbol of the Church he is serving.' Kant disputes the idea that a minister's task as an office-holder is dependent upon any historical-philosophical convictions he might hold as one learned in the subject. A preacher would be bound to abandon his office for this reason, only if he should find something flatly in contradiction of the 'inner religion', as he must understand it as a philosopher, in the teachings of his Church, but not if these teachings do not happen to correspond exactly with his historical-philosophical convictions. Even if such a conflict between the office-holder and the scholar in him should take place, the scholar can always explain that it is not completely impossible for 'truth to lie hidden' in the things he has to represent in the Church as one holding office.[2]

And with this we have arrived already at what, according to Kant, constitutes the material possibility of a biblical theology. Kant guards against the reproach that it seems as if his critical religious teaching is presuming to dispute revelation. This is not his intention, 'since it might be after all, that the teachings of revelation stem from men supernaturally inspired'.[3] He does not wish to assert that in matters of religion reason is sufficient unto itself, but acknowledges (let us think once again at this point of that letter to Jung-Stilling) that reason, after it has established in religion those things which it is fitted to establish as such, 'must await the arrival of everything else, which must be added beyond its capacity, without reason being permitted to know in what it consists, from the supernatural helping hand of heaven'.[4] 'Even at that point where philosophical theology seems to accept principles in opposition to those of biblical theology, e.g. in respect of the teaching concerning miracles, it confesses and proves that it does not assert them as objective principles, but only as subjective ones; they must, that is, be understood as maxims, *when* we merely wish to make use of our own (human) reason in judging of theological matters; and in so doing we do not dispute the miracles themselves, but merely leave them without restraint to the biblical theologian, in so far as he wishes to judge solely as a biblical theologian and scorns any alliance with philosophy.'[5] What Kant does dispute is the idea that the reality and possibility of revelation, its availability as data for human reason and its perception by human reason, are things which can be accounted

---

[1] Second draft.   [2] *Was ist Aufklärung?* (What is Enlightenment?), 9.
[3] *Disp. of the Facs.*, 44; cf. *Rel.*, 87.   [4] *Letters*, II, No. 542.
[5] *Draft of Writings to a Theol. Faculty*, 1793.

G

for by philosophical means, the idea that over and beyond the philosophy of religion there is a philosophy of revelation and of faith, and
that by its theology might be represented, or make its position secure.
At the same time, however, he disputes the philosopher's right to deny
revelation because it cannot be accounted for by philosophical means.
He therefore advises both the theologian and the philosopher 'not to
indulge his curiosity in those things which do not pertain to his office
and of which in general he understands nothing'. For him theology is a
'privileged body', which he quite plainly instructs to do precisely those
things in matters of religion which philosophy dare not do, and to refrain from doing precisely those things which philosophy is bound to do.

What may theology *not* do? It may not 'interfere in the free profession of philosophy and attempt to prove or refute its principles of
belief least of all, by philosophy', just as philosophy for its own part
has to resign itself that it cannot pass any definitive judgment upon the
authority and exposition of the Scriptures.[1] Theology 'does not speak
according to the laws of the pure and *a priori* knowable religion of
reason, for in so doing it would debase itself and set itself down upon
the bench of philosophy'.[2] It may not, 'in what concerns the fulfilment
of the divine commandments in our will . . . by any means count upon
nature, upon man's own moral capacity (virtue), that is'. The interpretive method of 'giving another meaning to something' is forbidden
for theology: theology cannot be entitled 'to give the sayings of the
Scripture a meaning which does not exactly suit what is expressed in
them; with a moral meaning, for instance', 'and since there is no human
expounder of the Scripture authorized by God, the biblical theologian
must rely upon a supernatural enlightenment of the understanding by a
Spirit which guides into all the truth, rather than concede that reason
intervenes'. 'The biblical theologian as such cannot and may not
prove that God himself spoke through the Bible, since this is a matter
of historical fact, and thus belongs to the philosophical faculty.'[3] He
must, as Kant at one point says, certainly not without malice, as a pure
(*purus, putus*) biblical theologian, be 'still uninfected with the accursed
free spirit of reason and philosophy'.[4] What, on the other hand, should
theology do? The answer: 'The biblical theologian is really the scribe
of the Church faith, which rests upon statutes; laws, that is to say, which
stem from the arbitrary choice of another authority.'[5] Theology
'speaks according to statutory prescriptions for belief which are contained in a book, preferably called the Bible; contained, that is, in a

---

[1] First draft of the Foreword to the *Rel.*   [2] *Disp. of the Facs.*, 106.
[3] Ibid., 62.   [4] Ibid., 63.   [5] Ibid., 77.

codex of the revelation of an Old and New Covenant of men with
God, which was joined many hundreds of years ago, and whose
authentication as a historical faith (and not, particularly not, as a
moral faith, for that might also be drawn from philosophy) should
surely be expected from the effects of the reading of the Bible upon the
human heart rather than from . . . proofs'.[1] 'The biblical theologian
proves that God exists by means of the fact that he has spoken in the
Bible.' He may, in the question of the realization of the will for good,
count only upon grace, 'which, however, man cannot hope to partake
of in any other way than by virtue of a faith which fervently transforms
his heart; which faith itself he can, however, in his turn expect of
grace'.[2] Theology, with these premises it has: the Church, the Bible,
historical revelation, and grace, should allow itself to be ranked together with other branches of learning and content itself with the
influence it can acquire as such by its own dignity.[3]

Such was the advice Kant had to give to the theologian. What comment should we make upon it? We should certainly not forget that it
was to some extent conditioned by the historical events of Kant's time,
and that it must be understood accordingly. His philosophy of religion
was written subject to the pressure, or in the shadow, at least, of Wöll-
ner's edict of religion. We must therefore certainly bear in mind the
fact that he was prevented from developing a decidedly anti-theological
absolutism by restraints imposed from without, too. But he cannot be
understood solely from this point of view either, unless we intend to
question his character in a way for which we have no reason. Once
again we must not fail to appreciate that kind of philosophical irony
with which Kant carried out this deeply serious segregation of the
matters in which the two faculties were to be considered competent,
on the basis of which he finds himself after all, unexpectedly in a
position to allocate to a biblical theology its place beside philosophy.
But what is the ultimate significance of this irony? Perhaps the placing
of philosophy and theology side by side is after all a matter which
cannot be spoken of without irony—and from the theological side
too! It is only to be regretted that there was apparently no one among
Kant's theological contemporaries who had the insight, the courage
and the humour expressly to draw the great man's attention, in all
respect, to the mutual quality of this relationship.

Be this, however, as it may: looking at the matter purely objectively
there is just the one question as to whether, behind Kant's segregation

[1] *Disp. of the Facs.*, 107.   [2] Ibid., 62.
[3] Second draft of the Foreword to the *Rel.*

of the philosophical and theological function, with or without irony, an *insight* lies hidden, which had, and still has, a right to be heard, an insight which, it is true, was of no direct usefulness within the framework of Kant's undertaking, but one in which that determination of the place of theology might well have its deep and justified reason. We do not overlook the fact that with more than one of the passages just quoted Kant may have laughed up his sleeve as he wrote them, happy not to be in the shoes of such a 'biblical theologian', and that for his part he need not take up his uninvitingly portrayed position. But it cannot be maintained that the old gentleman's smile by any chance detracts from the weight of the train of thought which was becoming visible as he wrote, whether he would have it so or not. We cannot see, however, why the smile of the old man should impair the importance of his train of thought, which willy-nilly becomes visible. Again we cannot see why his determination of theology's place should not be right simply because the place he indicates for the theologian is in fact such that in it the theologian—seen from the point of view of a philosophy attentive to the concerns of 'mere reason'—must right at the outset feel himself threatened and also probably an object of ridicule. It is only necessary to take quite seriously what Kant said half in mockery, in order to hear something very significant, even though we reserve in every respect our right to object to his formulations. Or is it not the case that the philosopher of pure reason has said something very significant to the theologian in telling him in all succinctness that '*The biblical theologian proves that God exists by means of the fact that he has spoken in the Bible*'?

V

HERDER

I. BEFORE and during the time when Kant was painstakingly engaged in writing the *Critique of Reason* other, completely different men had long been at work, who in a more daring and sweeping way than it was given to Kant were bringing the spirit and cast of thought of the eighteenth century to its culmination, and ultimately overcoming it. They were so different from Kant that turning to them after studying him is like suddenly finding oneself in another world, even though they were his contemporaries, and their assumptions and aims were ultimately the same as his. Kant's way of pursuing the path of the Enlightenment to its end, his striving for basing everything on principle, his severity and asceticism, the very method which led to a glimpse of new horizons beyond the Enlightenment and beyond the eighteenth century generally, were bound to have a limited appeal. It needed too much patient study and too little prejudice to discover that his work not only signified the fulfilment of the old era, but paved the way into a new one. Kant's works are so demanding that the majority even of his present-day readers remain unaware of the fact that his cold deliberateness was capable of hiding more enthusiasm than is to be found in any number of frankly enthusiastic proclamations. The air at the goal to which Kant's path finally led seemed too rarefied and chill; the gateway to the knowledge of the last things formed solely by the twin pillars of pure and practical reason, to which he pointed in conclusion, too narrow; the demand that we should actually persevere beneath this narrow portal to metaphysics, too inhuman. Further, even if Kant was well-acquainted with the message of the Christian Church, or at any rate acutely conscious of its significance, we cannot deny that it figured too imprecisely and too insignificantly in his scheme of things for his philosophical system to appear as necessary, meaningful and promising from the Christian point of view as it might otherwise well have done.

Thus it happened that Kant's work as a whole did not satisfy his contemporararies, however impossible they found it to escape its influence in detail. Kant was respected, admired and praised by all. Herder himself in his formative years experienced the exalting effects of Kant's personality as a thinker and a teacher, an influence which continued to affect his work even when he was devoting it to attacks, both direct and indirect, upon his former master. But even in those days it was probably only relatively few people who read Kant's work in detail and in its entirety, let alone truly accompanied him to his goal: and Herder was most definitely not one of them. In the very act of praising Kant his fellows began to chafe and argue against his conclusions, without always having used his guidance to think them out for themselves. They tried to circumvent him, imagining that they could turn his findings, and especially the negative ones, to a far richer and more fruitful purpose, and that they were already in a position to advance beyond him and put him behind them. The most that Kant could promise for the possibility of uncovering the secret of the existence of man and of the universe—an activity to be performed by man himself—had been his indication that only an ideal knowledge by pure reason understanding itself solely in the form of practical reason was possible. This was not enough to satisfy the yearning of the eighteenth century. No one, it is true, was capable of refuting the deductions of Kant's logic, and still less those of his ethics, which had shaped the final expression of his logic and determined its limits. But the yearnings mounted like a flood against the barrier of Kant's conclusion that the knowledge of the last things possible to man should now actually consist in thinking the *action*, in *thinking* the action, and that rational knowledge should be confined within such narrow limits.

Was it not the case that Kant himself in reaching this conclusion, and reason as he had defined it, had once again, and more than ever, encountered the secret, the unfathomable and yet undeniable secret, of man as he really is and of the real world? Had he not himself proved by this that reason knows and pursues also a way different from the one he had described as the only one? Do we live only in the interlacing of idea and action which seems to be Kant's single preoccupation, or do we not begin to live *until* we reach that stage? Does not man again and again push forward to the utmost limits of the possible, to the source of things, to the 'mothers', and to truth, and in doing so discover himself and the self's absolute power?—Does he not do this also in ways entirely different from the one described by Kant as the only one? Must thought and speech allow themselves, dare they allow themselves, to be restricted to the sphere of learning and morality, and to the postulates and hopes possible and necessary within the limitations of those two spheres? Was this not wrongly allowing a fount of reason itself to become choked, allowing a justification for human speech to be wrongly suppressed? Could it really be that we dare not recognize and may not speak of the very thing which is our true and ultimate source of life, beyond this interlacing of idea and action? Did this not mean that Kant had overlooked the most decisive, the deepest and most comprehensive possibility open to mankind, and that his philosophy, signifying a calamitous impoverishment, was therefore in need of the speediest re-orientation, a process which would, however, by no means injure its truth and greatness within its own particular field? Was there no other, better fulfilment of the Enlightenment in prospect, apart from and beyond that offered by Kant, and with it a different, better and new self-understanding of the eighteenth-century spirit? Was not the *sapere aude* capable of being interpreted far more deeply than Kant had interpreted it?

It was in discussing Lessing, in connexion with his reflections upon the significance of the historical element in Christianity, that we came across the concepts 'experience' and 'feeling', and the image of the decisive 'grateful shock of the electric current'. Lessing was sufficiently a representative of the Enlightenment, sufficiently a Kantian in advance of Kant, one is tempted to say, to refrain from pursuing this line of enquiry, from interpreting experience and feeling as means to an end, and reaching out after all to grasp the plain truth beyond the limits of human reason. It was Lessing's desire to leave pure truth to God, experience and feeling notwithstanding, and to be himself content with striving after it. We have already heard what Kant thought of the idea of introducing the concepts of experience and feeling into the teachings of religion: who is to convince us that an experience is even really an experience, if, as is the case with religious experience, we are unable to derive it from any principle of our understanding? 'The wish to feel the direct influence of the Godhead as such is a self-contradictory piece of presumption.'[1] 'Feeling is something entirely personal, and no one can assume its presence in others, which means that it cannot be taken as a touchstone for the truth of revelation. It does not teach us anything at all, consisting as it does merely in the effect of pain or pleasure upon one particular person, and cannot possibly form the basis for any knowledge at all.'[2]

It was the successful ignoring of this objection which formed the starting-point for the circumvention of Kant. That circumvention would be embarked upon with a low obeisance to his genius. It could

[1] *Disp. of the Facs.*, 103.   [2] *Rel.*, 165f.

be perfectly reconciled with his methodological starting-point, his enquiry concerning the 'capacity' of the human mind, and also with the
answer he discovered, the interlacing of idea and action. It was possible
for those carrying out the outflanking movement to declare that they
merely wished thought and action to be looked upon as relative things,
considered in relation to experience, within the totality of phenomenon,
of human reason that has to be taken into account; that they were only
proclaiming that which we sense immediately as a source of knowledge
of a higher order. They could let the Kantian concepts of science and
moral philosophy stand, grant their validity, as they were, in their
rigour and more or less understood, and content themselves with
saying that Kant had merely overrated their significance, depriving
them of their force by making evident the possibility of a quite different
kind of intellectual activity and communication, a far more fruitful
and much more promising one, that, namely, which is founded upon
experience and feeling, upon the lessons of life. In actual fact this
reducing of thought and action to a position of merely relative importance, and the award of pride of place to experience, had appeared
upon the European scene long since, in the person and writings of Jean-
Jacques Rousseau. It was when German philosophy with typical
German thoroughness, took its stand as a matter of principle in the
position Rousseau had discovered that the success of the circumvention of Kant became inevitable.

The master in the art of circumventing Kant was Johann Gottfried
Herder. He has been called the 'theologian among the classical
writers'. He was also truly a classical theologian, because he was the
first to discover in convincing manner a way of making a theology
possible which was able to bypass Kant. The possibility which Lessing
was too cautious to exploit, and which, according to Kant, was forbidden, is to Herder a joyous event, in the course of which, as I. A.
Dorner has well expressed it,[1] his mind stands like a help-meet beside
the masculine mind of Lessing. Herder's significance for those theologians who came after him can scarcely be rated highly enough.
Without him the work of Schleiermacher and de Wette would have
been impossible, and also the peculiar pathos of the course of theology
in the nineteenth century. Without Herder there would have been no
Erlangen group and no school of religious history. But for Herder there
would have been no Troeltsch. There are three different ways of
characterizing Herder's significance for theology and the emergence of
his philosophy of religion to take its place beside Kant's. I make the

[1] *Geschichte der protestantischen Theologie* (History of Protestant Theology), p. 737.

distinction without discussing the relative merits of each, but simply to help make the situation clear:

1. If Kant's philosophy of religion, because of the supreme place consistently accorded in it to the autonomy of reason, was a work of the *hubris* of the Enlightenment turning a somersault, then the reaction instigated by Herder brought about its nemesis with incredible rapidity and force.

2. If Kant's philosophy of religion, by the way it juggled away every revelation presenting itself to mankind, constituted a danger, temptation and difficulty for Christian theology, then it was Herder's incredibly sudden and forceful arrival as its saviour which rescued it, temporarily at least, from all its troubles.

3. If Kant's philosophy of religion, because of the clarity with which it at all events recognized and established the limits of humanity, represented a unique opportunity for theology to call itself to order and to recollect certain fundamental theological premises, then it was Herder, by his sudden and powerful influence, who took care that such an act of recollection did not at once take place.

Be that as it may: it was Herder who restored forthwith to theology the scope of its activities which Kant had apparently reduced to a painfully small space. It was thanks to Herder that the overcoming of the Enlightenment did not merely signify, as it did with Lessing, the overcoming of a system of polemic and apology without objects, by a reminder of the autonomy of ultimate knowledge; nor, as it did with Kant, the subjection of a freely proliferating speculation by arguments to prove that this ultimate knowledge was limited both ideally and practically. With Herder the vanquishing of the Enlightenment influence means the vanquishing of the supremacy of logic and ethics in general, of the categories of the understanding and of the categorical imperative as well, by means of the discovery of feeling and experience, the discovery that there is a form of knowledge and speech which arises directly from the events of life. This not only saved the discovery of man as the measure of all things which was common to Rousseau, Lessing and Kant, and to the eighteenth century as a whole, and ensured its passage into the new era, but meant that it was in turn immensely enriched and strengthened by the discovery of another potentiality inherent in man himself. Let us suppose religion should prove to be a matter of immediate feeling and immediate experience, perhaps in direct contrast to science and morality, and more deeply rooted than these; again, let us suppose religion should prove to contain the deepest meaning of the faculty for recording and applying the teachings of life, and thereby also the deepest meaning of the processes of thinking and willing. In this case does not the man who proclaims this truth, by virtue of an equal, nay a superior consciousness of self, take his place beside the man of the Enlightenment, beside the proclaimer of science and moral philosophy, and even beside the philosopher of self-criticizing reason? If this should be so then it erases the memory of Kant's smile as he presented theology with a task which he held to be impossible. Then it is possible once again to be a theologian, on the heights, and above and beyond the Enlightenment!

'I see no reason why theologians should not be just as open-minded and cheerful in their subject as students of the other branches of learning. Theology is in a certain way the most liberal of all the arts, a free gift of God to mankind, and one which has aided him in the acquisition of all the liberal benefits of reason, high-minded virtue and enlightenment. It was the theologians who were the fathers of human reason, and of the human mind and heart. It was from the sacred grove of theology that the first sages, law-givers and poets went forth, and it was only much later that the most diverse and lucid studies emerged from the old form of theology like flowers from the bud. . . . The divine revelation is the red sky of morning, the spring sun-rise for the human race, full of the spring's promise of light, warmth and abundance of life. What has this to do with the theologian's depressed and morose expression; as if this expression were in some way inseparable from the Bible and theology, as the beggar is from his sack?'[1] What tones are these, and what a language! And Herder wrote this seven years before the appearance of Kant's critique of religion. There can be no mistaking the fact that this was a new wind, swelling the sail from another quarter. He who speaks in this manner, remember, was one of the most celebrated thinkers and poets writing in the German language, whose influence gave an unprecedented stimulus not only to theology, but to history, the history of literature, and to natural science, even, as well; the General Superintendent (1776-1803) of Weimar, of all places, he occupied the pulpit beneath which Goethe ought to have sat at least from time to time.

But there was really no need for all these reminders to make us properly aware of what seems to have been here at stake. Herder's thinking underwent a long series of changes in the course of its development: from Kant to Hamann, Hamann to Leibnitz, Leibnitz to Spinoza, and when he was old (a sure sign that he might have pursued

---

[1] *Briefe d. Stud. Theol. betr.* (Letters concerning the Study of Theology), Herder's complete works, ed. B. Suphan, Berlin, 1877ff., vol. 10, 277f.

his previous path a little too hastily at times) there was a kind of weary return which brought him back close to the Enlightenment. We shall not stop to discuss this development here, but we shall try rather to get a rough idea, first of the general compass of Herder's thought, and then of the way he applied it to theology.

II. I am not here to think!—To be! To feel! To live! And to rejoice![1]

Thus Herder in the poem *St Johanns Nachtstraum* (St John's Night's Dream), written while he was at Bückeburg during the years 1771-6,[2] which has as its theme the idea that man is entirely alone, and yet not alone, in Mother Nature's great enchanted arbour. The middle and fixed thing between the two poles of this paradox, of this mysterious being alone and not alone, is nothing other than man's being, which is feeling, life and joy and all these things at once—and not thought, or at least not primarily thought! And even if it should happen to be thought, then it is the thought of one particular being, the language of the soul, being that of some person or other at a particular time and place, at a single point of the great process willed and created by God: the soul which is formed by its place as a link in the chain of this process, and which is yet, like the fire-fly, the original and unique 'glowing spark of God'. 'Syllogisms can teach me nothing where it is a question of the first entry of truth into the mind, which syllogisms merely develop once it has been received . . . the great spirit which breathes upon me and shows me the mark of one hand in great and small, and uniform laws in the visible and the invisible, is my seal of truth.'[3] That is one aspect of my being, my being alone, recognized by me by virtue of the inspiration of this great spirit. 'All God's works have this in common, that although they are parts of a whole too great for us to comprehend, they nevertheless all singly are a whole in themselves and bear the stamp of the divine character of their destiny.' God the all-wise 'does not compose any abstract world of shadows—in each one of his children he loves and feels himself with a father's feeling, as if each were the only one in his world'.[4] 'The most fundamental basis for our existence is individual, in our feelings just as much as in our thoughts.'[5]

---

[1] For original, cf. Appendix, p. 403.

[2] Stephan, *Herder's Philosophy*, Phil. Libr., Vol. 112, p. 249.

[3] *Vom Erkennen und Empfinden der menschlichen Seele* (Concerning the Knowing and Feeling of the Human Soul), 1778, p. 51.

[4] *Ideen zur Philosophie der Geschichte der Menschheit* (Ideas for a Philosophy of the History of Mankind), p. 139.

[5] *The Soul*, 75.

Forget your ego, but yet never lose
Yourself. It is the greatest gift
A bounteous heaven can bestow.[1]

Such is being alone. The other side, however, is the quality of not being alone:

To live alone?
The fire-fly is not alone,
And becoming what it will be
Will ne'er be so!
And I, rejoice?—Alone?
Great Mother Nature!—none to tell
How beautiful you are
In the love-heat of summer!
Having none to share with me
The music of creation, none to hear
The wheels' soft hum nor see the angel fly,
With me imagine immortality!—
Dream it together and together taste
This earthly life! In friendliness embrace!
Thy noblest spark, O wondrous Mother Nature![2]

Continuing in this vein, Herder finds himself able roundly to declare:

If peace your aim then fly, O friend, that worst
Of enemies, the personality!

.   .   .   .   .

Rouse up! But no, your soul is not your own,
You're integrated in the great, good All!

.   .   .   .   .

What were you otherwise? Not self; for each
And every drop of blood, each cell and every
Thought and impulse of your heart and mind,

.   .   .   .   .

Each word that issues from your lips, your very
Countenance are not your own, but yours
On loan, for passing use. It's thus man goes
By stealth; inconstant, ever-altered, bears
A wealth of alien source throughout his years.

.   .   .   .   .

'Tis only when the mind, which seeks to live
In all men's souls, o'erlooks the narrow bounds
Of self, when heart beats with a thousand more

---

[1] *Self*, 256; cf. Appendix, p. 403.
[2] *St John's Night's Dream*, pp. 249f.; cf. Appendix, p. 403.

That you are made immortal, powerful,
Like God invisible, the Nameless One.

.   .   .   .   .

So let us quell the spirit and effects
Of 'I', and let the better
Thou and He and We to banish it
In gentleness, and slowly free from I's
Harsh call; and may the first of all our work
Be self-forgetfulness! It's only thus
Our deeds will prosper, and each act be sweet.[1]

But the two aspects of our being, the quality of being alone and of not being alone, and everything they imply, belong together. They always become one again, and are one in experience. Herder has the same view of the whole of sensate nature, man and the animals and all the lower orders, as he has of the universe: both are moved and quickened by an influence like that of an advancing and receding tide. 'Man is made to receive and to give, to strive and rejoice, to do and suffer. In the well-being of his body he assimilates and gives forth again, conceives easily and achieves an ease in re-imparting what he has absorbed. He does gentle violence to nature, and she in her turn to him. It is this attraction and diffusion, activity and rest, which are the source of health and happiness.'[2] It is really the unity of all these things, their combination and combined effect and mutual dependence, preserved throughout every seeming contradiction, which is the secret of man's experience of himself which forms the hard core of Herder's thought. Our senses reach their object and the objects our senses through the medium of the questing spirit which seethes in us. The incomprehensible heavenly being which brings me all things and unites all things in me might also well be called flame or ether—it is this being in whom we must place our trust, in whom we must believe in the act of knowing, for 'unity, if God's hand be not at work here, where could it be?'[3] If we pay heed to know his works it is impossible for us not to sense on the one hand everywhere a similarity with ourselves in the great spectacle of nature as a living force; not to imbue everything with our own feelings, 'whether the truth of this analogy is a merely human one or not ("so long as I am on this earth I have no knowledge of any truth higher than the human one"), and on the other hand not to seek, implement and work out the analogy of our own nature with the Creator's, our likeness in his image'.[4]

Herder thought of this working out of the image of God in ourselves,

[1] *Das Ich* (The Ego); cf. Appendix, p. 404.   [2] *The Soul*, 54.
[3] Ibid., 62, 64, 65.   [4] Ibid., 50f.

so to speak, as a passing through a gateway: if we keep our minds and spirits open to the influences of the world, which is God's world, then we come to resemble God, as it were, of our own accord. 'The law of nature will not change solely on your account: but the more you recognize nature's perfection, goodness and beauty, the more her living frame will mould you after the model of the Godhead in your earthly life.'[1] It was for this reason that Herder was a great believer in the potentialities of modern science. 'The more the true study of physics increases, the further we shall emerge from the regions of blind force and lawlessness into those where a goodness and beauty which are stable in themselves rule with a most wise necessity.'[2] Necessity, according to Herder, is transformed in man's cognition of it into perfection, goodness and beauty. In human life also, and indeed in human life in particular, it is a question of accepting, discovering and truly implementing what is absolutely necessary. Herder's attitude of 'fervent delight' in feeling the 'balm contained in the laws of human nature, and watching it spread among men against their will'[3] is far, far removed from Kant's. Far removed from Kant he declares: 'Stimulation is the mainspring of our existence, and must remain so even in the case of the cognition of the highest things. What inclination or passion is there which is not susceptible of being enriched by the knowledge and love of God and our neighbour, so as to produce effects all the more noble, sure and strong? The dross is consumed, but the true gold shall remain. Every force and capacity for stimulation lying dormant within me shall awake and work solely in the spirit of him who created me.'[4] Therefore: 'Let no one despair concerning the purpose and effect of his existence; the more order it contains, the more it will act in accordance with the laws of nature, the surer will be its effects. Like God, it works in an almighty way, and cannot help but reduce to order a state of chaos surrounding it, and dispel darkness that there be light: it causes everything with which it comes into contact, and even, to a greater or lesser degree, everything hostile which it encounters to assume the beauty of its own form.'[5] The soul, 'the queen, whose thoughts and wishes are enthroned within us'[6] 'is the image of the Godhead and seeks to stamp everything about her with this image: she creates unity out of diversity, brings forth truth out of untruth, serene activity and achievement out of restless ease, and all the time it is as if she turned her gaze inward and with the joyous feeling, "I am the daughter of God, and his image" said to herself:

[1] *Ideas*, 124.   [2] *God*, 206.   [3] *Ideas*, 163.   [4] *The Soul*, 72.
          [5] *God*, 242.   [6] *Soul*, 66.

"Let us!", and holding sway, were engaged in asserting her will.'[1]

It is fitting, particularly at this point where we are trying to determine the concept which underlay all Herder's thought, that we should allow him to speak for himself at somewhat greater length. The fact that the piece is a poem is essential to his view of the matter. He wrote the following, entitled *Die Schöpfung* (The Creation) also during the time he was at Bückeburg (250f.).

> God's creation, now complete,
> Pauses, silent yet awhile,
> Looks within and fails to find
> What is creator, what created;
> Seeketh one whose mind delights.
> Source of joy unto himself,
> Seeketh one who God-like gazing
> Shineth all creation back!
> Inward, outward. And himself
> Radiates fatherly, reigns supreme
> Is a maker like his God!
> See, this is what God's creation
> Seeketh, having reached its goal,
> Transmits sense to what it misses
> And behold, man-God-exists!
> New-formed creature, how to call you?
> Teach me, Lord, God of creation!—
> But it's I, it is myself
> Who became God's image here!
>
> I, like God! Creation's scheme
> Fills me and expands, finds focus,
> Gathers force—the end is joy,
> Great rejoicing and fulfilment.
> I, like God! At this my soul
> Self-exploring, finds, conceives me!
> Re-creates itself and acts
> Freely, feels how free its God.
> I, like God! In kingly pride
> Beats my heart, and brotherhood.
> All life here is one, and man
> Feels himself the friend of all.
> Feels himself full of compassion,
> Reaches even to the flower,
> To the goal of man's God-seeming,
> Far and wide welds all in love,
> Reaches ever deeper, higher,
> I, the focal point of all,
> Flow through all things and it's I
> Who filleth all things in himself!

[1] *The Soul*, 68.

> To the meanest of God's creatures
> My sense extends and feels and tastes!
> The harmony of every creature
> Is one with me, yes, I am they!
> Sound of earth's ecstatic choir
> Flew on high through me and came
> To the ear of God, took shape,
> Grew to thought and deed—and man.
> Godly counsel, man, is in thee!
> Feel thyself and thou wilt make
> That creation feels itself!—
> Feel thyself and thou wilt feel
> God is in thee and God feels
> That in thee alone he is
> As no sun or animal can feel him
> Thus fulfilling himself in self! . . .[1]

This makes it quite clear to us that the most significant concept—perhaps with this despiser of the syllogism we should rather say, the most significant word, or sound, even—of Herder's thought, can be nothing but *humanity*. 'Just as our way of knowing is only human, and must be so if it is to be right, so our will can only be human too; something which arises from and is full of human feeling. It is humanity which is the noble standard by which we know and act.'[2] 'Man has no more noble word to describe him than man itself, in which the image of the Creator of our earth, as it was possible for him to become visible here, lives reproduced. We have simply to outline his form to arrive at an idea of his noblest duties.'[3] In doing this, however, we must once again bear in mind the aforementioned rhythm of attraction and diffusion and not by any chance confuse individual man as such with this human standard. 'Look upon the whole of nature, behold the great analogy of the creation! Everything senses itself and its kind: life intermingles with life. Every string vibrates to its own note, each fibre intertwines with its neighbour, animal feels in harmony with animal; why should not man feel in harmony with man? Our feeling for ourselves should only be the *conditio sine qua non*, the ballast which gives us stability, not an end, but a means to an end—but a necessary means, for it is and must ever be true that we love our neighbour only as we love ourselves. How can we be true to others if we are not true to ourselves? The degree of our sense of self is at the same time the measure of our feeling for others: for it is only ourself that we can as it were project into the feelings of others.'[4] 'It is in absorbing the love of the Creator and imparting love to others by means of the self, and in

---

[1] For original, cf. Appendix, pp. 404-5.   [2] *The Soul*, 72.   [3] *Ideas*, 116.   [4] *The Soul*, 72f.

continuing in this assured course, that the true definition of the moral sense, of conscience, consists.'[1] It is the sphere of humanity, 'the realm of these propensities and their development, which is the true kingdom of God on earth, the state which has all men as its citizens. . . . Happy he who can help to extend it, for it signifies the human creation in its true, inward sense.'[2]

But the extension of this kingdom is the history of the human race. That is why it is at this point that history becomes the chief of Herder's interests. That is why he proceeded to enquire into the origin of language, into the spirit of Hebrew poetry, and of Oriental verse in general, and why he was one of the first to study the old German folk-song. That is why he laments and condemns the Enlightenment's complete absence of understanding for history, and why he twice attempted to write a philosophy of history, in those days an unprecedentedly novel undertaking (the first, in 1774, according to a more original method, but one less comprehensive than that of the *Ideas* of 1784-91 which have become famous). That is why, by dint of considerable devoted study and receptivity he was also one of the first to appreciate the achievements of the European Middle Ages, an era the Enlightenment dismissed as one shrouded in darkness and barbarity,[3] and why it was given him to discover that the Reformation, and Luther in particular, represented an event of considerable importance, a view which, strange as this may seem to us, had likewise been completely lost sight of in the eighteenth century.[4] It was just those aspects of history which had made it particularly suspect, and an object of hatred even, to the Enlightenment, precisely those which the eighteenth century, in its tendency to absolutism, looked upon as the most irreconcilable with its tenets, that Herder illuminated and emphasized with love and care, counselling his contemporaries to esteem and respect them as the very ones which were absolutely essential to the concept of history. The ideas he put forward were:

1. That the significance of history is the principle of individualization: it is 'a pure natural history of human energies, deeds and impulses, according to time and place'.[5] 'Set down upon the earth living human forces together with certain local and temporal circumstances, and all the changes of human history take place.'[6]

2. History is composed of facts: in it humanity is not just an idea, a teaching or a kind of poetry, but in one way or another that which happens, no matter how simple or obscure a form the event may take. It

[1] *The Soul*, 72. [2] *Ideas*, 147. [3] *Auch eine Philosophie* (Also a Philosophy), 93f.
[4] Ibid., 100f. [5] *Ideas*, 145. [6] Ibid., 148.

is precisely this factual quality of history which, it seems, suggests to Herder the 'depth of obscure feelings, forces and urges' to which he wished to draw his contemporaries' attention as important sources of creative power.[1]

3. The wondrous nature of historical reality in its varying content, at the intersection of the co-ordinates of time and space, which is changing and fortuitous, and yet not fortuitous, but necessary in its fortuity: its wondrousness, in which at every point a miracle too lies hidden, the madness or half-madness which produces the greatest changes in the world and which must be given scope and allowed to have its way from time to time, without being either incensed or provoked.[2]

4. Most important: history means tradition. As historical beings we are not monads, but links in a chain, drops of water in a stream, the living cells of a growing organism; not the autonomous subject exercising thought and will, but the mother suckling the infant and encouraging its first attempts at speech, the father of the child, who has fought and suffered to safeguard its inheritance, and the child itself, whose most intimate possession in its totality is at once only what it receives from the father and mother—it is these who become of interest to the thinker in historical terms. 'Why should I become a mind of pure reason when my sole wish is to be human, and when in knowledge and belief I am just what I am in my being, drifting like a wave in the sea of history?'[3]

There can be no disputing the significance of these discoveries, made by Herder as they were in complete defiance of the extreme opposite views prevailing in the time before him. And how often have they been discovered again since Herder's time and proclaimed anew as the principles most precious and most fundamental to theology in particular! Talk in any way you please, just a little unguardedly, but it may be, perfectly logically in the 'rationalistic' Kantian tradition, and you will suddenly and inevitably find that you are consciously or unconsciously getting an answer which is entirely indebted to Herder's way of thinking, conjuring up his conception of history. It is as if his genius had been given the task of continually appearing behind Kant's like a shadow; sometimes as a necessary corrective, but sometimes like a rather excitable schoolmaster, which, of course, was just what Kant, when properly understood, did not require. Herder's genius (whether for good or bad it is no part of our task to decide), the new and

[1] *The Soul*, 59.
[2] *Briefe zur Beförderung der Humanität* (Letters for the Furtherance of Humanity), Suphan, 17, 231f.
[3] *Br. Theol.* (Letters concerning the Study of Theology), Suphan, 10, 290.

epoch-making quality of his mind, is precisely his complete, loving and
devoted understanding of the concrete reality of history. It was none
other than Goethe who, long after Herder's death, wrote the most
affectionate and understanding description we have of him, in the
Maskenzüge (Masked Processions) of 1818.[1]

> A man sublime, intent upon discerning
> The diverse emanations of the mind,
> Attentive to each sound, each word returning
> From each of sources countless in their kind,
> Both old and new exploring in his quest,
> He studies all things; spirit slow to rest.
>
> And thus he hears the music of the nations,
> The things that move them in their native air,
> And hears recounted all the good traditions,
> The generations' gift that all hold dear.
> And all he heard held both delight and lesson;
> And mood and action harmonized in one.
>
> Events that oft bring ease and often pain,
> A sudden discord or unhoped-for rest,
> Have ever found a similar expression
> In every tongue that ever man possessed.
> Thus sings the bard, thus myth and saga say—
> And move us now as much as in their day.
>
> When crags are veiled in gloom, and heavily
> Is born the dread lament of phantom shapes;
> Or when with sun-beams on the open sea
> The song sublime of ecstasy escapes—
> Their heart is pure—'twas only what we ought
> Each one of us to seek, the human things, they sought.
>
> Wherever it was hid he could reveal it,
> In solemn garb or lightly clad in play—
> With highest sense of time to come he'd seal it:
> Humanity be our eternal lay.
> Alas that he's no longer here to see
> The sorest evils healed by its decree!

In what concerns history, too, Herder shouted what Lessing had
whispered. History, for him, is nothing else but living experience understood in the macrocosmic and universal sense, instead of, as previously,
in the microcosmic and individual one. That is why, if I may make use
of a phrase adapted by a present-day theologian from Luther, God and
history are for him part and parcel of the same thing. That is why the
acquisition of a feeling for history constitutes *the* task and *the* hope to

---

[1] Jubilee ed., vol. 9, 350; for original, cf. Appendix, p. 406.

which he directs mankind: 'Our body decays in the grave, and that which bears our name is soon a shadow on earth; only when merged in the voice of God, in the tradition, that is, which shapes the future, can we actively live on, as an unconscious influence, even, in the souls of our fellow-beings', in the golden thread of man's store of knowledge, in which 'the human figure vanishes, it is true, but the human spirit survives, as a constant and undying force'.[1] And civilization, which is the task and source of hope for mankind as a whole, is 'the tradition of an education'.[2]

It is because he finds God in living experience, and this is based upon self-experience, which is itself embedded in the communal experience of history, that Herder is implicitly and unequivocally optimistic in his general view of history, and of its course and development—but in a very different way from Kant, who on principle gave these same ideas a very fragmentary treatment. Kant's doctrine of radical evil did not appeal to Herder any more than it did to Goethe. He fairly shouts the view that all evil is merely negative: 'In God's kingdom nothing evil exists that could be described as real. Everything evil is as if it were nothing. We, however, call hindrances or contradictions or transitions evil, whereas none of them deserve the name. . . . Viewed properly even our mistakes have a good purpose; for they soon reveal themselves as such, and by pointing the contrast, help those who commit them to find the way to more light, and purer goodness and truth and they do not do this haphazardly, but according to the eternal laws of reason, order and goodness.'[3] 'No force can be lost, for what meaning could there be in the words, a force is lost?'[4] 'Death brings life; individual decease furthers a higher order, and in physical nature nothing is really lost. Can it be otherwise in moral nature, the true nature, where all the main-springs and sources of power are housed?'[5]

Because this is so Herder finds in history 'progress, progressive development, even if no single thing should profit therefrom. Great things are in store! . . . the scene of a guiding intention on earth! . . . even if it is not given us to see the final intention, scene of the Godhead, even if visible only through gaps in the isolated parts of the action, and amid their ruins'.[6] 'The course of history shows that with the growth of true humanity the destroying daemons of the human race have actually decreased.'[7] Herder was for instance of the optimistic but strangely naïve opinion (Schleiermacher later thought so too) that

[1] *Ideas*, 141f.   [2] Ibid., 138.   [3] *God*, 246f.   [4] *Ideas*, 128.
[5] *Letters concerning the Study of Theology*, Suphan, 10, 346; cf. *God*, 246.
[6] *Also a Phil.*, 194.   [7] *Ideas*, 161.

even war was in the process of becoming humanized, 'the more it becomes a studied art, and especially the more technical inventions contribute to it'.[1] It cannot be said that this optimism of Herder's was based entirely in this world. Its prolongation into a kind of beyond, however, is brought about by the cry to the man standing terrified before death, the frontier of his existence: 'What the Giver of all life calls into being, lives—that which is a force is a force everlastingly, in its eternal harmony with everything else.'[2] 'If we look back and see how behind us everything seems to have ripened and developed towards the coming of man, and how, with his coming, the first promise and propensity of that which he is meant to be, and of the image upon which he was carefully modelled, are present within him, then we are bound to conclude that man also must pass onward if all nature's perfect order and all the evidence that she has a goal and intention are not to be dismissed as an empty illusion.'[3] There *is* therefore a passing onward in store for us; even our earthly blessedness and virtue are merely an education, a journey and an instrument—provided the order of nature and the postulate based upon it are not in fact an illusion.[4] 'All man's doubt and despair concerning the confounding of goodness in history, and its scarcely perceptible advance, have their origin in the fact that the unhappy wanderer is only able to see a very short part of the way before him.'[5] The fact that this very short part of the way happens to coincide exactly with the unhappy wanderer's one brief life on earth, and that in view of this fact Herder's optimistic idea of a cosmic embodiment, 'with great things in store', of the various causes of unhappiness was likely to be a poor consolation for those in need of comfort, seems to have worried him and most of his contemporaries very little, so far, at least, as can be judged from his writings. In his own life Herder found no justification for his optimism, and one is almost tempted to describe it as a consoling fact that he should have ended his life deeply disillusioned, not to say embittered, in a state of mind completely belying the trend of the ideas just described.

It should be clear that on the basis of those presuppositions Herder, as was said as an introduction, brought theology relief when it was hard pressed, gave it a chance, even, to survive and continue to remain active, and provided it with convenient and practical handholds. This will be the subject of our further discussion.

III. What is religion? 'Religion is man's humanity in its highest form.' This weighty sentence[6] says in a nutshell all there is to be said.

---

[1] *Ideas*, 164f.   [2] Ibid., 129.   [3] Ibid., 133.
[4] Cf. *Letters concerning the Study of Theology*, Suphan, 10, 397.   [5] *Ideas*, 166.   [6] Ibid., 122.

Kant too might have written this sentence; but how sublime, or how meagre, but, to be just, how unmistakably clear also, is the meaning Kant would have attached to it, as compared with the deeply generous but also of course generously ambiguous significance lent it by Herder! Let us at once hear a somewhat more detailed definition, in order to convince ourselves that we are here in fact in another world: 'Religion, even when looked upon solely as an exercise of the understanding, is the highest humanity, the most sublime flowering of the human soul. It is an exercise of the human heart and the purest direction of its capabilities and energies.'[1] Herder, to begin with, has the following idea of the genesis of this sublime flower: 'As soon as man learned to use his understanding when being stimulated ever so slightly, as soon, that is, as his vision of the world became different from that of the animals, he was bound to surmise the existence of invisible, mighty beings which helped or harmed him. These he sought to make his friends, or to keep as his friends, and thus religion, whether true or false, right or wrong, became the teacher of mankind, the comfort and counsel of a life so full of darkness, danger and perplexity.'[2] True religion, however, 'is a childlike service of God, an imitation of the highest and most beautiful qualities in the human image, and hence that which affords the deepest satisfaction, the most effective goodness and human love'.[3]

To Herder there is nothing easier than to pass on from this point to the concept of revelation. The notion of man free of revelation, as Kant ultimately tried to conceive him, is impossible from the very outset within the framework of Herder's thought. Man's distinguishing quality is the fact that he stands within history. And religious man's chief distinguishing quality too is the fact that he stands within history. 'Facts form the basis for every divine element in religion, and religion can only be represented in history, indeed it must itself continually become living history.'[4] We do not know what we were, and there are no physical data available to us to tell us what we shall be. Analogy forsakes us upon both sides. Thus history must truly take the place of arguments, and this history provides the record and commentary of revelation. Standing within history also means on principle standing in the stream of revelation. 'Here also tradition is the transmitting mother, of its religion and sacred rites as of its language and civilization.'[5]

[1] Cf. Dorner, *Geschichte der Protestantischen Theologie* (History of Protestant Theology), 739.
[2] *Ideas*, 123.
[3] Ibid., 124.
[4] *Letters concerning the Study of Theology*, Suphan, X, 257.   [5] *Ideas*, 143.

The fact, however, that we stand within tradition forms part of the notion of our existence. How often after Herder and up to our own times theology has thought further along these lines, without, it must be said, always carefully considering whether the path it was treading might perhaps end in a *cul-de-sac*! Herder's meaning was this: 'If we are now bent upon taking experience as our guide, then we observe that the soul does not contrive, know or perceive anything of itself but what its world contributes from within and without, and what the finger of God assigns it. Nothing returns to it from the Platonic realm of a previous world; it has not chosen to appear in the position it occupies, and does not itself know how it arrived there. One thing, however, it does know, or should know, which is that it perceives only those things which this position reveals to it, and that there is nothing in the idea of the soul as the self-sufficient mirror of the universe, or of the endless upward flight of its positive power in omnipotent selfhood. It is in a school of the Godhead which it has not itself prescribed; it must make use of the impulses, senses, powers and opportunities it has received by a happy and unmerited inheritance, or else it withdraws into a desert where its divine strength falters and falls. It seems to me, therefore, that abstract egotism, even if this be but an academic phrase, runs counter to truth and the apparent course of nature.'[1] In how many studies, where sat theologians who would willingly have believed at that time but were chagrined to find themselves at a loss to answer what Kant had pointed out, must such words have been joyful tidings and like a breath of morning air! Man's existence, according to Herder, with its historical quality, comprises his participation in God's revelation in a manner which is without doubt the most direct possible. With Herder nature in its historical development is the action and speech of the Godhead. 'Is there on this account no Godhead, or is it not precisely the Godhead which is at play so exhaustively, uniformly and invisibly in all its works?'[2]

We may not in these circumstances expect from Herder any precise answer about a criterion of the true religion and revelation. How, in face of the exhaustive, uniform and invisible deity, could there be any criteria? The dispute between reason and revelation, in the form in which it so greatly occupied Lessing and Kant, has its place on the borders of Herder's field of vision. He prefers to speak of it metaphorically as, for instance, that both are surely gifts from God and as such could not be opposed to one another, since two presents are better than one! Revelation is the mother, and reason the daughter she has

[1] *The Soul*, 67f. [2] *Also a phil.*, 92.

educated: 'The mother cannot be against the daughter, and the daughter, if she is the right sort, should have no wish to be against the mother.'[1] Humanity is to be compared with the outline of a statue, hidden in the deep, dark marble. The marble cannot hew and shape itself. 'Tradition and teaching, reason and experience should do this.'[2] Or: 'the book of sacred nature and of conscience was slowly unfolded, ordered and explained by the commentary of tradition.'[3] In the last quotation it is not even entirely clear whether it is reason which is looked upon as the book which provides the foundations, and revelation as the elucidating commentary, or vice-versa.

In his later years Herder came close again, strangely enough, to Kant's and Lessing's view, the Enlightenment view of the primacy of reason. And there can be no doubt that in his evaluation of Christianity as the religion embodying the highest humanity, this quality giving it its truth, he measured it, fundamentally, in sound Enlightenment fashion, by the ideal of humanity already postulated and known, and then he found Christianity, in inspired fashion, but from the well-known lofty watch-tower, to be in accordance with this ideal. The view most characteristic of Herder at the summit of his course is, I think, that in which reason and revelation preserve a mutual balance like the two arms of a see-saw, in a harmony resulting from equal tension, a relationship which cannot be explained intellectually, only experienced, and one therefore which leaves the question open, or disperses it in the gusty whirling of the spirit. We must get used to the idea that with Herder and with the whole line of theological development which began with him there is not that burning interest in the question of truth which we might at first expect where the establishment of a working basis for a theology is at stake which had to come to terms with Kant of all people. Herder's theology finds the reality of revelation so conclusively in living experience or history, in feeling or practical knowledge, that it thought it could dispense with the enquiry into its legitimacy. 'It is an inner token of the truth of religion that it is utterly and completely human, that it neither senses nor broods, but thinks and acts, and bestows the power and the means for thought and action. Its knowledge is alive, the sum of all its knowledge and sensations is eternal life. If there is a universal human reason and sensation, then it is in religion and it is precisely this which forms the most neglected aspect of religion.'[4]

This position *could* mean that theology was preparing to reflect upon

---

[1] *Letters concerning the Study of Theology*, Suphan, 10, 285f.   [2] *Ideas*, 147.
[3] *Letters concerning the Study of Theology*, Suphan, 10, 295.   [4] *The Soul*, 86.

its own basis for knowledge, upon the independence, in authority and in faith, of revelation. We may ask whether that may not be the ultimate significance of Herder's obscure utterances upon this point. For from time to time we find nuances in his writings which lead us to conclude that the thought was not quite foreign to him that revelation might not only signify the revelation of humanity, but also at least the revelation of a majestic claim to Lordship made upon mankind. I am thinking of the way he rejected the juggling away of the miracles in the Bible, stating as his reason that 'these miraculous *facta* cannot be reasoned away by any conclusion of our practical knowledge, nor can the analogy they themselves contain be defeated by any analogy drawn from our lives'.[1] I am thinking further of how he gave the Christian Church the task of 'preaching *God's* will, not our own, presenting his theme, and not our theme', and of the great energy with which he therefore maintained that the homily was the only form of sermon suited to the subject, and brought good reasons in support of this view.[2] To Herder the sovereignty of a revealed religion over all forms of apologetics and polemic was also apparent: 'Facts can only be documented and preserved by facts; the best proof of Christianity is thus Christianity itself, its foundation and preservation, and most of all its representation in innocence, active hope and in the life such as Christ lived.'[3] 'Shun disputes about religion like the plague: for there can be no disputing about that which is truly religion. It cannot be either proved or disproved by argument any more than we can hear light or depict spirit. The spirit of Christianity flees dispute and strife.'[4]

But we must ask, in face of such statements which perhaps may be understood as being full of promise, whether it is not obvious that reflection of theology upon the presuppositions peculiar to it, has become bogged down in its first stage, in the hasty equation, that is, of revelation and history, of revelation and experience. We must ask whether the enquiry of pure rationalism concerning the independence in authority and in faith of revelation thus affirmed could in the long run fail to come, or be suppressed and whether Herder's own emergence in the neighbourhood of the Enlightenment position does not, clearly, at least show one thing: that in principle he no more succeeded in overcoming the Enlightenment than Kant did in his philosophy of religion. In other words, is the extent to which Herder actually overcame the Enlightenment any greater than that we have encountered in Kant and Lessing, in spite of the fact that his was a different approach? We

---

[1] *Letters concerning the Study of Theology*, Suphan, 10, 164.
[2] Ibid., 11, 17f.   [3] Ibid., 10, 172f.   [4] Ibid., 10, 260.

can even wonder whether we could not say that Kant and Lessing overcame the Enlightenment more fundamentally than Herder, in so far as they, especially Kant, after all at least saw and acknowledged, in a much more basic fashion, the problem of a realm beyond the human one, containing a truth incomprehensible to us. In the theology of Herder, the saviour of theology and prophet of the religion of God, on the other hand, with its impetuous equation of human experience, religion and revelation, of the quality of being in the image of God and the quality of the Divine, that problem of a realm beyond the human, continually threatens, in spite of several starts in another direction, to founder completely inside this human world. It is enough that Herder decided upon Christianity as the true religion, 'the genuine religion of God, which honours the father as his child and loves him in his children'.[1]

It is clear that Herder's general assumptions were first and foremost bound to give him an entirely new key to the Bible. Whatever we may hold of Herder's conception of the Bible, it must be conceded—and this was something new in the world of learning of those days—that at all events he read the Bible lovingly and with delight, and that he certainly showed many people how to read it as he did. His approach was this—and how could it be otherwise?—the more human (in the best sense of the word) the way in which we read the Word of God, the closer do we approach to the goal of the divine Author, who made men in his image and acts humanly for us in all the works and acts of beneficence in which he reveals himself to us as God. In supposing that this book was written in heaven and not on earth, by angels and not by men, we do not do him honour, but outrage and harm.[2] It should be read, just so that we may be convinced of its divine quality, with eyes and ears as human as those we devote to the study of Horace, Homer, Sophocles or Plato. Nothing unnatural is of God, the things most supernaturally divine become the most natural, for God adapts himself to the creature with whom he speaks: On the other hand we should quite simply desist from all reflections about the inspiration of the Bible. I am 'far more inclined to acknowledge, sense and apply in living fashion the divine element in these writings, than to dispute and ponder its actual form and nature in the souls of those who wrote it, or on their tongues, or in their pens or pencils. Flee, my friend, the scholastic whims and subtle speculations upon this subject, the sweepings of old barbaric schools, which will often destroy for you the best natural impression of the spirit of these writings. From the moment when you

---

[1] *Letters concerning the Study of Theology*, Suphan, 10, 246.   [2] Ibid., 10, 7f.

bar yourself up at the bottom of a precipice and help to weave a
spider's web of philosophical questions and distinctions, instead of
enjoying and applying a healthy view and the living divine effects,
the spirit of these writings will depart from you. It is a natural,
free, happy and childlike spirit, and it does not love such caverns
and servile examinations. If you do not hear the sound of its footsteps as heralding the arrival of a friend or loved one but slavishly
seek to measure and grope out its stride, then you will not hear it
coming.'[1]

It is plain that behind these sentences—and they too have been
enthusiastically repeated, in countless variations, for more than a
hundred years—there is Herder's axiom that in the entire analogy of
nature the deity has never acted other than through nature.[2] It cannot
be said out of hand that it was essentially Herder's object here to arrive
at an aesthetic appraisal of the Bible, in so far at least as 'aesthetic', in
accordance with normal usage, would be taken to mean the same as
'artistic'. Even if he did without doubt read the Bible also from this
point of view, and wanted to have it read thus, this was nevertheless
only a means to his end. He was capable of calling the discovery of the
poetical element in the Bible in which he himself played a part, 'tinsel',
in tones of contempt, 'and whoever turns a Gospel of Christ into a
novel has done injury to my heart, even if he has done so with the most
beautiful novel in the world'.[3] He expressly declares: 'I would very
much deplore you, my friend, if, being unconvinced of the historical
truth of the earliest Christian history, you were to remain a student of
theology.'[4] Herder's aim, in the Bible as everywhere, was to discover
the 'course of history', the 'spirit of God', which with him means that
which was so peculiar, actual and miraculous that it could not have
been invented, as it was received and handed down as tradition by
this people Israel, and later by the apostles;[5] 'God's course over the
nations.'[6]

In this connexion Herder already felt the importance, as the true
focal point of revelation, of that feature which, much later, was called
the religious 'personality', and proclaimed with particular emphasis
by Carlyle, in a completely different sense from that in which Herder
conceived of it. 'God works upon earth in no other way than through
great and chosen men.'[7] 'Religion is dead in a group where it has no
living examples; the dead profession of faith, dead customs, pedantic

[1] *Letters concerning the Study of Theology*, Suphan, 10, 145f. [2] *Also a phil.*, 92.
[3] Ibid., 10, 218. [4] Ibid., 10, 169. [5] Ibid., 10, 139f., 143 and 11, 167.
[6] *Also a phil.*, 104. [7] *Ideas*, 141.

learning and the splitting of hairs, even if it were to perform its work in the original language and upon the lips of the founders, can neither represent nor replace this daughter of heaven, who must be alive in men, or she is no more.'[1]

Already Herder recommends further that we should distinguish in the Bible between the letter and the spirit, between teaching and life. 'What is written is after all only a copy of what is spoken.' It is necessary to bear in mind that behind the test of the Bible there was the living speech and listening, and that the oldest books of the Scriptures are young compared with the beginnings of the human race.[2] 'Never let yourself be diverted from the one truth in the Bible by the way in which its teachings are dressed from the one truth which lives in all its teachings as their soul. . . . In every case the dress is only a means to the teaching; the truth itself is the end, and only weaklings forget the end for the dress.'[3] This is the sense in which it is true that history is the basis of the Bible, 'the roots and trunk of the tree out of which the teachings spread like branches, upon which the duties grow like the flowers and fruit'.[4] This is the sense in which 'the basis for the whole of Christianity is historical event and the pure comprehension of the same plain simple faith actively expressed'.[5] The apostles' 'joyousness both in life and death came solely from the fact that they had, from sheer necessity, at the command of God, to preach a true history they had themselves seen, especially that of the resurrection. It was the very simplicity of this teaching as a certain fact which they had experienced themselves which contributed most to the revolution Christianity brought about.'[6]

And now we can already anticipate what Herder will have to say to us about Christ. 'As a spiritual saviour of his race he sought to form men of God who, whatever the laws to which they were subject, because of their pure principles, would further the good of others and, even suffering, would reign like kings in the realm of truth and goodness.'[7] That he is this saviour is perceived by the fact that the human quality in him speaks to the human quality in all of us. In no other way! Herder had a strong aversion to the Christology of the Early Church, which sought to determine in monastic terms what no human reason will ever be able to determine and thus obscured the 'healthy view' of the life of Jesus as it was presented by the Evangelists, without any such definition of terms. A hundred years before Harnack Herder already declares: 'Our Protestant Church has nothing to do with this Greek,

---

[1] *The Soul*, 79.   [2] *Letters concerning the Study of Theology*, Su., 10, 285f.   [3] Ibid., 11, 9.
[4] Ibid., 10, 258.   [5] Ibid., 10, 171.   [6] Ibid., 10, 169f.   [7] *Ideas*, 172.

monkish illusion.' In opposition to it he already recommends concentration upon the figure which was later called the 'historical Jesus': 'A divine phantom walking upon earth is something I dare not imitate in thought or deed . . . thus for every Christian and for every Christian theologian the human Christ is not some image in the clouds to be gazed at in wonder, but a perfect example upon earth for our imitation and instruction. Every written work which develops historically and represents morally this perfect example, the figure of the purest man on earth, is an evangelical book. On the other hand, all scholastic sophistry which contrives to turn it into something calculated to dazzle, something devoid of humanity, is diametrically opposed to the spirit of the writings of the New Testament and harmful to it.'[1] But how does it come about that here, and particularly here, humanity as the messenger of divine truth speaks to humanity? Here too Herder's general canon of the theory of knowledge must be applied, and this means, on the one hand, that 'it must be believed, that is to say, it must be experienced and sensed and shuns every form of linguistic generalization and abstract divination. If an object of which we have not dreamed, from which we have hoped for nothing, suddenly reveals itself in such close proximity to ourselves that the most secret impulses of our heart willingly obey it, as the tops of the grasses are moved by the wind, and the iron filings by the magnet, what is there here that we should ponder upon, or debate with argument.'[2] And, on the other hand, it means that the appeal takes root in the universal and pre-known ideal by which Jesus is measured, and which he was found to fit. Herder did this especially over against the person of Jesus. It is self-evident that an intention—of this kind (such as is manifested in the intention of Jesus in his earthly life) must be the sole aim of Providence towards our race, an aim to which all wise and good people on earth must and will contribute the more nobly they think and strive; for what other ideal of his perfection and blessedness on earth could man have except this pure humanity with its universal effect?[3]

It is of course the first of these two arguments which is typical of Herder, whereas the second, which yet again employs the idea of the Platonic recollection, of humanity as something abstractly divined, is to be construed as an unavoidable re-insurance in the style of the Enlightenment.

But it is precisely in the form of this unavoidable link with a secret *a priori* mode of thought that the theory of experience is characteristic

[1] *Letters concerning the Study of Theology*, Su., 10, 238f.   [2] *The Soul*, 60.   [3] *Ideas*, 172.

of Herder, and not only of Herder. Obviously it means something different from what it is in fact speaking of, something other than mere experience. It seems somehow as if what is meant is the autonomy and independence in faith which belief derives from its object, and only from its object. With Herder, as I said, one is always tempted to construe such pronouncements as evidence of an insight which truly and finally explodes the Enlightenment conception of religion. It is instructive to find that Herder, on his quite different course, was just as unable as Kant had been to avoid talking sometimes in such a way that a conception of things that could and must have directed nineteenth-century theology along quite different lines, seems to have been staring them in the face, just waiting to be taken hold of. But with Herder, as with Kant, we should be mistaken in assuming that such a decisively different conception had actually come home to him. For Herder's theory does not in fact extend beyond experience as such. He is far from basing theological knowledge upon the object of experience but bases it quite definitely upon experience as such. For the historical objectivity to which he appeals is quite definitely different from the objectivity which would, for instance, have to be taken into account in a theology of faith. The thing which interests him about faith is its assumedly intuitive *form* in sensation; and what interests him concerning the object of faith is its assumedly tangible and demonstrable *effect* in the state of mind already prevailing in the believing subject. 'Rebirth and faith are the principle, the true energizing force, the vital spark of a new creature for a new heavenly existence.'[1] And thus dogmatics are for him 'a system of the most sublime truths for the human race, relating to its spiritual and eternal blessedness . . . the most beautiful, significant and true philosophy'.[2]

Once this point has been reached, however, then the referring back to reason, the anamnesis, the appeal to the pre-known or to philosophy, has in actual fact become inevitable. At this point theology yet again expressly appears in the garb of a philosophy, at which its claim that it is the most beautiful, significant and true philosophy is clearly at the outset one very debatable assertion among others. On such a footing theology will not be able on principle to reject and deplore criticism from a philosophy which has itself become critical. The dispute of the faculties cannot by any means be decided by mere assertions. And so theology abandons, together with its peculiar duty towards its special object, a duty which could perhaps be the secret of a legitimate constituting of this discipline, also the peculiar dignity which might

---

[1] *Letters concerning the Study of Theology*, Su., 10, 355.   [2] Ibid., 10, 279.

perhaps accrue to it if it honestly sought to be a science of this object.

Thus the honour Herder won for theology seems from the outset to be at best an ambiguous one, and beset by perils. His theological point of departure is in itself, as a counter-blast to Kant's pure rationalism and the rationalism of the eighteenth century in general, understandable, and historically necessary. To be sure, Kant too had not been able to offer a true solution. But the counter-blast was set afoot in a dimension in which it was bound to be exposed to a possibly lethal counter-blast from the other side, in a sphere where pure rationalism was simply master and would in all probability again and again achieve the mastery. Whoever speaks of humanity, experience, history—and ultimately Herder and the scores of theologians after him who were supposed to be vanquishing Kant did not speak of anything else— does not, it is true, only speak of 'understanding'. But he too speaks of 'reason', and he who says reason must be prepared to give an account of himself before self-criticizing reason. Ultimately and at the deepest level, therefore, will anything remain for him but a retreat to the religion of reason, which Kant had worked out neatly enough in all conscience? A retreat upon which he would after all not be able to escape the temptations and dangers which outcast understanding will set in his path!

And then we must still ask whether it is not more clearly apparent from the standpoint of this self-critical reason (as the authoritative position in all circumstances primary to experience and history) in what a true counter-blast to pure rationalism, one that would destroy the sphere in which it held undisputed sway, would consist. The question arises whether Kant did not understand better than Herder what theology, in pure contrast to pure rationalism at all events, might be. I have said that Kant understood what the idea of a Church was, a knowledge which enabled him to understand what theology might be in certain circumstances in which he himself, admittedly, had no desire to be placed. And I further dare to say that Kant understood what grace was, in the sense of the Church of the Reformation. Without making use of this understanding! He was purely a philosopher and his philosophy is not in the least dressed in the garb of theology. But all the same, Kant would not at all events have let pass the attempt to dismiss the Christology of the Early Church as a Greek monks' illusion. How different things would be if it could be said of Herder, the inaugurator of typical nineteenth-century theology before its inauguration by Schleiermacher, that he too understood what Church and grace

were! But this can be said of Herder only with the greatest of reserva-
tions, in spite of every recognition of the great significance of what he
set out to do. And if in theology it should perhaps be above all a
matter of this understanding—it is not for us to decide upon this here—
then the fiery dawn of a new age which it was many people's desire to
see in Herder may after all have been perhaps only the transient glow
of a Bengal light.

VI

NOVALIS

I. ROMANTICISM was not the most profound, the most radical or the most mature form of the great intellectual movement which fulfilled and surpassed the Enlightenment and the eighteenth century generally, and established the typical way of thinking of the nineteenth century. Not the most profound: this was in all likelihood the philosophy of Kant. Not the most radical, which we shall come to discover in Hegel. Not the most mature, which we should have to recognize in the wisdom of life of the one and only Goethe. But of all these forms of that great intellectual movement Romanticism probably expressed this movement in its most characteristic and representative form; that in which the general trend was most clearly apparent. Nowhere, probably, were the final aims of the Enlightenment expressed in a form so plastic as to tend almost to caricature, as in this most angry and most thoroughgoing of all the protests against it. And nowhere was the secret of the man of the dawning nineteenth century, of his strength and weakness, of his greatness and of his faults expressed in so plastic a form as to be almost a caricature, as in this very part-manifestation of the great eruption which was establishing the new basis, this manifestion which, after flaring up briefly, was itself in its turn dispatched and extinguished. It was dispatched and extinguished with even greater fury and derision than that with which Romanticism itself had once imagined it could dispatch and extinguish the Enlightenment.

There is a French *bon mot*, which says, scratch the Russian, and you rouse the Tartar. It could equally be said of 'modern man' that you have only to scratch him to discover the Romantic. 'Modern man', and not present-day man! What manner of men are *we*? The question is one which, for the present, cannot be answered historically. I refer to the 'modern man' who once, in a manner typical of the apogee of the nineteenth century, thus consciously and euphorically described himself, who was at his height approximately between the years 1870 and 1914, and who served in theology as a point of orientation already for Ritschl and still for Troeltsch. He was something of a positivist

philosopher, this modern man, a coldly calculating technician, a
Manchester capitalist and Marxist socialist, an exact natural scientist,
relativist historian and impressionist artist—and in all these things he
was apparently worlds removed from the world of Romanticism.
But we must not allow ourselves to be led astray by the changed *décor*.
The melancholy sound of the post-horn and the ruined castle by moon-
light, the fairy princess, the blue flower and the fountains dreamily
playing in the splendour of the summer night—these are the things
which—not without cause—first spring to our minds at mention of the
word Romanticism. They are however nothing more than the stage-
properties of Romanticism as it first was, which to comprehend does
not mean that we have understood the true game that was played here
for all that they are certainly part of the game in their way. It was
possible to go on playing it with a completely different set of properties
and that is what happened. To illustrate what I mean I shall just
mention the names of five men who lived at the height of the age of this
modern man: Richard Wagner, Friedrich Nietzsche, Ernst Haeckel,
Leo Tolstoy, Friedrich Naumann—all five of them certainly modern
men to the core, and representative of their time. But at the same time
each of them was in his way a solitary, a modern man in a somehow
original way, and just because of this all the more representative of the
hidden striving of his age, which was apparently so far removed from
Romanticism. None of the five of them can truly be understood in
terms of Kant, or Hegel, or Goethe; but, if they are to be understood
at all as stemming from this turning-point in time, then only in terms
of Romanticism. And the golden base of Romanticism, which with
them shines forth from beneath various washes of another colour,
is not only their secret. There can surely be little doubt that ultimately
and finally, when its spirit matured, the unromantic century was after
all bound to have its Eugen Diederich Publishing House and its youth
movement, and that the last German emperor, if all our understanding
of him is not an illusion, was bound, like his great-uncle Frederick
William IV, to be 'a Romantic upon the throne of the Caesars'.
It is precisely for this reason that we cannot pass over Romanticism in
our attempt to discover the elements of the general intellectual structure
of the century.

What has just been said applies however to nineteenth-century
theology as well. It left Romanticism behind, but could not escape it.
Somehow in the last resort it is also Romantic theology. In so far as
it was ruled and determined by Schleiermacher there is no need to
prove this preliminary point. And it is not for nothing that the entire

era ends where it had begun: with a renaissance of Schleiermacher. I
spoke just now of the modern man of the turn of the century, as he
provided a point of orientation already for Ritschl and still for
Troeltsch. It should, however, be said that Troeltsch understood this
modern man considerably better than Ritschl. Ritschl took him far
too seriously as a positivist, etc. This was rather like making the blue
flower and the post-horn wholly characteristic of the man living
around 1800. This was one of the reasons that the school of Ritschl
was unable to survive any longer than it did. It is well worth noting
how Ritschl's most reliable pupil, W. Herrmann, was already unable
to get on without leaning heavily upon none other than the young,
Romantic Schleiermacher. The victorious element in the teaching of
Troeltsch, however, certainly rested last and not least upon the fact
that he took up Schleiermacher's programme once again and placed
a conception in the centre of his philosophy of religion, which was
basically the Romantic one. The decisive main stream of nineteenth-
century theology cannot therefore be explained in terms of Herder
alone.

What does stem from Herder in the newer theology is all that which
can be brought under the heading of psychologism and historicism,
its methodical point of departure in the correlation 'experience—
history'. G. Wobbermin, for instance, the inventor of the religious-
psychological circle, might easily be described as a very schoolmasterly
and extremely dull Herder. But if with Herder himself the departure
from this correlation was in the nature of a reaction, a counter-blow at
Kant's pure rationalism, in the theology following him, but not only
him, it rests upon the attempt at a more essential, profound and superior
understanding of this rationalism; it overcame it, or thought to have
overcome it, in passing through it. It sets out from the correlation
'experience—history', after previously setting out with Kant (but in a
way which was assumed to be, or actually was, more profound than
Kant's) from a synthesis which (assumedly or actually) surpassed,
transcended this correlation. It was probably this synthesis too which
Herder meant, when he spoke, as, for instance, in his work on the soul,
of the spirit. It was possibly also what he was getting at as the true
meaning of such outpourings as the *Hymn to the Creation*, for instance.
But Herder was too involved in the mere reaction to Kant to be able
to gain a clear sight of this Above and Beyond of experience and
history. He was too involved in it to be able to prevent himself, whenever he was speaking of the spirit or the soul and its likeness in God's
image, or of humanity, from sliding off into the psychological and

historical, or from falling back into the very *a priori* methods he was trying to combat. It was this which was bound to put him straightaway at a disadvantage not only with Kant; but also with those who, like Herder himself, were seeking to rise above the Kantian position. The deeper source of the newer theology which in its method is linked with Herder is, however, Romanticism. Thus regarding theology itself we have occasion to concern ourselves with Romanticism. We shall do so before approaching Schleiermacher, who was by no means only a Romantic, and whose Romanticism we must measure against Romanticism in its pure form in order to understand it.

I have taken Novalis (whose real name was Friedrich von Hardenberg) as my particular example just because he represents in a uniquely pure way the intentions and achievement of this entire group—and not because the theological aspect is particularly clear in his work. He did not, like Rousseau, write a *Vicar of Savoy*, nor, like Lessing, theological polemics or a *Nathan*; nor, like Kant, did he write a philosophy of religion. And he did not, like Herder, engage in biblical studies. His direct utterances concerning the problem of religion are few, and, outwardly at least, they carry no particular weight beside his much more emphatic and detailed remarks relating to every other conceivable 'province' of human intellectual life, as the favourite expression then was. Even his famous *Sacred Songs* would not in themselves be sufficient to secure him a place in a history of theology. But he does belong there because he, and really he alone, of all his fellows, succeeded in exposing the meaning of Romanticism with a certain unequivocality and finality, and with a clarity that demands judgment. It is possible to master Friedrich Schlegel, Tieck, Brentano and Eichendorff, but with Novalis it is not so easy. He proclaimed the concern of Romanticism in a form in which it must at least be heard. We cannot dispose of Romanticism without disposing of Novalis.

But that is precisely what has not happened up to now. It has been rightly said of him, that he alone of all the Romantics has assured for himself, through all the numerous changes of outlook of the nineteenth century, 'a singularly certain *succès d'estime*'.[1] We might well add that leaving Schleiermacher out for the moment, Novalis is the only Romantic whose work goes on seeming relevant and new. He is the poet whom we cannot silence by any historical relativizing, any more than we can silence Kant—who was so different—in that way. And it must further be said that we shall perhaps only be able to speak of a true Neo-romanticism for all time when Romanticism is once again

[1] Bölsche, *Novalis' Ausgew. Werke* (Novalis' Selected Works) Leipzig, 1903, p. viii.

seriously taken up in the sense that Novalis understood it and in his spirit.

The peculiar significance of Novalis is closely bound up with the fact that he can scarcely be said to have given the world a true life-work. Those of his works we do possess are a little book of poems, *The Apprentices of Sais*, a story of natural philosophy, a sketch in the philosophy of history entitled *Christendom or Europe*, the unrevised first part of a biographical novel, *Heinrich von Ofterdingen*, planned on a grand scale in the style of Wilhelm Meister, some attempts at a continuation of this work and finally a chaotic collection of 'Fragments',[1] i.e. isolated thoughts set down at varying length for later use.

Fundamentally all these works are fragments. Novalis died of consumption in 1801 at the age of twenty-nine. The lament for the work which by his premature death he was forced to owe his time and all time is understandable. But it is at least open to question whether he has not precisely thereby, in this beginning, which remained a beginning—like Wackenroder, his older contemporary and sharer of the same fate—said everything he had to say in a way truer and more essential than that in which he would have said it in a long life, which would have brought him beyond this beginning. Another reason why he is the pure type of the Romantic is that the Romantic principle hardly achieved in him any length or breadth but remained almost a mathematical point. Perhaps Romanticism is something which should not achieve length and breadth, but which should flare up in this meteoric way if it is to bring forth its concern in a manner impressive and worthy of credence. Would it be possible for a Romanticism which acquired length and breadth to end anywhere but in the psychologism and historicism of Herder, or back again in the pure rationalism of Kant?

Thus it might be that the old saying that those whom the gods love die young has in more than one sense been vindicated here. I am reminded of a scarcely more recent parallel in the history of theology; that provided by the Württemberg revivalist preacher, Ludwig Hofacker, who also, at thirty, at the most fruitful moment of his life, and when he had but given promise of his best, was snatched away as by the scythe. Is it chance that his sermons are still read today—a thing we can very rarely say of sermons, and particularly of those of the past—and that for the most part their effect is topical and relevant! The revivalism too—which incidentally was certainly not unconnected with Romanticism—was ill-suited to the Consistorial Councillor-type

[1] Classified Collection edited by Ernst Kamnitzer, Dresden, 1929.

length and breadth it acquired in the figures of Hofacker's longer-lived colleagues in the middle years of the century. How completely different Schleiermacher's *Addresses on Religion* would seem to us if their author had not the good fortune to be able to carry out, in his further thirty-five years of life, the programme he announced in them—or should we say if he had not had the misfortune to have to carry it out! No wonder Schleiermacher's contemporaries and followers—among the contemporaries, Klaus Harms and among the followers, W. Herrmann, for instance—again and again tend, so to speak, to shut their eyes to the later, more mature Schleiermacher, and to cling in nostalgic delight to the younger figure in its Romantic purity, which Schleiermacher himself, continuing in his life and influence, simply could not preserve. Perhaps this message was such that it could only sound strong and worthy of belief if it was proclaimed for a short time and abruptly terminated.

The second feature about Novalis, which he reveals in a manner both relevant to the moment and decisive for an understanding of the time which came after him, is the uniquely exact way in which he stands between the ages and between the great problems of the two ages. W. Bölsche wrote of him: 'Of all the figures of the great epoch of Goethe, he is the one who most plainly stands upon the border between the eighteenth and the nineteenth centuries. He is bathed simultaneously in the light of the setting and of the rising sun. He stands in this magic dual splendour as if steeped in an artificial glow. . . . He is an immeasurably concentrated figure, crowned and sometimes also a little bowed by the richness of the hour.'[1] But not only the eighteenth and nineteenth centuries are finely divided in him. Again and again we find ourselves compelled to ask, within the problem-complex of the old and the new age which moves him: Is it philosophy or is it art which is really his true sphere? And if it is both, if his particular problem is in fact the merging of the one with the other, is this philosophical art or artistic philosophy really directed towards nature or towards history? And if once again the answer should be that he is concerned with an attempt at a synthesis, is the personal expression of this synthesis love in the sense of the Platonic *eros*, or *agape* in the sense of the Christianity of Augustine and Roman Catholicism, the direct love for the distant object or the love emanating from this distant object being answered by love and loved again and therefore religion? And if yet again it should be a question of a synthesis, then will the word 'poesy', with which Novalis is in the habit of

[1] Bölsche, V.

defining the creative centre and unity of all these antitheses, remain comprehensively and decisively valid here also? Will it be Mary or will it be Christ—Novalis sang the praise of both of them—who will keep the central position? It is possible to decide all these questions either way with equal degrees of probability. It is just the way these questions remain open which is typical of Novalis, and of him alone in this fashion, and which makes him in particular into the pure type of the Romantic. Pure Romanticism is truly the border: between the eighteenth and nineteenth centuries as it is the border between philosophy and art, between nature and history, and between love and religion. Their border? Romanticism imagines it to be their unity. But strangely enough it is only in actually revealing their borders that it can actually make it plain that it is their unity which it has in mind. It is pure Romanticism only in so far as it draws up its programme, and not by carrying it out. It is surely no mere chance that the life-work of the last great Romantic in theology, Ernst Troeltsch, consisted chiefly in the proclamation and ever-renewed proclamation of programmes. Pure Romanticism must not wish to extend itself in such a way as to become a science or action, or—the science and action of which it is capable will signify its disloyalty to itself. Romanticism is pure as yearning, and only as yearning. That is why Novalis is a pure Romantic. That is why we can scarcely refute and dispose of him. And that is why he is scarcely to be imitated. That is why through him Romanticism became something which was perhaps unassailable, but which is perhaps also never to be recalled. Just in this way it became a word which continues to speak to us in an incomprehensibly real and relevant way. It has spoken also, and spoken in particular, to the theology of the new age. How could it have been otherwise? Possibilities seemed to offer themselves here to theology particularly, which held promise of making fruitful for the first time Herder's somewhat tumultuously inaugurated attempt to come to terms with Kant. Here there was something more than Herder. From this point it was for the first time possible to free Herder from the *cul-de-sac* in which he had landed himself. Only this was Schleiermacher's point of departure.

II. We shall in the first place consider the world of Novalis's thought, irrespective of its theological content. The form in which we find it in his literary remains and which in its incompleteness is its final and perhaps its most perfect form, is like a field of early corn in the spring: open to the view and yet with much that remains hidden from sight. This is also true because in its rather unfixed state of early development it delights, but can also confuse those who would know it at every step in its naturalness, in the apparent secret of a creative life which is reflected and represented there. And the way in which it does this is rare in what usually confronts us as mere literary reality, and unique even within the writings of the Romantics, of which we could generally say this. For the desire to proclaim the miracle of creative life, not without expressing openly the underlying thought that this is identical with the secret of the Creator, is something essential to all the Romantic movement. This intention also leaves its mark upon the language of Romanticism and its mode of presentation. The course of Schleiermacher's thought and his systematic method also has something of the life of a great organism, of a gigantic tropical climbing-plant, for instance, and this is not the least of the qualities which make for its recurring beauty and power of attraction. The novels of Eichendorff, too, seem to breathe—the fairy tales which the Romantics loved so much seem to bud and blossom before our eyes. What is uniquely moving in Novalis is the state of early development, of first germination, in which all his thoughts are to be found and in which they speak all the more eloquently of the creative power which is indeed their true object. We find here no world-tree, with its roots, trunk and spreading branches; here there is truly only a blue flower—which, to be true, is in the process (but only in the process!) of developing into a world-tree,[1] a pretentious lack of pretentiousness, against which we can say everything and nothing, which we should perhaps only look upon, and which perhaps, for all our doubts, we must simply like in order to understand it. I venture to speak in these unusual terms because we may be concerned here with the very heart of nineteenth-century theology, because it is perhaps just in Novalis that the question of the understanding of the entire age, and of the entire age of the Church, with which we are here concerned, is posed with an urgency which compels us to final decisions.

It is, I think, impossible to give an account of the world of Novalis's thought; only Novalis himself could do it if he returned among us. We can only make an attempt at a general survey, without claiming to present everything there is to be seen, much less interpret it all. We shall do this by attempting to see some of the systems of co-ordinates which, all at different levels, seem to weave a criss-cross pattern in Novalis's thought. I have already mentioned the antithetic unities which seem to me to be the most significant in that respect: art and philosophy, nature and history, love and religion. We shall finally

[1] Bölsche, IV.

come to speak of a last antithesis, which raises the problem as to whether it is likewise to be understood as an antithetic unity, or as a disjunctive antithesis, as an either—or: I should like to describe this last one as the Mary-Christ antithesis.

The first three antitheses are antithetic unities because each of them has an exact and therefore neutral and therefore superior centre. This neutral centre is common to all of them: the three systems of co-ordinates intersect, therefore, in such a manner that their points of intersection coincide. Or if instead of conceiving each of them as consisting of two straight lines intersecting at right-angles, we imagine each of them as the two end-points of a straight line, then in this case these straight lines are to be understood as diameters of a circle, which as such can only intersect at one point.

We would be completely mistaken if we thought that this mathematical description of the teaching of the blue flower is one ill-suited to it and contrary to its character. No description could in fact suit it better. It is precisely in its affinity with the spirit of mathematics that the spirit of the blue flower is no stranger on the threshold of the century of the exact sciences. Pure Romanticism regards itself as something of the strictest objectivity: 'The Romantic studies life as the painter, the musician and the engineer study colour, sound and power. It is a careful study of life which is the making of the Romantic.'[1] And it is precisely mathematics which is completely in keeping with this objectivity and care: 'A necessary postulate to the conception of mathematics is its complete applicability . . . its basis is the intimate connexion, the sympathy of the universe . . . its relationships are world relationships . . . true mathematics is the true element of the magician . . . in music it appears formally as revelation, as creative idealism . . . all enjoyment is musical and therefore mathematical . . . the true mathematician is an enthusiast *per se*; without enthusiasm there is no mathematics. The life of the gods is mathematics. All ambassadors of the gods must be mathematicians. Pure mathematics is religion. Mathematics can be arrived at only through a theophany. Mathematicians are the only happy people . . . anyone who does not pick up a book of mathematics with reverence and read it as if it were a divine book will not understand it.'[2] 'Every true system must be similar in form to the numerical system—the qualitative system or the denominator system too.'[3]

Let us return to the subject in hand. It should be clear that the fact that this neutral superior centre of these antitheses is a common one

[1] *Fragments*, Kamnitzer, 1,942.   [2] Ibid., 940.   [3] Ibid., 107.

will give rise to an abundance of mutual relationships, and indeed of new antithetic unities between the antitheses themselves too, so that, strictly speaking, with each single antithesis it is not only its two poles and its centre which we have to reckon, but because this centre is also the centre of all the others, we have at once indirectly to take all the others into account.

1. *Poesy.* Novalis sometimes, in accord with Fichte, defined this centre as the ego, which is confronted by the non-ego, the universe, consisting in the unity of every object of sense, but in such a manner that the positing of the ego is to be understood as a positing of the universe, and the positing of the universe as a positing of the ego.[1] 'It makes no difference whether I posit the universe in myself or myself in the universe.'[2] 'It is all one whether we suit ourselves to things or suit things to ourselves.'[3] That is why Novalis can say: 'One succeeded—he lifted the veil of the goddess at Sais—But what did he see? He saw— wonder of wonders—himself',[4] as well as, in the fairy tale of Hyacinth and Rosebud in the *Apprentices of Sais* having the youth who is seeking the same 'mother of things', find not himself this time but his Rosebud, abandoned and yet loving and beloved.[5] Novalis, therefore, advancing beyond Fichte, defined this centre better and more peculiarly as the life which consists precisely in its defiance of the attempt to comprehend it, because it has its being beyond the ego and non-ego, being and non-being, composed of synthesis, thesis and antithesis and yet nothing of all three.[6] Life is 'the stuff that truly and absolutely binds everything together'.[7]

At the point where he defines the centre as poesy Novalis speaks in terms which are completely characteristic of him and quite original. 'Poesy is that which is truly and absolutely actual. That is the core of my philosophy. The more poetic a thing is the truer it is.'[8] Novalis understood the concept of poesy primarily in its original sense of τοίησις, work, creation. 'The poetic philosopher is *en état de créateur absolu*.'[9] He posits subject, predicate and copula simultaneously.[10] 'Transcendental poetics treats of the spirit before it becomes spirit.'[11] 'The poet is *a priori* the inventor of symptoms.'[12] 'The true poet is omniscient, he is a real world in miniature.'[13] It is precisely for this reason that poetry is admittedly ultimately 'something completely personal and therefore indescribable and indefinable. Anyone who does not immediately know and feel what poesy is can never have any

---

[1] *Frag.*, 157.   [2] Ibid., 429.   [3] Ibid., 439.   [4] Bölsche, III, 95.
[5] Ibid., I, 148f.   [6] *Frag.*, 649.   [7] Ibid., 506.   [8] Ibid., 1,871.
[9] Ibid., 53.   [10] Ibid., 54.   [11] Ibid., 1,890.   [12] Ibid., 1,908.   [13] Ibid., 1,909.

conception of it instilled into him.'[1] The poet, the true poet, he of genius, and no other, is the true man: 'It is the poets, those rare nomadic men, who pass from time to time through our dwelling-places and everywhere renew the old and venerable service of mankind and of its first gods, of the stars, spring, love, happiness, fertility, health and gladness; they who are in this life already the possessors of a heavenly peace and not driven hither and thither by any foolish desires, only breathe in the scent of earthly fruits without consuming them and thus becoming bound irrevocably to the underworld. They are free visitors, whose golden foot steps gently and whose presence causes all men to spread involuntary wings. A poet, like a good king, is to be discerned by the joy and clarity of his countenance, and he alone it is who rightly bears the name of a sage.'[2]

Thus poetry by no means coincides with art and for this reason it would not be fitting in discussing Novalis to speak of 'aestheticism' in the customary meaning of the word. Poetry, according to Novalis, is certainly also art, but is at the same time distinct in principle from all other art, as the art of expression by means of the word. It distinguishes itself from painting on its right and music on its left by the fact that what it does is in no way produced with tools and hands. 'The eye and the ear perceive nothing of it . . . it is all achieved inwardly . . . through words the poet presents us with an unknown splendid world for our perception. Past and future times, countless human figures, wonderful regions and the strangest occasions rise up in us as if from deep caverns and tear us away from the known present. We hear unfamiliar words and are yet aware of what they should mean. The utterances of the poet exercise a magic power; the familiar words, too, appear in delightful assonance and bemuse the enchanted hearer.'[3] This, according to Novalis, is in fact, the essence of Romantic poetry: its way of 'pleasantly surprising art, of making an object strange, and yet familiar and attractive . . .'.[4] But this is something only poetry can do of all the arts, or which all other arts can do only in so far as they, too, are poetic. Making the stange familiar by means of making the familiar strange; this is nothing else but the rhythm of ego and non-ego, the rhythm of life itself, in which Novalis imagines he has discovered the essential nature of poesy, and of the creative process in general.

That is why poetry is the secret not only of this or that person, but the secret of man in general. 'It is a very bad thing, Klingsohr said, that poesy has a particular name and that poets form their own

---

[1] *Frag.*, 1,887.   [2] *Heinrich v. Ofterdingen*, Bölsche, II, 79.
[3] Ibid., Bölsche, II, 24f.   [4] *Frag.*, 1,941.

profession. There is nothing at all special about it. It is the way of acting peculiar to the human mind. Does not every man give birth to poetry and aspiration at every instant?'[1] Transcendental poesy comprises 'all transcendental functions and in fact contains the transcendental altogether. The transcendental poet is transcendental man altogether.'[2]

To summarize, the concept of the ego or of life or, significantly, poesy, and, therefore, the concept of the neutral superior centre is, with Novalis, to be defined as the endless becoming outward of endless inwardness, or also as the endless becoming inward of endless outwardness, in the way that these processes both can and should and do in fact take place in the human act of living. It is a principle which is not only systematic, which does not only organize, but which is a creative principle that we have thereby come to know. All other principles are applications of this one creative principle, and are identical with it in substance. That is why it and it alone can stand neutral and superior as the centre of all of them. Novalis stated his notion of this principle in a manner entirely and uncannily characteristic of him, in describing it finally also as a magic principle, and the poet, and thus man in general, as a magician.[3] We shall have to return to the question this raises in our third section.

2. *Art.* There can be no mistaking the particular affinity of this poetic or magic principle with art. We have already heard that the two do not simply coincide. But the poet in whom Novalis perceives the true man is yet, primarily at any rate, also the poet in the narrower sense of the word, one identifying him also as one of various kinds of artist. 'Art is the development of our effectiveness.'[4] 'The artist stands upon the man as the statue upon its pedestal.'[5] And on the other hand: 'The poet uses things and words like the keys of a musical instrument.'[6] 'The beautiful is the visible $\kappa\alpha\tau$' $\dot{\epsilon}\xi o\chi\acute{\eta}\nu$.'[7] 'Beauty is objective goodness.'[8] 'In every genuine art a spirit is realized—produced from within —the world of the spirits.'[9] And for this reason there also exists an artistic realism. In his doctrine of art especially, Novalis is very far from wishing to throw open the flood-gates of an unrestrained immediacy. The poet cannot be cool and composed enough. 'A confused babble results if a tearing storm rages in the breast and the attention is dissolved in a quivering abandonment of thought . . . the true state of mind is like the light, just as calm and sensitive, just as elastic and penetrable, just as powerful and imperceptibly effective as this precious element, which distributes itself upon every object in fine gradations

---

[1] *Heinrich v. Ofterdingen*, Bölsche, II, 97.   [2] *Frag.*, 1,875.   [3] Ibid., 669.   [4] Ibid., 1,771.
[5] Ibid., 1,778.   [6] Ibid., 1,904.   [7] Ibid., 1,788.   [8] Ibid., 1,792.   [9] Ibid., 1,793.

of intensity and allows them to appear each one in delightful diversity. The poet is pure steel, just as sensitive as a fragile thread of glass and hard as the unpliant 'pebble'. . . . 'Poesy requires above all to be practised . . . as a strict art. As mere enjoyment it ceases to be poesy. A poet must not idly wander about all day and go hunting after images and states of feeling. That is the wrong way entirely. A pure and open state of mind, skill in reflection and observation, and an adroitness in transforming all his abilities into an activity which in its turn enlivens the mind, and keeping them there; such are the demands of our art.'[1] It is only upon this condition that the identification of life with art, art with poesy, is valid. With this we have already cast a glance from art at the thing which makes it possible and orders it, the power of thought: without philosophy there can be no perfect poetry.

3. *Philosophy.* 'The division between the poet and the thinker is only an apparent one and is harmful to both. It is a sign of disease and a diseased constitution.'[2] Philosophy is only feeling when it is dreaming.[3] This statement is not meant in any derogatory sense. Dreaming, for the pure Romantic, is something to be treated in all earnestness. Philosophy is in its original form feeling. It treats of an object which cannot be learned, of no object, that is to say. That sets it apart from all the other sciences, which have as their objects things which can be learned. Philosophy is the reflected feeling, based on the self-consciousness of the ego, or,[4] seen objectively, it is the proving of things by relating them with the self-consciousness of the ego, in which man perceives the absolute basis for his own existence.[5] All philosophy begins at the point where the philosopher philosophizes himself, i.e. at once consumes and renews himself.[6] In this we further perceive the connexion between philosophy and poesy. 'In its truest sense philosophy is a caress, an attestation of the most fervent love of reflection, of the absolute joy in wisdom.'[7] 'Philosophy is actually nostalgia, an urge to be at home everywhere.'[8] It coincides, in the 'act of overleaping itself', with the original point, with the genesis of life.[9] 'It also, like the activity of genius in general, is not susceptible of description.'[10] And: 'There is no philosophy *in concreto*, because philosophy is intelligence itself.'[11] And it is precisely because philosophy in its perfect form is nothing else but poesy that it must now come together with art in the narrower sense, must conceive of itself as art, the art of 'producing all our ideas in accordance with an absolute artistic idea and of evolving

---

[1] *Heinrich v. Ofterdingen*, Bölsche, II, 92f.   [2] *Frag.*, 1,907.
[3] *Appr. of Sais*, Bölsche, I, 152.   [4] *Frag.*, 64.   [5] Ibid., 65.
[6] Ibid., 95.   [7] Ibid., 69.   [8] Ibid., 70.   [9] Ibid., 95.
[10] Ibid., 73.   [11] Ibid., 77.

by way of thinking a world-system *a priori* from the depths of our spirit, of using the organ of thought actively for the representation of a world to be comprehended only in thought'.[1] 'The poet closes the procession just as he opened it. If the task of the philosopher is only to order everything and put it in its place, the poet loosens every bond. . . . Poesy is the key to philosophy.'[2] Thus we are directed back from the second pole of this antithesis to the first one again.

4. *Nature*. Corresponding to the antithesis of art and philosophy on the ontological there is the antithesis of nature and history on the ontic plane. Nature is 'the quintessence of that which moves us'. It is 'that wonderful community into which our body introduces us and which we come to know according to the body's facilities and capacities'.[3] It is 'an Aeolian harp, it is a musical instrument whose sounds moreover are the keys to higher strings in ourselves'.[4] ' "Where is the man," cried the youth with sparkling eyes, "whose heart does not leap with delight when the inmost life of nature enters his mind in all its abundance, and when, at this, that mighty feeling, for which language has no other name but love and desire, expands within him, like a strong, all-releasing vapour, and he sinks trembling with sweet anguish into the dark, alluring womb of nature, his poor personality being consumed in the breaking waves of delight, and nothing remaining but a focal point in the immeasurable procreative power, a sucking whirlpool in the vast ocean." '[5] With Novalis, as his *Fragments* in particular show, such dithyrambs have as their background a true abundance of observations in natural science, drawn especially from the fields of biology, physics and chemistry, psychology and medicine. 'The essential qualities required of a true naturalist are a long and unrelenting association with the object of his study, free and ingenious observation, an attention to the slightest indications and tendencies, an inner poetic life, practised senses, and a simple and God-fearing mind.'[6] The most significant of these requirements is, however, once again, the 'inner poetic life'. 'The spirit of nature has appeared at its purest in poems. Upon reading or hearing true poems one feels an inner understanding of nature moving there, and hovers like nature's heavenly body, at once in it and over it. The naturalist and the poet, in that they speak a common language, have ever revealed themselves to be as one race and people.'[7]

It is precisely at this point, however, that one is tempted to see the

---

[1] *Frag.*, 1,793.   [2] Ibid., 1,875.   [3] *Appr. of Sais*, Bölsche, I, 154.
[4] *Frag.*, 498.   [5] *Appr. of Sais*, Bölsche, I, 160.   [6] Ibid., Bölsche, I, 144.
[7] Ibid., Bölsche, I, 141.

objectivity of that which is observed threatened, in spite of the realism which Novalis recommends here, too, by the stormy *eros* of the observing subject. And if this be in doubt then the balance of the rhythm of this entire system of thought is threatened also! There is a disturbing note in Novalis's proclamation: 'The secret path leads inwards. Eternity with its worlds, the past and the future, is within us, or nowhere.'[1] 'What need have we of laboriously journeying through the muddy world of visible things? For the purer world lies within us within this fountain-head. It is here that the real meaning of the great, variegated, confused spectacle is revealed; and if, full of these sights, we step into the realm of nature, everything there is familiar to us, and we have a sure knowledge of every form. We have no need of any long research; a light comparison, a few lines traced in the sand, are enough to ensure our understanding. Thus all things are like a great book to us, for which we have the key, and nothing takes us by surprise, because we know in advance the way the great clock-work runs.'[2] The study of nature seems to be dispensed with also, the instant it is laid down, when the following figure appears among the apprentices at Sais, who we are at first tempted to think are in an academy of the natural sciences: 'One of them was a child still, and no sooner was he there than he wanted him to take over the lessons. The child had big dark eyes with sky-blue depths, his skin glowed like a lily, and his curly hair was like wisps of cloud at the coming of evening. His voice pierced all our hearts. We would fain have given him our flowers, stones and feathers, everything. There was an infinite gravity in his smile and when he was there our spirits were strangely exalted. "One day he will come back again," said the teacher, "and dwell among us, and then there will be no more lessons." '[3]

We do not know whether Novalis would have continued further along this course, which was not without its dangers, or whether he might have more nearly approached the great maturity of Goethe's outlook upon nature. What is certainly intended, even in such striking passages, is, however, the proclamation of the referring back of the perception which is directed outwards to the principle of the centre. This is achieved by the proclamation of the necessary counter-pole to this world of nature, which presses in upon man in an overwhelming way. This counter-pole of nature coincides, however, in Novalis, with history. For it is not enough to be able to improvise upon nature, as upon a great musical instrument. It is only the man who understands the history of nature, its dimension of depth in time who understands

---

[1] *Frag.*, 593.   [2] *Appr. of Sais*, Bölsche, I, 146.   [3] Ibid., Bölsche, I, 138.

nature. History, however, means mind, as it is opposed to nature in the 'counter-image of humanity'. Nature would not be divine if it did not also have a history, did not also have a spirit. 'In order to comprehend nature one must allow nature to grow inwardly in its entire sequence . . . it is comprehensible only as the instrument and medium of the acquiescence of reasonable beings.'[1] Novalis seems after all to have had nothing else in mind but what Goethe said about the relationship between the inner and outer world in the contemplation of nature, however unguardedly and tempestuously he may have spoken of it.

5. *History.* It is now clear to us why Henrich von Ofterdingen, when journeying to fetch his bride, should have to meet nature and history one after the other in the shapes of a miner and a hermit. Nature and history are in very fact opposed to one another in an antithetic unity. In history, too, according to Novalis, in so far as it is now to be taken especially into account, man seeks and finds the ego in the non-ego, the familiar in the strange. It is characteristic of Novalis that with nature it is primarily a question of finding, and with history, of seeking the great $\times$, the $\times$ which is his subject the whole time. Once again there can be no mistaking the fact that the concept of a historical realism, which now truly seeks the familiar in the strange, is not unknown to Novalis. But far more important to him than an assessment of the significance of exact research into the details of history is here once again the polemic against its degeneration, against every study of history which is merely analytic, unphilosophic, unpoetic, and the canon that 'a student of history must also of necessity be a poet', and the assertion that there is more truth in the fanciful tales of the poets than in the learned chronicles.[2] A few verses from the *Hymns to the Night* might best show the pure Romantic's approach to history:

> What seek we in this world below
> With all our love and duty?
> The old is worthless, let it go!
> How shall the new bring beauty?
> O sad, forlorn and out of time
> Who warmly love the golden Prime.

> The golden Prime, when senses light
> In upward flames were glowing;
> When men the Father's hand and sight
> Felt, his own presence knowing;
> When high and simple thought was rife,
> And time showed forth the perfect life.

[1] *Appr. of Sais,* Bölsche, I, 157f.   [2] *Heinrich v. Ofterdingen,* Bölsche, II, 71.

The golden Prime, when blossomed full
The primal races flourished;
And children tried in death's pained school
The heavenly vision cherished,
And though life joyous accents spake
Yet many a heart for love would break.

The golden Prime, when glowing young
God came himself revealing,
In sweet love-life went among
And died young for their healing;
Nor drove he pain and grief away
That he might dearer with us stay.

Restless the golden Prime we see
In night's dark shade enveloped;
Nor stilled our burning thirst will be
By all in time developed,
But we to home must also go
To see that holy season's flow.

What still keeps back our late return?
The dear ones long are waiting;
Their graves shut in life's utmost bourne,
And all is sad and sating;
Nought's left for us to seek again,
The heart is worn, the world is vain.[1]

It becomes clear, in the last verse especially, how greatly, and once again how menacingly, for the equilibrium which seems to have been intended throughout this system of thought, poesy becomes master of this object, too: master to such a degree that the creative, all-too creative man finds himself driven more and more to the edge of an abyss of appalling loneliness. Novalis was capable of saying in the major key also what was said, in the verses just quoted, in the minor:

When signs and figures cease to be
For all created things the key;
When they who do but kiss and sing
Know more than sages' reckoning;
When life to freedom shall attain
And freedom in creation reign;
When light and shade, no longer single,
In genuine splendour intermingle,
And man in tales and poems sees
The world's eternal histories,
Then this corrupted state will flee
Before a secret word's decree.[2]

[1] *Hymns to the Night*, Bölsche, I, 30; for original, cf. Appendix, p. 407.
[2] Ibid., Bölsche, II, 143; for original, cf. Appendix, p. 408.

The same impression of an uncanny threat to creative man who is capable of achieving such a break-through, is conveyed also in the sole example of historical art Novalis has left to us, the essay *Christendom or Europe*, written in 1799. In it he draws a mighty circle from the boldly idealized, or perhaps imagined, picture of the peaceable and friendly single Church of the Middle Ages, through the Reformation, which declared a revolutionary government permanent, profanely identified the boundaries of the Church with those of the state, and introduced the highly alien secular science of philology into affairs of religion, on to the farthest point of the orbit, which in so far as it is the farthest point already heralds the return, the Enlightenment, with its hatred of the Church, the Bible, faith, enthusiasm and poesy, and finally back to the time just then coming, that of the resurrection, the conception of a new Messiah, in which one Brother in particular is described and lauded as the 'heart-beat of a new age', who has made for the Holy one, i.e. religion, 'a new veil', which 'clingingly betrays the divine mould of her limbs and yet veils her more chastely than any other'. Novalis awaits the revelation of this new age and with it the coming to life of Christianity, the bringing of awakenment and peace to Europe in every field, from the convocation of a 'venerable European council'. 'When?—and when most likely? That is not the question. Just be patient, the time will come, must come, the holy time of lasting peace, when the new Jerusalem shall be the capital city of the world; and until this day, be cheerful and courageous amid the dangers of the time, sharers of my faith; proclaim with word and deed the holy Gospel, and remain faithful unto death to the true eternal faith.'[1] Once again we see the pure Romantic standing in affecting isolation, and ask ourselves whether it might not be that his need is sprung from a tragic guilt; whether a view which has so largely renounced the ability to see could in fact end anywhere but in this convulsive hope which simply does not speak in tones worthy of credence. And we ask ourselves once again whether, if he had lived longer, Novalis would have proceeded further along these lines, or whether from this point he would have found his way forward or back to an ultimate historical wisdom. Suffice it to say that here the problem of history is at all events passionately felt to be a problem, and poesy, man's creative inward world, has shown itself to be the key to this book of mysteries as well.

6. *Love*. What art and philosophy are on the ontological plane, and nature and history on the ontic one, love and religion are on the personal or ethical plane. It becomes even more difficult than before to

[1] Bölsche, I, 135.

distinguish the antitheses to some extent, both among themselves, and from the creative centre.

It is part of the quality of Novalis as a phenomenon that his utterances concerning love in the most obvious sense have not the breadth which one might perhaps expect. Novalis was of little experience in the sphere of sexual love. His engagement to Sophie von Kühn only really acquired significance for his work by her early death. And his second engagement to Julie von Charpentier never became greatly significant either in his life or in his writings. But the intensity of the few things he said upon this cardinal theme of all poetry speaks all the more plainly for that. According to Novalis sexual love is the decisive event in human life because it is the revealed secret of reciprocal effect. Love is 'a mysterious flowing together of our most secret and most peculiar being'.[1] It is a question in life, in all art and philosophy, in nature and history, of ego and non-ego. Novalis, however, advancing beyond Fichte, wished to have the non-ego understood as Thou. It is, he finds, precisely love which is lacking in Fichte. Love understands the non-ego as Thou in understanding it as beloved and loving Thou and consequently as the 'centre-point of a paradise',[2] as the 'object of all objects';[3] consequently the propositions are valid that 'love is the most highly actual thing, the primal basis',[4] 'the final goal of world history, the Amen of the universe'.[5] 'I do not know what love is, but one thing I can tell you; I feel as if I were only now beginning to live.—My Matilda, for the first time I sense what it means to be immortal.—How deeply you shame me! For it is only through you that I am what I am. Without you I should be nothing. What is a spirit without a heaven, and you are the heaven which contains me and bears me up.—I can conceive nothing of eternity, but should think that must be eternity which I feel when I think of you.—Yes Matilda, we are immortal because we love each other.' Thus we hear the lovers speaking in *Heinrich von Ofterdingen*.[6] But what is decisive in this representation of love is not, after all, the way the lovers find each other for themselves, but the way in which, simultaneously looking at and beyond each other, they each discover in the object of their gaze the new secret world of poesy.

> A darkling pathway love did tread,
> Seen by the moon alone,
> The shadows realm, unfolded wide,
> Fantastically shone.

---

[1] *Heinrich v. Ofterdingen*, Bölsche, II, 100. [2] *Frag.*, 1,257. [3] Ibid., 1,260.
[4] Ibid., 1,677. [5] Ibid., 1,745. [6] Bölsche, II, 98.

> An azure mist with golden edge
> Around her hung in play
> And eager Fancy bore her fast
> Oe'r stream and land away.
>
> Her full and teeming breast rose up
> In wondrous spirit-flow;
> A presagement of future bliss
> Bespoke the ardent glow.[1]

The *eros* which is the subject of this poem has become the divine *Eros*, or is at any rate no longer merely that *eros* which unites two human beings. For when this *eros* reaches its goal the human couple, the man and the woman, have vanished in the eternally-human, that the one has found in the other, the romance is lost in the purely Romantic quality, for whose sake alone the romance shall and may exist, and the truth then, is that

> Love's kingdom now is opened full
> And Fable 'gins to ply her wheel;
> To primal play each nature turns,
> To speak with tongues each spirit burns.
> And thus the world's great feeling looms,
> Moves everywhere, forever blooms.
> For each thing to all else must strive,
> One through the other grow and thrive;
> Each one is shadowed forth in all
> While it itself with them is blending,
> Eager to their deeps doth fall,
> Its own peculiar being mending,
> And myriad thoughts to life doth call.—
> The world's a dream, and dream the world.[2]

And therefore by virtue of this passage through the creative centre the counter-pole must always shine forth in love, too, in magical identity with love itself. That is why the lovers' conversation goes on as follows: 'O beloved, heaven has given you to me to worship. I pray to you, you are the saint who carries my wishes to the ear of God, through whom he reveals himself to me, through whom he declares to me the abundance of his love. What is religion but an unlimited understanding, an eternal union of loving hearts? Where two are gathered together he is there. It is through you that I have to draw breath forever; my breast will never cease to draw you in. You are the divine splendour, eternal life in most alluring guise . . . I swear to be yours eternally, Matilda, as truly as love, God's presence, is with us.'[3] That is

---

[1] *Heinrich v. Ofterdingen*, Bölsche, II, 107; for original, cf. Appendix, p. 408.
[2] Ibid., Bölsche, II, 126; for original, cf. Appendix, pp. 408-9.   [3] Ibid., II, 98f.

why Novalis himself was able to write in his diary: 'I feel religion for Sophie—not love. Absolute love, independent of the heart, based upon faith; such is religion.'[1]

7. *Religion.* 'Through absolute will love can be transformed into religion.'[2] We were already prepared for that sentence. Like art and philosophy, like the study of nature and history, and like love, religion for Novalis is without doubt in the first place a work of man, something to do with Romantic civilization. 'There is as yet no religion. First of all a lodge for training in true religion must be founded. Do you believe that religion exists? Religion must be made and put forward by the union of a number of people.'[3] The concept of God is achieved 'from the union of every capacity for feeling' . . . 'by means of a moral revelation, a moral miracle of centralization'.[4] For the finding of God an intermediate link is of course necessary. But this intermediate link must be chosen by ourselves, and this choice must be free. Regarding the intermediary as God himself is idolatry. The intermediary is the organ of the Godhead, its sensory manifestation, and Novalis declares himself a believer in Pantheism in the sense that he wishes to understand by it the idea that everything can be the organ of the Godhead, the intermediary, if I exalt it to that position. He rejects monotheism, which seeks to acknowledge only one such organ, but believes it possible to unite pantheism and monotheism by making the monotheist intermediary the intermediary of the intermediate world of pantheism, through it centring this world, as it were.[5] I believe that it is these very sentences which justify my tracing of the line, in the introduction, from Novalis via Schleiermacher to Troeltsch. That is why we now find that Novalis furthermore thinks that the Bible is still in process of growing.[6] 'The history of every man is intended to be a Bible; will be a Bible. . . . A Bible is the highest task of authorship.'[7] 'There is no religion that would not be Christianity.'[8] 'Our whole life is service of God.'[9] No wonder Novalis speaks of 'the infinite sadness of religion': 'If we are to love God he must be in need of succour.'[10] No wonder he has given us, one might well say, an absurd philosophy of the Lord's Supper, the existence of which could not be well enough noted by the present-day adherents of symbolism. Its climax is contained in the sentence: 'Thus daily we enjoy the genius of nature, and thus each meal becomes a commemorative one, a meal which changes our soul just as it sustains our body, a mysterious means of transfiguration and deification on

[1] *Frag.*, 47.   [2] Ibid., 1,746.   [3] Ibid., 1,676.   [4] Ibid., 1,679.
[5] Ibid., 1,688.   [6] Ibid., 1,707.   [7] Ibid., III, 202.   [8] Ibid., 1,714.
[9] Ibid., 1,733.   [10] Ibid., 1,747.

earth, of a quickening intercourse with that which lives absolutely.'[1]
Let us hear this philosophy in its entirety in the following hymn, taken
from the *Sacred Songs*:

> Few men know
> The mystery of love,
> Feeling contentless
> Appetite and thirst.
> The Holy Communion's
> Divine significance
> Is a riddle to our earthly senses;
> But he who once
> Drew breath of life
> From warm beloved lips,
> Whose heart in trembling
> Waves was melted
> By the sacred glow;
> Whose eye was opened
> To survey the endless
> Ground of heaven
> Shall eat of his body
> And drink of his blood
> Eternally.
> Who has guessed the high
> Purpose of earthly flesh?
> Who can say he
> Understands the blood?
> All will be body once,
> One flesh,
> The blessed pair
> In holy blood imbued.—
>   O that the world-sea
> Might now redden,
> The rock break forth
> In fragrant flesh!
> The sweet repast is never ended,
> Love never will be satisfied,
> Never enough his own
> Can it possess
> The loved one.
> Constantly more tender lips
> Transform the joy to something
> Even deeper, closer.
> A more intense desire
> Besets the soul,
> Hungrier, more thirsty
> Grows the heart:

[1] *Frag.*, 1,766.

And thus the joy of love endures
From eternity to eternity.
If they of sober mind
Did taste it, though but once,
They would forsake their all
And join us at the table set
For those who yearn,
The never-empty table.
They would see the endless
Fulness of love
And praise the fare
Of body and blood.[1]

If we are justified in speaking of a *hubris* of the Enlightenment, then it is here, in the magic religious teaching of pure Romanticism, that it broke out, and if perchance it was precisely the religious teaching of pure Romanticism which was to become the esoteric secret of nineteenth-century religious teaching, then it is just in this event that the uninterrupted connexion with eighteenth-century absolutism would stand revealed. It is surely clear, indeed Novalis says it himself, that his teaching of religion is the teaching of love, of heavenly love indeed, but of love nevertheless. For all this, however, we should not perhaps bear him ill-will, in the last assessment, not even in a survey such as this. For precisely at this point a final problem obtrudes, a heterogeneous line of thinking providing a point of vantage from which we can see how his teaching on religion, if it does not annul—that indeed we cannot say—at all events calls into question in significant fashion his entire teaching, and, further, poesy as the last word of this teaching, as it celebrates its ultimate triumph in this religious teaching particularly.

III. Somewhere among Novalis's mathematical fragments there is enclosed in brackets the little sentence, fraught with meaning: 'God is sometimes $1 \times \infty$, sometimes $\frac{1}{\infty}$, sometimes 0.'[2] In the 'sometimes $1 \times \infty$, sometimes $\frac{1}{\infty}$' is contained the whole ideology of pure Romanticism, while the added 'sometimes 0' contains its whole problem.

1 of course represents the given quality of the ego or of life, or the reality of poesy, in which the individual affirms, engages, possesses and enjoys himself. And the multiplying and dividing of this 1 by ∞ signifies the rhythm of transforming things inwards and outwards, of gathering and deployment, of things becoming familiar and strange, in which poesy, and with it the individual, and with him the ultimately real,

[1] Bölsche I, 73f.; for original, cf. Appendix, pp. 409-10. [2] *Frag.*, 909.

and with it God, is actual. Seen from the opposite pole, seen, that is, through the constant 1, which is to be thought of as transparent, art and philosophy, nature and history, love and religion can just as well signify $1 \times \infty$ as $\frac{1}{\infty}$; the creative subject can just as well give his life, himself, the highest, as the least value, without, however—for even infinity cannot arrive higher than the highest once the basis 1 is postulated—abandoning or even only endangering his substance and therefore himself, in scaling the value either up or down. The extreme is reached now on the one side and now on the other—philosophy seems to be merged and to disappear in art, art in philosophy, love in religion and religion in love. But it always only reaches the extreme, and care is taken that there is always a safe return from whichever extreme it may be. The creative subject plays and dances, on a high wire in peril of its life, to be true, but it dances well, and will for this reason not fall in spite of everything. It achieves infinite rejoicing and infinite sadness. But that is all it does achieve. And why should not this $\times$, which can sometimes be $1 \times \infty$ and sometimes $\frac{1}{\infty}$ be God? Its beauty surely cannot be in dispute. It is surely a God at least, this dancer, this *perpetuum mobile*, a God whom to serve as God might make a human life truly rich enough, and in view of whom it might seem folly to begin to look out for another. Who needs yet more if he has that, having himself as a premise of the whole?

What could Novalis have been thinking of when he added that God could also be 0? The sentence could of course be intended to convey the negation: 'and there is no other God'—beside this dancer, that is, whom we have in having ourselves. Does not Romanticism truly seem to wish to raise itself to a denial of this other God? And if this is not its wish, is not this denial necessarily contained in the natural sequence of Romanticism? But even if the sentence 'God is 0' were intended to mean that, would it not after all, in saying it, have set up the notion of this other God, even if merely as a notion which is denied, and have placed it beside the true notion of God, the notion of God the dancer? And it now seems after all that it is not this negation which the sentence is meant to signify. Novalis placed that third 'sometimes' beside the first two in too disinterested and unpolemic a fashion for that. He seems to have intended it in the same positive sense: God can also be 0, just as he is sometimes $1 \times \infty$, sometimes $\frac{1}{\infty}$.

Do we not look upon Novalis in this as we would look upon someone who, for the sake of perfection or caution or beauty, or for some other reason, has walled up a bomb in the cellar of his house, with a fuse running up to his writing desk? Let us hope there is no accident! The

concept o is a dangerous thing to play about with. For o is certainly
not merely a harmless little point which is passed through between
$+ 1$ and $- 1$, between $+ \infty$ or $- \infty$, or between $1 \times \infty$ and $\frac{1}{\infty}$.
Novalis himself defined o as the 'positive non-determinate'.[1] o stands
at least as an emphatic question, not beside but above and below the 1,
cutting through the whole series of numbers perpendicularly from
above; above and below the 1 as it is above and below the million and
the billion, and above infinity even. What would it avail the 1 if it
were to gain the whole world, of what avail to it would be infinity, of
what avail any addition, multiplication and scaling-up, and (assuming
that it might be even more beautiful the other way round) any sub-
traction, dividing and scaling down, if it were not the 1 but the o
which is the ultimate reality? And together with the million and the
billion, and with infinity, the 1 stands in the light or shade of the o.
o is the end or the beginning, not the 1 and not infinity either, whether
it be infinity scaled up or down. o, if we have interpreted the $1 \times \infty$
and $\frac{1}{\infty}$ correctly as a mathematical formulation of the Romantic
dialectic, is the equally exact mathematical formulation of the question
which opposes the premise of the Romantic dialectic, this idea that
we have ourselves. And now this o is to be thought equivalent to God,
or at all events a possible equivalent to God. What weight the o which
confronts the 1 acquires in face of this possibility!

What does the sentence 'God is sometimes $1 \times \infty$, sometimes $\frac{1}{\infty}$,
sometimes o' mean? The third part evidently means a μετάβασις
εἰς ἄλλο γένος, conceived in a manner which could not be more
energetic or more dangerous. It signifies the most radical splitting-up
of the notion 'God', who is the subject of the whole sentence. God is
then on the one hand the x that can be everything between the extreme
values $1 \times \infty$ and $\frac{1}{\infty}$, on the basis, be it well understood, that would
be God the dancer. And God is then, on the other hand, the y which
opposes this very basis 1 as an irremovable question and exclamation
mark: it stands in opposition and does not dance at all (as x can dance
between art and philosophy, between nature and history, between love
and religion), the y which stands there like the visitor of stone in *Don
Giovanni* or like the Christmas angel among the shepherds, as the *dies
irae* or as the day of resurrection, in short, as the end of time whatever
its equal may be. In standing there God either makes the whole dance
completely impossible: 'Thou hidest thy face, and they are troubled:
thou takest away their breath, they die, and return to their dust'—or
he makes it possible: 'Thou sendest forth thy spirit, they are created:

[1] *Frag.*, 910.

and thou renewest the face of the earth.' What is to become of x, if there is also a y? x and y cannot be God in the same sense, and if they are God at all then they are God as differently as heaven and earth are different, as something and nothing, as creator and creature are different. Only one of the two can be the true God, God in the ultimate, true sense. A decision must be made between these two, or perhaps as the secret of this decision a revelation, as upon Mount Carmel: 'and the God that answereth by fire, let him be God.' We are not in any position, either as regards Novalis or any other person, to be able to know or say whether this decision or revelation has or has not taken place in his life, will and thought. But there can be no mistaking that the question of the o and the question of the God y underlying it played a definite part in his life, will and thought. And there are more eloquent indications that this was so than this 'sometimes o', which he wrote down so smoothly and without perhaps giving the matter overmuch thought.

There was in fact a very universally human factor which played a very special part in the life of Novalis, and one which stands in close relationship to this 'sometimes o': namely, death. It was of special significance for him first because his own early demise was brought about by an incurable disease, so that for him death cast its shadow a long way before. Its second and chief significance for him was, however, the fact that in the spring of 1797—a remarkable repetition of Dante's experience with Beatrice—he lost his intended wife, Sophie von Kühn, whom he had met three years before, when she was thirteen years old, and fallen in love with immediately. We have already seen how, as was indeed inevitable in the light of all Novalis's set theories, his erotic relationship with this girl was irresistibly sublimated and transfigured, even while she was still alive, into a religious one. At her death, however, it became characteristic of this love, that being that of someone himself doomed, it should become a love for a dead person. It is safe to say that the poet's second engagement, biographically so curious, which took place scarcely a year afterwards, is the best proof of the incomparable way in which this first relationship was set apart in his mind—set apart in such a manner that a second relationship of a quite different order was possible and perhaps even necessary beside it. Let it be noted that every more or less completed work which we have from Novalis: the *Apprentices at Sais*, *Christendom or Europe*, the beginning of *Heinrich von Ofterdingen*, the *Hymns to the Night* and the *Sacred Songs*, was written in the years 1798-1801, and therefore stands already in the shadow or light of this experience, or of the insight which the poet owed to this experience. It cannot, therefore, he said that this insight, falling like a frost in a spring night, beat or destroyed another tendency; instead, just as it precedes in time all Novalis's work which has some pretence to a finished form, so it was the beginning of this work, in principle and in content. Upon it stands everything, the entire teaching of poesy, which, anticipating, we have studied on its own. It is the high wire upon which, with Novalis, the dance of the Romantic dialectic takes place. It was the thing that made Novalis what he was.

What is the nature of this insight? It can be described by a linking up with the previously quoted definition of the concept o: it is a question of the insight into the 'positive non-determinate' of the ego, of life, of poesy. The Romantic doctrine of poesy proceeds, to begin with, from the point of determination 1: in poesy man posits himself as the ultimate reality. It is upon this basis that he dares to establish the Romantic doctrine of poesy, upon this basis that he makes $1 \times \infty$ and $\frac{1}{\infty} =$ God. But the secret wisdom which Novalis acquired in 1797 says that beyond this point of determination 1 there takes place the positive non-determinate! Let it be noted: *positive* non-determinate; this border, this Beyond of the Romantic synthesis requires therefore to be construed not merely negatively, but positively. It seems as if a new field of at least equally serious problems were unfolding itself, above this synthesis and its problems. It seems! For it is precisely this which we do not know, and we must take good care not to feel tempted to decide positively (just as little as we can decide negatively) whether this new field of problems really disclosed itself to Novalis's thought; whether a shaking of the somnambulist feeling of security with which we see the pure Romantic going his purely Romantic way, took place, therefore, or not. It may also be that as a result of this insight he felt himself yet again, all the more confirmed and strengthened in this security. It is also possible that he succeeded in relating the antithesis of life and death which revealed itself to him beyond the antithesis of love and religion, to the Romantic synthesis. He may have succeeded in dissolving death 'in a play of harmonies', in 'pointing to it as an arabesque in the poetry of each individual life', as Bölsche has approvingly remarked.[1] It may also be that the figure before whom he apparently desires to clasp his hands, having come up against this positive frontier, was after all only that of Mary and not of Christ. We must content ourselves with establishing the fact that it could, none the less, have been otherwise: it might also be (and judging by the nature of

[1] Op. cit., p. xxxviii.

the matter there are no strong indications against this) that a perception
of a radically different kind had announced itself, that the Romantic
synthesis in the entire splendour of its self-given sense of security
yet ultimately bore within it a great, fundamental and inescapable
flaw, capable of shaking, challenging, and even of destroying it, and
that, therefore, it was after all Christ and not Mary whom Novalis
encountered at this frontier.

The facts of the matter are these: In the *Hymns to the Night* Novalis
speaks of his discovery that in the conflict between the Daylight, the
most beloved of all the miraculous manifestations of space by those
living and endowed with sense—and the Night, the sacred, ineffable,
mysterious Night, it is the latter which should be accorded pride of
place and greater honour.

> Have you too
> A human heart,
> Dark Night?
> What do you keep
> Beneath your cloak
> That moves my soul
> With unseen power?
> You do appear but fearful—
> The poppies in your
> Hand dispense
> A precious balm.
> In sweet delirium
> You spread the heavy magic of your wings.
> And give us dark
> Ineffable delight,
> Secret as yourself.
> Joys which give us
> Sense of heaven.
> How poor and childish
> Is the light
> With its gaudy things,
> How blessed a relief
> The day's departure.
> For this alone, then,
> Since the Night steals from you
> These your servants,
> Did you sow,
> Among the widths of space,
> The gleaming globes
> Proclaiming your omnipotence,
> Your return
> In the time when you are far.
> I think the endless eyes

More heavenly
That Night unveils within us
Than these resplendent stars,
In that vastness.[1]

How did he come to make this discovery? The following hymn in prose gives us the answer:

'Once, when I was shedding bitter tears, hope melted in grief and drained away, and I stood lonely by a barren mound that concealed in a small, dark space her who was my life, lonely as no one else had ever been, driven by unspeakable fear, without strength, remaining nothing but a thought of wretchedness, as I looked about me for help, powerless to move either forward or back, and clung to the fleeting, extinct life with infinite longing, there came from the distant blue, from the heights of my former happiness a twilight tremor, and all at once the birth-bond, the fetters of light, were broken, earthly splendour fled away, and with it my mourning. My sadness was gathered into a new, unfathomable world. You, excitement of the night, slumber of heaven, did fall upon me. My surroundings rose softly upwards, above them hovered my liberated, new-born spirit. The mound became a cloud of dust, and through it I beheld the transfigured features of my adored one. Eternity lay in her eyes. I seized her hands and the tears became a sparkling, unbreakable band. Millennia vanished into the distance like blown storm clouds. Upon her neck I wept enrapturing tears in tribute to this new life—that was the first dream in you. It passed, but left its reflected glow, the eternal, unshakable belief in the night-sky and its sun, the beloved.'[2]

Novalis did not then renounce the world of light as a result of this discovery and change of attitude. On the contrary: it is Platonic, doubly reflected negation which is in question here.

Gladly will I move
With busy hands,
And ever look to see
Where you need me,
Praise the utter glory
Of your splendour,
Tirelessly pursue
The wonderful contrivance
Of your work.
Gladly I observe
The meaning course

---

[1] *Hymns to the Night*, Bölsche, I, 14; for original, cf. Appendix, pp. 410-11.
[2] Ibid., Bölsche, I, 17.

Of your great glowing
Measurer of time,
Plumb the regularity
Of forces
And the rules
Of the fantastic play
Of spaces numberless
And all their periods.
But my most inward heart
Remains the thrall of night
And of her daughter,
Creative love.[1]

For night is at once the secret, the true principle of the world of light.
Why are they who do not know it fools? Because they do not know its
creative significance for the world of light especially:

They do not feel you
In the grape's gold flood,
In the magic oil,
Of the almond tree
And in the brown juice of the poppy.
They do not know
That it is you
Who hovers round
The gentle maiden's bosom,
And makes a heaven of her womb—
Do not divine
That you come towards them from ancient tales
Revealing heaven,
Bear the key
To the dwellings of the blessed,
The silent messenger
Of never-ending mysteries.[2]

Novalis sings the praises of Night as the high proclaimer of a holy world,
as the nurturer of blissful love:

You come, beloved—
It is night—
My soul is entranced—
The earthly path is ended
And you are mine again.
I look into your deep, dark eyes,
Revealing nought but love and blessedness.
We sink upon the altar of the Night
Upon the gentle couch—

---

[1] *Hymns to the Night*, Bölsche, I, 18; for original, cf. Appendix, pp. 411-12.
[2] Ibid., Bölsche, I, 16; for original, cf. Appendix, p. 412.

> The veil falls,
> And fired by the warm embrace
> The limpid glow transpires
> Of the sweet sacrifice.[1]

But that, of course, is the earthly love which has already been purified by heavenly love, which has passed through the catharsis of death; it is only from the night that the world of light and its love acquires its possibility and truth; and even then it is possible and true only in a very preliminary sense and in the light of this its own transcendence:

'A heavenly weariness now never more forsakes me. The way to the holy sepulchre was long and toilsome and the cross was heavy. He whose lips have once been moistened by the limpid wave which flows in the hill's dark womb invisible to common earthly sense, the hill at whose foot the earth's sea breaks; he who has stood aloft upon this border mountain of the world and gazed across at the new country, the dwelling-place of Night; truly he does not return to the turmoil of the world, to the country where light reigns and constant unrest has its abode. He builds humble lodgings, huts of peace, up there, yearns and loves, gazes across, until the most welcome hour draws him down—into the spring's source. The earthly element rises to the surface and is washed down from the height, but that which was made holy by the touch of love flows liberated in hidden channels to the land on the other side, where, like clouds, it intermingles with departed loves.'[2]

That the Night which the poet thus extols is the night of death, as we just found suggested, is something which finds direct expression in that very artistic part of Novalis's poetry written in the form of a mythical history. Life was once:

> An endless feast
> Of gods and men.
> In childlike awe
> Each race revered
> The tender, precious flame
> As the highest thing in the world.[3]

But there is one thing which mars and irrestistibly, irreparably interrupts this feast:

> One thought alone was there,
> Which, its dread form amid gay revels showing,
> Did sudden fill their heart with horror wild;
> Nor means had all the gods within their knowing

---

[1] *Hymns to the Night*, Bölsche, I, 15f.; for original, cf. Appendix, p. 412.
[2] Ibid., Bölsche I, 17f.
[3] Ibid., Bölsche, I, 22; for original, cf. Appendix, p. 413.

To still men's troubled mind with comfort mild;
Mysterious ill the spectre e'er went sowing;
Nor prayer subdued his rage, nor gift beguiled;
For Death it was who all their merry cheer
Suppressed, with pain and anguish and with tears.

.　　　.　　　.

With daring spirit and impassioned breast
Man sought to beautify the mask of dying,
A pallid youth puts out the light and rests,
The end as gentle as a harp's low sighing—
And memory melts mid shadow-waves' cool crests,
The poet sang, to this sad need replying.
But still unfathomed was the endless Night,
The awful symbol of a far-off might.[1]

Until the great reversal of death actually came about:

The night became
The fruitful womb
Of revelations

.　　　.　　　.

The deep divining
Fertile wisdom
Of the East
Did first perceive
The new millennium's dawn.[2]

Christ was born and lived, an event which Novalis describes as follows:

The heavenly heart
A lonely flower unfolding,
Turned towards
The glowing source of love,
The Father's countenance sublime—
Resting on the loving-earnest mother's
Breast, which dreamed of blessedness.
The growing child's prophetic gaze,
With fervour to ensure divinity,
Was turned towards the future,
To his loved ones, future
Bearers of his name,
Not caring for the earthly
Fate in store.
Around him soon,
Miraculously drawn by
Love all-powerful
The child-like hearts assembled.
A new and unknown life

[1] *Hymns to the Night*, Bölsche, I, 22f.; for original, cf. Appendix, p. 413.
[2] Ibid., Bölsche, I, 24; for original, cf. Appendix, p. 413.

Grew up like flowers
Where he was—
From his loving lips
Undying words
And tidings most rejoicing
Fell like sparks
Of a divine spirit.[1]

And then Novalis causes this wondrous child to be addressed by a minstrel hailing from a far-off shore, and who then joyfully journeys onward to Hindustan, as follows:

The youth art thou who all these years hast stood
In thought inclined o'er graves of mortal beings;
A sign of comfort in dark solitude,
And of a higher manhood's glad beginning;
That which hath made our soul so long to pine
Now draws us hence, sweet aspirations winning.
In death eternal life hath been revealed,
And thou art Death, by thee we first are healed.[2]

For while Christ is dying, while his holy mouth, drawn in dreadful anguish, is draining the dark cup of suffering, the birth hour of the new world is drawing near him.

Awakened to new glory,
He ascended to the height
Of this new world made young again;
The old world that had died with him
With his own hand he buried
In the empty tomb;
And set upon it with almighty strength
The stone which no force can remove.[3]

Long ages since
Have passed:
Thy new creation grew
In ever-greater glory.
From out of misery and pain
A multitude has followed thee
In faith and longing
And in loyalty.
They reign with thee
And with the holy virgin
In the realm of love,
And serve within the temple
Of Death that is in heaven.[4]

[1] *Hymns to the Night*, Bölsche, I, 28; for original, cf. Appendix, pp. 413-14.
[2] Ibid., Bölsche, I, 25; for original, cf. Appendix, p. 414.
[3] Ibid., Bölsche, I, 25f.; for original, cf. Appendix, pp. 414-15.
[4] Ibid., Bölsche, I, 27; for original, cf. Appendix, p. 415.

I

Death sounds his bridal call;
The lamps are brightly flaring;
The virgins stand preparing
With oil in full for all;
If on the ear came falling
The far sound of thy train,
And all the stars were calling
With human tongue and tone!

To thee, Oh Mary, hallowed,
A thousand hearts are sent,
In this dark world and shadowed
On thee their thoughts are bent.
They hope for gracious healing
With joy more fully guessed,
By thee pressed, holy Mary,
Upon thy faithful breast.

.   .   .

By no cold grave now weepeth
A faithful love, forlorn;
Each still love's sweet rites keepeth,
From none will they be torn.
From heaven cherubs thronging
Hold watch upon our heart;
To soften our sad longing
Her fires doth Night impart.

Content, our life is hasting
To endless life above,
Now greater longings tasting
With sense transformed in love.
The starry host shall sink then
To bright and living wine,
The golden draught we drink then,
And stars ourselves shall shine.

Love released lives woundless,
No separation more;
While life swells free and boundless
As a sea without a shore.
One night of glad elation,
One hymn that cannot die,
The sun of all creation
Is the face of the Most High.[1]

And now in conclusion there follows that song of triumph in a minor key from which we have already quoted those verses of painful nostalgia for the wonderful 'golden Prime':

[1] *Hymns to the Night*, Bölsche, I, 28-9; for original, cf. Appendix, pp. 415-16.

Down into earth's dark bosom, down!
From realms of light departing;
The sting of pain, wild tortured frown,
Are signs of happy starting;
The slender bark will bear us o'er
Like lightning, to the heavenly shore.

Eternal Night! Then praised be thou!
Be praised eternal slumber;
The day has made us warm; pale now
Press cares we cannot number;
No more 'tis joy abroad to roam,
We rise to seek the Father's home.

.   .   .

Down to the soul's own sweetest Bride,
To Jesus, the Beloved!
Rejoice! the evening glimmers wide,
To hearts by sorrow proved;
A dream breaks all our bonds apart,
And sinks us in the Father's heart![1]

And now once again in truly triumphant tones the 'Song of the Dead'
in *Heinrich von Ofterdingen* can ring out:

First with us grew life from love;
Closely like the elements
Do we mingle Being's waves,
Pounding heart with heart.
Longingly the waves divide
For the strife of elements
Is the highest life of love,
And the very heart of hearts.

Whispered talk of gentle wishes
Hear we only, we are gazing
Ever into eyes transfigured
Tasting nought but mouth and kiss.
All that we are only touching
Change to balmy fruits and glowing,
Change to soft and tender bosoms,
Sacrifice to bold desire.

The desire is ever springing,
On the lover to be clinging,
Round him all our spirit flinging,
One with him to be—
Ardent impulse ever heeding
To consume in turn each other,
Only nourished, only feeding
On each other's ecstasy.

.   .   .

[1] *Hymns to the Night*, Bölsche, I, 29-31; for original, cf. Appendix, pp. 416-17.

And in flood we forth are gushing,
In a secret manner flowing
To the ocean of all living
In the One profound;
And from out his heart while rushing,
To our circle backward going,
Spirit of the highest striving
Dips within our eddying round.

O could men, our future partners,
Know that we in all their joyance,
Are about them and do share
All the bliss which they do taste,
They would burn with glad upbuoyance
To desert the life so hollow—
O, the hours away are streaming;
Come, beloved, hither haste.

Help to fetter the earth-spirit,
Learn to understand death's meaning
And the word of life discover:
Turn around but once.
Soon will all thy power be over,
Borrowed light away be flying,
Soon art fettered, O earth-spirit,
And thy time of empire past.[1]

The *Hymns to the Night* and this *Song of the Dead* are balanced by the two songs to the Virgin Mary and the thirteen Sacred Songs. Their thought-content is apparently the same as that of the first two works, the only difference being that now, instead of the ideas, night and death, it is the ideas, Mary and Christ, which occurred in the mythical-historical turn of the first train of thought, which acquire central importance, so that, accordingly, the positive, affirmatory significance of the entire new insight is stressed even more strongly and one-sidedly, being indeed the sole subject of emphasis. It is, however, precisely at this particular point inevitable, in face of this specifically religious, and indeed Christian writing by Novalis, that this entire final problem which he raises should once again itself become highly problematical, in so far as the *Song of the Dead* has not already made it so: problematical in its ultimate seriousness as regards the genuineness of the transcendence which, seemingly, makes itself noticeable here, and as regards the solidity of the ground upon which all the rest of his work, as a thinker and poet, is here seen to be standing. Has the 'awful symbol of a far-off might' in death become visible with such complete clarity here

---

[1] *Heinrich v. Ofterdingen*, Bölsche, II, 144-6; for original, cf. Appendix, pp. 417-18.

that the thought of the overcoming of death does not have the significance of a renewed attempt to beautify the gruesome mask of dying, with daring spirit and impassioned breast? Be that as it may—it is now the faith in the love for Christ which overcomes death, which is declared loudly, and with spirit and persistence.

> O what would I have been without thee?
> What would I not be without thee?
> Dark fear and anguish were about me,
> In all the world alone I'd be.
> No certain love had I been proving;
> The future, an abyss concealed;
> When sorrows deep my heart were moving
> To whom had I my care revealed?
>
> . . .
>
> But if now Christ, himself revealing,
> Has shown to me the truth, the way;
> The light of life, past all concealing,
> Drives anxious darkness fast away:
> With him is manhood crowned by duty,
> And fate through him doth glorious show;
> Ev'n in the north all India's beauty
> Must round this loved one joyous blow.[1]
>
> Of the thousand hours of gladness
> Which I found amid life's sadness
> One doth still supreme abide;
> One 'mid thousand sorrows growing
> Taught my heart its highest knowing:
> Who for me hath lived and died.[2]
>
> If I do but have him,
> If he is but mine,
> If even to the grave's dark rim
> His trust I ne'er resign,
> Naught I'll know of sadness,
> Only worship, love and gladness.[3]

It must be said that in all this things seem remarkably easy for the lover; here at all events it is remarkably easy to forget the passage from the abyss which he claims he has made in saying such things. For him there is no problem as to whether Christ is there for him to have; he takes it completely for granted that he can take hold of him.

> He died, yet with each day's appearing
> He and his love are heard anew,

---

[1] *Heinrich v. Ofterdingen*, Bölsche, I, 61; for original, cf. Appendix, p. 418.
[2] Ibid., Bölsche, I, 65; for original, cf. Appendix, pp. 418-19.
[3] Ibid., Bölsche, I, 66; for original, cf. Appendix, p. 419.

We can approach whate'er the place,
And fold him in a fond embrace.[1]

Boldly seize those hands appealing,
By his radiant face be won;
Turn to him with all thy feeling
As a flower to the sun—
If thou but turn to him, thy whole heart showing,
He'll prove thy faithful bride, his heart bestowing.[2]

That he is there for Christ, too, is something which seems to him to contain no problem either:

Then conquered sin did lose its terror,
And joyous every step was now;
And this pure faith to guard from error,
We wreathed about the children's brow.
And by it life new-consecrated
Flowed onward like a blessed dream;
And by eternal love elated,
The glad farewell no death did seem.[3]

We have already heard that 'the virgins stand preparing, with oil in full for all'.

If I do but have him,
The world as well I gain.
Happy as the heavenly boy
That holds the Virgin's train.
Rapt in contemplation
I'm safe from earthly consternation.[4]

It is only in respect to other people that some doubt or question can arise:

If all were faithless proving,
Yet faithful I'd remain,
That gratitude unmoving
Ne'er die on earth again.

.   .   .

Oft I go bitter weeping,
That thou in pain hast died,
While those thou lov'st forgetting,
Have not thy love descried;
Thy love alone constraining
Thy great work thou hast done;
No fame wert thou here gaining
And no-one thinks thereon.

But I:

[1] *Heinrich v. Ofterdingen*, Bölsche, I, 65; for original, cf. Appendix, p. 419.
[2] Ibid., Bölsche, I, 64; cf. Appendix, p. 419.
[3] Ibid., Bölsche, I, 63; for original, cf. Appendix, p. 419.
[4] Ibid., Bölsche, I, 66; for original, cf. Appendix, pp. 419-20.

I have felt thy goodness,
O leave me not again;
Let all the love that binds me
To thee for aye remain.
And yet may all high thinking
Look heavenward for its rest;
Men, brothers, in love sinking
And falling on thy breast.[1]

And thus after the fashion of the others this question also is resolved in the most direct manner imaginable:

O go ye out o'er all the highways,
And bring the wanderers gently in,
And even in the darkest by-ways
Let love's glad call the faithful win;
For heaven is now on earth appearing,
In faith we can behold it plain;
To all it opens who are loving
With us the truth that shall remain.[2]

For he really seems to be present everywhere and to offer himself to man always in a manner which will never admit of the smallest doubt that he is in fact there to be taken:

I see thee in a thousand pictures,
Oh Mary, lovably expressed,
But none of them can equal that
I find upon my soul impressed.
I only know that since I saw thee
My heart has banished earthly strife;
A heaven of undreamed-of sweetness
Holds my mind eternally.[3]

Our eyes behold the Saviour true,
The Saviour lights those eyes anew;
His head the fairest flowers adorn,
From which he shines like smiling morn.

He is the star, he is the sun;
The fount whence streams eternal run;
From herb and stone and sea and light
Shines forth his radiant vision bright.

His child-like heart, supreme affection,
Are universal in their action.
He hugs himself, unconscious, blest,
With endless power to every breast.[4]

[1] *Heinrich v. Ofterdingen*, Bölsche, I, 67; for original, cf. Appendix, p. 420.
[2] Ibid., Bölsche, I, 62; for original, cf. Appendix, p. 420.
[3] Ibid., Bölsche, I, 61; for original, cf. Appendix, pp. 420-1.
[4] Ibid., Bölsche, I, 72f.; for original, cf. Appendix, p. 421.

And we might well at this point call to mind again the hymn of the Lord's Supper, with its interpretation of the communion with Christ into the communion with the non-ego in general.

In short: Novalis has suddenly become remarkably ripe for the hymn-book. This is not without its more doubtful aspects. For it is certainly the modern hymn-book he has become ripe for. The Christian song we hear him singing is certainly not the first person plural song of the Reformation, praising the great deeds of the Lord, but a species, and perhaps the most pronounced species, of the first person singular song which has advanced mightily since 1600, in which the congregation thinks to find edification by letting each individual say and sing that he has felt the hand of God in such and such a way, and how his works have been of benefit to him, to him, to him.

We wonder where death is now, a figure full of menace, warning and promise, who after all confronts too this entire Christian heaven, in so far as it is part of earthly experience. Can it perhaps be that the poet does not intend to express this opposition as something so dangerous, so critical, so full of promise, as he seems to portray it in several passages? Has not death, after all, been resolved in a play of harmonies? And can it be thus resolved? Can the 'positive non-determinate' be included in such a manner; can it, after all, carried away by a powerful 'enthusiasm for Night', be included in the point of determination i? Was the poet's whole meaning no more serious than in this way when he spoke of the visitor, 'its dread form amid gay revels showing'? Can one dispose of him by simply, in the twinkling of an eye, giving him the name of Christ? And what has Christ become, if he is deemed just good enough to appear as a mythical symbol—or is the poet's meaning different?—at this point, where it is a question of replacing the negative by the positive sign? If it is possible to mention 'Jesus' and 'the sweet bride' in the same breath and sense? If the name Mary can simply be set down with equal meaning for the name Jesus? If he is omnipresent in this way and only seems to have been waiting for the inclination of our hearts, to become our own? Has the poet really seen the majestic distance between the $1 \times \infty$ and $\frac{1}{\infty}$ on the one hand, and o on the other, between the god x and the god y, or has it for a long time, or even from the outset, been submerged in the unity of the one true God x? Is there a knowledge here of the decision between Baal and Jehovah, or has not Baal been chosen unconsciously a long time previously—an act suppressing from the outset, perhaps, the question which flashed into the mind like lightning? Was Novalis in the *Hymns to the Night* and in the *Sacred Songs* singing another melody or was he not rather singing the same one as he usually sang an octave deeper: the song of the magic identity between the ego and the non-ego, with Night now additionally included, with death now additionally included, with Christ himself now additionally included? These things we can only ask. And we are not entitled to ask them as if perhaps we knew the answer. We do not know it. But in order to understand Novalis we must ask, sharply, remorselessly.

The question is concentrated with much symbolic force in the question concerning the meaning of the opposing of Christ and Mary. If the *Sacred Songs*, in spite of all the talk of Christ, are, in the final and decisive assessment, songs to the Virgin Mary, then that would mean that Novalis has in fact succeeded in understanding death too, and death in particular, as a 'romanticizing principle', as he once said,[1] as the ultimate principle of this great process of things growing more strange and more familiar, in making it part of the reality of this dancing god, and in including Christ too in the train of Dionysus. For if Mary is the final word—Mary in the sense of Roman Catholic Church doctrine, to which, upon this point, Novalis was receptive enough—then that means that the final word is the creature open to what is above, open to God, capable of participating in God. The creature thus described can at most be regarded with fervour, at most also with infinite sadness but by no means worshipped. In what concerns Mariology the Roman Catholic Church doctrine too in fact—whatever else may be said of it—is still confined within the frame of the ancient and ever new religion of immanence, which one hundred years ago was called Romanticism. The meaning of 'Star of the sea, I greet thee' may well be one of wondrous beauty, but is not sufficient to make plain the decision or the revelation.

Everything would be different if the *Sacred Songs* could really be referred to by the title they lay claim to, that, namely, of songs of Christ. As we have seen, however, there is a great deal which argues against this. But once again we do not have the final right not to recognize them as what they claim to be. Behind them lies a life that might well have known, and seems to have known, enough of the 'dreadful anguish' to compel us at all events to respect its confession of faith, for all the doubts it might awaken in us. Thousands and thousands of people over the last hundred years have believed that in these poems they have heard a most genuine testimony. Who would argue that they have not really heard it? The fact that *our* confession and testimony, for serious reasons, perhaps, cannot be this one is another question. At all

[1] *Frag.*, 660.

events the simple fact that Novalis wrote these *Sacred Songs* (and in such quantity, too, in relation to the sum-total of his output) is evidence that his gaze was in some way fixed upon the point which forms their subject, and fixed so strongly that it cannot be explained as the conduct of the pure Romantic, for whom things Christian also became a symbol, as has often been said. Certainly that aspect is also part of the matter. But the emphasis with which here just things Christian become a symbol, and the proximity in which things Christian find themselves to the critical concept of death, would still remain striking and singular, even if our final judgment must be that in the last resort the riddle of death has been juggled away once more and that Christianity has yet again been interpreted in humanistic terms. In that event we should be compelled to say that pure Romanticism, in order to mark out the field containing its particular problem, had inevitably to approach extremely close to this other quite different field of problems.

And now let us once again consider that Novalis's confession of faith and testimony is known to us only in the incomplete form in which the twenty-nine-year-old poet left it at his death. Truly it is much more question than answer! Novalis relates of the hero of *Heinrich von Ofterdingen* that, in the cave of the hermit, who personifies history, he came upon an old book containing pictures, and written in a foreign language. To his astonishment he suddenly found amongst its diverse pictures a picture of himself: he saw his likeness, in fact, in different situations. 'Towards the end it seemed to him that he looked bigger and nobler. The guitar lay in his arms and the countess handed him a garland. He saw himself at the imperial court, on shipboard, now in close embrace with a slender and beautiful maiden, now fighting with fierce-looking men, and again engaged in friendly conversation with Saracens and Moors. Frequently he was accompanied by a man of grave aspect. He felt a deep reverence for this august form, and was glad to see himself arm in arm with him. The last pictures were dark and incomprehensible; yet some of the shapes of his dream surprised him with the most intense rapture. The conclusion of the book, it seemed, was missing. This upset Heinrich considerably, and he wished for nothing more earnestly than to have and be able to read the whole book. He looked over the pictures repeatedly and was startled when he heard the company return. He was beset by a strange feeling of shame. He did not dare make known his discovery, closed the book, and merely asked the hermit generally about its title and language. He learned that it was in the tongue of Provence. It is long since I have read it, said the hermit; I do not now remember its contents very distinctly.

As far as I can recollect, it is a romance relating the wonderful fortune of a poet's life, wherein the art of poesy is represented and extolled in all its various relations. The conclusion is missing to the manuscript, which I brought with me from Jerusalem. . . .'[1]

The conclusion to this manuscript is missing. It is missing in every respect. And in so far as we all, as children of the age which began with Novalis, have something of the Romantic, or at least, it is to be hoped, the pure Romantic, in our blood, the same might well be said of us too. This manuscript cannot have a conclusion, and that, perhaps, is the best that can be said of it.

[1] *H. v. Ofterdingen*, Bölsche, II, 77.

VII

HEGEL

IT is well known that Hegel was of the opinion that his philosophy, unlike that of his predecessors from Descartes to Fichte, should be understood not as a stage, a particular period in the development of the course of the history of philosophy in general, leading to heaven knows where, but as the final culmination of this history, uniting and doing away with all previous knowledge within itself. The ridicule, open or subdued, regretful or malicious with which historians of philosophy generally describe this view of Hegel's, the astonishment greeting such an almost mythical or pathological sense of self-importance in a man who in everything else seems to have shown that he had some intelligence, the gratification at the thought that after Hegel's lack of success in thus assessing his own work nobody else would dare to say such a thing again—all these attitudes are fundamentally both petty and irrelevant.

For fundamentally the astonishing thing is not that Hegel believed his philosophy to be an unsurpassable climax and culmination. It is that he was not right in thinking that after him the development was possible of a school of positivism, of pessimism and even of materialism, of Neo-Kantianism and whatever else the other modern philosophies may be called. The astonishing thing is that nineteenth-century man did not acknowledge that his concern in the realm of thought, his basic intellectual concern, had truly achieved ultimate recognition in Hegel's philosophy. It was astonishing that he broke out and made off in all directions as if nothing had happened, and that he was not content with pondering Hegel's wisdom, at most constantly re-formulating it, perhaps cautiously correcting certain weaker parts, and for the rest thankfully applying it in everything. Why did Hegel not become for the Protestant world something similar to what Thomas Aquinas was for Roman Catholicism? How could it come to pass that, very soon after Hegel's death and ever more plainly from the middle of the century onwards, it was exactly his achievement which began to be looked upon, with a pitying smile, as representing something which was in the main already superseded? This happened, though the same people who pitied his achievement were still secretly drawing intellectual sustenance from certain isolated elements of his thought. How did it come about that as early as the eighteen-sixties those who professed Hegelianism openly found it necessary to be defiant, not to say embittered in tone—as for instance in the foreword of Biedermann's *Dogmatics*? How did it come to pass that pure Hegelians, Michelet, for instance (from 1829 to 1893 a lecturer at Berlin), became a species as rare as the ibex and were close to being figures of fun? And how is it that the Hegel renaissance in our day too is but one of many other renaissances and is far from being generally recognized, even in a limited way, as the one true and necessary renaissance as according to Georg Lasson, for instance, one of the faithful few, it should inevitably be? That is what is astonishing. That Hegel, at all events outwardly, should temporarily at least appear to have been put so much in the wrong by the events of history; that is the amazing fact. If the eighteenth and nineteenth centuries formed a unity in such a way that the nineteenth century was the fulfilment of the eighteenth, then it was Hegel who represented this unity in his philosophy as no other man did. Is it not in Hegel that the man who is free from all the ties of tradition and from all conflict with tradition, who rejoices equally in reason and in history, as Lessing, still groping and uncertain, had set him upon the stage—is it not in Hegel that this man has for the first time achieved complete, clear and certain self-awareness? Is it not Hegel who exploited and made fruitful to the last detail Kant's great discovery of the transcendent nature of the human capacity for reason? Is it not he in whom the extremely vulnerable attempt to form an opposition to Kant's real or supposed one-sidedness, as it had been undertaken by Herder and others like him, came most legitimately into its own? Is it not he who is above all the great systematizer and apologist of the concern of Romanticism, of the discovery of Romanticism, of the immediacy of the creative individuality, and of the dialectic of the way his life moves? Was not Hegel he who should come as the fulfiller of every promise, and was it worth waiting for another after he had come?

Such was the view of the new age itself, in the early days at least, in the years between 1820 and 1830, which were so remarkable in every respect. It was at such a time that the Prussian state, just struggling to power, and preparing to take the lead in things German and perhaps European, called Hegel to its first chair of philosophy at Berlin, and that the liveliest students from all Germany, and with them the educated of all ages, flocked to hear him with an enthusiasm of which we can scarcely form any idea today. Again, it was at such a time that learned literature in every sphere spoke something of his language, and that philosophy, and thus fundamentally concentrated knowledge in general, was actually thought to be synonymous with Hegel's philosophy, with a naïveté that almost succeeds in becoming credible again. Was Hegelianism really just another 'ism' among and before and after many others? Was it something comparable to a new fashion in dress? That is how it was regarded afterwards. But if all things do not deceive us it was precisely when it was utterly and completely ruled by Hegel that the new age best understood itself, and it was then at all events that it best knew what it wanted.

It was the first sign that the new time was growing old, the first harbinger, we might perhaps say, of the catastrophe of 1914, the first hint that men were themselves beginning to doubt their own desires, when they became unfaithful to Hegel, who had only just been glorified. It should not have happened. In making Hegelianism the subject of irony they were making themselves the subject of irony. In rejecting this Messiah they were rejecting the whole promise, the very thing they themselves had thought to have received as a promise. In doing so they declared their belief that the first culmination and overcoming of the Enlightenment, as it reached its peak in Hegel, had not succeeded, that a new start had to be made, a return behind Idealism and Romanticism. They declared their belief that the inheritance of the Enlightenment must be entered into once again, with the claim that they were as competent and capable of entering into it as the generation of 1770-1800, and with the risk that this time they might perhaps not attain either to the overcoming of the Enlightenment, which they sought, or to a true culmination of it.

And did this second attempt succeed half as well as the first which had been given up? The first half of the century was still chiefly under the sign of the first approach culminating in Hegel. In the second half of the century the desire was to go behind Idealism and Romanticism to link up with the Enlightenment again and make a better job of things. Today we are already, to a certain extent at least, in a position to survey the scene as a whole: can there be any question that the intellectual atmosphere of the first half of the century was distinguished from the second not only by a far greater sense of self-importance but also by a far higher standard, intrinsic value and dignity? We need only compare the representative figures of the two eras in our own field, the field of theology, the two church fathers,

Schleiermacher and Ritschl, to be shocked at once at the era of meaner things, of smaller stature, which has manifestly arrived. The resurgence of the exact sciences, both natural and historical, to which this new age, the supposedly adult period of the nineteenth century, can lay claim as its title of particular honour, was after all a modest substitute for the clarity and confidence in matters of principle with which the basis was laid between 1820 and 1830, a basis which was later to be abandoned, and with which, even into the forties, people worked at the German universities. It was a meagre consolation for the deep resignation with which as early as 1870 the more far-sighted representatives of this second era, like Frank Overbeck, for instance, did their work, aware that the new time had completely lost the ground beneath its feet. In the eighties and nineties this resignation began to lay itself like a paralysing spell upon all intellectual life, in spite of the thinly chirping pathos to which this age, too, on occasion was once more capable of rising.

At all events, and despite the outward splendour of the era of Kaiser Wilhelm which was just beginning, there can be no suggestion that a second spiritual peak was reached like that around 1830. Hegel's professorial chair was now occupied by Friedrich Paulsen; Schleiermacher's by Julius Kaftan, and in F. C. Baur's place Adolf von Harnack now determined how things stood with the 'essence of Christianity'. And with all due respect for such figures, that is a different matter, if we think of their specific weight. The century had become tired and somehow sad for all its enforced jollity. The age of Hegel and the age of the superseding of Hegel are related as is the battle of Sedan to the battle of the Marne. This time, too, there was an abundance of victorious bulletins, but something had gone wrong at the top, and there was a premonition that things would turn out badly. The century had denied its truest and most genuine son and since then it no longer had a good conscience or any true joyousness or any impetus. It would have liked very much to achieve these things, but it could not. Looking back became its typical attitude of mind, a somewhat aimless and unrelated looking back to various periods of the remote past, a historical stocktaking. It drew its sustenance from memories drawn from earlier centuries, but without taking the opportunity to make them material for a new basis; it did so impelled more by curiosity than by an inner affinity with the concerns of these earlier ages. The century reproached its own youth for having been neglectful particularly of this, for having been far too unhistorically-minded—completely overlooking the fact that in its youthful days it was not only young, but dared to take itself seriously, dared to live from its own resources, and could therefore afford the enthusiasm, the poesy, and the sense of self-importance, too, which it now looked back upon with a senile smile. It did not reflect that in those early days, even though it had less curiosity about history, the century perhaps thought and lived truly historically in a better sense, because it was claimed by history, because it was engaged in conversation with history. But however we may judge all that in its details, a synthesis, and with it a definite feeling for the needs of the age, such as was peculiar to the age of Hegel, was not achieved again once people thought they had left the age of Hegel behind them. In turning away from Hegel the age acknowledged that, having reached the summit of its desires and achievements, it was dissatisfied with itself, that this was after all not what it had intended. It set Hegel aside and tried again, but did not even reach such a peak a second time, and thus manifestly it was bound to be even less satisfied than it was before, although it pretended to be.

Where does the fault lie? In Hegel? Those who study him will not receive this impression. If it is a question of doing what the entire nineteenth century evidently wanted to do, then Hegel apparently did it as well as it could possibly be done. Or is the reason that afterwards the age of the great men was past, that there was no genius present in the second half of the century to carry out the better things which the century it seems had in mind in turning away from Hegel? But it is always a bad sign when people can find nothing to say but that unfortunately the right people were lacking. This should be said either always or never. Every age, perhaps, has the great men it deserves, and does not have those it does not deserve. The question only remains, whether it was a hidden flaw in the will of the age itself, perfect as the expression was that it had found in Hegel, which was the reason why it could not find any satisfaction in Hegel and therefore not in itself, and yet could not find any way of improving upon and surpassing Hegel, and therefore itself.

It might of course be possible that Hegelianism indeed represented in classic form the concern of the nineteenth century, but precisely as such came to reveal the limited nature of this concern, and the fact that it was impossible to proceed from it to the settlement of every other question of truth. And that for that reason it was, curiously, condemned. The rejection of Hegel might have been the fig-leaf with which man at this time sought to hide what he himself was aware of as his pudendum from his own sight, from the sight of others and from the sight of

God. It might of course be that Hegel was in fact the Messiah, the fulfilment of the age, as he himself thought, and was held to be in the eighteen-twenties, but this fulfilment would have been after all only the fulfilment of the promises which had been received, and as they had been received, whereas better or at any rate different promises, which we thought we could see round the edges of the pictures of Lessing, Kant, Herder and Novalis, and which could be much more clearly indicated in many other manifestations of the time, did not exist either for Hegel or for his contemporaries (in the narrower sense of the word). These latter promises did not receive their fulfilment in Hegel either, but were at best only reaffirmed as promises. It is possible that different needs made necessary new promises, different from those which figure centrally in the pictures we have so far studied, and which now in fact seem to be fulfilled in Hegel. It is possible, moreover, that these different promises are in fact present, even if at the edge, indistinct, and in the form of open questions, presented by Kant and Novalis as glimpses beyond the border: problems which were suppressed, which did not get their fair share of attention, and which were calling for treatment. Hegel, fulfilling what he could, did certainly not provide an answer to these problems, except for the fact that with him they are perhaps suppressed and did not get their fair share of attention in a particularly obvious way. If all this was the case, then both the triumph and the tragedy of Hegelianism were meaningful, seen in relation to history.

There would then have to be a break with the idea of a historical progress moving in a straight line, which was so important to Hegel particularly; and it would then have to be acknowledged that a time like the nineteenth century can also take some guilt upon itself for the way it worked out its own peculiar concern: the guilt incurred by the neglect, the overlooking, the covering up and denying of other concerns by the existence of which it was bound to feel itself hindered, limited and channelled in asserting its own concern; again, the guilt for a crime against the truth in not allowing such hindering, limiting and channelling to take place, but rather all too constantly affirming and asserting itself; a guilt all the more manifest the more classically the will of an age is expressed in its leaders and heroes. It is a guilt which must sooner or later be paid for, and which, naturally, will be paid for above all by its leaders and heroes, by those in whom the age itself was great. It will be paid for first in such a way that the age itself will, by degrees, or all at once, find the greatness of these leaders and heroes (and hidden in it its own greatness) unworthy of trust, repugnant, and rotten. This of course need not mean at all (and in the case of Hegel and the nineteenth century it did not mean at all) that the age itself has done penance and is about to perform a *volte-face*. What it does signify, objectively, is that judgment is about to be passed, that the inner impossibility of the crime committed is about to come to light, and that the way will then be free for remembering forgotten things, resuming neglected things, facing the problems which have been suppressed, and in so doing honouring the truth. The fact that this in its turn cannot be achieved without guilt is something that will perhaps be granted by this new age more willingly than Hegel himself granted it in relation to the age preceding him. Perhaps in fact the new age would prefer to dispense from the outset with the idea of historical progress. But precisely in this way will it then be possible really to become aware of the concern of the preceding age, in our case that of the age of Hegel, without failing to realize that that time is truly past.

Everything we have said so far must admittedly be put in parenthesis, for we do not know whether the age of Hegel is in fact entirely past, even if we should, in all seriousness, consider it to be so as far as we ourselves are concerned. It was only in the course of centuries that Thomas Aquinas acquired the position at present accorded him in the Roman Catholic world. It may be that the dawn of the true age of Hegel is still something that will take place in the future. But that would mean that we are in fact standing only at the beginning of the era of the man whom we here provisionally described as the man of the nineteenth century. The fact that people were weary of Hegel in the second half of the nineteenth century would then have to be judged a resting-period, brought about by a state of weakness in modern man, because he had not quite comprehended his salvation at that juncture. And the denial of Hegel, which to us today perhaps seems necessary in a more comprehensive sense than it did to man in the second half of the nineteenth century, would then have to be understood as a reactionary current approaching the point where it will be annihilated or at least rendered harmless, a current which might then only hope for its concern to reach fulfilment at a much later time. The day of judgment and of freedom, which somewhat boldly perhaps we previously set in the past, would then lie in a possibly distant future. Anyone who is aware of serious considerations which cannot receive justice at Hegel's hands, and which in fact Hegel suppresses, will not hesitate, while simultaneously paying his due respects to Hegel as a spirit of undoubted greatness and as the spirit of our time too, to associate himself already now with the necessary protest against him and against this time of ours, even if it is as the supporter of what is already a lost cause. Whether the age of Hegel is already past or whether it is still to come and to come even more than ever before, cannot perhaps be decided, and it is not necessary for us to know for certain.

I. Hegel's philosophy is the philosophy of *self-confidence*. It was because it at once postulated and affirmed this principle, which this age in particular found to the highest degree comprehensible, that it seemed so suited to its time, that it was so much a fulfilment in relation to what the whole century felt as a promise within itself. It was because this principle, for all the artistry with which it was developed and applied, was so startlingly simple that this philosophy seemed so grand and fruitful. And the reason why Hegel's philosophy seemed so convincing was that Hegel dared in all earnestness to pursue this simple principle, which every true contemporary in some way agreed with, to its ultimate conclusion and with all imaginable faithfulness. Anyone who has once understood that here we have a man who absolutely and undeviatingly believes in himself, who can doubt everything because he does not for a moment doubt himself, and who knows everything for the simple reason that he has complete trust in his own self-knowledge—anyone who has once understood *that*, has at least the key to this labyrinth, even if he cannot avoid the trouble of finding his own way about it. It is a question of philosophy and thus of the self-confidence of thinking man. Hegel puts his confidence in the idea that his thinking and the things which are thought by him are equivalent, i.e., that his thinking is completely present in the things thought by him, and that the things thought by him are completely present in his thinking.

He trusts that these two things are equivalent because he trusts—and this is the secret of his secret—in their *identity* which comes about in the performance of the act of thinking. The identity which exists between our thinking and what is thought, in so far as it is achieved in the act of thinking, is, with Hegel, called mind. So Hegel's brand of self-confidence is also confidence in mind which for its own part is one with God and the same with God. The characteristic thing about this, however, is that the confidence in mind or in God must also to the fullest extent and in ultimate seriousness be self-confidence, because there is likewise and in the same sense a final identity between Self and mind, as there is in general between thinking and the thing thought. It is the purpose of Hegel's philosophy to proclaim this confidence, and to summon people to it. He does these things because he does not conceive of it as a personal distinction to have occasion for such confidence, since there is no kind of inspiration or individual enlightenment behind it, because it is meant to be understood utterly and completely as confidence in universal human *reason*, the reason known and available to everyone.

Here Hegel takes up the inheritance of the Enlightenment: in fulfilment of the concern of the whole movement between himself and the Enlightenment, but also criticizing and correcting the courses it had taken acting in an independent direct relationship to the Enlightenment. In affirming this equivalence and final identity of things within and things without, of ego and non-ego, of the familiar and unfamiliar, Hegel affirms the insight of Romanticism. Of the minds we have studied here he is unquestionably most akin to Novalis. For just three years (Jena, 1801-3) he was closely associated with Schelling, the true philosopher of Romanticism, and even though he turned away from Schelling later this did not mean that he had rejected the things Romanticism wanted, but that he was attempting to provide for it a better system and apologetics than that of Schelling. He found the Romantic synthesis and identity to be lacking in a firm and universally valid basis. It seemed to him that the truth and force of this synthesis was imperilled by the mere appeal to poetry, to creative experience, to the individual genius. That was why he was also Schleiermacher's determined opponent and opposed his metaphysics of feeling, and the doctrine of faith which called this instance to witness. For him it is a question of understanding the synthesis which he also affirmed as Novalis, as Schelling, and as Schleiermacher wanted it to be, as solid knowledge, as a free, conscious and responsible act of the capacity for reason, which is in principle always and everywhere present in man and can be appealed to.

Hegel of course also affirms Herder's ideal of humanity and his experience of totality. He it was who put into effect the testament of Herder, and further, of Lessing, by his very thorough inclusion of history in the concept of reason. It has been regarded as Hegel's greatest achievement that in his concept of reason, which also embraced historical reality, he finally and justifiably overcame the dualism of transcendental and historical-empirical thought, the dualism of the eternal truth of reason and the accidental truths of history, of destiny and the idea, which had already been disputed by Herder. This was, however, the case because he actually achieved it within his concept of reason, and not by referring to some intuitive and emotional Beyond, which could not be apprehended, but only experienced! It is in fact

Hegel's criticism of Romanticism, solely and entirely, which distinguishes him from Herder. Hegel believed in the possibility, legitimacy and sovereignty of pure thought. He was never so fiercely aggressive as when, rightly or wrongly, he thought he could detect, behind the appeal to such supposedly given and yet inapprehensible instances, an example of lazy thinking, or fear of thinking, or mistrust of the power of thought. He would have had only the greatest contempt for a collective concept, like that, for instance, of the irrational, as it was evolved by a later age. It was not in a capitulation of the reasonable to the real, as to something which was unreasonable, or against reason, that he sought and found a way of overcoming the dichotomy which Herder had all too tumultuously disputed, but in the knowledge that the reasonable is just as real as the real is reasonable.

And Hegel of course also affirmed Kant's transcendentalism. He did so in the same sense that Fichte did; following in his footsteps, but excluding, admittedly, the specifically ethical turn Fichte had given to his affirmation. Reason critically understanding itself is reason which is self-established and liberated, which is now as a matter of principle the master of all things. But just for this reason Kant's critique of knowledge seems to Hegel to have after all rather the character of a carter's job, that had to be done sometime but could not have any lasting significance. It was in him to ridicule the demand for a theory of knowledge by saying there was as much sense in it as the demand of the Gascon who did not want to go into the water before he could swim. The interests of the theory of knowledge, he said, were best served in the act of a truly rational knowledge. 'If we are not to go to philosophy, to rational thought, before we have rationally known reason, then we can do nothing at all, for it is only in knowing that we rationally apprehend. Rational activity cannot be investigated before we are rationally active. In philosophy reason is for reason.'[1] In this act of rational knowledge the Kantian distinctions between the knowledge of ideas and empirical knowledge on the one hand, and between theoretical and practical knowledge on the other, also fall away, as necessary but secondary preliminary stages of mere reflection. All knowledge comprehending and surpassing these distinctions, is knowledge of God. True logic, including from the outset physics, is as such also the true metaphysics, the metaphysics of the mind which unites within itself thinking and the thing thought—the true metaphysics in mind. It is unnecessary to point out that Hegel's reaction to

---

[1] *Vorlesungen über die Philosophie der Religion* (Lectures on the Philosophy of Religion), ed. Lasson, Philosophische Bibliothek, Vols. 59-63, I, 57f.

certain elements of Kant's teaching, like his theory of postulates, for instance, or his theory of the theoretical unactuality of all knowledge of ultimate things, or his distinction between the religion of reason and historical religion, could only be one of sovereign displeasure. From Hegel's standpoint the good Kant is looked back upon as a manikin loyally improvising his resources, however sadly limited by the cave in which he plies his handiwork. Kant receives an honourable mention, and Fichte, as the man who with his teaching of the ego was the first to understand Kant better than he understood himself, receives a crown of oak: but we should on no account allow either of them to detain us. The distinction between knowledge and the thing in itself, between ego and non-ego is a provisional matter. Upon this point Hegel proceeds with Herder and Romanticism.

Hegel's direct, independent linking-up with the Enlightenment was done in this way: the confidence of the Enlightenment in the right and the power of rational thought was naïve, untested and therefore unsecured, stuck fast in half-truths and open to all kinds of counter-blows. Hegel called this confidence in the right and power of rational thought to self-awareness, worked out and defended its deepest truth *vis-à-vis* its own weaknesses as *vis-à-vis* its attackers, and in so doing exalted it from the level of a one-sided view of the world to a comprehensive world principle. We cannot of course name Hegel in the same breath as Christian Wolff, but we can liken him to Leibnitz, corrected and supplemented by Spinoza, the secret patron saint of all enlightened opponents of the Enlightenment. Hegel is the Enlightenment philosopher with an entirely good conscience, with a completely protected rear. These things the earlier philosophy of the Enlightenment did not have. Somehow it was still not at peace, it was still at loggerheads with the object as the object confronted it, in history particularly, with an irksome refusal to be dismissed. The reality of destiny, to which it shut its eyes, stood like a shadow behind it. That is why the fight against the Enlightenment was bound to emerge from the Enlightenment itself, as we saw it break out in Lessing's discovery of historical experience, in Kant's teaching of radical evil and of the primacy of practical reason, in Herder's protest against pure rationalism and in his enraptured hearkening to the voices of the peoples, and in the Romantic discovery of the immediacy of the individual. The Enlightenment had no safeguard against this assault upon it by opponents who were themselves enlightened, and it was therefore also ultimately unsecured against the never entirely suppressed opposition of such of its opponents as, in a manner which was not in tune with the age, did not even meet it upon its own ground. It was unsecured because the watchword 'Have the courage to use your own understanding' could only ring true when the idea of one's 'own understanding' was so deepened that the conflict with the object, the ignoring of history, and shutting one's eyes to the reality of destiny was superfluous, because all these things, the object, history and destiny, were included in it. God must not any longer be an offence or foolishness to one's 'own understanding'. The individual understanding had to learn to recognize that it must not be so diffident and defiant in understanding itself merely as *individual* understanding or merely as individual *understanding*, but that it must understand itself as *the one and only reason* which is already prevented from quarrelling with God, and which cannot be either openly or secretly atheistic, because as the one true reason of man it is *eo ipso* also the reason of God, a generic object which when thought out to its conclusion must necessarily be transformed into the generic subject, and in fact finally thus transformed. Because to Hegel the rational was historical and the historical rational, he completely and finally disposed of the God who had somehow stood in opposition to reason, who was in some way an offence and a foolishness to reason, and who could perhaps be denied through reason. He did not do this by denying him, and not even by denying that he stood in opposition, but by making the offence and foolishness of this opposition relative, by seeing that this relationship with God was something which was necessary but which was also provisional, by seeing that it could finally be resolved in the peace of reason, which is at once and as such the peace that is higher than all reason. That is what is fundamentally new about Hegel in relation to the Enlightenment, and in it Hegel brought the Enlightenment in its old form to honour in a way of which it would never have dared to dream.

And this makes for the peculiar momentum of Hegel's philosophy of self-confidence; it does not allow itself to be surpassed in cold-blooded rationalizing by any worldling, nor in depth of feeling by the most pious. It is Titanism to the highest degree and at the same time to the highest degree humility. The *self*-confidence it proclaims and to which it summons is at once and as such confidence in *God*, a qualified confidence, a most true and most actual confidence, imbued with the entire mystery and majesty of true confidence in God. Its intention is to give the honour as expressly as possible to *God* and not to man; and this it expresses quite directly and consistently not *only* in the form of a most naïve human *self*-confidence, but *also* in this form, as explicitly as possible. Every formal peculiarity of Hegel's philosophy can be understood when seen in this light. The method of thinking which is based upon the identity of confidence in God and self-confidence must become one that never fails, which is inexhaustible. As the result of the thought which is based upon this identity a *system* must emerge, a complete settling of the account with knowledge and the striking of a balance with truth. Based upon this identity questions which remain *open*, which play so large a part in Kant's philosophy of religion, for instance, simply cannot arise. Here problems are simply there in order that they may be raised and *settled* with all certainty. With this identity as the basis for his thought Hegel is able and indeed bound to be present himself as the man who has an implicit knowledge of *everything*, and is empowered to hale *everyone* before his judgment-seat. Based upon this identity there must be here a fierceness of controversy which is only possible otherwise in the form of a *rabies theologorum*. Wondrous to relate, it is accompanied by a fundamentally conciliatory spirit, and an open-mindedness towards all things. Of this spirit one is at first tempted to believe that it is thinkable only on assumptions which are to some extent theological. If all theology seems at first to pale beside this philosophy, then the reason is not that it confounds and disperses theology in a particularly dangerous and victorious way. Hegel had no thought of undertaking any such unfriendly task, and at bottom he remained throughout his life a loyal son of the Tübingen seminary. It is rather that everything that seems to give theology its particular splendour and special dignity appears to be looked after and honoured by this philosophy in a way incomparably better than that achieved by the theologians themselves (with the possible exception of Thomas Aquinas). Theology, taken care of once and for all, is here not surpassed in the act of this philosophy, but in fact surpasses itself.

Only someone who does not understand Hegel's philosophy can miss its peculiar greatness. Again and again we find we must think three times before contradicting it, because we might find that everything we are tempted to say in contradiction of it has already been said within it, and provided with the best possible answer. It is great in two ways: first, looked at in itself, because it has seized upon and imple-mented an idea that is at once simple and all-embracing, the at least relative truth of which is self-evident. It has done this so energetically, that whatever attitude we adopt towards it we cannot help hearing it and coming to terms with it. It is possible to bypass Fichte and Schelling, but it is as impossible to pass by Hegel as it is to pass by Kant. And the promissory nature of the truth Hegel enunciated and the ease with which it lends itself to equalization will perhaps be even greater than in the case of Kant for someone who, as a theologian, must finally say 'No' to Hegel.

The other great quality in Hegel's philosophy is the very fact that it is not at all the accidental discovery of one particular, gifted individual —this is what Hegel, in contrast to Schelling, did not wish to be—but the mighty and impressive voice of an entire era, the voice of modern man, or of the man who, from 1700 to 1914, was called modern man. 'Philosophy does not stand above its age in such a way that it is something completely different in kind from the things which generally condition the age; one spirit, rather, moves through the realm both of reality and of philosophical thought; it is only that the latter is the true self-understanding of the real. Or it is one movement which bears along the age and its philosophy. The only difference is that the things which condition the age still appear as accidental, are not yet justified and thus can still stand in unreconciled, inimical contrast to the truly essential content of the age, whereas philosophy, as the justification of the principle, is also the general tranquillizer and reconciler.'[1]

Quite apart from the intrinsic weight of the thought Hegel represents, it is impossible to pass him by, simply because we cannot pass by that modern man. We must not be led astray by the fact that modern man became unfaithful to Hegel. He meant and means what Hegel meant, even if he did, ungratefully enough, blushing, ashamed, and with a smile of embarrassment, turn away from Hegel; after Hegel, to his applause at first, had said that which he himself wished to say in a thousand tongues, but which he simply could not say nearly so well. Self-confidence, qualified as confidence in God, confidence in God given concrete form as self-confidence—where is the man who, with the blood of this modern man in his veins, would not listen to this and hear the finest and deepest echo of his own voice? If we wish to take this modern man seriously, to hear him and put his desires on record— if we wish to take ourselves seriously κατὰ σάρκα, but in the best and deepest sense of what must ultimately come under the notion of σάρξ, then Hegel also must be taken seriously. That is why it is fitting that he should have a place of honour in our investigation of the foundations of nineteenth-century theology. We ourselves are involuntarily thinking along Hegelian lines when we state that his greatness as a thinker consists in the objective and historical significance, the reasonableness and reality of his teaching, which are all present in equal measure, and which form a unity of mysterious clarity.

[1] *Phil. of Rel.*, Lasson, I, 53.

II. We have said that Hegel's philosophy is the philosophy of self-confidence. It is, first of all, the philosophy of the confidence of thinking man in the dignity, strength and value of his thought. And man, according to Hegel, cannot understand himself more deeply, more exactly, more definitely, than simply as thinking man. It is in thinking and in thinking alone that he is different from the animals, that he is, as man, himself. Thus in trusting in the dignity, strength and value of his thought he is in the most fundamental sense putting his trust in humanity, in his own dignity, strength and value. These qualities in his thought are based upon the fact that the act of his thinking, provided it is truly both an *act* of thinking, and an act of *thinking*, is identical with the event of reason, or of the concept or the idea or the mind. With Hegel all those things are synonymous, and indeed they are all synonyms for the reality of all reality, which is one and the same as God.

Reason understood in this sense is *absolute* reason, the concept in this sense the *absolute* concept, truth the *absolute* truth, the idea the *absolute* idea, mind the *absolute* mind. By absolute is meant set free from all, definitely all limitations, such as apply to history in relative contrast to reason, but also to reason in relative contrast to history, to Being in relative contrast to the concept, but also to the concept in relative contrast to Being, to reality in relative contrast to truth, but also to truth in relative contrast to reality, to experience in relative contrast to the idea, but also to the idea in relative contrast to experience, to finite nature in contrast to infinite mind, but also to infinite mind in relative contrast to finite nature. The qualities of absolute reason and its synonyms are absolute dignity, strength and value. That is to say, they are dignity, strength and value, which are not limited by any contrast, which cannot be called into question by any contrast, since they unite all contrasts within themselves, since they are in themselves in motion and at rest, since they stand in and of themselves, or rather set themselves up.

It is by virtue of the fact that the act of human thinking—provided only that it is truly both an *act* of thinking, and an act of *thinking*—is identical with the event of reason, that it merits this confidence, in its dignity, strength and value, a confidence which is therefore absolute, and not to be led astray by any quality of contrast, for this reason it is the occasion for the absolute self-confidence which is the secret of Hegel's philosophy. Identical with the *event* of reason, we say. And that really is the key to everything; that reason, truth, concept, idea, mind, God himself are understood as an *event*, and, moreover, only as an event. They cease to be what they are as soon as the event, in which they are what they are, is thought of as interrupted, as soon as a state is thought of in its place. Essentially reason and all its synonyms are life, movement, process. God is God only in his divine action, revelation, creation, reconciliation, redemption; as an absolute act, as *actus purus*. He is a graven image as soon as he becomes identified with one single moment, made absolute, of this activity. And reason, likewise, is unreason as soon as the process in which it is reason is thought of at any stage as something stationary, when any of the moments of its motion is identified with reason itself. Just because of this it is only the act of human knowing as such which deserves the confidence Hegel speaks of, because it alone is identical with the act of reason itself, and thus partakes of the absolute qualities of dignity, strength and value. Hence as soon as we seek to understand by reason something other than the act in which it is itself, the act in which the idea is idea, the mind mind, etc., we shall inevitably be guilty of treating Hegel with the grossest misunderstanding. The picture he had before his mind's eye in his great apotheosis of thinking, the picture of speculative philosophy in his sense, is not one that could be reproduced by means of a drawing in points, lines and outlines, however much the hints of this picture which Hegel himself gives over and over again seem to invite such treatment. Even in speaking of the Hegelian system we must not think of a rigid, stable construction. Relevant here is the fact that Hegel's terminology is in fact not so unambiguous as one might expect, especially from one who worshipped logic as he did, and it is certainly not as clear as the reader might wish. Anyone who has studied the textbooks of the history of philosophy and then begins to read Hegel, finds himself continually nonplussed and bewildered by the—so unlike the textbooks—overlapping in the application of the individual terms the master allowed himself, for all the consistency of what he wanted to say and did in fact say. And yet somehow it seems fitting, this freedom which brings with it the notorious obscurity of Hegel's writing and which does in fact cause considerable suffering in the reader. From page to page Hegel does in fact wrest from us the possibility to compromise for ourselves a tranquil picture of his views. With him we are only to look, and look again and again, and anyone who thinks he sees stable points and lines, quantities and relationships, is not in fact seeing what Hegel is seeking to show us.

Hegel sees life, the life of reason, of the mind, of truth, admittedly, but nevertheless life, in the full movement of life. Only a kaleidoscope or the moving film of the cinematograph could offer the visual quality that would be required. What is here called a system is the exact recollection of the observed fulness of life. It is only in the form of this recollection that it has permanency and validity, and only when the recollection is itself event, a continual re-creation of the picture itself. And what makes this system a system, that gives the order and regularity running through the whole of this recollection, is nothing but the rhythm of life itself, recognized as running through the fulness of history. This rhythm, considered in itself, is the regularity inherent in the system, its heart-beat, as it were. It is the famous dialectical *method* of thesis, anti-thesis and synthesis, in pursuit of which Hegel described, or rather reconstructed, in constantly new and changing aspects and insights the event of reason as the sole object of knowledge and learning. That this object is in fact an event, the event pure and simple, is as much as to say that the method here must be the one and all (*Eins und Alles*). Anyone unwilling to allow himself to be seized by the rhythm of the method, anyone seeking to acquire wisdom while standing instead of moving, would remain in ignorance, would not achieve the slightest glimpse of this object.

Nothing is more characteristic of the Hegelian system of knowledge than the fact that upon its highest pinnacle, where it becomes know-ledge of knowledge, i.e. knowledge knowing of itself, it is impossible for it to have any other content but simply the history of philosophy, the account of its continuing self-exposition, in which all individual developments, coming full circle, can only be stages along the road to the absolute philosophy reached in Hegel himself. But that which knowledge is explicitly upon this topmost pinnacle as the history of philosophy, the philosophy completed in Hegel, it is implicitly all along the line: the knowledge of history and the history of knowledge, the history of truth, the history of God, as Hegel was able to say: the philosophy of history. History here has entered so thoroughly into reason, philosophy has so basically become the philosophy of history, that reason, the object of philosophy itself, has become history utterly and completely, that reason cannot understand itself other than as its own history, and that, from the opposite point of view, it is in a position to recognize itself at once in all history in some stage of its life-process, and also in its entirety, so far as the study permits us to divine the whole. It is a matter of the production of self-movement of the thought-content in the consciousness of the thinking subject. It is not a matter of reproduction! The Hegelian way of looking is the looking of a spectator only in so far as it is in fact in principle and exclusively theory, thinking consciousness. Granting this premise, and setting aside Kierkegaard's objection that with it the spectator might by chance have forgotten himself, that is, the practical reality of his existence, then for Hegel it is also in order (only too much in order!) that the human subject, whilst looking in this manner, stands by no means apart as if it were not concerned. It is in his looking and only in his looking that there is something seen. It is in his looking and only in his looking that the something seen is produced. And the thing seen actually has its reality in the fact that it is produced as the thing seen in the looking of the human subject. Man cannot participate more energetically (within the frame-work of theoretical possibility), he cannot be more forcefully transferred from the floor of the theatre on to the stage than in this theory.

But what is the meaning of this self-movement of the thought-content which is identical with the self-movement of the thinking subject? In this we must most particularly bear in mind Hegel's dialectical method. Reason is concept, i.e. reason conceives, reaches within itself, and, in completely penetrating, embraces reality within itself, embraces it so much that reality is reality only within reason, only as conceived reality. That, however, is not simply so; it comes about. The concept, to be exact, the absolute concept, is event. Its absoluteness is not a result to be discovered somehow and somewhere but is the absoluteness, the unlimited necessity of its execution. And the self-execution in which the concept is an absolute concept, brings itself about according to Hegel, in an endless circling, in a triple beat in which we are meant to perceive the very rhythm or heart-beat of the Hegelian system. Here we have to deal with Hegel's boldest and most weighty innovation. This movement comes about because of the fact that the concept does not so much exclude the concept that contradicts it, as the fundamental axiom of the whole of western logic had previously held, but includes it. It comes about because the contradiction of the concept, far from neutralizing it, is on the contrary a necessary moment of the concept itself. As an absolute concept the concept not only can but must 'swing over' to its opposite, 'release' its opposite, as Hegel puts it. It must do this not, it is true, in order to allow this opposite as such to stand and be valid, but in order to have it swing over forthwith into a second opposite, and finally and thirdly, that it might adjust and reconcile both in itself, call both back into itself again, and dispose of them within itself. 'Dispose' here does not have the meaning of *tollere*, but of *conservare*, so that the 'play'—Hegel's own name for the process—that is now finished can and must begin again immediately. It must begin again because it is only in its eternal self-execution that the concept is the absolute concept, the concept which is unlimited and unsurpassable in dignity, strength and value, which is absolute reason, the mind, the idea, God himself. The concept is therefore absolute, it is God, in such a way that in being and remaining the *dictum* it is also always the *contra-dictum*, and always the contradiction of the contradiction and always the reconciliation and the higher unity of both: thesis, antithesis, synthesis—subjective-finite, objective-infinite, absolute-eternal—being in itself and of itself, existing in and of itself, and however else the three dialectical stages in Hegel are generally described.

Speculative thinking is defined as: 'dissolving something real and setting it in opposition to itself in such a way that the differences as determined by one's thinking are set in opposition and the object is conceived as a unity of both'.[1] All truth is to be found in the ceaseless completion of this circle, all error is contained in stopping and staying at one of the moments of the concept, which are necessary as stages, but are thought of not as points to be stopped at but as points to be passed through. Error, lying and sin, with Hegel, can only signify obstinate one-sidedness, a blind lingering and stopping which represents a departure from obedience to the self-movement of the concept.

There is no limitation or exaggeration, no folly or wickedness in the whole range of real human thinking, from that of the most distant times and places, right up to what is taking place here and now in the philosopher's study, which would not be in principle included in the rational quality of the concept which conceives all reality within itself. Even that which is most questionable in itself can appear in this context as the exponent of the mind. It was in this sense that Hegel wrote in 1806, after the battle of Jena: 'I saw the Emperor, this world-soul, riding out through the town to go on reconnaissance; it is indeed a wonderful feeling to see such a person who, concentrated here upon one spot, sitting on a horse, reaches out over the world and rules it.'[2] In this sense Hegel could even speak of the Devil in tones of unfeigned admiration. But precisely in being made relative in this way that one-sidedness is shown its limits, and the means of rising above it is displayed. *Tout comprendre c'est tout pardonner!* From the height occupied by the concept a soft and reconciling light can be shed upon everything and everyone, and even more than that *tout comprendre c'est tout admirer*, might well be added to the saying to embrace Hegel's meaning. But it must be said at the same time that one-sidedness must submit to being seen and described as such, to being shown up in its merely relative necessity and in the badness of its habit of stopping and staying. It must be content to be summoned and aroused to go on by the magic

[1] *Phil. of Rel.*, Lasson, I, 33.
[2] Überweg, *Geschichte der Philosophie* (History of Philosophy), IV, 85.

wand of self-knowledge, which is as such knowledge of God. Theodicy and categorical imperative, the discovery of the meaning of all history, and one's own continuation of meaningful history, to put it in terms of Christian dogma, justification and sanctification, coincide perfectly within the act of this knowledge, at whatever stage it is completed, and whatever point the individual takes as his point of departure—if only this departure from the realm of one-sidedness comes about. And forthwith, as soon as this departure is made, an outlook in principle presents itself, is made possible and real upon the entire inner life of the concept or of the idea or of the mind. The Hegelian universal wisdom is there, like Pallas Athene sprung from the head of Jupiter, the moment this departure from one-sidedness, and with it the entry into the self-movement of the concept, has come about. Accordingly science, the one and only science, must be:

1. Proceeding from immediacy to objectivity: natural philosophy.

2. Passing into the non-immediacy of reflection, of imagination: logic—

3. Turning back into itself, as pure knowledge taken up once again into the higher unity of these opposites: the philosophy of mind.

In accordance with the same principle of motion logic forms itself into the teaching of Being at the first stage, into that of Essence at the second, and at the third and highest stage into that of the concept— natural philosophy forms itself into mechanics, physics and organic sciences—the philosophy of mind forms itself into the teaching of subjective, objective and absolute mind.

Leaving logic and natural philosophy, which are always divided and sub-divided according to the same principle, let us further note from the ordering of the philosophy of mind, which represents the third and decisive moment of the whole course, that Hegel understands by the teaching of the subjective mind psychology in its most comprehensive sense; by the teaching of objective mind, once again in the most comprehensive sense, ethics, which in its highest stage unfolds into the teaching of the family, the society and—characteristic of Hegel—at the highest level, the State. Finally the teaching of absolute mind moves from aesthetics via the philosophy of religion to this philosophy κατ᾽ἐξοχήν, the history of philosophy, in which Hegel's own teaching is understood as the crown and conclusion of a development which had taken place over three thousand years.

That, presented in the roughest outline, is what may be called the

Hegelian system of knowledge. Involuntarily we ask ourselves at what place in the wide ramifications of this structure we could look for the central point, the decisive concern of Hegel's thought. It might be reckoned as logic, in so far as logic has its peak in the doctrine of the concept, which plays a decisive part throughout. But we learn just as well, or better, of the most significant qualities of the concept of the concept, which is, admittedly, central to the entire teaching, and of its life and activity, in different places, where it lives its life, as distinct from the place where its life as such forms the centre of the discussion. Hegel's logic seems to be one of the less significant parts of his system, or at all events one which is less heeded and effective than many others. Natural philosophy has no clear claim for consideration either: it must be the result of personality that the strength of Schelling and Goethe, a receptiveness for nature, did not constitute Hegel's strength to the same extent. Someone whose view of the history of mind is predominantly political will be inclined and also justified in his way, whether stressing it positively or negatively, to see the Hegelian teaching of the State, with its singular conservative streak, as the master's most significant achievement. But this doctrine of the State, as a possible and necessary consequence, is probably more characteristic of than enlightening about Hegel's actual intentions. It is usual, then, to lay claim to his philosophy of history, which in the system follows upon the teaching of the State, as constituting Hegel's most significant thought. It is true, and was revealed already in his youth (Berne), that his interest in historical matters was incomparably greater than that which he showed, for instance, in research in the natural sciences. But the fact that his philosophy as a whole is the philosophy of history, philosophy of the history of God, is more important, in principle at any rate, than the expositions, given under this particular title, of reason in history, of world-history as the judgment of the world, and of this historical reason as having had its childhood in the oriental world, its time of adolescence and adulthood in the world of Greece and Rome, and its mature old age now in the Germanic world, however stimulating and important these ideas may be in themselves. Hegel's scheme of aesthetics is also certainly highly typical. In it, in opposition to the symbolical art of the East, whose characteristic form is architecture, and to the classic art of Greece, whose characteristic form is sculpture, there appears the 'romantic' art of Christendom as the higher unity, in so far as in it for the first time the spiritual element, infinite subjectivity, is said to predominate, and a reaching of art beyond itself is said to take place, whose characteristic forms are painting, music and poetry, of which, once again, the last takes up the totality of all forms within itself. At this point Hegel's connexion with Romanticism becomes palpably clear, but clear also is his going beyond Romanticism. This is shown in the view he held that the appearance of Goethe meant the beginning of a complete revolution, in terms of what had gone before, in the sphere of art. All the same, once again it cannot be said that Hegel's thought was actually centred in his teaching of art more than anywhere else. Likewise the history of philosophy, which forms the summit of the whole, should probably be looked upon more as the characteristic exponent than as the organizing centre of the whole. Finally, if anyone has wanted to find this whole in Hegel's philosophy of religion, it must indeed be said that here, where it is expressly a question of the things which clearly claim to be the last things, the nerve of all that Hegel wanted is laid bare as nowhere else. Once again, however, it cannot be said that Hegel attached particular importance to this philosophy of religion. It is for him one concern among many others, antithesis to the thesis of aesthetics, subordinate to the synthesis of philosophy; no more and no less. The fact that the philosophy of religion, too, is a motive force and this particular motive force in the self-movement of the mind, makes it relatively important, but it is definitely not important as a motive force in this movement which in some way embraces the others.

We shall ultimately understand Hegel best by believing him that, even if he does not speak with the same weight everywhere, he does after all wish to speak quite weightily absolutely everywhere, and not merely at certain points. Fundamentally there can be no centre here at the expense of a periphery. Or rather: the centre moves with the thinker himself; it is always at the point where the self-movement of the mind in the consciousness of the thinking subject is taking place. There is no outer thing that drawn into this movement could not forthwith become the most inward; there is no second to the last or third to the last thing that could not here forthwith acquire the tone and central significance of the last. Where the triple beat of thesis, antithesis and synthesis rings out and it rings out everywhere the Hegelian universal wisdom resembles one of those old villages of weavers or lace-workers where once, day after day, the sound of the same machines could be heard from every house: where this rhythm sounds there is the whole and the centre of this philosophy, possessed of the greatest strength within the smallest space. It is not this or that discipline, not a particular aspect of life or of learning, not that of the State either, or of history, or of religion, which is here in itself the organizing centre. The only centre is the *method* which is to be applied and proves true in every discipline and in every field of life and learning.

One could perhaps go a step further and say that the really vital interest, the true life-force of the Hegelian method of thinking, does not lie even in the peculiar nature of this method as such, that it is this particular method of the triple beat which is given by the division and re-union of the concept. It is of course significant, and will concern us further, that what Hegel wanted and was capable of found and was bound to find expression in this particular method. But Hegel's will and achievement itself does not consist in the invention of the dialectical method as such, but in the invention of a universal method altogether. That is what makes for Hegel's genius, what makes him typically modern, and suited to his time: the fact that he dared to want to invent such a method, a key to open every lock, a lever to set every wheel working at once, an observation tower from which not only all the lands of the earth, but the third and seventh heavens, too, can be surveyed at a glance. That was the characteristic and specific desire and achievement of Hegel: the invention of a rule for thinking whereby one can arrive at the thought and its rule itself just as much as at the things in themselves as the object of thought, at the problems of natural reality just as much as at the incomparably harder concreteness of history, at the secret of art just as much as at the texts of the Bible, which was completely affirmed as revelation, at the most primitive paths of the human psyche just as much as at the decisions of the Lord himself. This was a rule of thinking which meant that riddles exist only to be seen through at once from above and solved. Hegel's method makes it possible for him to have to overlook, suppress or forget nothing, seemingly nothing at all. It enabled him to be open, free and just in all directions. By virtue of it he could meet every request and complaint, no matter how alien it was to him, with the answer that it had already been taken into consideration in its place, or at any rate could be considered. It enabled him to understand everything great, true, beautiful and good as singly connected—nay more than that, as one. By it he could somehow comprehend and welcome all imperfect things too, the defiant resistance of the Devil not excepted, in the positive quality of this unity, and would take them up and affirm them on the condition that they allowed their place to be pointed out to them in the process of life and therefore in the system of knowledge.

Is not a principle which promises and offers such things, which emits such force and splendour, really the quintessence of dignity, strength and value? Does thinking not merit confidence, if its principle is shown to be identical with this principle? Is self-confidence, the highest possible self-confidence, not possible and necessary if we ourselves are capable of thinking thus, and of thinking this? Once again we are confronted by the mystery: why did not modern man once and for all stretch out his hand and take this key to every lock which Hegel's method offered him? Even if Hegel's method was disputable, and the system unfolded by it—what did that matter? How could modern man, how dared he let it drop before another had been invented which, even if in a better way, perhaps, promised and offered at least the same and was just as universal, just as superior and fertile, just as possible to apply as Hegel's? It is of course true that the philosophers both before and after Hegel believed they, too, could make keys to fit every lock. But how one-sided, how abstract or material were the offerings which were made before Hegel, how many questions of truth, even those held by someone like Kant, seemed to be simply brushed aside! And why was it not noticed that the attempts made after Hegel, although they sought to achieve the same, once more fell short of Hegel's achievement, that they all have the significance of being mere relapses into the one-sided modes of thinking which Hegel had overcome? Again: how, after Hegel, could materialism, positivism, pessimism, neo-Kantianism become possible? Could Hegel's picture, once it had really existed, be forgotten again? Could the prodigal son, once he had returned to his father's house, and had eaten of the fatted calf, really depart again and fill his belly abroad with husks?

Or was it in fact not his father's house to which he then had returned? Had he become the victim of a second great illusion when this picture, Hegel's picture, which seemed perfectly to correspond with and to gratify his own desire, became real? Did the self-confidence which was presented to him by this picture prove finally to be without strength or foundation? If so, then it was certainly not because of the failings which might be part of the Hegelian system as a historical quantity, as they are part of every other, nor because of the questionable things by which the Hegelian method, in the peculiarity of its nature, might be surrounded. Failings and doubtful points of detail can be no reason for rejecting a scheme such as this.

In the depths of the consciousness of the time a violent shock must have befallen the will common both to Hegel and to it, the attempt to make a key to every lock must itself have come under suspicion, a deep resignation must have been born not only as far as the How of the Hegelian method was concerned, but also as regards its That, as regards the possibility of such a universal method at all. There is no other way of explaining the retreats which now began in every sector of the front. The natural scientists withdrew into their laboratories. The historians retired to a consideration of the none-too-subtle question: how was it in those days? The philosophers fell back upon psychology and the theory of knowledge, the theologians upon the historical Jesus and upon the history of religion in general.

There is no other way of accounting for the complete bursting asunder of the *Universitas litterarum* which Hegel had once again saved. It was not only that people had happened to tire of Hegel, but that they had become fundamentally weary of the path which leads to a universal knowledge in general. They were frightened by the ideal that had been achieved, and it seems that they could not think of anything else to do but to drop it. They contented themselves once again with knowing this or that, rejoiced to think that their knowledge was at all events much greater than that of the eighteenth century, and they gave up the idea of knowing one thing, the whole, with those who wanted to surpass the eighteenth century. From this time on their habit of speaking of a scientific method as if it were a unity was but a fond illusion. Fundamentally from this time on not only theology and the other sciences but philosophy and the other sciences, even the science of history and the natural sciences among themselves, stood again helplessly confronting one another. The time was now beginning when the more people talked of method the less they could be content with any method at all, however well founded and worked out it might be; and the more the method, the one method that alone would allow them to speak of a single science, a single culture, was conspicuous by its absence. The self-confidence of modern man which still wanted to assert itself and seems to assert itself even in these changed circumstances, could only be a broken self-confidence. Anyone seeking to look at the intellectual situation of the age after Hegel as an advance upon the age of Hegel himself—and the possibility of interpreting it thus is not precluded— will not be able to seek this advance in the line in which the Enlightenment and the surpassing of the Enlightenment took its course up to and including Hegel. Measured by this line, in the light of the question of whether we have advanced along this line, the intellectual development which has taken place since Hegel can only be regarded as a decline and a retrogression.

The two questions with which we began will now perhaps have become clearer: Why did Hegel meet with no belief? Why did not his philosophy of self-confidence, a self-confidence which was unbroken because it was founded in itself, in a homogenous method, assert itself and win through? Was not his offer, even if he had been in fundamental error, still better, incomparably better as a fulfilment of the promise in which modern man still claimed he believed, than everything that came after? Or should the time of its effectiveness which we can survey perhaps be still too short? Is the time only coming, in which Hegel will meet with belief, in which his offer will be accepted?

III. Hegel is also the great perfecter and surpasser of the Enlightenment because he brought the great conflict between reason and revelation, between a purely worldly awareness of civilization and Christianity, between the God in us and the God in Christ, to a highly satisfactory conclusion. Is it any wonder that Hegel found a following above all among theologians? It seemed that after a long winter a theological spring had come such as had never been known. What had now become of all the arguments against theology which it had had openly or secretly to face since the time of Descartes, indeed for even longer, since the men of the Middle Ages who had disputed revelation? All criticism of revelation was evidence of a lamentable one-sidedness, and the wretched limits within which Kant and Lessing were still prepared to grant it validity were also evidence of one-sidedness; these were all murderous attempts upon the wealth and depth of the truth. Hegel put down each and every one of them. In a most thorough fashion Hegel himself showed the disturbers of the peace, and not least the theologians who were capitulating to them, who was master. He produced a philosophy, as we have seen, in which theology seemed to be taken better care of than in theology itself. 'Because of such a finite perception of the Divine, of that which is in and of itself—because of this finite conception of the absolute content it has come to pass that the basic teachings of Christianity have for the most part vanished from dogmatics. It is now philosophy, not alone, but chiefly, which is essentially orthodox; it is philosophy which maintains and safeguards the tenets which have ever been valid, the basic truths of Christianity.'[1] 'Much more of dogmatics has been preserved in philosophy than in dogmatics in theology itself.'[2] For it is a fact 'that the content of philosophy, its requirement and interest, is also completely that of religion; its object is eternal truth, nothing else but God and the explanation of God. Philosophy, in explaining religion, is only explaining itself, and in explaining itself it explains religion . . . Thus religion and philosophy coincide . . . philosophy is itself in fact an act of divine worship'.[3]

[1] *Phil. of Rel.*, Lasson, III, 26.   [2] Ibid., I, 40.   [3] Ibid., I, 29.

Could theology demand more than such a declaration of solidarity, indeed of a complete identity of interests from its ancient foe?

And the fascination of the form of this declaration lay in the fact that at last, at last it did not mean what the philosophizing of theology had meant during the Enlightenment, and what it had still meant with Kant. There was no de-historicizing, no forsaking of what had once actually happened in history in favour of the timelessly rational. It meant that at long last the historical element in Christianity was not only brought into a tolerable relationship with the rational one, a relationship to some extent in accordance with its dignity, but that it was actually exalted to the position of the most significant factor, that the universal quality, reason itself, was understood entirely historically. The concern which Herder particularly had expressed was given the most thorough consideration here. Anyone who thinks that he can help theology by establishing an organic relationship between revelation, faith and history, should be quite clear in his mind that it has long ago received this help from Hegel. And with history it was dogma, mystery, and primarily those teachings of Christianity which were most profound and most inaccessible to rationalism, which were splendidly rehabilitated by Hegel's philosophy of religion and which were honoured and received protection against the assaults of philosophy and of the faint-hearted among the theologians themselves.

The offer here made was, however, not only that to help save Christianity, or theology. The Middle Ages had possessed a uniform culture, which even the Reformation had not destroyed. What did destroy it was the relentless progress of the intellectual movement of the Renaissance, of the seventeenth and eighteenth centuries. The emancipation of culture from the Church which compelled the Church's emancipation from culture seemed an accomplished fact. The entire intellectual surge of the Enlightenment, but the struggle against the Enlightenment, too, had had the effect of widening this rift. It meant a threat not only to the Church, but also, truly, to culture. In spite of Kant and in spite of Goethe there could be no really quietened cultural conscience, no assured self-confidence for modern man, so long as religion was behind him in the *rôle* of an insulted enemy. A mere 'treaty' such as Schleiermacher wanted to propose to the opposing parties, along 'let us depart in peace' lines, and suggesting that faith must not hinder scientific research and that scientific research must not exclude belief—such a treaty could truly not suffice here. It did not restore what had been lost since the Middle Ages, the unity of the human and the Divine. It still caused man to appear as a spirit divided within himself, and still set up in opposition to free thinking a threateningly independent authority. At the back of Schleiermacher's proposed treaty was admittedly something quite similar to the Hegelian declaration of solidarity, and indeed of an identity of interests, as we shall see. But Schleiermacher, with his teaching of the feelings as the seat and basis of religion, remained too deeply rooted in Romanticism to be able to make clear the unity he too had in mind. This decisive achievement was something of which the speculative idealism of Hegel could alone be capable, and it did not fail in bringing it about. How indeed could it have been otherwise, after all we have seen of it? Hegel wanted to do justice to both sides, with an equity and a circumspection such as none had summoned before him. He wanted to be a modern man, without forsaking or conceding anything, and we must also credit his other desire, his wish to be a Christian, and indeed a Lutheran Christian, without forsaking or conceding anything. He acted as a true attorney, or judge, rather, between the two parties.

He had therefore to make demands of both parties. In his eyes these demands required no sacrifice, nor any compromise or concession. They rather required, upon both sides, a deeper, more radical understanding of its own case by each party, an achievement of greater self-awareness, and upon this basis the arrival at mutual understanding, at a new mutual recognition. It was perhaps the strongest expression of Hegel's self-confidence that he felt able to point out this basis and make the demands upon both sides which rested upon it. These demands were finally rejected by both sides. Modern man, without knowing of a better unity than that proposed by Hegel, yet split himself once again, as oil and water separate, into the Christian and the man. The grip whereby Hegel sought to unite him in himself turned out to be premature, too strong, or too weak, even, to prevent the centripetal forces of both sides from once again shattering the unity. That was probably the deepest, and perhaps the tragic meaning of the catastrophe of Hegelianism.

Let us begin with the demand which Hegel's philosophy of religion made upon modern cultural awareness. Hegel certainly made this demand to its own best advantage, as its own advocate, but also as its judge, in so far as, in the depths of which it had no knowledge, he sought to understand it at the same time as Christian self-awareness. Hegel interpreted modern cultural awareness to itself in an unprecedented fashion by saying that at the deepest and ultimate level it was concerned with the claim of truth. This claim takes a form possible only if the truth is God, and God is the Master of men. This is the meaning of the Hegelian apotheosis of thinking, thinking as distinct from mere feeling; this is the meaning of Hegel's intellectualism, which has so often been condemned: man lives from the truth, and only from the truth. Truth is his God, whom he dares not forsake if he is to remain human. Truth is necessary to him, and, indeed, necessary to him in its unity, in its entirety, in the divine rigour inherent in it. Such was the claim which Hegel hurled at modern man more forcibly than any theologian, at any rate, had done for centuries, although it was without doubt fundamentally a theological claim. 'Our subject', the *Philosophy of Religion* begins, 'is that which is utterly truthful, that which is truth itself, the region, where every mystery in the world, every contradiction confronting deeper thought, every emotional pain, is resolved, the region of eternal truth and eternal peace, absolute truth itself.'[1] The Enlightenment, and thinking since the Enlightenment, had admittedly also been concerned with truth, but where was it concerned in this manner with the imperious and indeed imperialistic claim of truth, with the premise that it, and ultimately it alone, formed the agenda? Where was it concerned with this unity, entirety, rigour, and divinity of truth? 'Knowledge is not only knowing that an object is, but knowing also what it is, and not only knowing in general what it is, and having a certain knowledge and certainty of it, but knowing of that which determines it, of its content, in which the necessity of the relations between these things determining it is known.'[2] The simple principle of philosophical knowledge itself should now be 'that our consciousness knows immediately of God, that knowing of the existence of God is a matter of utter human certainty . . . that reason is the place of the spirit where God reveals himself to man'.[3] 'God is not *a* concept, but *the* concept.'[4] Will modern man recognize his joy in truth, his quest for truth, his fanaticism for truth (we are reminded of Lessing) in this looking-glass? Will he put up with being taken so seriously, with being thus seized upon in his penchant for truth? Will he affirm that it was just this, something of such deadly seriousness, which was the object of his intention and desire? Or will he shrink back before the last things, which are pointed out to him as his own; before the discovery of the revelatory nature of absolute truth and all real knowledge, and still, now as ever, seek to fall humbly into the left hand of God, instead of exalting his thinking to a divine service, as is here demanded of him?

Hegel's demand consists secondly in his insistence on having truth and with it knowledge most strictly understood as a movement, as a

[1] *Phil. of Rel.*, Lasson, I, 1.   [2] Ibid., I, 50.   [3] Ibid., I, 49.   [4] Ibid., III, 42.

history. Science to Hegel means knowing and he enforces this definition with an adamant consistency and exclusiveness. Science is present only in the deed, in the event. The concept, the idea, the mind, God himself is this event—not anything outside this event. Science is applied method, and that means the applied method of truth itself, the method of God which lays claim to man in the ultimate sense. This science cannot have assured results, cannot pause for rest after achieving its discoveries. It cannot proceed from axioms unsurpassable in their certainty, from established presuppositions which lie behind it. It is nothing less than everything which is in question, and everything must continually be in question, the ultimate included, for the ultimate too, in the self-movement of truth, must ever and again become the first. This understanding, too, of truth towards all truths apparently rests upon a theological premise. The truth can only be so menacing, so disquieting, all truths can only be so unstable, all science can only be so relativized, if truth, as Hegel constantly assumes, is identical with God himself. Will modern man suffer this threat, permanent in its nature, to all certain science, this dissolution of all science into the act of knowing, into method? Will he acknowledge that Hegel has told him nothing new, but has only described the actual situation of modern man in all his research into truth? Or will he hide his eyes and not be willing to admit this after all? Will he turn away in disgust at having the background to his actions thus disclosed, and devote himself anew to his positive, exact, detailed work in history and the natural sciences, convinced that one can have a wonderful trip on Lake Constance when it is frozen, without having to think every instant where one is going?

And Hegel's demand consists thirdly in the fact that he asserts the contradiction as the law of truth understood as history. It consists in the fact that he thought he could show that the dialectical method was the one which alone exhausted and comprised the truth. The truth is God, God, however, is God only *in actu*. This means for Hegel, only as the God who is Three in One, the eternal process which consists in something distinguishing its parts, separating them, and absorbing them into itself again. Life itself is not a unity resting in itself, but a perpetual $a = non$-a, in despite of the whole of western logic. It is, quite simply, the task of logic—and of science with it—to order itself according to life, and not the task of life to adapt itself to logic. The unity of truth—and no one fought for it more vigorously than Hegel—is the unity of contradictions, more, the reconciliation which is effected between them. It is their reconciliation, but also the establishment of their basis, their necessity, and their adjustment and dissolving. It is not in the setting aside of contradictions, but in the act of making them relative that the absoluteness of mind consists. This means that it exists in the mutual relationship between the contradictions of being and thinking, object and idea, nature and spirit, object and subject, etc., the relationship they have both among themselves and with their higher unity, the unity which must, however, forthwith emit them again, and in fact itself set them up.

Looked at from this point of view, too, Hegel's demand can be understood only as a theological one. His doctrine of the Trinity, unsatisfactory as it may be from the theological point of view, is anything but a retrospective adaptation of his philosophy to comply with the wishes of the theologians. The leading theologians of Hegel's time had absolutely no desire for a renewal of the doctrine of the Trinity, and least of all for such a one as Hegel's, which threatened to place them yet again and now more than ever in conflict with all single-line logic. In propounding it Hegel was theologizing in his own way, alone and acknowledging no master, against the philosophers and against the theologians. The meaning of his dialectic method is apparent, much clearer than Schleiermacher's meaning, for instance, since Hegel in contrast to Schleiermacher presented his method under the sign of a necessary and certain knowledge of truth: the knowledge of the Creator of heaven and earth, of the Lord over light and darkness, over life and death. Knowledge of God could be the knowledge of irreconcilable contradictions and their eternal vanquishing in the mind. Knowledge of God could mean the passage through the contradictions of reason to the peace that is higher than all reason, and the emergence into these contradictions in comforted despair. Knowledge of God could make this method possible and necessary. It is a question of whether the definitions with which Hegel surrounded his method allow us to recognize that which he intended and achieved, as knowledge of God. There can be no denying that knowledge of God was what he meant, and that he was speaking from very close to the heart of the matter. But once again: will modern man tolerate such a theological invasion, and one of such a particularly menacing aspect? Will he recognize himself in this looking-glass? Was it really this which he had wanted and intended? Or had not Hegel already understood him in far too deep and far too Christian a way, by demanding of him that he should thus found his philosophy upon theology, and eventually allow his philosophy to be transformed into theology?

This partner, modern cultural awareness, did in fact let Hegel down. It neither sought to understand itself thus in its own depth, nor did it want to be reconciled in this depth with Christian awareness in such a way as Hegel thought it should be. Why not? Because the demand was too great, its conditions too theological? That in fact is how it was felt and how it is usually represented. It could also have been for the other reason, that the demand was still not radical enough, that there was not too much, but too little theology in it, for it to seem worthy of belief.

This leads us to the other demand, the demand which Hegel's philosophy of religion presented to theology. We must first of all establish that with what we have come to know as his Christian opposite to modern consciousness, Hegel had something of decisive and lasting importance to say, or to recall, to theology, and not only to the theology of his age. A theology which is jostled by philosophy—and what theology is not—is just the one which has often forgotten and still forgets that truth should not concern it less than philosophy but, on the contrary, much more. It should not be concerned with manifestations of life in general, with some kind of expressions, declarations, avowals, assertions and symbols attempting to express the inexpressible in some form or another, nor with a kind of verbal music-making, nor with a description of conditions and circumstances, nor even with a view of essentials, however deep, but with truth, with a kind of knowledge which does not have its foundation in some kind of given thing, as such, but in the link of this given thing with the final origin of everything given. If theology does not speak the truth in this sense, then in what sense can it assert that it is speaking of God? Can it perhaps absolve itself from the earnestness with which Hegel equated the knowledge of truth and the knowledge of God? Dare it fall short of Hegel in this respect, if it is not to stand—for all the supposed independence of its source of knowledge—in the shadow of philosophy, philosophy being regarded as something much more important. A theology whose basis was merely historical, merely psychological, merely phenomenological, could in fact stand in this questionable shadow. And did not nineteenth-century theology to a large extent stand indeed in this shadow when and after it passed by Hegel's doctrine?

Secondly, theology too and theology in particular was and is reminded by Hegel of the possibility that the truth might be history, event; that it might always be recognized and discovered in actuality and not otherwise. Theology might and should have known, not less well but better than Hegel, that its knowledge, its knowledge in particular, was only possible in the form of a strict obedience to the self-movement of truth, and therefore as a knowledge which was itself

moved. It could let itself be reminded by Hegel that the source of
knowledge of Reformation theology, at all events, had been the Word,
the Word of God, the word of truth. But this also means, the event of
God, the event of truth. An event that comes and goes, like a passing
thunder-shower (Luther), like the angel at the pool of Bethesda, an
event at which the man for whom it is to be an event must be present;
an event, which by repetition, and by man's renewal of his presence,
must ever become event anew. Should not theology have let itself be
reminded, by what Hegel had said to it and beyond what he said to it,
of the biblical concept of revelation, of the God who presents himself
to our knowledge, and can be known, only as the Living God? Did
not theology fall short of Hegel in this respect as well, instead of
surpassing him? Did it not, together with his strict concept of truth,
also lose sight of the concept of real history? Could this loss be made
good by the fact that, in the time which followed, theology was capable
of surpassing Hegel by means of an understanding of the historical as
such that was in fact more extensive than his? Of what use to theology
was all knowledge of reported history, that of the Bible too, and of the
Bible in particular, if at the same time it was incapable of recognizing
real history, of recognizing the Living God?

Thirdly and finally, theology was reminded by Hegel of the contradictory nature of its own particular knowledge. How on earth was
it possible for theology after Hegel to allow itself to become involved
once again in the discussion on the rational and historical qualities of
Christianity. More than that: how could it allow itself to be pushed
into the problem of the natural world and the world of the spirit?
How was it possible for it to enter into the fight against materialism,
just as if it stood and fell with the spirituality materialism was attacking? How was it possible for all its hopes and plans to be directed
towards finding a humble refuge beneath the sheltering wings of the
so-called science of the spirit? How was it possible for theology to be
exactly at the same point again around 1900, at which Kant had
arrived a hundred years before, at an *a priori* way of thinking, within
which it imagined it was well housed and secured in producing a
special, religious *a priori* method? Could it not have understood Hegel
better than he perhaps understood himself? Could it not have understood, namely, that Hegel with his concept of mind, must wittingly, or
unwittingly have been thinking of the Creator of heaven and earth,
the Lord over nature and spirit, precisely by virtue of the unity and
opposition of *dictum* and *contra-dictum*, in which Hegel had the spirit
conceiving itself and being real? Did the theologians, if they knew

about God, need to be so superstitiously respectful of natural science, and so eager to present themselves as scientists of the spirit, as they were—so typically for the theology of that period—in the second half of the nineteenth century? And if they knew about God ought they to have allowed the other Hegelian synthesis, that of reason and history in Christianity itself, to be wrested from them again? Was it really impossible to take up and make fruitful the entire Hegelian concept of the synthesis, so soon as it was taken seriously, more seriously perhaps than Hegel himself took it, with the realization that it could be a question only of the incomprehensible synthesis of God?

Doubtless, theology could and can learn something from Hegel as well. It looks as if theology had neglected something here, and certainly it has no occasion to assume an attitude of alarm and hostility to any renaissance of Hegel which might come about. It might then perhaps open its eyes more than the first time to the most highly positive element in this philosophy, to what is theologically at least indirectly significant in it. It might perhaps for that very reason be more capable than the first time of avoiding its undeniable pit-falls and temptations.

With this we come to the other thing we must say here. It may in fact be that the Hegelian demand is unacceptable to theology for good reasons, or rather that it can only become acceptable and salutary to theology if it is very vigorously translated and transformed. In order to keep sight of the complete picture we shall once again take as our guide the three landmarks of Hegelian thinking which we have already singled out: truth, the moving cognition of truth, and the dialectical character of this movement.

The first question which arises is whether the Hegelian concept of truth can do justice to theology. Hegel thinks of truth as the thinking which is conceived as the pinnacle and centre of humanity. But has humanity *this* centre? *Has* it any such centre at all? Does not man always exist at the invisible intersection of his thinking and willing? Did not Kant's doctrine of the primacy of practical reason at least put forward a reminder of this unity in man? Was it not this with which Schleiermacher's teaching of the central significance of feeling was truly concerned? It was a reminder—Hegel was right in this—which should of course not be allowed, by discrediting thinking, to lead to a vitiation of the notion of truth, but one which must protect the notion of truth from one-sided theorizing. Is a theory of truth which builds itself up upon the inner logic of a thought which is divorced from practice still the theory of man as he really is, the theory of his truth? Can the theory of truth be any other theory but the theory of human practice? From the point of view of theology perhaps it really cannot. But then doubt arises about the uninhibited way in which Hegel, at two decisive turning-points, used to think further, unperturbed—at points where a theory of practice would be bound to stop, and precisely in doing so prove itself as a theory of truth. Hegel in his paraphrase of the relation of man to God did not call a halt before the concept of sin. He included it in the unity and necessity of mind. He sought it in the finite nature of man as such, and in the freedom of mind. He thought he could see one point whence it could be understood at once as fate and as guilt, and at one and the same time the poison-cup of death and the fountain-head of reconciliation.[1] He thought he could understand sin as a 'point to be passed through in a moment or longer'.[2] He accordingly understood reconciliation not as an incomprehensibly new beginning, but simply as a continuation of the one eventual course of truth, which is identical with the existence of God himself. 'The idea of mind is this: to be the unity of divine and human nature. . . . The divine nature itself is but this: to be the Absolute Mind, that is to say, to be the unity of the divine and human nature.'[3] The consciousness of reconciliation 'completes religion as the knowledge of God as mind; for he is mind in the differentiation and return which we have seen in the idea, which implies that the unity of divine and human nature is not only significant in determining human nature, but equally so in determining divine nature'.[4] If the basis of theology for knowledge should be revelation; and of revelation should be the revelation of God to man who is lost in sin, and the revelation of God's incomprehensible reconciling, then here, where we seem to be permitted to think beyond the mystery of evil and salvation, and where it seems to be permitted and possible to solve in this way this dual mystery we have before us another basis for knowledge, a concept of truth which cannot be acceptable to theology.

That leads us to something further. The Hegelian self-movement of truth is identical with the self-movement of the thinking of the human subject, and in so far as the human subject is to be considered entirely himself while he is thinking, it is identical with the self-movement of this subject altogether. The Hegelian doctrine of the Trinity coincides with the basic principles of Hegelian logic, which is at the same time quite explicitly the basic principle of Hegelian anthropology and the Hegelian teaching of life. 'God is this: to distinguish oneself from oneself, to be object to oneself, but to be completely identical with oneself in this distinction.'[5] Certainly, but Hegel might just as well have

[1] *Philosophy of Religion*, III, 110.   [2] Ibid., III, 105.   [3] Ibid., III, 38.
[4] Ibid., III, 131.   [5] Ibid., III, 6.

said that knowledge is this and man is this. Hegel did not dispute the positive and historical nature of revelation, the uniqueness of Christ; rather he emphatically affirmed it. But with Hegel God and man can never confront one another in a relationship which is actual and indissoluble, a word, a new word revelatory in the strict sense, cannot pass between them; it cannot be uttered and cannot be heeded. It is only in so far as 'everything which exists for consciousness is objective to it that there is an objectivity of revelation. Everything must come to us in an outward way'.[1] Revelation therefore, like all knowledge of whatever kind, also passes through objectivity, inasmuch as knowledge also comprises the moment of perception. And this objectivity, and similarly and to the same degree the objectivity of revelation, is anything but indissoluble. It is distinguished as a stage of revelation upon the level of the mere 'imagination', which it is the task of philosophy, as being the delegated authority of mind, to raise to the form of thought as the form suited to the reality of mind. This also means, however, that philosophy has to reduce it to its purely logical content,[2] even if, now as before, those who are still immature are still allowed to perceive pure thought in the form of the imagination. Reason, whose ordained task it is to perform this operation, and which must set about performing it without being able to stop, is just as much divine revelation as is the imagination.[3] When God manifests himself the philosopher of religion has already understood him in the preliminaries of this act, and he already has the lever in his hand which he has only to depress to advance from God's act of revealing to the higher level of God being manifest, in which every given thing, all duality, is annulled, all speaking and listening has lost its object and been transformed again into pure knowing, the knowing of the human subject, as it originally proceeded from him. Hegel's living God—he saw God's aliveness well, and saw it better than many theologians—is actually the living man. In so far as this living man is only after all thinking man, and this abstractly thinking man might be a man who is merely thought, and not a real man at all, it is possible that this living God, too, Hegel's God, is a merely thinking and merely thought God, before whom real man would stand as before an idol, or as before a nothing. At all events he would stand in boundless loneliness, 'without a God in the world'. The self-movement of truth would have to be detached from the self-movement of man—and here it is equated with it with the utmost explicitness and rigour of logic—to be justly regarded as the self-movement of God.

[1] *Philosophy of Religion*, III, 19.   [2] Ibid., I, 67.   [3] Ibid., I, 54.

And the third thing there is to be said is that the identification of God with the dialectical method, even if it did not signify that he was identified with man's act of life, implies a scarcely acceptable limitation, even abolition of God's sovereignty, which makes even more questionable the designation of that which Hegel calls mind, idea, reason, etc., as God. This God, the God of Hegel is at the least his own prisoner. Comprehending all things, he finally and at the highest level comprehends himself too, and by virtue of the fact that he does this in the consciousness of man, everything God is and does will be and is understood from the point of view of man, as God's own necessity. Revelation can now no longer be a free act of God; God, rather, *must* function as we see him function in revelation. It is necessary to him to reveal himself. 'A mind which is not manifest is not a mind.'[1] 'God is utterly manifest.'[2] The finite consciousness, which partakes of revelation, thus shows itself as a motive power in the concept, in the process of God himself. Creation is necessary, and reconciliation too is necessary. The Church is necessary to God himself, for in it he can be the mind of the Church; and it is this alone which first makes it possible for him to be mind and God. If he were not the mind of the Church he would not be God. And he is God only in so far as he is the mind of the Church. I am necessary to God. That is the basis of Hegel's confidence in God, and the reason why this confidence can immediately and without further ado be understood as self-confidence as well, and why it did thus understand itself. Hegel, in making the dialectical method of logic the essential nature of God, made impossible the knowledge of the actual dialectic of grace, which has its foundation in the freedom of God. Upon the basis of this dialectic the attempt to speak of a necessity to which God himself is supposed to be subject would be radically impossible. But at all events the dialectic in which we ourselves exist, a method which we are ourselves at all times capable of using—this is not the actual dialectic of grace. Hegel did not open the gate-way of this knowledge to theology, and it seems that it remained closed to his own perception too. That is probably the weightiest and most significant of the doubts about him which might be raised from the theological point of view. The two points previously mentioned, the single-track nature of his concept of truth and the confusion of human with divine self-movement also have their origin in this: in the failure to recognize that God is free—one might perhaps say in all succinctness: in the failure to recognize double predestination. They have their origin in the fact that Hegel's dialectic cannot, by theology at all

[1] *Philosophy of Religion*, III, 35.   [2] Ibid., III, 6.

events, be acknowledged as a dialectic which could be accepted in all seriousness.

Theology was just as incapable of accepting Hegel's philosophy as was modern cultural awareness. Of course it cannot be said that it rejected him at that time because it knew better and because it clearly recognized the things which were unacceptable to it in his teaching. It would only have been able to do that if it had previously allowed itself to be taught by him much more thoroughly. Ultimately theology rejected him merely for the same reasons which also made him unacceptable to modern cultural awareness. Who knows whether it was not in fact the *genuinely* theological element in Hegel which made it shrink back? Conversely, openly or secretly, it adopted at any rate enough of the very things that were questionable about him, without being able to overcome their effects by means of his genuine insights. Theology had, and still has, no occasion to throw stones at Hegel, as if it had not trodden the same path as he, only not in so firm or so logical a manner as he did. When we come to consider Schleiermacher we shall have to ask very seriously whether his secret is a different one from that of Hegel, only that with Hegel it might be a secret which was to a great extent more respectable and at all events more instructive than that of Schleiermacher. And we shall also find strong traces of Hegel elsewhere and not only among Hegelians, but in places where people considered themselves to be far above Hegelianism. All too much had he, the misunderstood one, taught those things which his whole century, and the theologians of his century as well had at heart. Would modern man and the modern theologian have understood him better and accorded him a better reception, if there had not been these known theological objections to be raised against him, if he had at once gone one step further all along the line, and if he had at once been a little more in earnest from the theological point of view? Many and great things would then have assumed a different aspect in the intellectual life of the nineteenth and twentieth centuries, and perhaps in their political and economic life too. But in that case Hegel would not have been Hegel, and we must therefore be content to understand him as the man he was: as a great problem and a great disappointment, but perhaps also a great promise.

VIII

SCHLEIERMACHER

THE elder Gass, impressed by a reading of Schleiermacher's *Doctrine of Faith*[1] once wrote to its author saying: 'There is no one who can make me waver in my belief that your dogmatics herald a new era, not only in this one discipline, but in the whole study of theology in general.'[2] And A. Neander went even further, saying to his students on the day after Schleiermacher's death: 'From him a new period in the history of the Church will one day take its origin.'

These prophecies have been fulfilled. The first place in a history of the theology of the most recent times belongs and will always belong to Schleiermacher, and he has no rival. It has often been pointed out that Schleiermacher did not found any school. This assertion can be robbed of some of its force by mention of the names of his successors in Berlin, August Twesten, Karl Immanuel Nitzsch of Bremen, and Alexander Schweizer of Zürich. But they are correct in so far as Schleiermacher's significance lies beyond these beginnings of a school in his name. What he said of Frederick the Great in his Academy address entitled 'What goes to make a great man' applies also to himself: 'He did not found a school, but an era.'[3] The man who published an essay in 1907 called *Schleiermacher der Kirchenvater des 19. Jahrhunderts* (Schleiermacher, the Church-father of the Nineteenth Century), was speaking the historical truth. The nineteenth century brought with it many deviations from Schleiermacher, and many protests against him; often his ideas were distorted to the point of unrecognizability, and he was often overlooked and forgotten. But in the theological field it was nevertheless his century. After describing all sorts of curves, both great and small, it none the less always returned to him. His influence did not decrease, it increased as time went on, and his views established themselves more and more. He was studied,

[1] *Der christliche Glaube, nach den Grundsätzen der Evangelischen Kirche im Zusammenhang dargestellt* (The Christian Faith, systematically set forth according to the principles of the Evangelical Church). References in this chapter to the *Doctrine of Faith* (*Glaubenslehre*) are to this work, known in England as *The Christian Faith*.

[2] *Briefwechsel* (Correspondence), ed. W. Gass, Berlin 1852, p. 195.

[3] *Philosophische Werke* (Philosophical Works), Berlin 1835, III, 83.

honoured and made fruitful much more in 1910 than in 1830, when people outside the closest circle of his acquaintances had no hesitation in naming him in the same breath with theologians like Daub, Marheineke, Bretschneider and others like them. Even if at this time, when he was producing his greatest work, he doubtless stood in the shadow of Hegel (when the young D. F. Strauss, just arrived in Berlin on the journey customary for Tübingen seminarists, heard in Schleiermacher's study of Hegel's sudden death he wounded him with the unreflecting painful words: 'But it was on his account that I came here') his star rose all the brighter after the fairly rapid passing of the age of Hegelianism. From that time on, after the stimulation of Hegel had, partly rightly and partly wrongly, been withdrawn, only Schleiermacher could be the saviour. The great exception, the original school of Ritschl, was also but a proof of this fact. And it is truly a sign of the extraordinary extent of his influence that E. Brunner, in 1924, was the first man writing against Schleiermacher whose premises were really different, really free of him (even if they were perhaps only relatively free of him!). Until then every attack had shown such a close similarity of content with his own writings that an effective antithesis had been impossible. Nobody can say today whether we have really overcome his influence, or whether we are still at heart children of his age, for all the protest against him, which now, admittedly, has increased in volume and is carried out according to basic principles.

If we ask ourselves how it was that Schleiermacher could become so much our—and perhaps really still *our*—man of destiny, we are once again faced by the mystery of the great man, which possibly consists in the indissoluble unity of his timeless individual power on the one hand, and on the other of the temporal, historical conditions into which he was placed.—We have no occasion to adopt the style of that man Lülmann, who in his work on 'Schleiermacher the church-father of the nineteenth century' referred to Schleiermacher as a 'gigantic personality', and then, as if this were not enough, as a 'priest and prophet in one person and a king in the realm of the mind' (p. 12). But it is impossible to consider Schleiermacher thoroughly without being very strongly impressed. Indeed one is more strongly impressed every time one does consider him—by the wealth and magnitude of the tasks he set himself, by the moral and intellectual equipment with which he approached them, by the manly steadfastness with which he trod the path he had once embarked upon right to the end as he had entered upon it, unheedful of the favour or disfavour of each passing decade—and by the artistry which he displayed, playfully, and endowing it by this very playfulness with the ultimate gravity of all true art—an artistry he showed in all he did, almost down to his last Sunday sermon. We have to do with a hero, the like of which is but seldom bestowed upon theology. Anyone who has never noticed anything of the splendour this figure radiated and still does—I am almost tempted to say, who has never succumbed to it—may honourably pass on to other and possibly better ways, but let him never raise so much as a finger against Schleiermacher. Anyone who has never loved here, and is not in a position to love again and again may not hate here either. H. Scholz wrote with perfect truth of the *Doctrine of Faith*: 'Schleiermacher did not succeed in everything; but his achievement as a whole is so great, that the only threat to it would be a corresponding counter-achievement, not a cavilling criticism of detail.'[1] This counter-achievement, and indeed the man who could not only criticize Schleiermacher but measure himself against him, have not yet appeared. Let it be said in warning that with every step which exceeds careful listening and the careful asking of questions one may, not inevitably but very easily, make oneself look ridiculous. That is the first thing there is to be said about the secret of Schleiermacher's peculiar position: the drawing of attention to Schleiermacher himself, who indeed won for theology a little more honour in the circle of the classic writers than the good Herder had done before him.

The other thing we have to do in trying to assess Schleiermacher's merits is to remember his time, with some outlines of which we have become acquainted in the first part of this book. We may bear in mind Lessing's advances in the direction of the concepts 'history' and 'experience', or the straits into which theology had been driven by Kant's philosophy of religion, or the concern which Herder, stammering rather than saying anything of real importance, produced in opposition to Kant. We may remember the discoveries in the mysterious wealth of the centre, on the basis of which Novalis, rather suddenly as we saw, attempted to proclaim Christianity with a new voice, together with much mathematics and love and poetry, or the greatness and downfall of Hegel's philosophy. Positively or negatively we can draw lines from everywhere leading to Schleiermacher; from every point we can come to understand that for his century he was not one among many others, with his theology and philosophy of religion, but that it was possible for him to have the significance of the fulness of time. I do not say it was inevitable that he should have this significance,

---

[1] *Christentum und Wissenschaft in Schleiermachers Glaubenslehre* (Christianity and Learning in Schleiermacher's Doctrine of Faith), 1911, p. 201.

but possible. Whether the century understood itself rightly in thinking it heard the liberating word from Schleiermacher, whether it might not have been possible to gain further insights of an entirely different kind from all the points which Schleiermacher had touched upon— that is a different question. With all the figures we have so far considered we have tried not only to look from them to Schleiermacher, but wherever possible to look from them to points beyond Schleiermacher, to look out for the possible answers to the questions raised there which Schleiermacher just did not provide. But one thing is certain, that this century could and did hear from Schleiermacher a liberating word, in some way an answering word. If it is not in itself certain that 'the man who has done justice to the best men of his age has lived for all time' it is beyond doubt that Schleiermacher, in the theological sphere, really did do justice to the best men of his age. And for that reason he did really live, for that age at all events, and still lives, in so far as we might perhaps still find ourselves within this age. He will in fact live for every age, if we construe his age, too, as an age of the Church. That is the other thing that must be said here.

We shall now attempt to look at some of the most important motifs, as regards content, which played their part throughout while Schleiermacher's life work came into being, and which must be borne in mind throughout the appraisal of it. We shall attempt both to see them and to see them in relation to each other.

I. The factor which is decisive in making a theology theology does not belong to the motifs whose presence can be asserted or denied in anyone's work. Even of Luther or Calvin it cannot simply be said that they represented and proclaimed the Christian faith, the Gospel. The Gospel in the full sense of the word, according to the *Confessio Augustana*, Article V, is represented and proclaimed *ubi et quando visum est Deo*, not at the point where, applying this or that yardstick, we feel we can affirm the Christian quality of a theology or philosophy—however superficially or thoroughly we are observing. The Christian quality of a theology does not belong to the motifs of a theology which can be vouched for, just because it is always the motif, with Calvin and Luther too, which is to be questioned. It is not on the same plane with the motifs of a theology that can truly be vouched for. I say all this in opposition to Brunner. He plays off 'the Christian faith' as a solid quantity against the other effective motifs in Schleiermacher's work in a way which, carried to its logical conclusion, would mean that the Christian quality would inevitably have to be denied to the theology of Luther and Calvin as well. Upon this point, which is admittedly a decisive one, one can only speak of indications. This also applies to Schleiermacher with whom we are possibly more tempted to ask questions than with Luther and Calvin, and one must then, in order to be fair, not only treat the positive indications as seriously as the negative ones, but even more seriously, provided one wishes to treat with Schleiermacher also within the sphere of the Church and not elsewhere. However weighty the questions we wish to put we must reckon without reserve with the fact that Schleiermacher was a Christian theologian at all events as well. We must remain true to the indications which support this fact. I do not mean to say that we should consider that these indications go to prove it. Led by these indications we should, however, believe it of him, just as we are led by indications which are perhaps stronger, to believe it of Luther and Calvin. I should like to point out four things which should be considered here:

(a) Schleiermacher, who proved by distinguished achievements in the field of philosophy, and above all of philology, that he had a mind which offered him other great possibilities, chose theology in his youth as his life's profession. He allowed himself to be led still deeper into it, into Enlightenment theology at first, as a result of the dénouement of his relationship to his father and the Moravian brethren. He did not allow himself to be led out of it again either by all the intensive investigation he then began of the intellecual life of the time, which was indeed unfavourable to theology, or by an intensive study of the history of philosophy, of Plato especially. And we cannot overlook the fact that he felt himself responsible for the interest of the Christian Church in this very field of learning, in answering the question of truth which was directed also at Christian preaching. We must remember that he dedicated to this interest what was after all a considerable part, and quantitatively at all events the greatest part, of the strength and work and time he had it in his power to dedicate. We must not overlook these things even if we feel that he was not the best man to protect this interest.

(b) We cannot be mindful enough of the fact that Schleiermacher was not one of those theologians who are in the habit, under some pretext or other, of dissociating themselves from the most difficult and decisive theological situation, that in which the theologian, without security of any kind, must prove himself solely as a theologian. I refer to the situation of the man in the pulpit. Schleiermacher did not only not avoid this most exposed position, but actually sought it, throughout his life, as the place for his 'own office'.[1] He sought it 'with enthusiasm', as one of his friends avowed in 1804, almost with astonishment.[2] More than one of the pupils of his who understood him best have testified, and Dilthey, his biographer, has added his historical testimony to their contemporary one, that it was precisely in his sermons that Schleiermacher's characteristic desires and achievements were made evident at any rate in their liveliest and most impressive form. To be true, it sounds terrible to us to hear Schleiermacher's pupil Sydow praise his sermons because they presented 'the outloook of a highly-gifted and thoroughly educated personality in the moments of its most noble expression of life'.[3] But we must not be prevented by that and the even more enraptured effusions of the dreadful Bettina von Arnim from seeing what there is to see here. Whatever may be said of and against the content of these famous sermons, one thing is certain. It is that in accordance with the sound Reformed tradition from which he sprang, Schleiermacher saw the *Kirchen-regiment* (Church polity), for which theology provides the premise, as consisting essentially in the office of the preacher, and that he did not only declare himself consistently for this belief theoretically, but—equalling Luther and Calvin—in un-interrupted practice—without, be it said, achieving extraordinary outward success. Those who know what preaching and academic work involve should be truly impressed by the fact that together with all the other things that claimed his attention, Schleiermacher managed to perform this office year in and year out, almost every Sunday. Nobody does that who does not feel impelled to do it, which at any rate is remarkable. All the questionable things we learn from the *Addresses on Religion* and *The Doctrine of Faith* about Schleiermacher's fundamental idea of this office: namely that the decisive factor is a 'self-imparting' of the preacher—cannot alter the fact that Schleiermacher performed this office with a noteworthy loyalty, whether or not his idea of it was correct.

(c) In academic theology, too, Schleiermacher did not make things easy for himself. In the history of Protestant theology the nineteenth cen-tury brought with it the none too dignified sight of a general flight, of those heads that were wisest, into the study of history. From the safe, distant regions of the history of religion, the Church, dogma and the mind the practice of theology is a gentle exercise, if one has the neces-sary equipment. Schleiermacher set a different example in this, at all

---

[1] *Schleiermacher's Leben in Briefen* (Schleiermacher's Life in Letters), Berlin, 1859-63, II, 16.
[2] *Letters*, III, 376.   [3] *Predigten* (Sermons), VII, p. viii.

events. What decides whether theology is possible as a science is not whether theologians read sources, observe historical facts as such, and uncover the nature of historical relationships, but whether they can think dogmatically. Schleiermacher attempted to show that theology was possible as a science by writing his dogmatics—it was really his only large work, apart from his lectures. Questionably enough, he called it a *Doctrine of Faith* and conceived of it as a historical discipline. At bottom it is perhaps more apologetics than what, by pointing to its better part, could be understood as comprising a doctrine of faith. It raises a most urgent question whether with these very dogmatics theology was not consigned to a branch of the general science of the mind, so that the historicizing of theology was most thoroughly prepared for. But all this does not alter the fact that Schleiermacher at least attacked the problem of theology at the point where it must be attacked if it is to be attacked at all: with a basic consideration on what the Church may, can and should teach in its prevailing present, in connexion with the biblical norm upon the one side and with the Church's past upon the other. We must compare Schleiermacher's attitude with the thorough distraction with which Troeltsch was a theologian a hundred years later. We must set the doctrine of faith of the one beside that of the other, in order to discover which of them had his work completely at heart, and which of them had it definitely less at heart. Then we can grant Schleiermacher what even the most negative judgment upon the theological content of his work must grant: that he was deeply in earnest, not only concerning theology in general, but in the trouble he took to safeguard the specifically theological quality of theology.

(*d*) One thing at all events must be said of the content of Schleiermacher's theology: he did at least see the danger of a theology which is essentially apologetic in its approach—its impending metamorphosis into a philosophy; and if there was one thing he fought almost desperately against as an academic theologian, it was this danger. He saw also what the offence was wherewith he had to present philosophy, or at least the philosophy of his own time, if he wanted to be a theologian, and he did in fact dare to offend it in this way. It is the problem of Christology which is here at stake. It can be asked whether what he wanted to say about the relation of God and man could possibly be said also in the form of Christology. And it can, moreover, be asked whether Christology can possibly serve as the form for what Schleiermacher wanted to say. The Christology is the great disturbing element in Schleiermacher's doctrine of faith, not a very effective disturbance, perhaps, but a disturbance all the same. What he wanted to say might perhaps have been said better, more lucidly and more concisely, if he had been able to say it in the form of a circle with one centre, instead of as an ellipse with two foci. But Schleiermacher could not avoid this element of disturbance. He could not present his views in any other way; he had to present them as he did. Jesus of Nazareth fits desperately badly into this theology of the historical 'composite life' of humanity, a 'composite life' which is really after all fundamentally self-sufficient; in Schleiermacher's sermons, too, Jesus only plays the striking *rôle* he does because, one is tempted to think, he is simply there. He obviously gives Schleiermacher, the professor and preacher, a great deal of trouble! But nevertheless he is in fact there. And the professor and preacher goes to this trouble, swims ceaselessly against his own current, and wishes under all circumstances, and be it at the cost of certain artifices and sophistries, to be a Christocentric theologian. Whether he really is, who can say? Perhaps in fleeing from one kind of philosophic speculation he became all the more deeply embroiled in another. Perhaps after all he avoided the offence of a real Christology.

Perhaps after all he transformed *pistis* into *gnosis*. There is much to support this view. Schleiermacher, as we know, on his death-bed celebrated Holy Communion with his family: with water instead of wine, which the doctor had forbidden him to drink, and recalling that Christ, in blessing wine, had also blessed water. It can be asked whether the water in the wine was blessed in order that in the last resort it could take the place of wine, or whether it all ceases to be the Lord's Supper when the one is exchanged for the other in this way. But there can be no doubt of the fact that Schleiermacher wanted to celebrate the Holy Communion. He wanted in his Christology, whose content might perhaps be compared with the water, to proclaim Christ. And the fervour with which he did it, as a dogmatician and preacher, is also beyond all doubt in the minds of all who know him. If anyone was most deeply in earnest in this matter then it was Schleiermacher. That cannot of course be regarded as a last word upon the subject; the theological question of truth must remain open here as everywhere, even in the face of the greatest personal sincerity. But we must bear in mind the phenomenon of this personal sincerity, which cannot be overlooked, just as we must bear in mind the other indications. Ultimately we can only believe that Schleiermacher, too, was a Christian theologian; that, I repeat, is something he has in common with Luther and Calvin and (lest it be forgotten!), upon the lower plane, with all of us.

II. The quality of being a Christian is the motif in Schleiermacher's theology for which there are indeed indications that it is present, but which we cannot vouch for and the presence of which, therefore, with him as with all other theologians, we can and must ultimately take upon trust.

But the second motif which we shall now discuss is one that can without doubt be vouched for. At the same time as he sought to be a Christian theologian Schleiermacher also felt responsible—I should like to understand and weigh this as earnestly as possible—for the intellectual and moral foundations of the cultural world into which a man was born at the end of the eighteenth century. He wanted in all circumstances to be a modern man as well as a Christian theologian— we must not seek to decide whether he was striving for the former aim with the same or perhaps with even greater earnestness than that with which he sought to be a Christian theologian, at any rate he did so with similar earnestness. The fact that in his famous first work he addressed himself to the educated among the despisers of religion is something which would have been characteristic of his own position, even if he had not at once, in the first lines of the book, emphasized that 'one of those who have raised themselves above the common level and are steeped in the wisdom of the century' here demanded their attention. With him his participation in the cultural awareness of his time, and indeed his participation in its deepest possible content, in its strictest possible form and liveliest expression, was a deeply serious concern which was not suspended for an instant. But it was not only his passive participation as an educated person, but also his participation as one who himself educated, as one who helped sustain this cultural awareness which is here in question. He affirmed its presence in feeling that he had received a call to struggle, together with his best contemporaries, for an ever-increasing depth in its content, for an ever-greater strictness of its form, for an ever-greater liveliness of its expression. He took part in the philosophy, science, politics, social life and art of his time as if they were his own concern, as the man who was responsible in all these fields, the man who was called to achieve and to lead in the general achievement. He wants to be and is entirely this man, the man moved by this concern. And he wants to be and is this man also as a theologian—and indeed in the pulpit just as much, and perhaps even more so, than in the professorial chair. It was only in his time, the time which fulfilled and overcame, overcame and fulfilled the Enlightenment, that this personal union became possible: beyond Rousseau's outbreaks, beyond Lessing's struggles, beyond Kant's critique, in the time which found it possible to take Hegel's synthetic philosophy as its sign. Schleiermacher so wonderfully fulfilled that time of his, in realizing the possibility of the theologian's being at the same time entirely a modern man, with a good, and not with a divided conscience. How, as a modern man, he was at once a theologian with a good conscience, is something that will be discussed later, under Point 3.

For the time being we shall continue to discuss the first thing: the fact that Schleiermacher was a theologian did not hinder him in the slightest from also wanting, seeking and effecting, all the things that, wisely understood, were best in what the non-theological world of his time was wanting, seeking and effecting. He did not do this retrospectively, trotting behind the times, as theologians so often do, but in advance of the time, as a born man of the age, and, further, as 'one dedicated to the achievement of a better future'. To say that it 'did not hinder him in the slightest' is to put it much too mildly. Precisely because he was a theologian, and precisely upon the basis of his interpretation of Christianity he felt himself compelled to be a modern man with all his heart, with all his feelings, and with all his strength. He did not achieve any synthesis; he lived from a unity which had been completed for him, he loved this modern man in himself and in the others with all the strength of a love which is just as sincere as it is a matter of course. And thus we find him at the turn of the century among the Romantics, the Berlin hospital chaplain, who yet found it possible also to come and go in the intellectually advanced circles of the capital without acquiring that rather unfortunate flavour of the clever eighteenth-century abbé—as one who, honestly and as a matter of course, belonged there. And thus we find him at Halle, devoting at least as much attention to his translation of Plato and researches into this philosopher, as to his studies of St Paul and the beginnings of his dogmatics, inspired to the writing of his *Weihnachtsfeier* (Celebration of Christmas), as he himself attests, by having heard a flute concerto, of all things. And so we find him at the height of his career, in the years 1809-34, in Berlin once again, at least as much at home in the Academy of the Sciences as in his pulpit in the Church of the Holy Trinity. Schleiermacher, so to speak, had no distance to go from the one concern to the other, from the one activity to the other. By birth and upbringing in its innermost sanctuary his theology is cultural theology: in religion itself which is the true object of his theology, it is the exaltation of life in the most comprehensive sense, the exaltation, unfolding, transfiguration, ennobling of the individual and social human life which is at stake. Civilization as the triumph of the spirit over nature is the most peculiar work of Christianity, just as the quality of being a Christian is for its own part the crown of a thoroughly civilized consciousness. The kingdom of God, according to Schleiermacher, is utterly and unequivocally identical with the advance of civilization. The way in which Schleiermacher himself realized in his own person this idea of religion and Christianity, as researcher, teacher, author and preacher, and what he was as an intellectually and morally thoroughly educated person, what an *opus ingens* the *Doctrine of Faith* was, for instance, which was in its way of intellectual achievement possibly completely unique: all these things are in fact so far above the average that to anyone who does not know them one can only say that he should go and learn here what civilization might be. It is very necessary for theologians that they should have ever before them a clear and lively notion of it, in order to make sure that they do not talk nonsense if, unlike Schleiermacher, they seek to find the secret of Christianity at some point beyond all culture.

But what interests us here is the principle Schleiermacher proclaimed along these lines to others, to the Church, and to society. Above all, it is clear that as a theologian Schleiermacher is relentlessly in earnest down to the last line, in the material sense, too, about thinking and speaking in terms of the premises achieved by the philosophy and history and natural science of his day, and on no account in any others. In the case of the conflict between the Christian and the modern quality of his thoughts this can lead to concealments and ambiguities in his writings. There is in fact no lack of them in his *Doctrine of Faith* and in his sermons. But we can be assured that within this certain element of obscurity—whatever becomes of the Christian quality— the feeling of responsibility for modernity was at all events consistently maintained, either openly or secretly. Schleiermacher did not permit himself any real concessions from this sense of responsibility to any other claim. This participation of his in modern cultural awareness was not only an actual one and not only a defensive one. He did not only advocate modern civilization, but proclaimed and demanded it. In order to become acquainted with Schleiermacher we must not neglect to take as our guide the *Philosophical Ethics* and the *Christian Morality*, and above all the sermons as well as the well-known *Address* and the *Doctrine of Faith*. We must do this if only because in these better-known works it is not nearly so clear as in the former writings that Schleiermacher as a theologian wanted something quite definite from his hearers and readers, something in relation to which everything else he propounded was only in the nature of a means to an end, as the lever is to the load to be moved.

What did he want? He wanted to draw men into the movement of education, the exaltation of life, which at bottom is the religious, the Christian movement. I venture to assert that Schleiermacher's entire philosophy of religion, and therefore his entire teaching of the nature of religion and Christianity, the things we first think of when his name is mentioned, was something secondary, auxiliary to the consolidation of this true concern of his, the ethical one. The fact that, in academic theory, he ranked theology below ethics, is but an expression of this state of affairs. With Schleiermacher it is not a matter of doctrine, nor of his particular doctrine, or a matter of his particular doctrine only for the sake of the end to be achieved; with him it is a matter of life. The life he means is not, as a superficial observer might suppose, a life playing itself out in the inwardness of the soul, a life which takes pleasure in itself, and is essentially passive, a mystical introspection.

This might well be the impression given by the famous introduction to the *Doctrine of Faith*, and perhaps also by the *Addresses on Religion*. But it must not be forgotten that in the *Addresses* and in the introduction to the *Doctrine of Faith* it is a question of Schleiermacher's apologetic representation of religion, and not actually of his objective one. And we must not overlook the remarkable Paragraph 9 in the introduction to the *Doctrine of Faith* where Christianity is suddenly described— contrary to all the expectations the reader acquires from the previous paragraphs—as a theological religion, one, that is, which is determined in the direction of activity, in which the consciousness of God is entirely related to the sum-total of the states of activity in the idea of a kingdom of God. After the apologetic beginning of the introduction such a description of Christianity as the highest religion should have been impossible: the feeling of complete dependence, which had been the definition of religion in this beginning, could only have found its fulfilment in the aesthetic, i.e. passive type of religion. It is by deviating in this way that Schleiermacher returns to the understanding of Christianity he presented when he was concerned with it objectively, and not apologetically.

We must therefore take the greatest exception to Brunner for completely failing, as the very title of his book *Die Mystik und das Wort* (Mysticism and the Word) shows, to look in the place where Schleiermacher was truly at home, the place whence he exercised his decisive influence. For just as Schleiermacher did not seek to identify Christianity with mysticism (although this was in fact what he did achieve as an apologist) but with the movement of civilization, so the theology of the nineteenth century which took over from him is least characterized by its affinity to mysticism, and most definitely by its unqualified and direct affirmation of modern cultural consciousness. Schleiermacher's entire intellectual attitude, as we have it in his writings, and as it must personally have influenced his contemporaries, is, after all, so completely unlike that of a mystic. This can best be observed in Schleiermacher's doctrine of prayer, which no pious person with a true bent for mysticism could accept. For the moment of withdrawal into self, the gathering of internal forces, the severing of connexion with the outside world, the achievement of a pure stillness, which he describes as the one aspect in the process of prayer, and describes, be it said, with great power, is only the beginning of transition to a quite different activity. In seeking and finding God in prayer man reaches, as it were, the watershed between receptivity and self-activity. In reaching it he has already passed beyond it, and he also once again finds himself, now more than ever, upon the ground of his own free, creative activity. In prayer there takes place, as it were, a crystallization of religious life into a particular act of life, which is forthwith dispersed and dissolved again, at the climax of this process, in the communion with God, in which the general act of life can and should take place, and will take place again after this concentration. It is only for the sake of this second state that Schleiermacher describes the first one. He prays because he wants to work; he is a mystic because without mysticism there could not be any civilization. Thus, Schleiermacher does not seek this particular act of life as such, but its dispersal and dissolution for the benefit of the general act of life taking place in the communion with God. The prayer of this moment is the anticipation of the enhanced will for civilization of the next. It is the *homo religiosus* himself who is in the deepest sense involved in the process of education. He must pass through the mystical sanctuary—but he must really only pass through it, and quickly and without delay—just at the point where the true mystic likes to stop and likes best of all to stop finally, in the pure confrontation and oneness of God and the soul; it is here that Schleiermacher unmistakably urges us speedily onwards, from the act of introversion to the act of forming, from contemplation to construction.

If Schleiermacher considers the first step to be important, then he undeniably sees the second as being even more important and the first is important only for the sake of the second. It is here, in this tendency towards an ethical interpretation, that I am moreover tempted to see the true cause of the undogmatic character, using the word in its usual sense, and indeed the anti-dogmatic, anti-intellectualizing, anti-doctrinal character of Schleiermacher's theology. What strikes us in a study of Schleiermacher's sermons is the fact that whenever he engages in true polemics these are always directed against the same three things: against all over-assessment of the importance of religious doctrine and of the religious word altogether, against every kind of particular religious excitement, and against the tendency associated with this, to religious sectarianism of individuals or whole groups. This must not only and not ultimately be understood as arising out of Schleiermacher's concept of religion, which does, it is true, coincide with that of mystical theology, but definitely as the result of the teleological, activistic intention of his theology, which affirms civilization. Schleiermacher's favourite interpretation of biblical miracle was that it was the prophecy of the astonishing victory of spirit over the natural world, which was being fulfilled more and more in human history, and especially in the present, and was thus, far from being important in itself or in need of repetition, the incitement for us to devote our energies to the achievement of this victory.

In this connexion Schleiermacher first and above all celebrated the *state* as the guardian of order and of peace. Although throughout his life he supported the idea that the Church should be independent of the state this did not mean at all that he thought that the Church particularly, as the free community of those moved by religious feeling, should not affirm, tackle and further in the most ideal sense those desires which had already found their powerful embodiment in the modern state. Schleiermacher no less than Hegel admired and loved the modern Prussianism, and cherished and proclaimed the myth of Sans Souci. But his whole frame of mind in his relation to the state, was incomparably more liberal than Hegel's, and the idea of progress he proclaimed, in this as in everything, was much more in the nature of an ethical demand than it was with Hegel, although with Schleiermacher too it was at the same time borne up by the glorification of a victorious historical destiny. Together with Fichte, Arndt, Scharnhorst and others Schleiermacher, in the years 1806-13, as is well known, became through his sermons—in a way quite different from that of Goethe and Hegel—one of the educators of the generation which sustained the wars of freedom, and some of the unpleasantness this generation had to face in the time of the Students' Association movement affected him also.

The second ethical point that Schleiermacher constantly stressed in his sermons concerned the civil *profession* in the exercise of which the

Christian is called to prove himself as such. Here Schleiermacher, after his own fashion, was taking up a motif of the Lutheran Reformation. Of this motif it has often been said quite wrongly that it was first given renewed prominence by Albrecht Ritschl. And it did not matter to Schleiermacher to turn the clearest New Testament texts into their opposites when he wanted to state this motif once more.

Schleiermacher's third sphere of interest embraces the problems of marriage and family life, to which, even as early as in his Romantic period, he devoted a penetrating attention, and to which in 1818 he dedicated his famous Household Sermons, which we may, I think, be justified in taking as a perfect example of what Schleiermacher meant by the exalting, ennobling and transfiguring of human life.

Fourthly, there is the social problem, mentioned here with special emphasis because there is scarcely any mention of it in the literature on Schleiermacher. This must have been an object of his strong concern, expecially in his last years, in connexion with the events of the July revolution. Within the frame of an outlook which today would probably be described as that of Social Liberalism he appealed very definitely and courageously to the sense of responsibility of the upper classes towards those placed at a material disadvantage by the advance of civilization. He expressed his belief in economic equality, in social insurance, and in social services (as a right, and not as a benefit!). He demanded a shortening of the hours of work for the lower classes. He gave numerous warnings of the possible dangerous consequences of a further uncorrected social development.

These are things which the great revivalist preachers of his time did not say, and did not even see. We need not mention the complacency with which the Church in general confronted the development which had its origin in these things! Whether his social ideas would have been adequate for the then incipient great conflict between the giants Capital and Labour is another question. But it is in order for us to ask whether one or two things might not perhaps have turned out differently if the educated German public, and if, for example, Schleiermacher's candidate for confirmation, Otto von Bismarck, had really heard and taken to heart what Schleiermacher evidently wished to say upon this subject.

So much, then, about Schleiermacher's positive concerns, the things that can definitely be verified, and which at all events we must see to understand his theology.

III. Apologetics is an attempt to show by means of thought and speech that the determining principles of philosophy and of historical

and natural research at some given point in time certainly do not preclude, even if they do not directly require, the tenets of theology,
which are founded upon revelation and upon faith respectively. A bold
apologetics proves to a particular generation the intellectual necessity
of the theological principles taken from the Bible or from church dogma
or from both; a more cautious apologetics proves at least their intellectual possibility. About the extent and content of these principles
opinions may of course vary among the apologists themselves, and
within the same period of time.

We found that Schleiermacher wanted to be a Christian theologian,
and we found that he wanted, come what may, to be a thinking man
of his time. These two facts inevitably led to his third concern for
apologetics. He formulated the apologetic question, in a famous passage
in his open letter to Lücke,[1] as follows: 'Shall the knot of history be
thus loosed: Christianity with barbarism and learning with unbelief?'
It is clear that his only answer to this question can be, No. His interest
in both Christianity and learning was so great that he even considered
the appeal to the origins of the Protestant Church suitable material to
help underline this No, and thus continues, several pages later: 'If the
Reformation, from whose first beginnings our Church took its life, has
not the aim of establishing an eternal covenant between the living faith
and scientific research, which is free to explore upon all sides and works
for itself independently, so that faith does not hinder research, and
research does not preclude faith: if it has not this aim then it is not
adequate for the needs of our age and we require another Reformation,
no matter how, and as a result of what struggles it may develop. I am,
however, firmly convinced that the basis for this covenant was already
laid in those days, and that all that is needed is to bring about a more
definite awareness on our part of that task in order to be able to
achieve it.'[2]

The intention of achieving this task, and thus fulfilling the contract
in question, is certainly the first clear motif meeting the reader who
traditionally begins with the *Addresses on Religion*, and perhaps also
attempts to work his way into the *Doctrine of Faith* by way of studying
its great introduction. I think I have shown that this intention must
not be understood as a primary motif; and even less primary are the
objective views about the understanding of Christianity which we shall
come to speak of later, which have of necessity emerged from this
secondary theological intention of Schleiermacher's. But let us not be
mistaken: anyone convinced, as Schleiermacher was, that he must, as a

[1] Ed. Mulert, 1908, p. 37.   [2] Mul., 40.

L

Christian theologian, affirm and proclaim the insights and ethos of modern man, must similarly have been convinced that he could and should, as a modern man, be a Christian theologian. It was doubtless only in his maturity, in the two works on ethics and in the sermons, particularly those of his old age, that what he primarily and truly wanted achieved clear predominance. It is none the less understandable, however, that not only in the theological work of his youth, in which he first had to prepare the way for what he really wanted, but also in the most significant part of his *summa theologica*—and such, in fact, is the introduction—he was bound to be concerned with stating this second conviction, that is, with performing the apologetic task.

If we first enquire quite generally into the standpoint which Schleiermacher as an apologist of religion and Christianity sought to take up and did take up, then the first thing we find is certainly that the approach to this task meant for him a certain relaxation of, and indeed detachment from, the essential theological task of interpreting and proclaiming Christianity—however, in general, he might conceive of and execute this task. He declared quite plainly already in the first section of the first paragraph of the *Doctrine of Faith* 'that all the propositions which will occur here cannot be in themselves also dogmatic ones'. The standpoint of the Schleiermacher who later, from Paragraph 32 onwards, was to present the Christian doctrine of faith, and himself represent the Christian faith, is different from that of the Schleiermacher who in Paragraphs 1-31 is explaining what the Christian faith and the teaching of the Christian faith can and should be about.

Paragraphs 1-31 of the *Doctrine of Faith* are written in precisely the same sense as the theological work of his youth, the *Address on Religion*. But what does '*on* religion' mean? It need not mean at all that they are not also talks *out of* religion, but this in fact, according to their actual basic intention, is precisely what they are not. While still a young man, Schleiermacher wanted to show the educated among the despisers of religion that by virtue of their education they are enabled and summoned to understand the nature of religion better than it has been understood previously; and further that it is worthwhile taking note of the nature of religion. Further, that with religion it is a question of the realization of an original, universal and necessary disposition of mankind as such. Further, that of the forms of religion the Christian religion is relatively the highest, the most dignified and the purest. Further, that the intellectual situation of the time, particularly in Germany, is especially favourable to the recognition of these statements and thus to a rebirth of religion among them, the educated. In brief, the speaker on religion seeks an admission from the educated people to whom he is speaking that religion in general and the Christian religion in particular is the highest value in life, something which is not only possible, but real and necessary beside science, art, the Fatherland, etc., something which is already existing in latent form, and only requiring their correct recognition; and that civilization without religion, without the Christian religion, is not a complete civilization.

The standpoint from which Schleiermacher could speak in these terms, and could speak of the nature and value of religion, is evidently the following. Schleiermacher was not now concerned, directly at least, with the thing itself, but with the phenomenon of religion as seen from the outside, and as something which is to be interpreted, understood, perhaps misunderstood, and perhaps better understood from the outside. Just as he was about to proclaim Christianity he realized to his sorrow that his fellow men of the day were not listening at all, or at best shaking their heads over what he had to say. So he left the text he has already turned to in the Bible to take care of itself for a moment, and came down from the pulpit again to debate first of all with his congregation which for this particular moment transformed itself into an audience. He did this in order to make plausible in advance, apart from what he was going to say later, the possibility and necessity of saying it; in order to convince them that religion, Christianity and the Church were not at all the insignificant or absurd things they considered them to be, and that they should, if they did but understand themselves aright, give this phenomenon a joyous welcome.

The possibility of taking up this second standpoint, different from that of the proclaimer of Christianity, evidently had a certain prerequisite. Anyone who seeks to negotiate between faith and a cultural awareness which at first is assumed to be unbelieving, and then bring about a lasting covenant between them must, at all events while he is doing this, take up a position which is in principle beyond that of both parties, a superior position, from which he can understand both parties and be the just advocate of both. He must, even if he himself belongs to one side at least carry a white flag in his hand when approaching the other for a parley; he cannot at that moment be engaged as a combatant. To put it unmetaphorically: as long as he is an apologist the theologian must renounce his theological function. In so far as the apologist approaches the educated among the despisers of religion from the standpoint of theology he must not desire to speak only from faith and with only the faith of his hearers in view. He must present himself to them in a part which is provided for in their categories, which really occurs or can occur there.—To judge from Schleiermacher's early work, the part which the apologist, the speaker on religion, must play is that of the virtuoso in religion. Faced by the Romantics, Fichte, Schelling and the others Schleiermacher would have felt incapable of negotiating simply as a theologian, as a preacher. But why should the *religious virtuoso* not be possible within their field of vision as well, together with the virtuosi of philosophy, of art, of morality? Why should he not exist within the general frame of virtuosity in life? Can he base his claim upon the Church, his ecclesiastical office, his ministry, the Bible, dogma? No. But can he refer to a special kind of virtuosity which had previously not been well known or recognized as such, can he refer to 'the inner irresistible necessity of my nature'? Can he base his claim upon the notion of a 'mediator', indispensable at first, in matters affecting a particular newly-interpreted universal concern of mankind, upon the possibility of an ideally understood priesthood, a religious heroism? Why not? From this position the educated man could and had to and did allow himself to be spoken to.

In his later works Schleiermacher made legitimate the apologist as the confidant also of the opposite side, in an objective way—not so much replacing his former merely personal legitimization as supporting and establishing it. It is true that he did not show the reality of theology, but he did show its possibility and necessity: the space for theology in a comprehensive system of learning. He supported true theology by a philosophical theology, which was meant to demonstrate that the existence of Churches—not the Christian Church in particular, nor any particular Church—was 'an element necessary to the development of the human mind', and not by any means an 'aberration'.[1] And he saw this philosophical theology as founded for its own part in a philosophy of religion which in its turn can be shown to be an integrant feature of ethics—ethics as the science of the principles of history as opposed to those of nature. That is why the introduction to the *Doctrine of Faith*, as Schleiermacher expressly states, proceeded by means of arguments taken first from ethics, secondly from the philosophy of religion and thirdly from apologetics as a branch of what Schleiermacher called philosophical theology. Set in this relationship concretely Christian theology becomes possible as the positive science of this particular Church and its faith. This entire construction, however, evidently implies no more than that which Schleiermacher had already

[1] *Kurze Darstellung des theol. Studiums* (Short Account of the Study of Theology), para. 22.

said in the *Addresses on Religion* about the legitimation of the theologian and his playing the part of the apologist respectively: that together with other virtuosi there are also religious virtuosi who may, like the others in principle justly allow themselves to be seen and heard, according to the judgment also of people who do not profess this virtuosity. The preaching of the Church is no more an aberration—one might also say, an offence—than any other human possibility which can be accounted for in its nature and value from the point of view of ethics as the science of the principles of history.

This white flag, which the theologian must carry as an apologist, means of course for the theologian himself that in so far as he is an apologist he must, as Schleiermacher once more expressly states, take his point of departure (standpoint) above Christianity (in the logical sense of the word) in the general concept of the community of pious people or believers.[1] As an apologist he is not a Christian theologian but a moral philosopher and philosopher of religion. He suspends to that extent his attitude to Christianity, and his judgment of the truth or even absoluteness of the Christian revelation. Together with the other educated people he looks upon Christianity as being on the same level as the other 'pious communities', as being subject to the points of view from which 'pious communities' are to be regarded here. He therefore regards the Christian Church too as 'a community which arises only as a result of free human actions, and can only continue to exist by the same means'.[2] The time will come for him to return completely to his subject and speak as a Christian theologian. Then he will no longer speak *on* religion, but *ex officio out of* religion. Then the nature and value of religion and Christianity in its own inner logic and necessity will no longer interest him. That will be the time for all the things there are still to be said about the concept of the Church and which have to be said also in a completely different way. As an apologist he must say the other things, he must regard the Church as a pious community which has arisen and lives from human freedom, and has to demonstrate its possibility and necessity as such a community.

But what now, according to Schleiermacher, is the meaning of the apologetic act that is to be carried out from this place? What kind of lasting contract is to be concluded from it? At the beginning we distinguished a bolder and a more cautious approach to the apologetic task. The question about which of these two types Schleiermacher's apologetics belongs to cannot be definitely answered.

[1] *Short Account*, para. 33; *Doctrine of Faith*, 1st ed., para. 6.
[2] *Doctrine of Faith*, 2nd ed., para. 2. 2.

At first it might seem as if with Schleiermacher it could only be a question of the second, the more cautious kind of apologetics, which seeks to show only the intellectual possibility of the principles of Christianity. In the *Open Letter* to Lücke[1] Schleiermacher says that his aim in writing the *Doctrine of Faith* was to show 'that every dogma truly representing an element of our Christian awareness can also be formulated in such a way that it leaves us uninvolved with science'. In fact Schleiermacher's labours in apologetics can largely be understood along the following lines. He is as a modern man and therefore as a thinker and therefore as a moral philosopher and therefore as a philosopher of religion and therefore as a philosophical theologian and therefore as an apologist and therefore finally as a dogmatist determined on no account to interpret Christianity in such a way that his interpreted statements can come into conflict with the methods and principles of the philosophy and the historical and scientific research of his time.

Schleiermacher's activity as a 'cautious' apologist, and the proof that he was such an apologist consists chiefly in the fact that he himself wrote his dogmatics in such a way that even to someone not so well acquainted with the subject it must be self-evident as something at all events thinkable. The peculiar aesthetic language of the *Addresses* should already be understood as apologetics in this sense. With this language, more musical than argumentative as Schleiermacher himself once said, he adapted himself to the language which the people he was addressing, chiefly the Romantics, happened to love and which they spoke themselves. The very form of the *Doctrine of Faith*, which cannot be sufficiently admired, is also apologetic in this sense. Its strict, artistically ingenious system and the rigid discipline and high intellectual quality of this work are doubtless in themselves meant to form an argument, to justify and defend the content of the work, to speak and testify for it. The feature which is, however, above all distinctly apologetic in this sense is the objective form in which the content of religion and later of the Christian faith is presented, both here and in the *Addresses*. Here the theologian is not only concerned with his subject-matter but as a mediator also with his readers. Indeed he is concerned with readers of a certain intellectual make-up and tendency which is accepted from the beginning by the theologian *qua* apologist. This is revealed at every turn by the fact that this representation of Christianity systematically removes, or is at all events intended to remove (of course he cannot judge in advance the effect of this) each and every stumbling-block which their own intellectual make-up and tendency might

1 Mul., 40.

prepare for them in such a representation. Christianity is interpreted in such a way that it acquires room by this way of interpretation, that it acquires room in the kind of thinking which is assumed to be authoritative by Schleiermacher's contemporaries, without causing any friction. Whether his readers move into this cleared space, whether they are able and willing to consider and accept this unexceptionable representation of Christianity as part of their own thought; that is of course a question that cannot be answered. But Christianity is prepared for them in such a way that in the author's eyes there no longer exists any obstacle in principle, against the occupation of this space. There must now be other reasons, reasons which are not essential from the standpoint of the cultural awareness as such, which guide them, if they fail to do this.

And now the significance of the fact that the apologist as apologist has to take as his point of departure a point above Christianity becomes clear. It certainly does not mean in itself that for once in a way the apologist has to think like a heathen or atheist in order to convince heathens or atheists of the excellence of Christianity. *De facto*, of course, it can mean this. It should, however, only mean—but this, of course, is in fact meaning quite a lot—that the apologist is a complete master of Christianity, in a position, as it were, to look into it from above just as much as modern cultural awareness is; able to elicit its nature and assess its value. Without having to worry about prejudicing the content of Christianity itself he is in a position to take a pencil to the stock of doctrine he has inherited and boldly 'erase and alter what might in untimely fashion (!) oppress the apparatus of dogma and hamper the living faith in its attempt to walk hand in hand with onward-marching science'.[1] 'Schleiermacher attacked the task of apologetics in the confidence that he knew what Christianity was, and could not be brought to depart from this basic feeling by any church doctrine, no matter how well established the latter was.'[2] It is not right to accuse Schleiermacher of consciously betraying Christianity to science, to the cultural outlook of his time, by always saying when there was a conflict between the two, that civilization was right and traditional Christianity wrong. The only alternative, however, if this accusation is to be avoided—and we must avoid it—is to say that as an apologist of Christianity Schleiermacher really played upon it as a virtuoso plays upon his fiddle: he played the notes and airs which, if they did not cause his hearers to rejoice, could at least be acceptable to them. Schleiermacher did not speak as a responsible servant of Christianity but, like a true virtuoso, as a free master of it.

[1] Scholz, p. 122.   [2] Ibid., p. 121.

Thus the great possibility which has arisen in classic form in Schleier-macher the apologist is that the anxious care to conserve, the advocacy of Christianity at all costs, which had still characterized the apologetics even of the Enlightenment period, can be abandoned. Christianity can be mastered at least in so far as, using the insight we have into its nature and value, we can treat, control and rule the Bible and dogma with unrestricted freedom. It is possible to be a Christian and theologian as one is a philosopher or artist: that is, one can also approach the material of theology in a creative and systematic way, illuminating it in principle, penetrating and forming it out of one's very own power. Like the other secrets of life this secret too can be interpreted. The interpreter need not take into account the fact that it might perhaps be seeking to interpret itself and that the Bible and dogma might perhaps be binding pointers for the understanding of this self-interpretation. And so, creatively forming and interpreting in this manner, and therefore knowing in advance just as much about Christianity as Christianity itself, it is indeed possible to be a Christian and a theologian also as a modern man.

This apologetics is, so to speak, immanent and negative, and in practice essentially turns its point against the Christian tradition itself, and would in fact be of the type of cautious apologetics. But after all it represents only one side of the picture which we can see here. The other appears already in the *Addresses* and is still present in the *Doctrine of Faith*. It is represented by an admittedly strictly limited approach towards a positive proof, an approach towards showing the intellectual necessity of the principles of Christianity. An approach in that direction, I say, and more it is not permissible to say without saying something quite wrong and completely out of keeping with Schleiermacher.

Schleiermacher did not give theology or the principles of Christianity a speculative basis. He did not, that is, conceive of them and treat them as principles to be derived necessarily from the idea of human knowledge. This, as expressed in a much-admired review which he wrote as early as 1803, was what separated him most decisively from Schelling, not to mention Hegel. Schleiermacher, it is true, also had his system of pure knowledge (as presented in his philosophical ethics and in his dialectics), but in this system knowledge and being are set in opposition in such a way that they are held together objectively only by the idea of God, and subjectively only by the feeling correlative to this idea, accompanying all knowledge and action; or, rather, by the dialectician's knowledge of this correlation. In so far as this synthesis of God and feeling as a bracket beyond the antithesis of knowledge and being exists for Schleiermacher, he too is a philosopher of identity, approximating to Schelling's doctrine of the point of identity as the point at which the ideal and the real are seen to be as one, and approximating also to Hegel's philosophy of the mind as the synthesis of logic and natural philosophy. But Schleiermacher did not, like Schelling, consider possible as a proof of Christianity a speculative theology as the science of the point of identity, nor did he, like Hegel consider a philosophy of religion, replacing theology, as the penultimate stage at least in the dialectic of absolute mind, possible as such a proof. 'I shall never be able to accept the idea that my belief in Christ stems from knowledge or philosophy, whichever philosophy it might be.'[1]

We ascertained while discussing Hegel that this rejection of speculation on Schleiermacher's part also has something to do with the fact that he was not very interested in the truth of theological tenets as such. For he was in the first place interested in the active life of religion, and then in feeling as the true seat of this life, and only thirdly in the tenets by means of which this life—always in fundamentally imperfect form—expresses itself. Schleiermacher quenched his intellectual thirst for truth as a philosopher in fields remote from his theological statements. But this alone is not enough to explain his lack of interest in speculative theology. There is something in him which protests in favour of the peculiar and underivable nature of these very tenets, against the omnipotence of deduction in the thinking of his contemporaries just mentioned, against the elimination of 'high arbitrariness', which might possibly, from one side, at any rate, be the key to Christianity, as he expressed it in his argument against Schelling.[2] And he fears that a theology which is capable of being understood and based upon philosophical terms would lead to the introduction of the un-Christian opposition of an esoteric and an exoteric teaching, of a *gnosis* ranked higher than *pistis*, a 'hierarchy of speculation'.[3] He wished the assertions of the *Doctrine of Faith*—not of the introduction, of course, but of the part which contained the proper representation— to be understood as 'quite simply and honestly solely empirical' (p. 21). The representation itself was meant simultaneously to be the vindication of the *Doctrine of Faith*, 'for everything in it can only be vindicated by being represented as a correct statement of Christian self-awareness' (p. 56). But all the same, this empiricism is that of a science, not rough and unscientific. If it were otherwise, Schleiermacher explains, he would personally, if faced with the choice, decide for a speculative

---

[1] *Open letter to Lücke*, Mul., 38f. [2] *Letters*, IV, 586.
[3] *Open Letter to Lücke*, Mul., 39f.

vindication of religion, although with the gravest misgivings (p. 39).
But Schleiermacher is not faced by this choice. His representation of
the Christian faith to be true, does not rest upon the basis of a highest
knowledge of God, whose more or less adequate expression it claimed
to be. To this extent his apologetics are not of the bolder type, seeking
to give positive proof.

Schleiermacher's representation of faith certainly rests, however,
upon the basis of a highest knowledge of human feeling or immediate
self-awareness in its correlation to God, upon the basis of a highest
knowledge of the nature and value of faith and the diversity of ways of
believing altogether. It is not the Christian religion, but certainly the
type to which this phenomenon belongs, religion as a necessary manifestation of human intellectual life, which is for Schleiermacher an
object of speculative knowledge of an *a priori* kind. And this knowledge
does not only provide him with a frame within which to establish
the nature of the Christian religion as empirically understood, but
also with a yardstick by which its value can be measured. To that
extent he is in a position to discover and present—and he did this
in the *Addresses* just as much as in the Introduction to the *Doctrine of
Faith*—not only the necessity of religion, in terms of the science of
mind, as completely determined human self-awareness, but also the
superiority, relatively at least, of Christianity, as regards its nature and
value, when compared with the other religions. Without that highest
unity of intuition and feeling, as Schleiermacher said in the *Addresses*,
or without the feeling of utter dependence, as he puts it in the *Doctrine
of Faith*, cultural awareness would be incomplete, a headless torso.
Of the various historical forms this feeling has taken it is the Christian
one, the Christian faith, which is the highest and most perfect. It is not
the absolute form, the one which is alone true, but it is indeed the
highest and most perfect among many which are relatively true as
well. In so far as Schleiermacher considers he can show this without
fear of objection, to the extent that, as was previously shown, he thinks
he can base his dogmatics upon philosophical theology, philosophical
theology upon a philosophy of religion, and the philosophy of religion
upon ethics as the universal science of mind, he also not directly, but
certainly in an indirect way proves the intellectual necessity of the
tenets of Christianity. It is a question of the intellectual necessity
which is possible within the framework of his system, which is essentially
more restrained than those of Schelling and Hegel. It is a question
of a relative determined, indirect intellectual necessity of thought to
accord with his more cautious conception of speculative identity. The

latter, however, is quite definitely in question and to this extent
Schleiermacher in fact has as his chief support cautious and negative
apologetics but also, without entrusting too much of his weight to them,
toys with the bolder, positive kind. And it is not impossible to see this
relationship as reversed, with positive apologetics as the main prop. For
it must certainly be said that it is only by having as his background the
positive vindication of the doctrine of faith by means of the science of
mind that Schleiermacher is able to form this doctrine of faith into an
apologetics in the way we have previously described: by means of this
bold virtuoso playing on the instrument of Christianity, by this complete freedom in the handling of the store of Christian tradition, and
by the brilliance of the system he applied to it. If Schleiermacher did
not descend from this height 'above Christianity', how should he be
able to appear as a virtuoso and master of Christianity? Thus the
best way of understanding the significance of this third, this apologetic,
motif in his theology, is to imagine him pacing—to continue with the
image of the two props—alternately supported by one of them and
using the other in order to take a step forward. And nobody can deny
that this particular traveller did in fact advance most vigorously
upon his way, after his fashion.

IV. Before proceeding to consider the two motifs in the content of
Schleiermacher's theology which were almost bound to arise from the
attitude he takes in his apologetics, I should like to call attention once
again to yet another of its formal features, which will illuminate the
necessity of the two motifs of the content from yet another angle. The
two motifs of the content, which we shall assess in conclusion, are
experience and history. It is between these two poles that Schleiermacher's interpretation of Christianity takes its course, because these
two poles are also the secret of his general concept of religion; because,
as an apologetic interpretation of Christianity, it cannot take any other
course but one lying between two poles. But why must the secret of his
general concept of religion be that of these two poles in particular?
Why must his philosophy of religion and ethics present him with this
particular polarity, and why must there be this polarity at all?

Here we must reflect that Schleiermacher, the Christian apologist,
was not only one educated and educating in his time, but that his
origins in this respect lay first with the Moravian brethren and secondly
with the Romantic school. Both these facts mean that for Schleiermacher being educated and educating must definitely mean *mediation*
—mediation, uniting vision, synthesis, and peace not only between this

and that opposite, but ultimately between all, even between the most pronounced opposites. Schleiermacher sprang from the Moravian brethren, and was certainly correct in once saying of himself that all his life he had been a 'Moravian of a higher order', to the extent that he had become familiar there with a Christian standpoint which was in principle synthetic, with a Christianity beyond the historical differentiations of Christianity, with the bold idea of a union before union comprising the various confessions merely as various choirs or divisions of the one Church of Christ—and at the same time with the bold idea of a Christianity in which the Saviour and the individual soul as well as the Saviour and the Christian communion were brought, in a correlation quite definitely compared to a form of play, into a synoptic, mediated, polar relationship. And Schleiermacher, passing briefly through the Enlightenment, went from the Moravian brethren to Romanticism. We have already seen what a part the principle of the centre, which was announced already in Herder, played with Novalis. It was the moving principle, in method, with Hölderlin too, and with Schelling and Hegel. Without this principle there would have been no speculative idealism, and no philosophy of identity. Schleiermacher applied it not in Hegel's way, but in his own way, to theology. In doing so he could call to witness the procedure of the Moravian brethren. What he made of it, however, subject as he was to the powerful stimulus of Romantic philosophy, was not a Moravianism merely of a higher, but of the highest order.

It is probably no mere coincidence that precisely in the last years of his life, when he was preparing to publish his *Dialectics*, there was one notion and concern which dominated every other in Schleiermacher's sermons. It can be characterized by the word 'peace'. If he is zealous as a preacher—we have already considered this from another angle— then he is zealous in attacking everything which can divide the Church, or can set the individual hearer at loggerheads with himself, because it calls to mind the idea of irreconcilable contradictions. There are no such irreconcilable contradictions and therefore there cannot and may not be any unpeaceful state either in general or in particular, outwardly or inwardly. Schleiermacher dealt with the most diverse moral and religious themes from the point of view that the truth lies in the middle, in reconciliation, in the point of no distinction, in the 'simplicity of the mind of Jesus', in 'common feeling', in the 'equalizing common note' between the supposed opposites, and that we must see the relative nature of the opposites, the fact that their quality as opposites is only provisional and capable of being annulled. That is why Schleiermacher does not like the Old Testament—because he saw in the notion of the Law which he thought prevailed there the division between heaven and earth, between grace and sin, which is removed in Christ, and may not be renewed again. That is why he has little liking for the figure of John the Baptist in the New Testament either. 'The one word of peace does in fact contain everything', he once declaimed.[1] The divine Spirit or communion with God or the kingdom of God is, according to his express declaration, the One from which the two proceeded, and into which they must again be converted.

This helps us to understand why Schleiermacher claimed so emphatically that his *Doctrine of Faith* was the first dogmatics at all events of the Prussian *Union*, and why the union between the Reformed Churches and the Lutherans was to him something which was indeed decisively necessary. And his further strongly marked aim over and above this union was the uniting of the orthodox-pietist and rationalist parties, which were coming into ever-sharper conflict in the twenties, within the United Evangelical Church. It was as a result of this tendency that the *Doctrine of Faith* did not take another form which, according to Schleiermacher's explanation, it might have taken,[2] and which might have decisively increased its influence and usefulness to the Church. The *Doctrine of Faith* is divided, as we know, into a first part, consisting of the generally religious premises (the Christian ones included, it is true) and a second specifically Christian (Christological-soteriological) part. Schleiermacher pondered the idea of reversing this relationship, of moving the first part, which at least approximated to a natural theology, and upon which the eye of the reader must first alight, to the end, as a kind of epilogue, as a definite *a posteriori*. He did not do this partly in order not to lend his support to the 'forcing out from our church membership' of those worthy men who are called rationalists, and he did not want to do this 'for natural fear that the little boat in which we are all sailing might capsize'.[3] He thought that he was thereby serving peace and by doing this was also serving the Church and God himself.

What Schleiermacher calls peace in his sermons and in church politics, however, coincides in content with the ultimate and highest principle, both in form and in content, of his philosophic teaching. This teaching is characterized by a method of division and unification of all principles. He carries it through by dealing with subject and object, knowledge and being, reason and nature, ethics and physics, speculative and empirical knowledge, and everywhere the transitions,

[1] *Sermons*, III, 468.   [2] *Open Letter to Lücke*, Mul., 46.   [3] Ibid., 44.

in contrast to those of Hegel's dialectic, are flowing from the one opposite to the other, and are quantitative. The truth—once again in contrast to Hegel—is not to be found in some definable third thing, but in the indefinable centre between the first and the second, at the point where peace reigns, a point to which from all sides only approximations are possible. In feeling and—for figurative thought and speech, which is of course inadequate—out of feeling, peace exists also between the ultimate and highest contradiction, that between the infinite and therefore identical being and knowledge of God and our finite and therefore divided, non-identical being and knowledge. World-wisdom and world do not, it is true, coincide in an absolute knowledge, as they do with Hegel, but Schleiermacher does in fact have his dialectic, as knowledge of a unity which can be felt, i.e. of the presence of God felt in human awareness. Seen from this aspect the principle of the centre is at once identical with the strongest and most decisive lever of Schleiermacher's apologetics. The Moravian and Romantic was bound to have recourse to this kind of apologetics and to no other!

From here we can also gain an insight into the essential content of the two *loci classici* in Schleiermacher's theological doctrine of principles: the second *Address* on religion and Paragraphs 3 and 4 of the *Doctrine of Faith*. In the second *Address* religion is described as the moment of the unity of intuition and feeling, which takes place beyond all thought and action. Intuition is the receptive, and feeling the spontaneous side of the act of awareness, in which man in his finite quality comes to partake, as Schleiermacher put it at this time, of the infinite quality of the universe. Intuition and feeling is the opposition of that which affects religiously, and the state of being affected religiously. The overcoming of this opposition, the One in the middle of these two, is the esential nature of religion. 'Intuition without feeling is nothing . . . feeling without intuition is likewise nothing: both are only anything if and because they are originally one and undivided.'[1] Paragraphs 3 and 4 of the *Doctrine of Faith* state, however, that: 'The piety which is the basis of all church communions (and which is therefore common to them all, and underlies all expressions of piety, no matter how diverse these may be) is, looked at purely in itself, neither a piece of knowledge nor an action, but a determination of feeling or of immediate self-awareness. It is that determination by virtue of which man is aware of his own self as utterly dependent or—what comes to the same thing—as in connexion with God.'

What Schleiermacher expressed in the *Address* by means of the dual

[1] *Addresses*, pp. 72f.

concept of intuition and feeling he characterizes here by means of the concept of feeling, which has now been widened and comprises the moment of intuition, in which that which affects, that which explains the origin of man's utter dependence is already posited. Because feeling in itself is the victorious centre between knowledge and action, because, in contrast to these functions, it is itself the true self-awareness and by virtue of this fact alone is at least the subjective representative of truth; again, because feeling as pious feeling is man's feeling of utter dependence, i.e. the feeling of his connexion with God, Schleiermacher's theology is the theology of feeling, or to put it more exactly, the theology of pious feeling, or the theology of awareness, or to put it more exactly, the theology of pious self-awareness. That is why Schleiermacher in 1832 found that the text of St John, 1.51: 'Hereafter ye shall see heaven open, and the angels of God ascending and descending upon the Son of man' was expressly affirmed 'by the most perfect and blissful experience of a faithful spirit', for which there is no longer any division between heaven and earth.[1] Piety does not only seek, does not only hope, does not only expect, does not only worship, but is this centre, this peace which passeth all understanding. That is why for Schleiermacher proclaiming God means proclaiming one's own piety, that is why for him preaching consists essentially of a self-imparting by the preacher.

And since what is to be proclaimed here is indeed a determination, but a determination of feeling, Schleiermacher gives to the Word, and with the Word, to intellectual truth, only a position of secondary importance. The tenets of the Christian faith are simply only 'conceptions of states of mind of Christian piety, represented in speech'.[2] The tenets are only derivatives of the original thing, the inner state.[3] The divine is ineffable. Talk about religion will one day be succeeded by 'the soft silence of holy virgins'.[4] Of the three modes of speech, the poetical, the oratorical and the didactic, the poetical is the highest; and what is higher than all of them together, and better, is music. 'Singing piety is the piety which ascends most directly and most gloriously to heaven.'[5] Thus theology, if only because it is merely the human word, and only, of all its forms, the didactic human word, is free, capable of transformation, and relatively non-binding—not bound in respect to its subject. That is why Schleiermacher finds it possible to adapt his theology so carefully to the educated awareness of his time, without worrying too much or nearly so much about whether his

---

[1] *Sermons*, III, 167f.   [2] *Doctrine of Faith*, para. 15.   [3] *Open Letter to Lücke*, Mul., 34.
[4] *Addresses*, 9f.   [5] *Christmas Celebration*, Phil. Libr., Vol. 117, p. 23.

theology was doing justice to its subject, to Christianity. That is why for him dogmatics is nothing more nor less than the 'representation of the opinion of the Church',[1] a branch of the church lore of the present, paraphrasing historically and empirically in systematic order the reality of the pronouncements, which are possible and necessary at the time, of the spirit affected by the Christian religion.

Truth in the strictly intellectual, expressible sense, which is because of these very qualities only the provisional truth, remains the concern of philosophy; truth in the ultimate, decisive, but also ineffable sense is reserved for mute feeling, the feeling which in the best event sings, and only as a last resort, and then inadequately, speaks. Schleiermacher's real and serious opinion was that all theological pronouncements were strictly theological to the extent that they were intended and meant to be received as pronouncements of religious feeling, referring to this feeling itself and to nothing else. Or, to put it negatively, that they declined in theological severity in proportion as they referred—as pronouncements upon some human knowledge or action—simultaneously to the objects of human knowledge or action. It is precisely as they enter upon the field of what is objective and to that extent expressible, that they become, according to Schleiermacher, potentially inadequate, as it were, by having lost their sure footing, the centre which represents the peaceful, ineffable truth.

This fear of objective and expressible pronouncements which are made inadequate by these very qualities, a fear which was determined by the Romantic principle of the centre, now provides the basis for a special methodic teaching in the *Doctrine of the Faith*, which is typical of Schleiermacher's theology as few other things are. I refer to the teaching of the three forms of dogmatic tenets. These, according to para. 30 of the *Doctrine of Faith*, can either be conceived of as descriptions of human states of mind or as notions of divine qualities or ways of behaving, or as pronouncements about certain ways in which the world is constituted. The feeling of utter dependence is never present in itself and isolated. It is present as real awareness filling out time, and always in such a way that it is linked with a time-filling, sensory form of self-awareness. Thus in the first place every formula for the feeling of utter dependence as such must at the same time be a formula for a certain state of self-awareness, a certain human state of mind. Every such sensory form of self-awareness must, however, be made to refer to a certain form of the world, such as typifies this form, this time-factor of self-awareness; i.e. it must be made to refer to something outside

[1] *Doctrine of Faith*, para. 19, suppl.

self-awareness, to a certain form of the not-self. Thus in the second place every formula for the feeling of utter dependence which is real in this sensory form can at the same time be a formula for the world, as it is real in this particular modification. And now the feeling of utter dependence is not what it is in and of itself, for God too is posited in self-awareness: thus the formula concerning the feeling of utter dependence can at the same time be understood as a formula for God himself. To express it more simply, and in a concentrated form, in a little variation on the theme of pious self-awareness: from intellectual reflection upon pious *self*-awareness there emerge the statements concerning the pious state of mind as such and in itself. From reflection upon pious self-*awareness* there emerge the statements about the world. From reflections upon *pious* self-awareness emerge statements about God. The form of the first group of statements, which always form the first section, the actual corpus of the exposition, in the individual sub-divisions of the *Doctrine of Faith*, Schleiermacher calls the dogmatic basic form, because their content necessarily rests upon pure self-experience, whereas the content of the statements about the world and God could in themselves always be understood either in the scientific sense or as an expression of metaphysical speculation. For this reason these latter statements must show that they are true theological statements by referring back to the first form of statements, i.e. that they can ultimately likewise be understood as pure pronouncements upon the religious state of mind and for this reason also, looked at according to their form, they are called tenets of the dogmatic subsidiary forms. The groups of statements upon the qualities of God and features of the world which come within these subsidiary forms always form the second and third sections in the individual sub-divisions of the *Doctrine of Faith*. If it were intended to present the content of the *Doctrine of Faith* in the form of a table, then, taking the longitudinal section of the whole, these second and third sections would have to be placed to left and right on either side of their respective first sections. This method means that the doctrine of God, for instance, extends throughout the whole work and is only finished when the book is finished. In the section on 'The way the world is constituted in relation to redemption' the entire doctrine of election, of the Holy Spirit, of the Church and the whole of eschatology is dealt with.

These are just some of the singular features this method involves. It must, however, be said that as a method it accords very well with the intention and spirit of the whole book. And Schleiermacher, without actually achieving this, wanted to advance even further in this direction. When he began to busy himself with the new edition in 1829 he considered the possibility, as is shown by para. 30 of the second edition and above all by the second open letter to Lücke, of cutting out the two subsidiary forms in favour of the main form, because they were 'superfluous really, in the strict sense'.[1] That, he expressly states, would be dogmatics in the peculiar form it had fashioned for itself in him.[2] He had, however, not done this, he says, in order to preserve, for one thing, the 'historical attitude' and 'church character' of his work, and further in order not to let slip the possibility of a critique and reduction of the doctrine of God, cosmology and anthropology as contained in the old dogmatics. These are reasons which cannot be described as very weighty or very much a question of principle. Schleiermacher takes leave of these unexecuted thoughts with a reminiscence taken, this time, from the Old Testament, that of the dying Moses' sight of the land of Canaan. 'I rejoice at least', he concludes in writing to Lücke, 'in the conviction that I have seen from afar at least the form for a freer and livelier way of treating our teaching of faith.'[3] This future ideal way of treatment, this Canaan, would thus consist in the disappearance of even the semblance of the idea that the subject of dogmatics was anything else but human states of mind. This semblance has not entirely disappeared in the form in which Schleiermacher left his work. But even so Schleiermacher approached very near to his ideal, and the fact that we know from his own pen what his true intentions were, may console us in some measure for the imperfection of what he actually achieved.

V. In conclusion let us enquire about the objective basic motifs of content in Schleiermacher's theology. We have called it a theology of feeling, of awareness. Thus we have already named one of these motifs of content, and indeed the one which is the original, primary and characteristic motif of content of this theology, and we have elucidated it in the foregoing.

The great formal principle of Schleiermacher's theology is at the same time its material principle. Christian pious self-awareness contemplates and describes itself: that is in principle the be-all and end-all of this theology. But what is this Christian pious self-awareness? The principle of mediation we have discussed already hints that the definition of Schleiermacher's theology as the theology of feeling or awareness cannot in any case imply that the formal and material principle of this theology is human feeling or awareness in such a way that this

[1] Mul., 47f.   [2] Ibid., 49.   [3] Ibid., 51.

feeling is understood as an indivisible unity. For it is a certain feeling, the feeling of piety, which is referred to. Feeling or awareness is here the centre in such a way that it distinguishes itself from another feeling or awareness outside it, in such a way that it shares its own unity voluntarily, as it were, with this other feeling or awareness, that it allows itself to oppose this other feeling or awareness in relative tension and is what it is only in the mediation between itself and the other feeling or awareness, and not in a pure identity with itself. This must in fact be so, if only as the result of the premises of Schleiermacher's dialectic, according to which there is no pure identity in finite self-awareness. And Schleiermacher was after all a Christian theologian to the extent that it was clear to him, and remained clear to him, that theology must in some sense have two motifs of content, that it must speak of God *and* man, of man *and* God. As has now become plain, man, human self-awareness, determined namely as pious self-awareness, was doubtless for Schleiermacher the central subject of his theological thought. In the very places where the theology of the Reformation had said 'the Gospel' or 'the Word of God' or 'Christ' Schleiermacher, three hundred years after the Reformation, now says, religion or piety. But Reformers did not neglect to split as it were their theological centre and to oppose it by something relatively different from it. They powerfully confronted the Word of God with the human correlate of faith, even though this correlate had its basis entirely in the Word of God, and was created and sustained by the Word of God. And in a similar way Schleiermacher's theology, too, is not centred in one point, in the sense that in that case it would not be aware of any other motif. Since by birth and upbringing he thinks in terms of man, just as the Reformers had thought in terms of God, this second motif with him must manifestly be identical with, or be the same in intention, as that which was primarily for them: God, Christ, revelation or what you will.

It is noteworthy that, by acknowledging the dualism of two basic theological motifs, Schleiermacher, in principle, enters into the course of Trinitarian theological thinking together with the Reformers. Even if he does not go beyond this, the fact must not be overlooked in the assessment of his undertaking. Trinitarian thinking compels theology—even a theology which cannot perhaps do much directly with the idea of the Trinity—to be completely in earnest about the thought of God in at least two places: first, at the point where it is a question of God's action in regard to man, and, secondly, at the point where it is a question of man's action in regard to God. It is aware of God as the Word of the Father which is spoken to man and as the Spirit of the Father and of the

Word which enables man to hear the Word. It cannot seek to have merely one centre, one subject, just because its subject is God. To the extent that it sought to resolve itself into a mere teaching of God's action in regard to man, into a pure teaching of the Word, it would become metaphysics. And to the extent that it sought to resolve itself into a teaching of man's action in regard to God, into a pure teaching of the Spirit, it would become mysticism. The one, however, would be just as little a pure teaching of the Word of God, as the other would be a pure teaching of the Spirit of God. A pure teaching of the Word will take into account the Holy Spirit as the divine reality in which the Word is heard, just as a pure teaching of the Spirit of the Son will take into account the Word of God as the divine reality in which the Word is given to us. It was with this thought in mind that the Reformers propagated the teaching of the Word of God in its correlation with faith as the work of the Holy Spirit in man.

Schleiermacher reversed the order of this thought. What interests him is the question of man's action in regard to God. We must not condemn him for this out of hand. If we call to mind the entire situation of theology in the modern world then we shall find it understandable that it fastened upon the point which had come to the centre of the entire thought of modern man. This point was simply man himself. This shifting of interest did not necessarily have to mean man without God, man in his own world. It could also mean man in the presence of God, his action over against God's action. A genuine, proper theology could be built up from such a starting-point. We may ask the question whether it was a good thing that Schleiermacher adapted himself to the trend of the time in this way and took up his position at the spot where he was invited to do so by the prevalence of the Copernican world-picture, by its execution during the Enlightenment, by Kant, by Goethe, by Romanticism, and by Hegel.

There was in fact no need for the Copernican conception of the universe to acquire the significance of a command that theology should in future be anthropocentric theology. It might perhaps have been both more spirited and wiser to take up and carry through the Reformed theology of the Word more than ever at this time, in instructive opposition to the trend of the age. For indeed this Reformed theology had not been founded upon and conditioned by the Ptolemaic conception of the universe and, as a pure theology of the Word, it offered opportunity enough to do justice to the tendency of the age by an honest doctrine of the Holy Spirit and of faith. There was ambiguity in the fact that theology took the trend of the times as a command which must be followed as a matter of course, and in its inability to do justice to the tendency of the age other than by becoming anthropocentric in accordance with the changed picture of the universe. The suspicion arises whether this does not betray the fact that theology forgot its own theme over against all world-views. But this reversal of theology's way of looking at things was not necessarily bound to mean that theology was now no longer theology, or had even become the enemy of true theology. Again, a genuine, proper theology could be built up from such a starting-point. Theology could remain true to its own theme while it went with the times and thus completed this reversal. What Schleiermacher constructed by means of his theology of awareness by planting himself in the centre which for the Reformers had been a subsidiary centre, *could* be the pure theology of the Holy Spirit; the teaching of man brought face to face with God by God, of man granted grace by grace. If it was this, then as a theology it was just as much justified as the theology which was orientated in the opposite direction, the theocentric, Reformed theology. The fact that Schleiermacher intended it as such (even if he did not perhaps execute it in this way) is revealed by the fact that he is very much aware of a second centre beside his original one, and seeks to grant it its full validity. In doing so he enters in principle into the course of Trinitarian thinking. The only question can now be, whether he will be in a position, in Trinitarian terms, to recognize and ensure as much validity for the divinity of the *Logos*, which forms for him this second centre, as for the divinity of the Holy Spirit, which is his actual centre or rather is apparently meant by what he presents as his actual centre. Will this show if it is not only intended to be, but if it is in truth the *divinity* of the Holy Spirit which forms this actual centre of his? Reformation theology, starting in reverse fashion, from the *Logos*, passes this test: as a theology of the Word it is at once a theology of the Holy Spirit to such a degree that it can largely be understood as a theology of faith too, and it is this very fact which proves that it is the divine Word that forms its true centre. Will Schleiermacher's theology also pass this test, thus proving that for all the great reversal which is its starting-point, as compared with Reformed theology, its proceedings are theologically unexceptionable? Here we must make two preliminary points:

1. The task of taking into account this second motif and making it valid, which Schleiermacher does not wish to avoid, is an unmistakable source of embarrassment and care to him and something he finds particularly strenuous. The car must certainly continue to run, and it

does in fact do so where in this theology and proclamation it is a question of speaking of Christ, of divine action as such, of the Word, and of the objective moment of salvation. But—to speak in the technical terms of the motor-car—from time to time the second, hill-climbing gear has to be engaged. This is betrayed to the layman as well because of the increased noise, suggesting a greater strain, coming from the dialectic mechanism.

In some way or other, for instance, it emerges from the *Christmas Celebration* of 1805 that in fact Christ is, and is intended to remain, the subject of the celebration of Christmas. The exaltation of the religious disposition, which is there in the first place, certain and blessed in itself, is never questioned in the slightest. But at the same time this other motif, after having been questioned at the outset, must first be worked out and established by means of difficult considerations which encounter all sorts of significant doubts. Similarly in the *Addresses* and in the *Doctrine of Faith* and the sermons there can be no mistaking that for Schleiermacher the theologian, the historical element in religion, the objective motif, the Lord Jesus, is a problem child, one which certainly must be brought to honour, and which is somehow brought to honour—but which is still a problem child. Schleiermacher, the apologist, is forced to go to considerable trouble to understand and present this on the one hand in such a form that it is as far as possible safeguarded from the objections of modern awareness, thinking in anthropocentric terms. He has to work on the image of Christ provided by the Biblical and dogmatic tradition like a sculptor working a block of marble, in order to produce the statue, the particular Christ who might be considered adequate from this point of view. And he has to go to similar trouble to show that seen from the basic fact of pious feeling the figure, now made unassailable, which is the product of his Christology is really important and necessary; and that we should not, as might be thought, be just as well-off without it. He succeeds in both things, both in working out a tolerably modernized Christology, and in showing, in tolerably convincing fashion, that this Christology is indispensable. He does not succeed without sometimes resorting to artifice. He does not succeed consistently nor perhaps in a way which is ultimately convincing and worthy of credence. But all the same, he succeeds somehow. It is just that it was a piece of extremely hard labour in apologetics—and this is a shadow which remains come what may—which was necessary to bring about this success.

This cannot be said of the Reformation in regard to its subsidiary centre. It would be absurd to say of Luther's doctrine of faith that it

had in itself cost him a particular dialectic exertion. From the outset
his teaching of the Word is so constituted that he can and must speak
with an inner objective necessity not only of Christ but of faith too.
With Luther the divinity of the *Logos* demands in the most direct way
possible the divinity of the Spirit. The relationship between the two
motifs is open, self-evident, and alive, although as with Schleiermacher
there is a difference of emphasis, in that here it is the first one which
forms the centre-point. Luther certainly did not speak as an apologist
of what for him was the second motif. He neither needed to model the
concept of faith to comply with a certain world view, nor did he need
first to work out the indispensable nature of this concept. The concept
of faith, rather, is already posited, both in its content and in its range,
in and with his conception of the Word, and all his theological labour
could only be devoted to showing this right, which stood firm from the
outset and inwardly, and the self-evident dignity of what for him was
the second motif. It is impossible, *mutatis mutandis*, to say this of Schleiermacher's theology. Whatever else we may think about it, it is impossible
to dispute the fact that it is a product of art. This fact alone is sufficient
to cause us at least to wonder whether in his theology the divinity of
the *Logos* is pre-supposed as unequivocally as the Reformers posited
the divinity of the Spirit, and whether, if this was not the case, the
divinity of the Spirit which seemingly formed the centre of his theology
was really the divinity of the *Holy* Spirit.

2. To overcome the difficulties with which he was faced by his
acknowledgment in principle of the second motif Schleiermacher used
the principle of mediation, which we have already considered as the
most significant formal motif of his theology. But why is it so difficult
for him to acknowledge and ensure the validity of this second motif?
Because apparently it did not escape him that the first and the second
motifs were, in the Reformed theology at all events, related to each
other in such a way, and were opposed to each other in such strict
distinction, as the Incarnation of the Word and the pouring out of the
Holy Spirit are, or, to go still higher, as the second and third persons of
the Godhead as such oppose each other. In this opposition both were
strictly characterized as moments of the divine revelation and protected, each by its correlation with the other, from being confused with
a mode of human cognition. Schleiermacher could not acquiesce in
this opposition, because it was not his intention at all strictly to
characterize these two moments as revelation, nor to protect them from
being confused with a mode of human cognition. As an apologist he
was bound to be interested in understanding revelation not strictly as

revelation, but in such a way that it might also be comprehensible as a mode of human cognition. As an apologist he was thus bound to look upon this opposition as an inconvenience, and to look for a means of overcoming it. And the means he found was this principle of mediation.

The efficacy of this principle is at once shown by the fact that Schleiermacher presents as the theme of theology, as seen from the anthropocentric point of view, not the outpouring of the Holy Spirit—this might in itself have been possible—but religious consciousness as such. Faith understood in this way, not as God's revelation, but as man's experience, allowed, nay demanded, that the second objective moment should be understood accordingly, i.e. not presupposing a strict opposition to the first, and not as a correlate to the concept of the Holy Spirit, as understood in the Trinitarian sense, but as a correlate to this human experience. It was in accordance with the line of thought pursued by Kant and Lessing that Schleiermacher allowed his first moment, as the psychological one, to be opposed by his second moment as the historical one. Historical knowledge, too, is a mode of human cognition, even if it is a different one from that of psychological knowledge. Between these two motifs mediation is possible. Seeing them together cannot be altogether out of the question. The great difficulty Schleiermacher had in acknowledging and explaining his second motif was determined by the old teaching of the *divinity* of the Logos and of the Spirit. After he had mastered this teaching by interpreting it in the relationship of the historical to the psychological, there then remained the smaller difficulty of bringing these two things into connexion with one another, that is to say of overcoming Lessing's big ditch, and showing in opposition to Kant that the historical element in Christianity was more than a temporal vehicle of timeless reasonable truth. Because of his principle of mediation, he was able to show this better than Herder had attempted before him. For basically it is a question of nothing but carrying out Herder's programme. In carrying out this programme, in demonstrating that faith and Christ, equated with experience and history, are the foci of an ellipse, Schleiermacher turns the Christian relationship of man with God into an apparent human possibility. It is apparent because a mode of human cognition corresponds to it on both sides, because these two modes can be brought into a peaceful, mediating relationship, and because they were thus treated by Schleiermacher.

They are not in fact related in this way in the theology of the Reformation, and they are not subjected to such an interpretation there. The sole mediation which enters into consideration there is the recognition of the Father in the Son through the Spirit in the strict irreducible opposition of these 'persons' in the Godhead. This mediation cannot be made comprehensible as a mode of human cognition. It is unusable in apologetics. But the question is whether the theological concern can be preserved, other than at the expense of the interest of apologetics. And conversely the question must be asked whether with Schleiermacher the concern of apologetics has not been preserved at the expense of that of theology. The fact that Schleiermacher's theology was anthropocentric is not in itself a sufficient justification for this question, let alone that this fact should be made the subject of a reproach. What certainly does make this question necessary is the way Schleiermacher immunized the concept of revelation, as he has done by this interpretation, and the way in which he made possible for himself the mediation between his anthropological centre and the other, the Christological centre, by means of this interpretation. Let us now try to see in concrete fashion how this came about.

(*a*) In order to describe the way Schleiermacher understood the relationship between the two motifs we have used the image of the ellipse with its two foci. This image must be supplemented by the further remark that the ellipse tends to become a circle, so that its two foci have the tendency to coincide in one centre-point. But at the same time it is unlikely that this centre-point will lie mid-way between the two foci, since the power of attraction of the first focus is from the outset much stronger than that of the second, and since the second, once the circle has been achieved, might perhaps have vanished altogether, having succumbed entirely to the first. When Schleiermacher speaks of Christ and Christians and their mutual relationship, what he primarily has in mind is neither the one nor the other, but one single concept embracing both, namely the 'composite life', humanity, the history of 'human nature'. In this history it is a question of the 'redemption' of human nature. This redemption, however, is at the same time its fulfilment. It is a question of the furtherance of its 'higher life', of its gradual ascent from the sensory to the spiritual state, from a dim to a powerful consciousness of God. To this extent it is a question of its approach to the way in which man was originally determined, which was thrown into question by sin. Piety is the condition of being involved in this approach. And if this approach is that which is brought about by Christ then the condition of Christian piety is that of complete piety in as much as the approach which is brought about by Christ is

the most complete of all. For the dignity of Christ consists in a consciousness of God which is utterly powerful, which precludes all sin,
and which is posited together with Christ's self-consciousness. The
statement that religious consciousness is Christian consciousness is as
much as to say that it refers to Christ, which in turn is as much as to
say that what is real in Christ in its original and perfect form ('arche-
types'), is likewise gradually imparted to this consciousness. That is
redemption through Christ. Redemption is the higher human life of
the Christian, which did not have its beginning with the creation, nor
in Adam, but perfecting and crowning creation, first in Christ, and
which now also reaches the Christian as an impulse, as movement, as
the life of the spirit of Christ in his Church.

That Schleiermacher put the historical element before the psychological at first seems plain: the first influences and the second is
influenced. But this does not prevent Schleiermacher from summarizing
the whole—inevitably disconcerting us at the first glance—in the title
'Concerning the state of the Christian, in so far as he is aware of the
divine grace', as if Christology for all that were merely a smaller circle
within the greater one described as 'the state of the Christian', etc. Is it
not so? Does Christ mean significantly more to Schleiermacher than
a special and admittedly most important way of more nearly determining the state of the Christian? Schleiermacher himself does not seem
to think it a vain question to ask whether the exaltation of life, as the
process in which we are involved, might not be primary, and the figure
of Christ merely the symbol, the reflex, projected back into history, of
this original light. This is asserted without contradiction by one of
the speakers in the *Christmas Celebration*. Nor does the other question
which was also raised in the *Christmas Celebration* seem a vain one. I refer
to the one as being whether the figure of Christ is anything but the
historical point of departure, discovered in retrospect, of that unity of
the human and the divine, such as comes about in the self-consciousness of humanity as such. If this putting Christ before Christians is to
stand (and at all events Schleiermacher declares this to be his intention),
then according to the way he approaches the problem these questions
must surely be asked and left open. This giving of precedence, and
together with it the distinction of the two motifs, is relative. The
distinction is made, but as soon as the point is reached where the
relationship between the two distinguished motifs is to be represented,
it becomes plain that their distinction is conceived as a fluid one. It
is fluid within the composite phenomenon of the higher life inaugurated
by Christ. But this is in process of developing within ourselves, within

the composite phenomenon of the single effect of Christ, which embraces his effect just as much as our being affected. Where the one begins and the other leaves off is something as difficult to determine as the question of where with Novalis, art begins and philosophy leaves off, where religion begins and where love leaves off. Redemption, according to para. 11, 2 of the *Doctrine of Faith*, is, passively, man's transition from the bad state of restricted activity of the higher self-consciousness to the better one of a relative liberation; actively it is the aid given to him to this end by another.

This 'transition' and this 'aid' can in fact be distinguished only relatively the one from the other. Even if Schleiermacher, too, finds that there exists between them an opposition as between what is and what should be, between receiving and giving, between the continuation and the beginning, the imitation and the prototype, the general and the particular, we do not lose sight for an instant of the fact that these antitheses are mediated: that they are mediated by means of their belonging together in the comprehensible composite phenomenon of the higher life. At some point or other they must coincide. And it is only with the prospect of this final coincidence and from this point of no distinction that they are distinguished at all. It is this which justifies our speaking of the mystic element in Schleiermacher. It also makes it fitting for us to recall in this context Schleiermacher's proximity to Hegel. His placing of things in opposition is as seriously meant as Eckhart's distinction between God and the soul, as Hegel's distinction between thesis and anti-thesis. It is meant as seriously as any opposition can be meant whose elimination is pre-supposed and which is therefore bound to come about. Anyone who is in a position to focus Christ and the Christian together, as a composite phenomenon, manifestly knows of a third thing above both, and will thus be capable of distinguishing between them in this manner, only relatively; and putting one before the other is bound to remain questionable in principle, even if he wishes to do so and does in fact do so.

(*b*) According to Schleiermacher Christ is the Revealer and Redeemer in so far as he effects the higher life. It is this idea of effecting the higher life which we must now investigate. In it Christ, as the cause, is obviously distinguished from the higher life in us, as the effect. The 'higher life' means: the development of our existence, and—since our existence significantly comes about in our consciousness of our existence, or self-consciousness, our self-consciousness, however, being significantly determined as pious self-consciousness—the development of our piety. In so far Christ should be the cause of our piety. Piety, according to Schleiermacher's general definition, is nothing but the feeling of an effect, the feeling of utter dependence. Consciousness of this utter dependence of ours is the same thing as consciousness of our connexion with God. According to para. 4 of the *Doctrine of Faith* man knows that in respect to the world he is relatively free and relatively dependent. If in this relative freedom and dependence in respect to the world he feels that he is at the same time utterly dependent upon something else, which is not the world, then he is pious; he is aware of his connexion with God. The other thing, the Whence of our being, in respect to which we feel that we are utterly dependent, is God. But we cannot actually say 'in respect to which', since feeling, in contrast to knowledge and action, has not anything standing in opposition to it, has not any object. It is only in the feeling of his effect that God is given to us as a cause, and not in any other way. If he were given to us in some other way, if he were given to us in some way as an object, then a counter-effect on our part would come about too, in respect of him, so that there would be freedom and not utter dependence. We should then not be dealing with God, but with the world. God, therefore, is not given to us as an object. God signifies rather one of several factors shaping man's feeling, and it is this factor upon which we 'throw back' its being determined as pious feeling. The consciousness of God thus remains 'shut up' in feeling, so that the expression of the idea 'God' cannot signify anything else but the expression of feeling concerning itself, the most immediate self-reflection. And this quality of God as not being given as an object, to represent the Whence of our being is, according to Schleiermacher's express declaration, identical with God's 'original revelation'. With the utter dependence of his being, which pertains to man as it does to everything which is in being, he is also given, as a man, immediate self-consciousness, which is engaged in the process of becoming awareness of God; he is thus given God, and his piety is only the advance of this process which is peculiar to his human existence as such.

This determination of God's quality as the cause, as seen within the general conception of religion previously posited seems to present Christology with the following dilemma. *Either* Schleiermacher's view of the matter allows and demands that we should substitute Christ in the very place where he was speaking of God. This would then decide the fact that 'Christ' is not to be understood as an objective quantity, but only as this factor which also determines feeling itself, as the Whence of our existence that cannot be distinguished from our feeling itself. For as an objective quantity Christ could not be that upon which we are utterly dependent, and thus could not be God. Hence he can only be this other thing in our feeling itself, upon which we 'throw back' its determination as pious feeling. Thus in speaking of him we are speaking immediately of our feeling itself. Thus he is identical with this quality God has of being given, by virtue of which self-consciousness quite naturally becomes consciousness of God. And he is identical with this original revelation of God, which precedes all history, and is given with our existence itself. It would therefore be impossible to speak of a distinction between him and pious feeling as the self-consciousness which becomes consciousness of God, especially if his divinity were to be treated seriously. *Or* on the other hand Schleiermacher's view allows and demands that we should at all events understand Christ as an objective quantity, and thus distinguish him from pious feeling as such; that we should not equate him with the timeless original revelation, but grant him his historical individuality and think of him in this individuality as a temporal point of reference for pious feeling. This, however, directly implies that he is part of the world, i.e. that he is of the quintessence of all that in relation to which we have relative freedom, and upon which, therefore, we are only relatively dependent. This is to deny the only thing which, according to Schleiermacher's way of thinking, could be his Godhead—for all that, within the world, this figure might represent a highest point, a point, perhaps, of unique excellence, significance and effect he is in this case the climax, the possibly incommensurable climax of the divine power in mankind as such, and hence the stimulator, the possibly incommensurable stimulator of the divine power in all others. His ability to stimulate and the others' ability to be stimulated is then, however, not seated in himself, but in the hidden higher thing, in the consciousness and possession of God, as the bearer of which he would ultimately, even if in a particularly distinguished way, be aligned with everyone else.

Schleiermacher did not opt for the first, but for the second of these possibilities. He renounced the idea of a purely speculative Christology, but precisely in so doing, according to the premises of his conception of religion, he was bound to renounce the idea of the Deity of Christ or, to put it differently, to understand the Deity of Christ as the incomparable climax and decisive stimulator within the composite life of humanity. And it was not possible to arrive at an unequivocal opposition of Christ and Christians from this angle either. The antithesis between the two is seen through even before it is elaborated, and cannot be a final one. The first thing, and therefore the final thing too is the unity between the two, and the point at which this unity can be perceived is not by any means Christ, but the Christian, the view of Christ being in principle a view back towards him.

We are bound to ask a question concerning the entire concept of Christ's 'effecting', of the relationship of cause and effect, which Schleiermacher first called upon in order to describe the relationship between God and man in general, and then the relationship between Christ and the Christian. The question is whether this concept, in view of its certain naturalism, is not already right from the outset a symbol for the fact that, according to the premise of his principle of mediation, Schleiermacher, while he wanted to accord precedence to the first of these two factors, and asserted that this precedence existed, was in fact incapable of putting this idea into effect with anything like an ultimate seriousness of intention.

(c) This distinction of Christ above Christians is that of the 'original fact' of the whole of Christianity, of the 'archetypal image', as Schleiermacher was also fond of saying. Christ is the principle of individuation of this religion. He is that power, formed in a certain way, which, thought of as determining and forming, makes this religion precisely what it is. For as Schleiermacher already said in the *Addresses*, feeling is not without intuition. It is not without the stimulation provided by a certain something which affects religiously, by the action of which there comes about a certain state of being affected religiously. Outside of this correlation no religion exists. According to Schleiermacher there is no religion in itself, no natural religion. Or to put it more exactly: natural religion, that original state of being pious, which coincides with the original divine revelation, is for ever real only in a definite, concrete and temporal way. It is in the Finite, in this or the other concrete, temporal intuition that the Infinite for ever reveals itself. There can be no original divine revelation without the temporal exponent of historical revelation. Religion begins with an incomprehensible fact, with something worthy of thought, with a single, isolated intuition in the sphere of nature, of history or of society, or also in the sphere of a man's own inner life. Religion is always real as positive religion. It is only when one settles in one such form of central intuition that one acquires a fixed address and active citizen rights in the religious world. But this world is 'a perfect republic', in so far as none of the forms of central intuition which are possible in it excludes in principle even one of the others which are possible in it, and in so far, rather, as innumerable intuitions of different kinds, and therefore determinations of feeling, have their right, equal in principle, to exist beside and after each other, as the 'glorious branches into which the heavenly tree of the priestly art has distributed its crown and top'. The one thing which reveals itself in all of them admittedly has its reality only in each individual one, in this or that positive religion. But because it is the individual one each is not for that reason the only one, since it has its truth only in the one thing which is also real in all the other individual religions.

It is thus, according to para. 10 of the *Doctrine of Faith*, that the impulse proceeding from Christ imparts to Christianity colour and tone, historical breadth and the possibility for its existence. Religion in this determined impulse is real as Christian religion. But its truth, its content, is none the less nothing but the feeling of utter dependence, at its highest level, in its stamp as awareness of redemption. Revelation, i.e. here Christ, is the individualizing element in this religion, and to this extent the effective, realizing element. It has nothing to do with the antithesis between things true and false. All, and no, revelation is true. Revelation is the excitement of feeling in an individual, which, moving, conveys itself to others and thus allows a development from the religious individual to a religious type, a religious species, a religious community, a Church. In the case of the Christian religion this dominating individual, who impresses himself upon all others and is effective in the after-effects of his spirit, is Christ. That was what Schleiermacher meant when he defended the 'high arbitrariness' of Christianity against the attacks of Schelling. He fought against the same opponent in the natural religion of the Enlightenment: Christianity is not a universal religion of reason, it is positive, revelatory religion. But its positive quality, its character as revelation, is exhausted in the individuality it receives from the manifestation of Christ and his after-effects. Christ is the archetypal image, the original source, the original fact. These things mean that he is the historical beginning of this religion, this Church, and as such he is the beginning which is decisive for every age. Christ as the archetypal image is primal, productive, singular, just as in other fields, that, however, of religion included, every original image or archetype is primal, productive and singular. There is no doubt that Schleiermacher sought to assert something like the absoluteness of Christianity, and continually asserted it. Strangely enough it was in the pulpit particularly that the problem again and again crossed his path: why Christ in particular? Why can we not manage without him? Why can we not manage with someone else? Perhaps with someone else who is yet to come? The answer consists in the constantly repeated protestation that everything we have of higher life we have from him.

There can be no doubt about the personal sincerity of this assertion. But it is just this which is in question—whether this assertion can be considered as objectively valid, whether the strength of this assertion can be some other strength beside that of the asserting believer himself, or of the composite life of the community of the Christian Church, from out of whose heritage the preaching believer speaks. Schleiermacher does not seem to be able to say that there is an eternal significance of Christ, an absoluteness of Christianity. At the back of even his most forceful protestations, unrevoked, and irrevocable, unless he is to abandon his basic premise, there stands the fact he established in the *Addresses* that the basic outlook of every religion is in itself eternal, since it forms a supplementary part of the infinite whole of religion in general in which all things must be eternal. The sincerity and strength of the distinction which pious feeling is inclined and determined until further notice to accord to Christ in relation to itself stands and falls with the sincerity and strength of pious feeling itself. The original fact of Christ and the fact of my Christianity are links in a chain, and the relationship of mutual determination which links in a chain necessarily have makes it plainly impossible to assume that the effect they have on one another cannot in principle be reversed. From this angle, too, the way Schleiermacher approaches his task makes it necessary for us to content ourselves with a distinction and an according of precedence which is relative, fluid, and challengeable in principle. The posing of the question of truth can at every instant become a danger to this distinction.

To summarize: Schleiermacher's Christology has as its summit the indication of a quantitative superiority, dignity and significance in Christ as opposed to our own Christianity. This is as much as to say that just because the point with Christ is that he has only an incomparably greater quantity of that which we see in ourselves as our Christianity, this indication is ultimately linked with the assertion, the self-assertion, of our own Christianity. The two foci of the ellipse draw relentlessly closer to one another, and how is the dissolution and disappearance of the objective moment in the subjective to be prevented? *The Word is not so assured here in its independence in respect to faith as should be the case if this theology of faith were a true theology of the Holy Spirit.* In a proper theology of the Holy Spirit there could be no question of dissolving the Word. Here, quite seriously, there is a question of such a dissolution. The only thing which prevents it is Schleiermacher's good will in not allowing things to develop so far. This good will must once again be formally acknowledged, but that in no way alters the fact that we feel ourselves here in all seriousness threatened by this dissolution. Thus it seems necessary for us after all to begin to consider whether what has happened here is that it is not the Holy Spirit, but, as Schleiermacher claims, merely man's religious consciousness which has after all become the theme of theology. In some depth of his mind Schleiermacher must have intended otherwise. This different intention must then have become submerged in the stormy need of the apologist to make plain the working of the Holy Spirit in the familiar form of religious consciousness. And when he had done this the only thing left for him to do was to equate the objective moment, the Word, with the form, likewise familiar, of that which is historically effective and original, thus arriving at the relative opposition with which he could do justice to modern cultural consciousness, but possibly not to Christianity.

Not in explanation, but in order to illustrate this situation, I should like to recall in conclusion yet another correspondence in Schleiermacher's theology, the execution of which raises doubts similar to those which have just forced themselves upon us. I refer to his teaching of sin and grace. What about this antithesis, forming as it does the theme, and providing the principle according to which the second part of the *Doctrine of Faith* is divided? According to the way Schleiermacher himself explains it sin and grace are comprised together in the one outer bracket of the consciousness of redemption: sin as the restricted awareness of the higher life, as the absence of ease in originating pious moments of life, as the non-domination of the feeling of utter dependence—and grace as the ease with which we are capable of reading into the various sensory stimuli of self-consciousness consciousness of God; consciousness of sin being at the same time that of a human deed, and consciousness of grace being at the same time that of a divine impartation. There is no true Christian consciousness in which these two states would not be contained, in the relationship of a More and Less, and thus once again in a quantitative relationship, and indeed in 'fluid differentiation'. Schleiermacher does not consider an objectless, absolute relationship with God, either in the negative or the positive sense, as a possibility that need be taken seriously into account. Our pious self-consciousness simply sways between these two extremes, sharing the inequalities (of development and restriction, pleasure and pain) of temporal life. The Christian is always aware of sin *and* grace both in and with one another. That means that with Schleiermacher there can be no question of man's knowing that he is earnestly adjudged a sinner, and equally earnestly ultimately pardoned.

M

And this, together with the absence of the vision of man which Luther and Calvin had in the teaching that man was in himself completely sinful and in Christ completely righteous, probably helps to explain the fact that we cannot reckon, in Schleiermacher, with an ultimate opposition between God and man, between Christ and the Christian.

The question as to how it was that Schleiermacher himself was not alarmed by this result, and how he could think—as he did in fact think —that he was not destroying Reformation theology, but taking it up and continuing it in a way suited to his time; how he failed to notice that his result challenged the decisive premise of all Christian theology in a way which had not been known, perhaps, since the days of the ancient Gnostics—this question presents us with a mystery which cannot be solved. We can only establish that the classic representation which the Christian doctrine found in the great moment when the spirit of the eighteenth century was fulfilled and overcome resulted in the development of an obscurity in its very statement, in the opposition of God and man, an obscurity within which every identifiable sign points to the fact that here man has alone remained master of the field to the extent that he alone is the subject, and Christ has become his predicate. The only consolation we can draw from this discovery is that this cannot be what the Christian Church intends, and therefore could not be what Schleiermacher intended either. The consolation we draw at this point, a point decisive in the history of recent theology, is however provided by what is truly a maxim of faith and not a maxim of historical knowledge. That which is historically knowable would leave us here ultimately without comfort.

IX

FEUERBACH

FEUERBACH was an outsider; not a theologian, but a philosopher engaging in theology. There are few philosophers who have not at some time and in some way engaged in theology. But Feuerbach, the philosopher, engaged in nothing but theology. 'Strictly speaking, all my writings have only one aim, one sole motivation, and one sole theme. This theme is religion and theology and everything connected with it', he once said. His love seems to have been an unhappy one, for in effect what he practised was anti-theology. But he practised it so knowledgeably, and with such relevance to the theological situation of his age, throwing such clear light upon it, and, moreover, in a way so interesting in itself, that we must allow him to speak together with the theologians.

Ludwig Feuerbach was born in Landshut in 1804, studied under Daub and Hegel, became a *Privatdozent* (unsalaried lecturer) at the University of Erlangen in 1828, and died near Nuremberg in 1872 as a private scholar. Of his numerous writings the most important are: *Das Wesen des Christentums* (The Essence of Christianity) (1841) and *Das Wesen der Religion* (The Essence of Religion) (1851). His aim was a simple, but big one: he sought to take Schleiermacher and Hegel seriously, completely seriously, at the point where they concurred in asserting the non-objective quality of God. He wanted, that is, to turn theology, which itself seemed half-inclined towards the same goal, completely and finally into anthropology; to turn the lovers of God into lovers of men, the worshippers into workers, the candidates for the life to come into students of the present life, the Christians into complete men; he wanted to turn away from heaven towards the earth, from faith towards love, from Christ towards ourselves, from all, but really all, supernaturalism towards real life.

In his eyes even Kant, Fichte and Hegel are still supernaturalists, to the extent that they are seeking the divine Being in reason, separately from man. The true man is not the man sundered from nature, abstracted from the world of the senses, but the man who is identical

with the totality of his body. It is man in this sense whom Feuerbach
would like to assist in acquiring his birthright. He does not want to
think as a thinker, but to think, as he expressly says, in 'existence', i.e.
as the living, actual being which he finds present, as himself, in the
world, and co-existing with it. Only the distinction of I and Thou is
real. And it is precisely in the experienced unity of this distinction that
man's essence is to be found. The concept of the object is nothing else
but the concept of an objective I, and thus of a Thou. By the consciousness of the Thou I become conscious of the world, and with the
world, of myself. And this consciousness is imparted by means of the
senses; truth, reality, the world of the senses, and humanity are
identical concepts. The secret of being is the secret of love in the most
comprehensive meaning of the word; which means that ultimately
head, heart and stomach jointly seek and find one object. With this
premise as his starting-point Feuerbach sets out to transform the
theologians into anthropologists—but this time in earnest.

Feuerbach does not deny either God or theology. In denying the
existence of an abstract divine Being, divorced from nature and man,
he is merely affirming God's nature as man's true nature. And in
denying a false theology distinguishing theological and anthropological
tenets, he is merely affirming anthropology as the true theology. The
weight of Feuerbach's feeling is positive. He, too, is singing his *Magni-
ficat*. He affirms, loves and praises man and his will for life, the will
revealed in the needs, desires and ideals which prompt man to rise
above his dependence, his limited and threatened state, to distinguish
between the valuable and the worthless, to struggle for what is valuable, and against what is worthless. And he affirms, loves and praises
man's tendency to make absolute the reason, necessity and right of this
will for life of his, and thus to become religious in the most diverse
ways. Feuerbach would wish us only to perceive and acknowledge that
the name of 'God', in which all man's highest, worthiest and most
beloved names are concentrated, actually first sprang from the human
heart, and that religion is thus in the deepest sense concerned with man
himself; he would have us perceive and acknowledge that with God it
is a question of man's own will for life, and not of a second, different
thing in opposition to it. 'God, as the quintessence of all realities or
perfections, is nothing else but the quintessence, comprehensively
summarized for the assistance of the limited individual, of the qualities
of the human species, scattered among men, and manifesting themselves in the course of world history.' The interest I feel in God's
existence is one with the interest I feel in my own existence, and indeed

in my own everlasting existence, and this latter interest is fulfilled in
the consciousness of the species, the consciousness to which I exalt
myself in positing God as existing. God is my hidden, assured existence
as a member of the human species. There is no quality or capacity
attributed by theological dogmatics to God, which would not be better,
or more simply conceived of as a quality and capacity of the human
species, of man as such, which I have occasion in varying degrees to
affirm, to aim at, and to believe in in my concrete existence as a man.
Theology itself in fact admits in Christology that God is entirely
human. He is human—and this is the true Christ—in the consciousness
of the species, in which we actually partake together of redemption,
peace and fellowship. The Word of God should be understood as the
divinity of the human word, in so far as it is a true word, a self-imparting of the I to the Thou, and thus man's essential nature, and hence
again the essence of God himself. Baptism and Holy Communion, in
which Feuerbach took an especial interest, are manifestly a ceremonial
recognition of the divinity and healing power of nature, the divinity of
the objects of the pleasure of the senses. And thus the Holy Spirit is
the personification of religion itself, the groaning of the creature, the
religious feeling's mirrored self. In short: Why search afar? Behold,
the good things lie at hand! What man, contradicting and doing
violence to himself a thousand times, seeks in and from a divine object—
these things are his own predicates, or alternatively those of his species.

That is the liberating truth Feuerbach seeks to express, at a time
when, as he never tires of stressing, this truth has long since shown
itself to be self-evident, through the actual historical course which
religion, the Church, and theology have taken. 'Theology has long
since become anthropology'—from the moment when Protestantism
itself, and Luther in particular, ceased to be interested in what God is in
himself and became emphatically interested in what God is for man.
Theology's course of development has irresistibly proceeded in such a
way that man has come more and more to renounce God, in proportion as he has come to proclaim himself. And it is an open secret that
Christianity in its theological form has long since disappeared, not only
from the sphere of reason, but also from the actual life of mankind; and
that man's awakened self-consciousness has meant that Christianity in
this form is no longer taken seriously. Religion exists. Religion is possible and necessary. But it is man who is the beginning, the middle and
the end of religion—man and man alone.

Whatever else it may imply, this anti-theology of Feuerbach represents a question; a question put by him to the theology of his time, and

perhaps not only in his time. In our previous discussions we have seen how theology was influenced by the belief in humanity which was developing in opposition to it and suffered itself to be driven into the corner of apologetics. We saw that its whole problem had become how to make religion, revelation and the relationship with God something which could also be understood as a necessary predicate of man, or at any rate how to demonstrate that man had a potentiality, a capacity, for these things. To Feuerbach at all events the meaning of the question is whether the theologian, when he thus formulates the problem, is not after all affirming the thing in which the ascent of humanity seems to culminate in any case, namely man's apotheosis. It was in this sense that, making up his mind quickly and fully approving of it, he wanted to understand and adopt the true aim of that theology. If theology was to be understood in that sense, he wanted to be a theologian himself.

Was he in fact completely in the wrong? Had not the theologians themselves tended to work in this same direction before him? We are reminded of Schleiermacher's doctrine of the relationship between God and pious excitement, which, as he expresses it, is manifestly not one which has lost all the characteristics of an encounter. We are reminded further of Schleiermacher's doctrine of the three dogmatic forms, of which the second and third, the utterances concerning God and the world, might just as well have been left out; and we are reminded of the same author's Christology and doctrine of atonement, seemingly projected back from the personal experience of the human subject. We think too of de Wette, who had already caused the word 'anthropology' to be pronounced and adopted as a slogan within theological circles themselves. We think of Hegel and his disciples, and of the might they bestow upon the human mind in its dialectic self-movement; a might which eventually and finally prevails over God too, and his revelation. We think of Tholuck, with his proclamation that it was the 'heart' which was the seat of divine wisdom in man. The question arises whether Feuerbach does not represent the point of intersection where all these lines converge, little as this may have been the intention of their originators; the question whether, taking into account the premises established at that time, the drawing of this unwelcome conclusion could effectively be avoided; the question whether the theologians themselves could at least protest to this anti-theologian that he had mistaken their intentions, and that they were seeking something else.

But it is not only in the relevance of what he said for his own time that Feuerbach is interesting. The question he represents becomes acute whenever incautious use is made in theology of mystical ideas, of the union of God and man; in fact, whenever these ideas are used other than in an eschatologically ensured connexion. And there is something here which should give us Protestant theologians special food for thought. Feuerbach preferred to call to witness for his interpretation of Christianity, not his theological contemporaries but Luther of all people. First he called to witness Luther's concept of faith, in which faith had acquired the nature of a divine hypothesis, and might upon occasion be called the 'creator of the Godhead' in us. Secondly, and chiefly, he called upon Luther's Christology and doctrine of the Lord's Supper. Luther taught, with the over-emphasis of genius, that the Godhead should not be sought in heaven but on earth, in the man Jesus, and then again that Christ's nature as the God-Man should substantially be sought in the sacred elements of Holy Communion. And Lutheran orthodoxy has cast this inspired doctrine into the dogma of the *communicatio idiomatum in genere majestatico*, according to which the predicates of the divine glory, omnipotence, omnipresence, eternity, etc., are to be attributed to the humanity, as such and *in abstracto*, of Jesus; and this it has expressly called the 'apotheosis' of Christ's humanity. In principle this clearly meant that the higher and lower positions, those of God and man, could be reversed. And what the theologians of old had seen as being right for the person of Christ was now, to more modern and even less restrained speculating minds, capable of seeming proper for man in general. German theology had for centuries guarded itself perhaps all too rigidly against the Calvinist corrective, so that it was bound to become uncertain now whether the relationship with God had really in principle to be thought of as irreversible. Hegel, as we saw, emphatically declared that he was a good Lutheran, and so did Feuerbach, in his own way and upon his own level. In the light of Feuerbach's interpretation of Luther, we must ask whether it may not be advisable for us to reflect, as regards the non-reversibility of the relationship with God, upon some things which Luther, in establishing his doctrine, seems to have neglected to ponder. And today especially it should certainly be useful for us at least to be aware that the doctrine of I and Thou was put forward as early as 1840 in the strongest possible form, with Luther as its authority, as the true *via regia* of faith and revelation. But it was put forward, be it noted, with this particular interpretation.

The question raised by Feuerbach further becomes acute at the point where it is opposed to all spiritualist understanding of Christianity. The very thing which might at first sight seem to be the weakness of Feuerbach's position, namely its sensory and natural quality might at any rate be also its particular strength. In speaking of man's reality as consisting in the unity of head, heart and stomach, Feuerbach is obviously concerned with the same ideas as Menken. It was man's existence, and indeed, as he stressed with passionate exaggeration, man's sensory existence, which interested him. He sought to have God's Beyond transposed into this human life. This might have been a denial of God's Beyond and thus a denial of God himself. But a denial or neglect of the relationship of God's Beyond with human life might also signify a denial of God; it is precisely a one-sided idealism and spiritualism which might cause us in a particularly dangerous way to suspect that the teaching of God is a human illusion. The question arises whether it might not in fact be this whole man, soul and body, of whom Feuerbach clearly sought to speak, who really corresponds to God. The question arises whether Feuerbach, with his protest, might not after all have upon his side the radical Easter belief, the belief in the resurrection of the flesh, which prevailed in early Christendom and still exists today in the Eastern Churches. One thing is certain here: the fact that a common concern unites him with J. T. Beck and the two Blumhardts, and with the theology typical of Württemberg as a whole. It is doubtful whether we can answer Feuerbach, who might upon this point also be in the stronger Christian position, if we fail to take this concern fully into account. Perhaps, to serve as a basis whereby a standpoint inwardly superior to Feuerbach's illusionism might be gained, a very real faith in resurrection corresponding to a real faith in God is necessary.

Feuerbach's doctrine was possible because there were several things which he failed to see, just like his contemporaries and opponents in theology. It was impossible for his contemporaries at any rate to point out his mistakes to him. It would have been possible to object, in terms just as basic and sweeping as those Feuerbach himself used in speaking of man and his existence, that 'man's essential being', the 'consciousness of the species' which he made the measure of all things and in which he thought he saw man's true divinity, might be a supernatural fiction in exactly the same way as Hegel's concept of reason, or any other abstraction. This objection was in fact raised by Max Stirner, a Hegelian living at the same time as Feuerbach, and tending even further to the left than Feuerbach himself. The true man, if he is to be thought of in completely existentialist terms, should surely be individual man. Like all the theologians of his time, Feuerbach discussed man in general, and in attributing divinity to him in his sense had in fact not said anything about man as he is in reality. And Feuerbach's tendency to make the two largely interchangeable, so that he speaks of individual man as if he were man in general, and thus dares to attribute divinity to the individual, is evidently connected with the fact that he does not seem sincerely and earnestly to have taken cognizance either of the wickedness of the individual, or of the fact that this individual must surely die. If he had been truly aware of this, then he might perhaps have seen the fictitious nature of this concept of generalized man. He would then perhaps have refrained from identifying God with man, the real man, that is, who remains when the element of abstraction has been stripped from him. But the theology of the time was not so fully aware of the individual, or of wickedness or death, that it could instruct Feuerbach upon these points. Its own hypotheses about the relationship with God were themselves too little affected by them. In this way they were similar to Feuerbach's, and upon this common ground his rivals could not defeat him. That was why the theology of his time found it ultimately possible to preserve itself in face of him, as it had preserved itself in face of D. F. Strauss, without summoning an energetic cry of '*God* preserve us!'

X

STRAUSS

D. F. STRAUSS was born at Ludwigsburg in Württemberg on 27th January 1808, and studied in Tübingen under the Supranaturalists, Steudel and Bengel (grandson of the famous Johann Albrecht of the same name), and under F. Chr. Baur, who was active there from 1826 onwards. He was also taught by Ecshenmayer, the mystic and mantic scholar. His studies in theology and philosophy led him 'from the steppes of Kant and his expounders to the more succulent pastures of natural philosophy',[1] to a highly personal union, that is, of the influences of Jakob Böhme, Schelling and Justinus Kerner (the author of the *Seherin von Prevorst* (Wise Woman of Prevorst)); then on to Schleiermacher and thence to his temporary goal, which he found in Hegel. In 1835 and 1836, repeating his course at Tübingen, he wrote his *Leben Jesu, kritisch bearbeitet* (Life of Jesus, a Critical Treatment), a work which made him at once and for many years to come the most famous theologian in Germany and ensured that he would never in his life be considered for any post in the church or in the academic world. In the following years he published a series of polemics in which he sought to defend what he had written and yet was able to give it a milder tone. His appointment as professor of theology in Zürich in 1839 came to nothing owing to the opposition of the conservative element there. Zürich was forced to pension him off. At this he completed his denial of the Bible, Church and dogma, in the two-volume work *Die christliche Glaubenslehre in ihrer geschichtlichen Entwicklung und in ihrem Kampf mit der modernen Wissenschaft* (The Christian Doctrine of Faith in its Historical Development and in its Conflict with Modern Science), (1840-1), and disappeared for a while from the theological arena, becoming a freelance journalist. This was the time of his unhappy marriage, which ended in separation after four years, to the famous Bohemian singer Agnes Schebest, whose excessive jealousy made his life a misery. The memory of this marriage inflicted upon Strauss a melancholy he was never able to shake off again. Thus it was that his attempt, in 1848, to

[1] *Gesammelte Schrifte* (Collected Works), 1876, I, p. 125.

enter politics brought him more grief than joy. In 1864 he felt compelled to enter into the theological discussion once more, which had
taken a new turn through the intervention of the Tübingen school, and
wrote a second *Leben Jesu* (Life of Jesus), this time intended 'for the
German people'. In 1865, with *Die Halben und die Ganzen* (The Halves
and the Wholes) he attacked Schenkel's *Life of Jesus* and the liberal
theology of the Protestant League; during the Franco-Prussian war he
conducted a celebrated patriotic correspondence with his French
counterpart, Ernest Renan, and concluded his theological writings
with *Der alte und der neue Glaube* (The Old and the New Faith), in 1872,
a work whose almost unanimous rejection in every camp embittered
the last days of his life, following as it did upon a long period of loneliness. He died in his native Ludwigsburg on 8th February, 1874.

We shall first attempt to draw a general picture of his theological
character. Afterwards we shall turn our attention to the practical
problem which will remain unforgettably connected with his name, and
which he was the first to bring to the notice of theology with axiomatic
distinctness, especially in his first *Life of Jesus*—an achievement parallel
to that of Feuerbach concerning the problem of religion—I mean the
problem of God's revelation in history.

'Strauss must be loved in order to be understood', Albert Schweitzer
has said.[1] As things stand, however, this can only mean that we must
feel sympathy for him. Strauss is not a tragic figure. We must have
sympathy for him chiefly because those things in his life which involuntarily give rise to honest regret in the beholder are unconnected
with any great and albeit perhaps guilty aims and since they are rather
more accidental in their nature than necessary, more trivial than
daemonic, more liable to evoke head-shakings than fear, and because
the sympathy without which we cannot in fact understand him, can
scarcely ever be mixed with admiration for the way in which he
suffered, since this once again evokes yet more pity for him, rather
than any respect.

But of course: sympathy here, particularly, cannot by any means
mean the pity of the objective observer. It may well be that in David
Friedrich Strauss, just because there was no tragic quality in him, a
secret ailment of the whole of modern theology is focused and represented in a special way, so that it was not without justice that he was
probably the best-known and most influential theologian of the
nineteenth century, in non-theological and non-church circles. We may
reflect upon the great practical problem he raised, which caused him to

[1] *Geschichte der Leben-Jesu-Forschung* (The Quest of the Historical Jesus), 1926, p. 69.

be so violently rejected, and think how he was in fact unable to find an effective counter to this rejection; we may observe him in the grief and loneliness which was brought upon him on the one hand by the truth he unwillingly represented, and on the other by the insufficiency and lack of fertility of his zeal for truth. Observing these things we involuntarily see not only him, but in a certain aspect the typical theologian of the century, so that we are not then content, like Hausrath, to establish that Strauss was 'essentially a pathological figure'.[1]

Strauss's most significant achievement lies in the historical sphere. It cannot be said that he was a historian in the sense that F. Chr. Baur was, nor one of such standing. He found it possible to write, as early as 7th April, 1837: 'I am beginning to find the manner of pure science a dry one. I was not really meant to be a scholar; I am much too dependent upon mood, and far too self-occupied.' Over and over again he made similar statements about himself. The discovery in historical method he undoubtedly made in his first *Life of Jesus* he hit upon more by chance than anything. This is shown by the fact that he did not abide by it, in its most decisive feature, in the second, in 1864, and indeed rather found means to adapt his method, in this very decisive feature, to the criticism that had been noised in respect of the first *Life of Jesus*. How did this come about? 'The mood was no longer there, in which I had written the book originally.'[2] The other, smaller historical works mostly biographical in content which we have from Strauss are not governed by the spirit of cohesive historical research either, or by an actual feeling for the past. In presenting Hutten or Voltaire, Frischlin or Schubert, he was much more concerned, once again upon his own confession, with the dream-image of his own existence than with the historical material as such. 'I am not a historian; with me everything has proceeded from dogmatic (or rather anti-dogmatic) concerns.'[3] The hero of a Strauss biography 'had to show intellectual interests, had to have intellectual accomplishments which could be pointed out, and indeed in a direction related to mine; he had to be facing the light, and freedom; an enemy of despots and the priesthood'.[4] Thus his serious attempt to write a biography of Luther was also bound to come to grief simply because he could not but consider Luther's concept of faith as 'something purely irrational, and indeed horrible'.[5] 'A man

---

[1] *D. Fr. Strauss und die Theologie seiner Zeit* (D. Fr. Strauss and the Theology of his Time), 1876, Vol. 2, p. 390.

[2] *Collected Works*, I, p. 6.   [3] Letter of 22nd July, 1846.

[4] *Collected Works*, I, p. 31.   [5] Letter of 24th December, 1857.

in whom everything proceeds from the consciousness that he and all men are in themselves utterly depraved, and subject to eternal damnation, from which they can be redeemed only by the blood of Christ and their belief in its power—a man with this consciousness as his core is so alien, so incomprehensible to me, that I could never choose him as the hero of a biography. No matter what other qualities I might love and admire in him, this inmost consciousness of his is so repugnant to me that there could never be any question of the sympathy existing between him and myself which is indispensable between the biographer and his hero.'[1] Speaking in this way he had in fact, with hostile acumen, seen in Luther what the historians as a rule either cannot or will not see, but he was not himself a historian.

Strauss has been called a speculative mind. This is only true if we look upon Strauss not so much as one who thinks as one who broods, with a passionate, shrewd, and skilful, co-ordinating brooding. Upon points of detail Strauss was without doubt clever, amazingly clear-sighted, stimulating and often amusing in description and debate. What he completely lacked was the 'thinker's' ability to build up consecutively, to construct, to synthesize.

In this respect he failed in a way which was nothing short of disastrous no less than three times in his life. Each time it was when writing one of his three most important works. The first time was on the occasion of his first *Life of Jesus*. This work, faithful to the Hegelian tradition, was really only intended as a critical analysis of the naïve conception of Christ, as furnished by tradition, to be followed by a speculative reconstruction of Christology as the true turning-point of the book. The first part of the programme, the antithesis, was meticulously executed. What was to be the actual positive achievement, however, the very part which Strauss, according to a letter of the 6th February, 1832, considered, strangely enough, to be the easiest, remained unwritten, apart from the often-quoted allusions to it in the final section of the second volume. The same thing happened again in 1840-1 in his *Doctrine of Faith*. What was intended and promised in the polemics preceding it was a positive representation of dogma following a critical reduction of dogmatics, a dogma conclusively intellectualized by speculation, but justified too by this process, in the manner, perhaps, in which A. E. Biedermann later did it in the third part of his dogmatics. All Strauss was able to do, was to steer the ship of dogmatics carefully on to the rocks of a somewhat facile confrontation with Spinoza's and Hegel's philosophy and have it founder there

[1] *Collected Works*, I, p. 41.

with all hands. The 1,400 pages of this second work were not followed
by a positive second part either. The same inability to keep to a system
was shown yet again in 1872 in *The Old and the New Faith*, in which
Strauss finally achieved an exposition of the new faith, but in the form
of a journalistic conglomeration of a little Darwin, a little Goethe, a
little Lessing, a little art criticism, and a great deal of anonymous,
flatly bourgeois morality so incoherent that one would suppose its
author to have been forsaken by any idea of the form, even, of the art
of philosophy. It was indeed too easy for Nietzsche, in the well-known,
devastating first part of his *Unzeitgemässe Betrachtungen* (Untimely
Observations), to bring about the old man's literary and philosophical
demise, a few weeks before the latter met his physical end. Certainly
there can be few who have thought more, more industriously, and more
existentially than Strauss in their lives; but even more certainly he
was not a thinker.

Furthermore, Strauss has been represented as the quasi-daemonic
type of cold, dry, intellectual logic, particularly by his opponents, and
he has been made the object of a horrified amazement. And he himself,
in fact, seems to have thought that his strength lay in this direction.
He imagined he had discovered in himself the gift of 'dialectic thought',
as a substitute for the creative imagination which he lacked.[1] When
he went on his first train-journey (between Heidelberg and Mannheim) in 1841, he had, according to a letter of 24th May, 1841,
'no fear, but the feeling that the governing principle of such inventions
was most closely related to my own . . . this abstraction, this tearing-
away of the individual by a universal might, such as occurs with these
colossal, gigantic machines is exactly the same principle which we
represent in the study of knowledge'.

We can certainly gain the impression that here is a logic proceeding,
as it were, on rails, by consulting any piece of Strauss's work; the great
declaration of bankruptcy of *The Christian Doctrine of Faith*, for instance.
But if we look at his life-work as a whole, we find the term 'spiral',
which Hausrath used to describe it, too suggestive of a unity. At this
time it was Feuerbach who was characterized by the intellectual logic
of the things he wanted, and not Strauss, who wrote of himself on the
17th March, 1838, that 'every six years or so an old scholar dies off in
me'. Strauss was clever, but not clever as F. Chr. Baur, who was able to
lay hold of an idea, and pursue it singly in perhaps very varied form.
Strauss was clever, rather, in a very illogical fashion, first in one way,
and then in another, just as the cleverness happened to come as a

[1] *Collected Works*, I, p. 12.

result of all kinds of determining factors which were of an outer rather than an inner nature. At the time when he was becoming a Hegelian, for example, he was able to preach in a faultlessly orthodox way and unobjectionably and successfully answer a prize question of the faculty of Catholic Theology of Tübingen, mark you, upon the resurrection of the flesh. 'With complete conviction I proved the resurrection of the dead by exegesis and natural philosophy, and as I made the last point it was clear to me that there was nothing in it at all.'[1] Between 1836 and 1840, in consideration of his outer situation too, he was prepared to make concessions, and to compromise about his *Life of Jesus*, the effects of which had surprised him himself. Then contrariwise in 1840, in anger about his experiences at the hands of the people of Zürich, he notoriously performed a reduction of the *Doctrine of Faith*, instead of a reconstruction, and in the same mood also took back his concessions concerning the *Life of Jesus*. Then as a private author he advocated a liberal Church and theology once again, in spite of his book of 1840-1. This in no way prevented him from attacking the Liberals from the rear in the sixties, once again chiefly because he had been personally disillusioned. This was precisely the most difficult time that liberalism had in church politics. It did not prevent him from playing off Hengstenberg against Schenkel, and thinking that this very work (*The Halves and the Wholes*) was 'the best I have ever written in polemics'.[2] On top of all this he finally, after forty years as an idealist, fell among the materialists 'like Karl Moor among the robbers' (Hausrath), and indeed among the scientific materialists, and of these among the Darwinists, of all people. Arrived at this point Strauss, the pupil of Hegel, was finally unable to recall any argument against man's origin with the apes. Thus, with the best will in the world, we cannot say that Strauss's life-work has a particular tendency or character. The tendency it does have is to take the line of the most obvious, of least resistance, of finding the easiest opportunity for striking out at theology or the Church, and justifying again and again the writer's own departure from their murky kingdom. One's final impression—which is Hausrath's too, who was very well disposed to him—does little to bear out convincingly Strauss's realism. It is that, deprived of his grounds for feeling ill-used and given a respectable professorship somewhere, like all the others he would have been capable of different achievements in questions of decisive importance, and certainly of taking another ultimate course. In these circumstances it is impossible for us to admire him as the champion of intellectual logic.

[1] Letter of 8th February, 1838.　　[2] *Collected Works*, I, p. 62.

And only now in fact do we come to the most important point. Strauss offered to his time the sight of the theologian who has become an unbeliever, for all to behold and without denying it. From 1839, at the latest, he wrathfully and zealously stood in opposition not only to the Church, but to God himself, like Michael Kohlhaas going to law, finally continuing to fight his case as an outlaw, having made of this dispute his life's profession. And contending even beyond the grave, he forbade any participation by a clergyman at his funeral already ten years before the event.[1] The denial he gave, as for instance in his *Doctrine of Faith*, is truly a very angry one. 'I have encircled and assaulted theism from every side, and bested the language of pantheism from an open position', he triumphs in a letter of 27th February, 1840. The chapter on the Church concludes with the frank declaration[2] that theology today could only still be productive by carrying out the task of destruction. Its task at the present time was to demolish a building which no longer fitted in with the architectural plan for the new world, and to demolish it in such a way that, even if it was not brought down upon the heads of its inhabitants, their gradual departure would be in part awaited, and in part accelerated. The study of theology, once the path to the ministry, was now the best way to become unfit for it. For as dogma was the outlook upon life of an idiot consciousness, theology being however the knowledge of this consciousness, this knowledge had at the present time become so critically penetrating, owing to the influence of philosophy, that anyone arriving at such a science would of necessity abandon that of which it is a science, namely the outlook upon life of an idiot consciousness. We should soon be reaching the state where the only people who could still be considered for the office of clergymen would be religious idiots and those theologically self-taught, those speaking and presiding at pietist gatherings.

'The religious chord in him gave forth no sound', Hausrath laments, and considers it to be Strauss's greatest failing that he simply did not understand that religion was not a matter for thought, but for feeling: 'a way of sensing God, and tuning oneself to the world'.[3] If it had been a matter of feeling, sense and mood he would inevitably have been the most faithful theologian, for with these things he was richly endowed, indeed to the point of over-sensibility. If this had been in question, then we might still have held it to his credit that in the time before he became critical, at the end of the twenties, he too experienced a revival —it was, after all, not for nothing that he lived at the same time as

[1] Letter of 22nd May, 1863.   [2] Vol. 2, p. 624.   [3] Op. cit., I, p. 6; II, p. 391.

Ludwig Hofacker, Albert Knapp and the other fathers of Württemberg neo-pietism—and sang of it in a poem, the last verse of which runs:

> Yes, be Thou sun, and I the tree,
> But hopeful gazing up to Thee;
> Be Thou the streamlet on the lea,
> And I the grass-blade close to Thee;
> O let me ne'er be rich and mine
> But only, Jesus, poor and Thine![1]

We should be deceiving ourselves if the many angry words which Strauss put on paper about the Church and theology and everything that has to do with them were to tempt us to think straightaway of those souls which, according to the Calvinist doctrine of predestination, are hardened from eternity. Strauss did make such a markedly anti-Christian impression upon not a few of his contemporaries. Above all he himself continually flirted with his unbelief in such a way that we cannot help taking the phenomenon into account. But I strongly advise anyone who today is still perhaps tempted to behold in him something like the spirit which constantly denies, to read his *The Old and the New Faith*. For the impression this work gives is that this heretic and unbeliever, who appears to be so dreadful, is in fact basically nothing but a Central European rejoicing in his learning, but not, unfortunately, quite content with himself and the world about him. The hell which quite properly seems to contain him is more like a 'home, sweet home' or *Gartenlaube*[2] than an inferno such as Dante or the cheerful Angelus Silesius saw and described. The book has four parts:

1. Are we still Christians?—Answer: No, because first it is no longer necessary for us to be Christians, and secondly, it does not suit us any more.

2. Are we still religious? Answer: 'Yes or No, according to what you mean by religion.' And yet Yes, in so far as, in spite of Schopenhauer, we are happy in a feeling of dependence upon the All, for which in the face of such pessimists, we demand most decidedly the same piety as the pious man of former times demanded for his God. 'Our feeling for the All reacts, if it is done injury, in absolutely religious fashion'[3]—after all, then: Yes!

3. What is our conception of the world? Answer: We arrive at it by a free interpretation of Kant-Laplace, Lamarck, Darwin, Haeckel—

---

[1] 1827 or 1828, *Collected Works*, XII, p. 96.
[2] *Lit.*: arbour; title of a once popular illustrated German family magazine (Tr.).
[3] *Collected Works*, VI, p. 97.

i.e. as infinite, animated matter, engaged in an ascent to ever higher forms.

4. How do we order our lives? Answer: In determining ourselves in accordance with the idea of the species! This is then elucidated by a loosely-linked series of observations on the necessity of monogamy, but also on the right to divorce, on the justification for war and capital punishment, on the excellence of the feeling of nationalism as compared with all cosmopolitanism, on the rights of the monarchy and nobility (although the author himself is proud that he is a bourgeois), on the dangers of a social democracy, on the sanctity of private property, and on the necessity for a corresponding limitation of the right of universal suffrage. All this is well in keeping with the fact that Strauss was so deeply shocked by the revolution of 1848, almost before it was there, as only a good Conservative could be at that time, and that he expressly yearned for 'the old police state';[1] further, that when, like Christoph Blumhardt fifty years later, he had, paradoxically, become a member of the Württemberg Parliament, he spoke, upon the occasion of the shooting of Robert Blum, emphatically against a demonstration of that parliament in his favour, and, finally, that he openly declared[2] that he would rather be governed in the Russian than in the democratic manner. In conclusion there is a description of how those for whom the book is supposed to have been written spend their Sunday, as distinct from those who profess the old faith: they do this with political discussions, and then with studies in history and natural science, with edification from *Hermann and Dorothea*, and finally with performances of works by Haydn, Mozart and Beethoven. 'A stimulant to mind and spirit, humour and imagination, such as leaves nothing to be desired. Thus we live, thus we pass blissfully upon our way!'[3]

Strauss, we tell ourselves on reading this, was not the Antichrist by any means. And almost the last thing there is to be said about the non-tragic quality of his general attitude—and this is just what evokes our sympathy—is that he did not even have the qualifications and the stature of a true evil heretic. It is that the result of all his negations was by no means an appalling Promethean uproar, but for all his attempted flat denials of God always only this self-conscious intellectual bourgeois quality, which was always morose, without the slightest notion of all the true heights and depths of life, the bourgeois quality in its specific national German form at the sunset hour of the age of Goethe, upon which Nietzsche then poured such cruel scorn as the embodiment of

---

[1] Letter of 13th April, 1848.   [2] Letter of 26th February, 1852.
[3] *Collected Works*, VI, pp. 198f.

the 'philistine of culture'. I quote in conclusion two very good speci-
mens of Strauss's poetry:

> I longed to travel; now I do not leave,
> And yet I do not know, if I shall stay.
> Certain it is that here's a foreign land:
> And where my true one is, I cannot say.
> I think I once had children, two, and dear;
> But yet I know not if it was a dream.
> A wife I spurned, if love to hatred turned,
> A hatred turned to love, I do not know.
> Books I used to write, or so they say—
> If they speak truth, or mock, I cannot tell.
> I hear, an unbeliever I am called:
> I know not if I am not rather pious.
> The thought of death has never caused me fear:
> I know not if I am not long since dead.[1]

> He to whom I thus lament
> Knows that I am not lamenting;
> She to whom I thus comment,
> Knows that I am not near fainting.
> Like a light we fade today,
> As a glow that dies;
> Slowly we are borne away,
> As a sound that flies.
> May this final flicker,
> May this sound but be
> Pure and clear for ever
> However weak it be.[2]

We certainly cannot read these poems without a sense of sympathy
for a fellow human being. It must and may, however, be said that this
is not the speech of the Antichrist; nor of Prometheus; nor of any true,
perilous spirit of rebellion. It can in fact only be the speech, always a
little haughty, and always a bit disillusioned, of the true nineteenth
century. And if there are those who are perhaps inclined to admire and
praise the 'truthfulness' of such language, and that of Strauss's language
altogether, then they should at all events grant that Albert Schweitzer[3]
was right in describing it as an 'uncreative truthfulness'.

If that were all there is to say about Strauss then the question, the
admittedly serious question, with which we should have to take leave of
him, could only be the one to which we have already alluded: whether
it was not that with him something was nakedly revealed to the light

1 1848, *Collected Works*, XII, p. 64; for orginal, cf. Appendix, p. 421.
2 29th December, 1873, *Collected Works*, XII, p. 226; for original, cf. Appendix, p. 422.
3 Op. cit., p. 78.

which remained more or less hidden in those more brilliant and more fortunate figures—or those, rather, who did not lay themselves open so much as he did, who were his close neighbours in theology and, further, whether the common hidden element in all nineteenth-century theology which became manifest with Strauss was not so much a particular sin of wickedness, but just one of an extraordinary weakness?

But this does not conclude our discussion of Strauss and his significance for the theology of more recent times. We turn our attention now —and here our task becomes more difficult—to the author of the *Life of Jesus*.

First, as a general appraisal of this work, I shall relate some of the characteristic things which Strauss said in the second book with this title, the *Life of Jesus* of 1864. Paragraphs 33 and 34 are concerned with 'the religious consciousness of Jesus'. Jesus's religious consciousness, Strauss begins, must have been there first, as the original thing, his consciousness that he was the Messiah being the form this religious consciousness only subsequently took. According to the meaning of the Gospel according to St John, which could not be explained away, Jesus considered himself as the personal divine Word of the Creator, which had been with God from eternity, which then became man for a while, for the sake of redemption, and then afterwards returned to God. We cannot possibly suppose that Jesus really did this. For first, in the accredited story no example of such a consciousness is known to us. But if we were to meet a man with such consciousness, we should take him to be a half-wit or a deceiver. Jesus as described by St John, with his 'he that seeth me seeth him that sent me', and 'I and my Father are one', must inevitably be as contemptible to us as Louis XIV with his, 'I am the state'. The finer a man's religious sense is, the less he will be able to forget, for all the liveliness of his feelings, that in the equation between his human self-awareness and his awareness of God there is always an indivisible remainder. Thus we can do nothing with the speeches of the Christ of the Fourth Gospel. 'A Jesus who takes it upon himself to say such things does not exist as an object of historical study.' Things are different if we take the Synoptic Gospels as our guide. Here we learn, from the Sermon on the Mount, particularly, that Jesus saw in him whom he felt and conceived as God, and described as the 'heavenly Father', 'indiscriminate goodness'. This indiscriminate goodness was manifestly the basic mood of his own nature. He was aware of his similarity with God in having such goodness, and transferred it to God as the basic determining feature of the divine

nature as well. If men are the children of this God, then they are
brothers to one another, and to this extent Jesus's consciousness may
also be described as a human mood of love transcending all the hindrances and limitations of human life, a mood which then gave rise to
an inner feeling of happiness, compared with which all outward joy
and suffering was deprived of its meaning. Serene and cheerful,
unbroken, and acting as the result of the delight and joyousness of a
beautiful nature, Jesus had, 'to use the poet's words, absorbed the
Deity into his will', thus uniting in himself the best of the Hellenic and
of the Mosaic heritage. This harmonious composure of mind certainly
did not come about in Jesus without violent exertion, but it certainly
came about (as distinct from Paul, Augustine and Luther) without an
inner struggle. He appears as a fundamentally beautiful nature, whose
only development comes from within, which only needed to grow ever
more clearly conscious of itself and to become ever firmer in itself, but
which did not need to turn back and—apart from isolated waverings
and errors, and the necessity for a progressive, earnest endeavour for
self-vanquishment and renunciation—begin any other life. This,
according to the Strauss of 1864, was Jesus's religious consciousness, as
it historically really was, according to the Synoptic Gospels. With
regard to the Messianic form of this consciousness, too, which for all
this cannot be removed from the Synoptics, Strauss was able to judge
at this time with understanding mildness: 'Did Jesus believe that he
would come again in the clouds of the heavens? . . . Are we not thinking
too much in western fashion, if we cannot conceive of the conjunction
of such an idea with great wisdom in an Oriental?'[1] What points of
view such deliberations might eventually have stimulated even in
respect of the Christology of St John's Gospel!

Let us follow this with what Strauss finds to say in the final paragraphs, Nos. 99 and 100, of the same work, about the significance of
this Jesus for us. Our historical information concerning him is incomplete and uncertain. It is out of the question that faith and salvation
can depend on things only the smallest part of which are not in doubt.
And, in any case, it is a matter of principle that there should be no
such dependence. 'Just as certainly as the destiny of man is a universal
one and accessible to all, so the conditions upon which it is to be
achieved . . . must be accorded to every man'; the perception of the goal
must 'not only be an accidental one, a historical perception coming
from without, but a necessary perception of reason, which each man
can find in himself'. The distinguishing of the historical from the ideal

[1] Letter of 9th November, 1862.

Christ, i.e. the original image of man as he should be, which resides in human reason, and the transference of the faith which saves from the first to the second figure, is the imperative result of the more recent development of mind. It is 'the continued development of the religion of Christ to a religion of humanity, towards which all the nobler endeavour of our time is directed'.

This does not imply that this original image, the ideal Christ, could be present in us to the same extent, if a historical Christ had never lived and exercised his influence. The idea of human perfection, like other ideas, is at first given to man only as a disposition, which is then gradually developed in its actual form. It is those who variously advance the human ideal, among whom Christ in every case predominates, who serve the development of this disposition. 'He introduced features into this ideal which were previously lacking, or which had remained undeveloped, curbed others which opposed its universal validity, and by the religious form he gave it he bestowed upon it a higher consecration; by its embodiment in his own person, a most lively warmth.' Even if he was not the first or the last of his kind, and even if important aspects of the human ideal, e.g. regard for the family, the state, and art, are missing from his shaping of it, yet all the features with which it would be desirable to supplement this ideal can be added to his version of it in the happiest manner, 'if only we have once understood that Jesus's version is itself a human achievement, and thus something which is as in need of development as it is capable of it'. On the other hand, to conceive of Christ as the God-man can only hinder us in thus making fruitful his moral and religious greatness. The purpose of critical research into his life is therefore the removal of all that which makes of him a more than human being. This is something which is a well-meant and at first perhaps beneficial illusion, but which, in the long run, is harmful, and nowadays quite destructive. Critical research must also aim at the restoration of the picture of the historical Jesus in his simple, human features, in so far as this can still be accomplished; and, for the good of their souls, the direction of men to the ideal Christ, this pattern of moral perfection. Concerning this pattern the historical Jesus has indeed thrown light on several salient features, but as a disposition it just as surely belongs to the universal heritage of our species, as its further development and completion can only be the task and work of humanity as a whole. This, then, according to the Strauss of 1864, is the significance of Jesus for us.

To summarize: in 1864 Strauss thought that there was a historical core to the 'life of Jesus', which was shrouded in a veil of myth. With

John it was a thick veil, with the Synoptics not so thick, but on the whole it was not impenetrable. It was difficult but not quite impossible to distinguish the core as such. This core consists in a human personality which made actual to a high degree the religious disposition, and to this extent the disposition of man as such. Together with others of its kind this personality should be assessed by us not, indeed, as the basis, in the strict sense, for our achievement of our human destiny, but certainly as the means towards this end.

If Strauss had said this in his first and famous *Life of Jesus* in 1835-6, it would definitely not have become famous, and it would not have cost its author his place at the university. As something which at that time could be regarded as having the attraction of a certain harmless novelty it would have brought him to the heaven of a university post in the usual way; and nothing would have been known of the great vexation which the name D. F. Strauss symbolizes in theology to this very day. In contrast to the first, Strauss's second *Life of Jesus* became neither infamous nor famous. It might perhaps have got him his desired chair at the eleventh hour, as the document of a definite, but none the less only mildly sinning common or garden liberalism, which had, in the meantime, long become the common cry, if the stir which the famously infamous book of 1835-6 had caused had not still lingered on and blinded the people of the time to the fact that the true offending element of the first book, that of its method, had to all intents and purposes been removed in the second. For in principle and in method this second book was in fact a *Life of Jesus* of the kind any number of others have written both before and after him.

The historical element in Christianity, that is, concretely, Christology, had admittedly given the founders of the theology of more recent times some trouble. But they had all managed to cope with it in one way or another. Quite naïvely they thought man could be conscious and possessed of religion, of the consciousness of God, the experience of transcendence, the Christian quality within himself, as something which was there and given, something which could be joyfully reckoned with. They thought man could be conscious and possessed of the historical basis for religion in the same way, no matter whether one understood it like Schleiermacher, more as a historical beginning, or, like Marheineke, more as a metaphysical origin, or lastly, like Tholuck and Menken—the 'Positives' of that time—more as the supernatural divine imparting of religion. They used history just as unquestioningly as they used psychology. They were unquestioning in their belief that it was possible truly to assume in individual man something like, for example, the feeling of utter dependence, with God as the content of its object. On the other hand they were unquestioning in their belief that somewhere in the related whole of man's history there might be something like a perfect archetypal image of this, man's own possession, something given, to which—in accordance with the correlation between Christ and faith handed down by the Church— the thing given within man himself could equally calmly and surely be referred back. The Romanticism and the rationalism which allowed the men of this age to discover the presence of God's miraculous quality in their hearts, or God's reason in their heads, also enabled them to assume that this miracle or reason very probably had its absolute place in history too, and to state, in accordance with church tradition, that this place was in Jesus of Nazareth. The age which could not produce and consume enough biographies and auto-biographies to the glorification of that which the man of that time found within himself—this same age inevitably hit upon the idea of a *Life of Jesus*, and put it into effect, both before and after Strauss, with the daring peculiar to it for such undertakings in the most varied forms; and always with the assumption that the one was as possible as the other. In detail, it was possible to proceed in varied ways with this: it was possible to read and evaluate the sources in the naïvely historical or in the critically historical manner. If the latter method was chosen, as Schleiermacher and Hase did, one could give preference to the Gospel according to St John at the expense of the Synoptics. Or one could reverse this relationship as gradually became the accepted method after Bretschneider's *Probabilia* of 1820. Then again it was possible to accord the rank of the oldest reporter among the Synoptics to Matthew, as Strauss did in 1864 and as F. Chr. Baur too wanted to do, or it was possible, as came to be the vogue at about the same time, to join the 'lions of St Mark', with or without assuming the existence of a source of sayings supplementing his Gospel. Or, like Eichhorn, one could think of an original Gospel which had been lost, or, as in Schleier-macher's theory of diegesis, which is once again becoming interesting today, of a great number of anecdotes and gnomic sayings circulating singly as representing the New Testament in its original form.

Further, it was possible to conceive of the relationship between the reports and the events reported, particularly as regards their largely miraculous nature, in such a way that one attempted to interpret them in some manner, i.e. to explain them as things which really happened. This could be done by juggling away the supernatural element in the reports as misunderstanding of all previous exegesis, or as a misunderstanding of the reporters himself, thus evolving a life of Christ which could be concurred in even if one's name happened to be Wegscheider (this was done in classic fashion, for the rationalists, by Paulus of Heidelberg). Or one could take refuge (this was the course of the so-called supranaturalists, also that of Tholuck and Neander) in the allusion to all kinds of as yet unknown forces of nature, to the hastening of natural processes, and above all to a dominion, incalculable in its effects, of mind over matter, as providing the explanation—a solution which was assured of great interest and applause in those decades, when magnetism, occultism, and everything connected with them were the subject of a deep fascination. One could also proceed by mediating or combining these two methods. Schleiermacher, for instance, had a foot in both camps, being a supranaturalist as far as all the miracles of healing were concerned, and a rationalist, for example, in the question of Jesus's resurrection, which he fairly openly explained as an awakening from a deep coma, in the pulpit too.

Finally, since in those decades the words 'poetry' and 'poetic' also had a quite individual, and indeed, a good sound, one could bring in the concept of myth, the idea that a story did not really happen, but was invented to illustrate a religious truth. The concept of myth was introduced at about this time by de Wette, at first for research into the Old Testament. It was, however, ventured upon only hesitantly, and applied only to the stories of the childhood of Jesus and of his resurrection—and then only by a few. It was possible to concede that the historical events might largely be surrounded, and perhaps permeated to their very core by such myth, without being deceived that between the cloud at the foot and the cloud at the summit of the mountain there was yet a great deal of the mountain visible in between, a lot of material which was no doubt historical, or which could at least be interpreted historically by either of these two methods. And then again differences were possible in the evaluation of the life of Jesus established in this way. It was possible to evolve a figure very similar to the God-man of the old dogmatics, and to which his soteriological predicates could be transferred with relative ease; the only difference was that the attempt was now made to understand this figure quite decisively as a divinely powerful one in the history of the world and of mankind as such. With Wegscheider, it was possible to revere in him the *doctor divinus* of the truth of reason common to all men, or with Schleiermacher, the productive archetypal image of one's own experience or that of the Christian Church, or, as we have just heard in discussing the Strauss of 1864, the religious genius, to whom one could then perhaps again ascribe, in retrospect, some of the predicates of the God-man. It was possible to present and illuminate the once-for-all-ness and necessity of the revelation which came about in none other than this Jesus—once again with variations in strength, and by the use of various arguments.

All these possible methods of writing a Life of Jesus are in part strikingly divergent, but there are five points which are agreed upon in all of them:

1. As faith has its reality in the immanence of human consciousness, so its correlation to Christ is a connexion within the immanence of history. As we have faith in the same way as we have other capacities or experiences, so we have Christ in the same way, in principle, as we have other people.

2. We have Christ as a person of a distant by-gone time, in so far as we have 'sources' of his life. For the Gospels are sources. They were written as such, or it is as such that they interest us; at any rate it is as sources that we now use them. We can employ them as sources in the same way—even if perhaps we subject them to the same provisos—as someone interested in the history of the kings of Rome would employ the books of Livy.

3. We are seeking the historical Jesus—for we want to have him historically, as we have other historical personages. He can be distinguished from the sources (or how else, indeed, could they be sources?). He can be recognized according to the sources, from the sources, and upon the basis of the sources as he lived and as he was, at a certain time and in a certain place. He can be perceived as clearly or as dimly as we can perceive his contemporary, the emperor Tiberius. He stands and becomes visible behind the sources: in such a way, in fact, that historically it is not merely Matthew or John whom we have, but in truth Jesus, as 'the historical core' of what they have imparted.

4. Jesus is a human personage who is in principle accessible to historical knowledge in precisely the same measure as Tiberius is accessible to it. The way in which he was conscious of himself is a form of self-consciousness which is at least conceivable, which is possible—perhaps not quite in the way in which John presents it, but at any rate in the way in which it is shown in the much more innocuous Sermon on the Mount—but who knows, the positive theologians say, perhaps as depicted by John too!

We can, as has been shown, in some way come to terms with his miracles, with virgin birth and resurrection, divesting them of their true miraculous character by describing them as misunderstandings, hidden secrets of nature, or as myth; or by somewhat enlarging *ad hoc* the concept of what is historical, calling historically real something one would never otherwise be prepared to call historically possible. In one way or the other: by regarding the miracle as a frame from which the content can be distinguished. The content, however, is the man Jesus, who was certainly a religious genius, and as such an extraordinary, an astonishing man, a man to be adored, but one who, like all men, is accessible to our understanding, and comprehensible as an object of historical knowledge. Let us constantly remind ourselves: if something like the feeling of utter dependence can find a place in the picture we form of ourselves, then why cannot someone like Jesus Christ also find a place in our picture of history? It will be a Jesus reduced in stature and hammered into shape, perhaps, a Jesus who is perhaps a trifle groomed, domesticated and made practicable when compared with all the strange things which are said of him in the texts, even in the 'Life of Jesus' versions of positive theology. But it is precisely in this way that he will find a place there, even if only just so that a historically immanent connexion between him and our faith becomes possible in principle.

5. As a personage who is so possible and comprehensible historically Jesus in fact is of the highest value for us, as can once again be established historically. He is then a central person, or the central person, the man who was perfect to the extent that we can call him a revealer of God, and indeed the chief revealer, as Strauss too concedes in 1864, from among all those whom people believe they can thus designate apart from him.

These then are the common assumptions for modern research into the life of Jesus. Strauss's *Life of Jesus* of 1864 no longer diverged from them; as far as they were concerned it no longer offended. For in it Strauss found a way of coping with the problem of Christology which was no better and no worse than that of any of the others. That was why it was not the famous Life of Jesus. That was why, although it could not further its author's reputation with the public and with the authorities, it did it no more damage either. That is why its only significance for the history of theology is that it helps, by contrast, to illustrate what the name of D. F. Strauss really stands for. Let us turn our attention now to the author of the first *Life of Jesus* of 1835-6. The name of D. F. Strauss stands for no more and no less than the breaking-up of this concerted body of opinion about research into the life of Jesus, the protest against its method, the declaration that its entire undertaking was impossible to execute. This is important enough to warrant a point by point demonstration with reference to the five headings we have just drawn up.

1. In 1835 Strauss demands from the biographer of Jesus, as his first duty, an observation and thinking which is without premises—which is not, that is, burdened in advance by faith. If he really wants to write a biography of Jesus, if he wants to have Jesus as we can have other men, then he has to choose not faith, but an observation and thinking which has no interest in faith. For we cannot expect to find what we believe, as such, in history. And that which we wish to seek in history must as such be accessible to this disinterested observation and thinking. By making this distinction Strauss challenged from the outset the historical immanence of the connexion between Christ and faith. It is now a question of whether the object of faith on the one side, and that of observation and thinking on the other, will prove to be one and the same.

2. In 1835, condemned by every New Testament scholar who followed him, Strauss does not begin with a critique of the sources as such, by establishing the order of precedence of the four Gospels, or their dependence upon one another, or with hypotheses concerning original pre-manuscript sources or some such thing, as in fact as a historian it was his duty to do, and has been done universally since. Even afterwards he accorded the labours his colleagues directed to this end little more than an ironical scepticism. He himself mentions[1] that it was only seven years after his book appeared that he had the idea of pasting together a synopsis according to Luther's translation! For him John and Mark and 1 Corinthians 15 are all equally damned in advance when judged by the canon of critical historical thinking with which he approaches them, and which can be roughly formulated in the following questions: To what extent can what is recounted be reconciled with the logical, historical and physiological law, otherwise known and valid, governing all events? To what extent can parallel reports really be reconciled with one another in what concerns time and place, the number and names of the participants in what is reported, in that which concerns the circumstances and material for these affairs themselves? And then, above all: To what extent does the poetical character of a representation or its content as far as it is contained also in other sources (e.g. in the Old Testament or in pagan saga and myth) make its historical nature not unlikely? We can imagine what the answer is: Upon all points, so to speak, the form of the New Testament narrative is not that of a historical report, but simply that

[1] Letter of 27th January, 1843.

of a myth. So strong is Strauss's impression of the particular nature of these sources that he makes their disqualification as historical sources the starting-point for his method. And all he has to say about them, simply as regards their content, without testing them further as historical sources—is that none of them, with the exception of scattered remnants, stands firm before this canon, that they cannot derive from eye-witnesses and thus cannot come from the apostles, unless we care to regard them as deceivers.

3. It is for this very reason—and this was the chief thing which made Strauss's first *Life of Jesus* so celebrated and notorious—that he not only does not discover a 'historical core' to the life of Jesus, but does not even begin to enquire after it. He does not deny that a historical core is a possibility, as Bruno Bauer did later, and as Kalthoff and Artur Drews have done in our century. But neither does he assert and demonstrate a historical core to the life of Jesus. Strauss is not interested in it. His work is purely critical. He is only concerned with showing the presence and origin of myth, whatever might be 'behind' it. That is what went home to the hearers of 1835 and had an effect in all directions. Here as well it was only that something was being challenged. But it was challenged comprehensively and thoroughly: where was the possibility of a method which made the historical correlate of faith uncertain in the same way as Feuerbach's psychology of religion made its metaphysical correlate uncertain. The supporting staff—from this aspect, history—could also be a reed to pierce the hand. That is why the Strauss of 1835 had everyone against him: from Hengstenberg to de Wette, who had yet himself admitted the enemy, the concept of myth, at least into the forecourt, into scientific research into the Old Testament. That is why the cry could now be heard even from those who were supposedly orthodox: Better Paulus the rationalist than Strauss the explainer of myth! Paulus, even if his interpretation did make things a trifle shabby, at least let everything stand as historical, whereas Strauss made everything, without exception, historically uncertain.

4. Strauss, as may be easily understood, did not go to any trouble, either, to work out a character picture of Jesus. He was lacking in the vision which perceives, to use Weinel's words[1] 'that what truly gives human history its greatness, worth and power is the great personality of genius'. He had not yet read any Carlyle! Does not the problem of personality interest him at all? This can scarcely be maintained of a man who afterwards, as a historian, preferred to occupy himself in the

[1] *Jesus im 19 Jahrhundert* (Jesus in the Nineteenth Century), p. 42.

biographical field. Or perhaps he is not interested in the person of Jesus? Or is he perhaps hampered by the fact that the Evangelists themselves are much more interested in something quite different from the actual character of Jesus, these miracles, for instance, which are the cause of so much offence? So that he thinks, perhaps, that he has no material for such a picture? Suffice it to say that the picture is not drawn. The very cause, that is to say, for the sake of which the other researchers into the life of Jesus, before and after Strauss, marched out with sword and lance, is neglected. Jesus should be accessible, understandable as a man, so that we could 'have' him, as we have other men. But Strauss's lack of concern and his silence upon this point made it seem as if Jesus were inaccessible and incomprehensible as a man, and as if we might not, therefore, be able thus to have him.

5. The Strauss of 1835 also quarrelled with the view that it was possible, with the instruments of observation and thinking, to ascribe to this historical phenomenon in particular, to Jesus of Nazareth, a qualified highest value, a unique and absolute quality. The final section of his second volume (1836), in which he expresses himself upon this point, is so important for the history of theology, that here we should allow him to speak for himself a little: 'If reality is ascribed to the idea of the unity of divine and human nature is this as much as to say that it must once have become real in one individual, as it was never again either before or since? This is by no means the way in which the idea realizes itself, pouring out its whole abundance upon one example and begrudging itself to all others. Rather it likes to unfold its wealth in a diversity of examples which complement each other, in the interchange of individualities one in decline, the other rising.' Humanity is the absolute, the true content of Christology. This content has been made to be attached to the person and history of an individual only, but this has been done for the subjective reason, first, that this individual, by his personality and the things which happened to him, became the occasion for the lifting of this content into the universal consciousness, and, secondly, that the intellectual level of the world of former times, and of a nation at any time, is only capable of contemplating the idea of humanity in the concrete figure of an individual. . . . The knowledge we have acquired in our age, however, can no longer suppress the awareness that the connexion with an individual is but the form of this teaching relating to a certain time and a certain people.'

The positive element in Strauss's position, which becomes visible in the fifth point, could and still can be disconcerting, and yet it cannot be overlooked that its negative side had enough weight behind it to lay the axe at the root of the naïveté with which the rest of theology at that time thought it could master revelation in the same way as history in general is mastered. Something absolute as a part of world and of human history as such is a sword of lath. Strauss's book made this very plain and well understood, and those who read it were shaken to the core, for it was precisely upon the card of history that they had staked no less than half their means, the other half being on that of religious consciousness. The situation was such that in running away from Feuerbach they ran straight into the arms of Strauss. And if they managed somehow to escape Strauss they were still not free of Feuerbach. That was the deeply disturbing feature of the state of theological discussion a hundred years ago: the deeply disturbing background to the history of theology in all the ensuing decades. Strauss is also similar to Feuerbach in that he was equally devoid of humour, and similarly incapable of criticizing his basic positive outlook, whereby his negations might first have acquired theological content. But unfortunately Strauss was unlike Feuerbach in that he was uncertain of his case in expressing these epoch-making negations. He was in fact not certain of his case in principle.

When the storm of hostile reviews and works against his first *Life of Jesus* set in, Strauss at once (in his smaller pieces of this time and above all in the third edition of the book in 1838) began to retreat in the direction of the position in which we have found him in the *Life of Jesus* of 1864. He does indeed hurl himself in his polemics, with all the power of his pungent pen, upon weaker opponents like Steudel, his former teacher at Tübingen, and grinds them to powder, but cannot avoid making important concessions to more serious representatives of the official theology, like Ullmann, Neander, and Tholuck. They relate particularly to the fifth point of the series we drew up. Strauss now suddenly recalls the saying of Hegel: 'In the forefront of all actions there stands an individual' and concedes:

1. That religion belongs to an incomparably higher sphere of human intellectual activity than science, art, etc., and that the man who has achieved the highest in this sphere therefore does not stand upon the same plane as the others, but has a claim to stand at the centre-point of the circle, in the closest proximity to the source itself;

2. That a higher realization of the religious idea than Jesus cannot historically be demonstrated;

3. That the union of the human individual with God in his immediate self-consciousness, and therefore God's becoming man in this

individual, is not philosophically impossible, and that its reality is only a historical question.[1]

In conjunction with this he is now also prepared—in 1864, impressed particularly by the works of F. Chr. Baur, he did not go so far again—to listen to a discussion concerning the genuineness and credibility of the Gospel according to St John. 'We have no way of knowing whether a mind of the religious fervour of Jesus might not have been able in the reflex of the imagination to form the communion with God, of which he was aware, into a recollection of a former dwelling with God.[2] 'I would not venture to assert that there is anything in the sayings in John which would decisively resist explanation partly as the result of John's personality, and partly from the fact that he wrote the Gospel at a very advanced age.[3] The same weakening of the historical canon makes its effects felt as regards the question of miracles. Renewing his earlier interest in natural philosophy Strauss now finds all kinds of things historically possible which three years previously had only seemed comprehensible to him as myth. And it is in the Gospel of St John, of all things, that he too now thinks he can demonstrate a historical core, which afterwards split up into the three-fold synoptic account. He also does not now scorn the harmonizing of the Gospels quite so much, which three years before he had so sharply proscribed. And, in a free version of Schleiermacher we are tempted to say, he now defines Christ along the lines that he was 'the man in whose self-consciousness the union of the human and the divine first appeared with an energy which thrust back to the infinitesimal minimum within the whole range of his mind and life all restraint upon this union; who to this extent stands unique and unrivalled in world history. This does not mean that the religious consciousness which was first achieved and expressed by him should be allowed to withhold itself in detail from purification and further development in the progressive advance of the human spirit.'[4]

We must be clear about the significance of the fact that Strauss's negotiations with Zürich and the disaster which befell him there came about just at this period when his critique was engaged in this backward movement! Influenced by these events, and embittered by the fact that in spite of his concessions he was still not trusted (far from it indeed, for Tholuck, for instance, was now quite openly triumphant that the critic's once pure, clear voice was beginning to break, so that the distinct 'No' was now a quavering upon 'Yes and No') he then

[1] Hausrath, I, 304f. and 324.   [2] *Life of Jesus*, third ed., Vol. I, ρ. 539.
[3] Op. cit., p. 741.   [4] Op. cit., p. 778.

ab irato not only wrote his *Doctrine of Faith*, but undertook a *restitutio ad integrum* in the next editions of the *Life of Jesus*. He has done himself an injustice, he has ground flaws into the blade of his own trusty sword, he now confesses in the fourth edition, and he restores the critical attitude of the first and second!

It is all the stranger that in spite of this we should meet him again, in 1864, at the spot where we did meet him: upon the broad highway of research into the life of Jesus, engaged in an attempt to extract a historical core from the shell of the sources.

And now the strangest thing of all. When he saw that this new course was making just as little impression upon the theological profession and the Church as that of 1838-9, he followed up his second retreat, in *The Old and the New Faith* of 1872 in which a section is also devoted to the life of Jesus, by a third advance. Here the true meaning, apparently, of the first and second advances too comes to light trivially but with a clarity which does not leave anything to be desired. As a historical man was Jesus such that he still determines our religious feeling? the old man now asks. He answers 'No', for we know too little which is reliable about him! 'Anyone who has once been made a god has irrevocably lost his human quality. It is an empty illusion to imagine that accounts of a life which, like our Gospels, apply to a supernatural being, can ever provide, by any process whatsoever, material for a natural, consistent and harmonious picture of a man or of a life.' 'All the efforts of the most recent authors of works on the "Life of Jesus", however much they may lay claim to show by means of our scriptural sources a human development, an arrival and growth of insight and a gradual widening of comprehension in Jesus, show themselves by the absence of any supporting reference in the records . . . to be pieces of apologetic artifice devoid of any historical value.'[1] If there is anything historical at all to be taken from the Gospels, then it is the fact that Jesus, a mere man, expected to appear in the clouds of the heavens in the very near future, in inauguration of the kingdom of the Messiah proclaimed by him. It was this which made the decisive impression upon his disciples, and not any sermon upon pureness of heart or the love of God or our neighbours. According to our concepts he was a noble spiritual fanatic whom we do not seek to choose as the guide of our lives since he could only lead us astray, just as it was only the manufacture of the idea of the resurrection of the slain master which saved his work at that time: a 'humbug of world-historical proportions',[2] which did at all events bear witness to the strength and

[1] *Collected Works*, VI, pp. 50f.   [2] Op. cit., p. 45.

N

persistence of the impression he made upon his followers. By what means? By the irrational and fantastic quality of his own nature, and of his own ideas, about which, incidentally, he perhaps had doubts at the end. In face of these we must indeed mourn him, with regard to his end, for the sake of the excellent qualities of his heart and striving. But we cannot escape the judgment that 'such a fanatical expectation only gets its just deserts if it comes to grief by ending in failure'.[1]

Who should seek to decide which was the genuine Strauss: the Strauss of the two retreats or the Strauss of the three advances? The naïve and a trifle boring liberal Strauss, who can however be talked to, or Strauss the savagely angry critic, who refuses to negotiate? One thing is certain. The unmistakable feebleness of the first figure only serves to throw into high relief the strength with which the second confronted theology with a series of questions upon which, just as with Feuerbach's questions, it has not, right down to the present day, perhaps, adequately declared itself.

Once again we formulate them, in five points:

1. Is it not a fact that if we conceive of the Christian faith as a relation which is historically immanent, thereby making faith a matter of history, we destroy it as faith?

2. Is it not a fact that the New Testament records are useless as 'sources' of a pragmatically comprehensible picture of a man and of a life? For it is from the very first word that they seek to be something quite different, namely testimonies to a 'superhuman being', corresponding feature by feature to the prophecies of the Old Testament, a being whose image must defy all historical reconstruction.

3. Is it not a fact that a 'historical Jesus' established behind the so-called sources, and therefore quite independently of the witness of the New Testament, can only be comprehended as such if we remove those predicates of his which are essential to this witness: his consciousness of himself as the Messiah of Israel and as God's eternal Son, his proclamation of the kingdom of God and expectation that he would come again, and his resurrection from the dead? Is it not a fact that the sentimental, moralizing description of character which is indispensable to the establishment of this figure has nothing at all to do with the faith of the Apostles?

4. Is it not a fact that according to the representation in the Gospels the so-called personality of Jesus is so indissolubly linked with these predicates that the historian aiming at a Life of Jesus cannot escape a fatal dilemma? He has either to undertake this erasure of the predicates

[1] Op. cit., p. 51.

and give a moralizing interpretation, or, like Strauss, he has to conceive of Jesus as a noble spiritual fanatic. He must do this unless he prefers to call a halt at the Early Church in Palestine as the last historically accessible date, and apply the concept of myth to everything or nearly everything lying beyond it—in which case he must at least take into account the possibility that Jesus never lived as Drews' thesis did.

5. Is it not a fact that the goal of historical research can at best only be a historical Christ and that this implies a Christ who as a revealer of God can only be a relative Christ? Is it not a fact that such a Christ can only be a helper of those in need, who as such requires all sorts of associates, and figures to supplement him, who at best could only be related to a real, eternal revelation to mankind as a most high and perhaps ultimate symbol is related to the thing itself, who could on no account be the Word that became flesh, executing God's judgment upon us and challenging us ourselves to make a decision?

This is what D. F. Strauss asked theology, just as Feuerbach asked it whether the Godhead man sought and thought he had found in his consciousness was anything but man's shadow as it was projected upon the plane of the idea of the Infinite.

Strauss was no great theologian. It is precisely when we take him seriously, that is when we hold him to his attitude in the first *Life of Jesus*, the *Doctrine of Faith*, and *The Old and the New Faith*, that we are still bound to conclude that his theology ultimately only consisted in the fact that he saw through a bad solution of the problem of theology, gave up any further attempt to improve upon it, abandoned the theme of theology, and departed from the field of action. 'The only aim of all my theological writing was to free me from the black folds of the cassock; and in this it succeeded perfectly.'[1] Blessed with a little impudence, any child can do the same, and we really have no occasion to worship such people as great theologians. The strangest thing of all is that this rather cheap 'freeing from the folds' was never so successful that Strauss at any time really had any peace from theology, that he never really managed to put it behind him as something completely settled. The problem he had so ostentatiously abandoned pursued him to the last like a fate: and the more intensively it followed him the less he knew what to do about it. It was as if this problem had an interest in him. He repaid this interest by meeting it coldly, unreceptively and helplessly in some way, but he could not, after all, detach himself from it and he continually became excited about it. He was continually impelled to react—always differently and always unsuitably—but still

[1] Letter of 1st October, 1843.

to react. He could only suffer from it. That was his misfortune. And that, negatively, it is true, might be described as his greatness in theology. It might have been better if many theologians, positively greater ones, both of his time and of other times, had suffered at least a little more from the problem of theology. The fact that Strauss, for all his determination to shake it off, in fact stood so passively and helplessly before it, reveals in a unique way the urgency of this problem, and this is after all some justification for this man, a justification which is not quite so obvious for many who were more energetic in their approach to the problem.

In conclusion, may I present yet another argument in apology for Strauss? I am not unaware of its personal nature, but for the sake of completeness I cannot hold it back. I am in fact not quite certain that Nietzsche's invectives have really said all there is to be said upon the subject, not even in respect to the Gartenlaube[1] into which Strauss finally fled, and in which he was probably at bottom most intimately at home. It seems worth remembering that in the midst of the calamitous song of praise which Strauss dedicated to 'culture' he again and again avows, in a variety of ways 'that for our age the music of Mozart occupies the same position as Goethe does in poetry. He is ὁ πάνυ, the universal genius. Next to him the best of the others only distinguish themselves by the fact that in them this or that single quality of mind or aspect of art has been further developed, but just for that reason developed one-sidedly.'[2] Anyone who has understood that can be pardoned much tastelessness and much childishly critical theology too. In this poor Strauss really seems to have chosen the better part, as against Nietzsche, who, as is well known, was the helpless slave of the dreadful Wagner at the time of his great deriding of Strauss.

Be this as it may. It is simply the case that together with Feuerbach, Strauss is the theologian who was most significant for the situation of theology in the time after Schleiermacher's death. It is a fact that he and no other man has the merit of having put this question, the historical one, that is, to theology, with such a grasp of the basic issue. Since then theology has talked round it in many and various ways; which was, rather, evidence of the fact that it had not heard his question. Many people have not been able to overcome Strauss to this day; they have simply by-passed him, and to this very day are continually saying things which, if Strauss cannot be overcome, should no longer be said.

I should now like to adapt the words of Albert Schweitzer, quoted

---

[1] Lit.: arbour; title of a once popular illustrated German family magazine. (Tr.)
[2] Letter of 5th March, 1868.

at the beginning, as follows: One must love the question Strauss raised, in order to understand it. It has been loved only by a few; most people have feared it. To this extent the name of Strauss together with the name of Feuerbach signifies the bad conscience of the theology of more recent times. To this extent Strauss was perhaps not so very wrong in calling his first *Life of Jesus*[1] an 'inspired book'. And to this extent the fact that they did not make him a professor of theology, but self-right-eously, and with an all-too-easy mind, banished him *extra muros*, was all things considered scandalous. I imply by this that Alexander Schweizer, at all events—I name him in particular as one of the positively 'great' theologians of that time—did not have the inner right to oppose Strauss's appointment to Zürich in 1839. Proper theology begins just at the point where the difficulties disclosed by Strauss and Feuerbach are seen and then laughed at. Thus such men and their questions are 'loved'! Alexander Schweizer and his kind neither saw these difficulties, nor were they capable of this laughter. In such a situation, however, Strauss could not and must not be pensioned off.

[1] *Collected Works*, I, p. 4.

XI

RITSCHL

I T has been said of Ritschl that in the history of theology since Schleiermacher he is the only one who, in the true sense, has given birth to an
epoch. This is not true because all the strivings proceeding from
Schleiermacher, who was, despite all argument, the only one who
really gave rise to an epoch, continued on their way in a very significant fashion beside Ritschl, and were even more than ever taken up
again after him. As has already been said, Schleiermacher's influence
was incomparably stronger in 1910 than in 1830, and one does not have
to be a prophet to observe that if the older age of theology were to
remain master of the field today, or conquer it anew, then it would do so
under the banner of Schleiermacher, or perhaps of Hegel, and on no
account under that of Ritschl. Ritschl has the significance of an episode
in more recent theology, and not, indeed not, that of an epoch. If it
were possible for us to continue our account in the way in which it has
been presented up to now, then we should have to depict Ritschl amid
his contemporaries and opponents to left and right: Luthardt, Frank
and von Oettingen on the one side, and Biedermann and Lipsius on
the other. We should, however, also have to point out, in the figure of
Lagarde, who also belonged to this generation, the turn events took
immediately after Ritschl, and which brought everything once again
on to the course characterized by the name of Schleiermacher. We
should then have to discuss the theologians born from the eighteen-
thirties to the eighteen-fifties, that is to say, Overbeck, Pfleiderer, and
Lüdemann on the one hand, and Cremer, Kähler, Schlatter, Ihmels
and Seeberg on the other, who in the main only managed to speak, or
were only heard, after Ritschl's death; and we should have to show that
Ritschl's followers, Schultz, Herrmann, Kaftan, Haering, Kirn, Katten-
busch, Harnack, Rade and others, who were also of this time, did not
dominate the picture quite so completely, even towards the end of the
century, as the historians of Ritschl's school would have us believe.
And we should then have to study the complete return to the main
tendency which Ritschl forsook, in those who were born in the sixties

and seventies, who were the men of the day in 1910, and still are in part today, men like the band of historians led by Troeltsch; namely Gunkel, J. Weiss, Bousset, Heitmüller, Wernle, and further the similarly orientated systematic scholars Otto and Wobbermin, men who are opposed from the right by E. Schaeder and C. Stange, a generation in which people like Johannes Müller and Rittelmeyer, Kutter and Ragaz could not be overlooked either. In the development thus hinted at the school of Ritschl played the undoubtedly important *rôle* of a reaction. It is thus, however, and not as the beginning of a new epoch, that it distinguishes itself from the flood of events and personalities, and that we are thinking of its leader as we bring this account to its provisional close.

The practical significance of this reaction is as follows. Ritschl rejected all the previous attempts to overcome the Enlightenment which were centrally determined by the tendency of Romanticism. Instead he energetically seized upon the theoretical and practical philosophy of the Enlightenment in its perfected form. That is, he went back to Kant, but Kant quite definitely interpreted as an antimetaphysical moralist, by means of whom he thought he could understand Christianity as that which grandly and inevitably made possible, or realized, a practical ideal of life. In this his abandoning of all knowledge which could not be rendered comprehensible within this framework is seen properly as the characteristic thing about his theology, provided we hold up beside it the positive determination with which on the one hand he apprehends and affirms this practical ideal of life as such, and with which on the other he makes the interpretation of Christianity, the Bible and particularly the Reformation, serve the founding and strengthening of this ideal. We must not allow ourselves to be blinded by sight of the extensive material Ritschl drew from the Bible and the history of dogma to the fact that this, and ultimately this alone, was his chief concern. Nobody either before or since Ritschl, perhaps—Wegscheider was the one exception—has expressed the view as clearly as he, that modern man wishes above all to live in the best sense according to reason, and that the significance of Christianity for him can only be a great confirmation and strengthening of this very endeavour. One could of course ask whether this will, soberly and honestly expressed by Ritschl, was not universally present, somewhere in the background of the theology of the whole century, except in certain outsiders, and whether all else was not more like an artificial fog surrounding this will than actually another will. We can ask whether the entire theological movement of the century resulted not at all in an overcoming of the Enlightenment, of its decisive interest of man in himself, but in its fulfilment.

But even if we understand it in this way we should still have to admit that the production of this artificial fog on the part of others had at least betrayed people's disquiet who for all that did not in fact want to admit that this will is the truth or, at least, that it is the whole truth. Ritschl, on the other hand, feels no trace of this disquiet. He stands with incredible clearness and firmness (truly with both feet) upon the ground of his 'ideal of life', the very epitome of the national-liberal German bourgeois of the age of Bismarck. That distinguishes him from those who went before him and from those who came after him. The passion with which he was attacked both from left and right is quite understandable—this self-assurance of modern man was not to everyone's taste, even between 1860 and 1890—and quite understandable too was the fact that he and his school could not long sustain themselves, once the jubilation over Columbus's trick with the egg had died away.

And yet perhaps the views of those who stood to left and right of Ritschl, who went before and came after him, were not basically very different from his. It was not hypocrisy, but this deeply-rooted disquiet which caused everyone before him and after him, and those on his left and right, to agree in the conviction that these views could not at any rate be expressed in this way. The plan for the overcoming of the Enlightenment had to be taken up again, after it had been postponed for a while, while theologians were blinded by Ritschl's simplification. The plan had to be taken up again with the risk that they would have to link up once again with Romanticism, and that they might perhaps not be able to find any better guidance from this source than the first generations of the century had done, with the risk that, far from managing this better, they might manage things even worse than their predecessors. It was Ritschl's great merit that with his reaction he showed that it was possible to abandon the Schleiermacher-Hegel approach, and he thus for a moment clearly illuminated the point of departure for the complete development, the perfected Enlightenment; though he then showed in effect that if theology did not wish to place itself in far too exposed a position, it could only employ the Schleiermacher-Hegel approach upon the basis of this point of departure; that a different approach would make necessary the choice of another point of departure, that it would, in fact make necessary a true overcoming of the Enlightenment. To this extent Ritschl is not at all a bad person with whom to conclude our account.

Albrecht Benjamin Ritschl was born in Berlin in 1822, and went to the universities of Bonn, Halle, Berlin, Heidelberg and Tübingen. First, at Tübingen he became a historian in the manner of Baur. In 1846 he qualified as a lecturer at the University of Bonn. The second edition of his book *Entstehung der altkatholischen Kirche* (The Origin of the Old Catholic Church) in 1856 brought him into conflict with Baur. He became an associate professor in 1852, a full professor in 1859, and was transferred as a systematic theologian to Göttingen in 1864, where from the end of the seventies onwards he was the head of the school bearing his name. He died in 1889. Chief consideration must be given to his two works, *Rechtfertigung und Versöhnung* (Justification and Reconciliation), 1870-4, and *Geschichte des Pietismus* (The History of Pietism), 1880-6. He set down his thoughts in condensed form in his *Unterricht in der christlichen Religion* (Instruction in the Christian Religion), 1875, in the lecture *Die Christliche Vollkommenheit* (Christian Perfection), 1874 and in the treatise *Theologie und Metaphysik* (Theology and Metaphysics), 1881, all of which appeared in several editions.

In order to understand Ritschl we must lay the emphasis upon the final word of the title of his chief work, *Justification and Reconciliation*. With Ritschl reconciliation, to put it baldly, means the realized ideal of human life. It is the intended result of justification (*Instruction*, para. 46). All Ritschl's thinking springs from this result. It is this result and this result alone in which he is interested. Completed reconciliation consists in God's confronting the believer as his Father and justifying him in his child-like feeling of utter trust,[1] giving him spiritual dominion over the world and engaging him in the work in the kingdom of God. This state is the state of Christian perfection. Religiously it consists in faith in divine providence, in humility, in patience and in prayer; morally it consists in activity in one's profession and in the development of personal virtue. In it 'the individual person acquires the value of a complete whole, which is superior . . . to the value of the entire world'.[2] In Christian perfection a man's life becomes a life-work accompanied by a justified sense of one's own work.[3] His perfection perpetually includes within itself an insight into a certain imperfection, but he may in principle 'be comforted' about this, since will and action would not be possible if his imperfection were the final word that could be said of him.[4] The quintessence of the task imposed upon man, which at the same time is his highest good and his own final

---

[1] *Instruction*, para. 46. [2] Ibid., para. 59.
[3] *Christian Perfection*, p. 13. [4] Ibid., p. 1.

aim, is the kingdom of God, in which the love of one's neighbour is activated.[1]

But the kingdom of God can only be lived for within the communities which have been naturally determined, particularly in the regular working activity of one's moral profession, and not outside them,[2] so that loyalty to one's profession is at once the true fulfilment of the model of Christ.[3] Where there is no reconciliation in this sense, as the realization of the ideal of life, or where reconciliation in this sense is not activated, there is no justification either. Ritschl finds he can express this, somewhat in the Pelagian manner, by calling man's conscious activity in reconciliation, and therefore in the kingdom of God and therefore in his profession, the 'condition' for the forgiveness of sins.[4] Or he can put it in an Augustinian way too, by simply equating the effect of grace and the impulse to corresponding self-activity; good conduct and the effect of grace.[5] But on no account may the balance for imperfection of moral conduct be sought in the certainty of justification or of the forgiveness of sins, but only in the resolve and implementation of a greater endeavour to improve,[6] whereas the meaning of the forgiveness of sins and of justification is entirely and alone that of placing man in the position where this activity is possible and demanded. There must not therefore be any thinking or any action which is not directly, perfectly or imperfectly activity in the kingdom of God and thus activity in one's profession and the development of virtue. There must not be any action directed towards God which by-passes this activity.

It was from this standpoint that Ritschl became the ferocious opponent of Pietism—which he accused of returning to the tendency of monasticism—and the opponent of all metaphysics in theology, which instead of holding solely to the effects of God which can be experienced, seeks to hold also, or indeed predominantly, to a God in himself. Again, it was from this standpoint that Ritschl became the opponent of mysticism as a religiosity which overleaps the will of God and of man. Christianity is an outlook upon life and it is morality, but in no way is it an immediate relationship with God. Roman Catholicism and every form of Anabaptists' faith is dispatched at one blow by virtue of the fact that they think they know of a Christianity, and perhaps indeed of a more perfect Christianity beside that provided by the consciousness and realization in the moral sphere of the fact that we are children of God.

---

[1] *Instruction*, paras. 5f.   [2] Ibid., paras. 27f.   [3] Ibid., para. 56.   [4] Ibid., paras. 45f.
[5] *Justification and Reconciliation*, III, para. 36; *Instruction*, paras. 39 and 55.
[6] *Instruction*, para. 46.

According to Ritschl there should strictly speaking not be any Sunday, and no eternity either, or at any rate no silent eternity, and he did in fact define God's eternity as the constancy of God's will for the creation and maintenance of his Church, overcoming the barrier of time.[1]

Justification is related to reconciliation, thus understood, as the great guarantee and realization, apprehended in faith, of this ideal of life. Reconciliation is event in the Christian Church as in the communion of the faithful, and faith is, simply, faith in the divine justification which in principle turns man from a sinner into a non-sinner.[2] Sin is deed and only deed. It is man's deed, performed in opposition to the action taking place in the Kingdom of God. In content it is selfishness, or a seeking after things which are of an inferior rank—i.e. an upsetting of the scale of things.[3] In form it is enmity to God, and lack of reverence and trust.[4] Its consequence is a reduction of the right to be a child of God, and, in conjunction with this, man's subjection to the evil as a restriction of his freedom in achieving his life's goal.[5] In origin it is ignorance,[6] which is strengthened by the existence of a realm of sin, i.e. by the mutual effect of the sinful conduct of all men upon one another, which with Ritschl takes the place of original sin.[7] Justification does not mean the removal of the power of sin dominating the individual—this must be combated and removed by the decision of the individual will, a process for which religious redemption can only pave the way. Justification rather means forgiveness.

In this sense Ritschl understood and affirmed the Reformation doctrine of justification as forensic. The intercourse between God and man, terminated by sin, is resumed by God. Upon the basis of the conditions he has to fulfil man may, unhindered by guilt or the feeling of guilt, join in the building of the Kingdom of God as something which is his own final goal.[8] This forgiveness of God's and this permission granted to man which is based upon it are the particular possession of the Christian Church. In justification God assigns man his place in his Kingdom, in spite of man's sin and upon condition that he should now desist from it. In so doing he makes him into a Christian. And everything there is to be said about God, according to Ritschl, is comprised simply in the statement that God wants, creates and maintains the Church in which this possession is to be received, in which, that is, men are admitted to the Kingdom of God with this intention and in

[1] *Justification and Reconciliation*, III, para. 37; *Instruction*, para. 14.
[2] *Instruction*, paras. 26 and 35.   [3] *Justification and Reconciliation*, III, p. 317.
[4] Ibid., III, para. 40.   [5] Ibid., para. 42.
[6] Ibid., para. 43.   [7] Ibid., para. 41.   [8] *Instruction*, paras. 44f.

this manner; that is, in which they are called to be active in this king-dom. God is love. That is, he did not have to make man's true goal into his own goal, but, as he is love, he has this goal originally as his own.[1] God—with regard to the fact that God's kingdom is indeed nothing else but man's own goal—God is 'the power which man worships because it upholds his spiritual sense of his own worth against the restrictions imposed upon it by nature'.[2] His omnipotence is his 'care and presence of grace for pious men'.[3] His righteousness is the logical manner in which he leads them to salvation.[4] His personality gives evidence of the value which religion attributes to the spiritual life of man.[5] Similarly God's creation of the world has of course taken place solely for the sake of the Kingdom of God, i.e. for the sake of men's own goal, and is to be understood only in this sense. And the idea of a wrath of God, and indeed even of a holiness of God which should be distinguished from his righteousness would manifestly imply a negation of his love and thus of man's own goal, and is there-fore to be regarded as an idea which was already vanishing in the Old Testament, but which in the New Testament can only be maintained eschatologically, that is, only as a description of God's attitude towards the unjust.[6]

What distinguishes Christianity from every other religion is that it answers the question all religions ask. Man knows himself as part of the world and at the same time he is predisposed to spiritual personality. How can he then establish the claim to dominion over the world which is based upon this predisposition, against the limitation imposed upon him by the world?[7] How can we, by appropriating the divine life, make assured the value of our spiritual life within its limiting involve-ment with nature or in the world?[8] That is the meaning of an apologetics of Christianity: to demonstrate this significance of Christianity for the realization of the ideal of human life—to demonstrate that the Christian idea of God is the first to offer the necessary connexion of ideas between our outlook upon life, which is dependent upon the perception of nature with all its limitations, and our necessary moral self-judgment and that therefore to this extent it fills a gap which philosophy leaves open, and must of necessity leave open.[9]

But the knowledge of God as the God of love, and thus as the God who forgives sins, who removes our natural limitations, who admits

---

[1] *Justification and Reconciliation*, III, p. 259.   [2] *Theology and Metaphysics*, p. 11.
[3] *Instruction*, para. 15.   [4] Ibid., para. 16.
[5] *Justification and Reconciliation*, III, p. 173.   [6] Ibid., II, paras. 12-15 and 16f.
[7] *Instruction*, para. 8.   [8] Ibid., para. 59.
[9] *Justification and Reconciliation*, III, para. 27; *Instruction*, para. 29.

us into his kingdom and makes us his children, free, but also bound in duty to him—this knowledge comes about in the form of a judgment which is completely different from all the judgments of science in the form, namely, of a value judgment. A value judgment is a judgment in which a certain aspect of being is expressed concerning a certain object of human experience with regard to the value, i.e. the practical significance, which it has for man, a certain aspect of being which, apart from this practical significance, could not be expressed concerning the object. Now the object of human experience which has for man the value of Godhead, and concerning which, therefore, in a certain sense we can venture to pronounce: 'He is God'—this object, and therefore the occasion for the knowledge of God as the God of love, is the historical phenomenon Jesus of Nazareth. Jesus, in himself being in surpassing fashion the bearer of grace as well as of dominion over the world[1] is the archetypal image of the humanity which is to be united in the kingdom of God[2] and his vocation is simply to reveal the God who is love. In so far as he exercises this vocation upon us, or in so far as we experience and evaluate his historical existence as an action revealing God, he is himself God. It is not through a command, and not through directly divine authority, but as a prophet: through his morally effective sayings and as priest: by the way in which his action is ready to serve, that he exercises the *munus regium* as God and substantiates to us his divine right of dominion. He realizes his own goal which is identical with God's own goal, which, once again, is identical with our own goal. It is in the recognition and expression of this connexion that this decisive value-judgment, which provides the basis for Christian theology as such, comes about; we obtain justification, that is, we obtain admission to the kingdom of God, that is, we obtain the realization of our own purpose of life in no other way but through Jesus in his Church; and thus and in this sense we have God in Christ.

The rounded, transparent and compact quality of this train of thought makes it very understandable that Ritschl should have found followers and support. The reasons why he could not establish himself have already been alluded to and need not be repeated. There were very real reasons why all his contemporaries, apart from the adherents to his school, and the history of theology after him showed themselves to be governed by the determination not to allow his words to hold sway as the final and characteristic words of the entire age, no matter how genuine and impressive they might be in their own way.

[1] *Instruction*, para. 24.   [2] Ibid., para. 22.

APPENDIX

I. MAN IN THE EIGHTEENTH CENTURY

p. 43. Goethe: *Symbolum*

> Des Maurers Wandeln,
> Es gleicht dem Leben,
> Und sein Bestreben,
> Es gleicht dem Handeln
> Der Menschen auf Erden.
>
> Die Zukunft decket
> Schmerzen und Glücke
> Schrittweis dem Blicke
> Doch ungeschrecket
> Dringen wir vorwärts.
>
> Und schwer und ferne
> Hängt eine Hülle
> Mit Ehrfurcht. Stille
> Ruhen oben die Sterne
> Und unten die Gräber.
>
> Betracht sie genauer!
> Und siehe, so melden
> Im Busen der Helden
> Sich wandelnde Schauer
> Und ernste Gefühle.
>
> Doch rufen von drüben
> Die Stimmen der Geister
> Die Stimmen der Meister:
> Versäumt nicht zu üben
> Die Kräfte des Guten!
>
> Hier flechten sich Kronen
> In ewiger Stille,
> Die sollen mit Fülle
> Die Tätigen lohnen!
> Wir heissen euch hoffen.

II. ROUSSEAU

p. 99 Goethe: *Harzreise im Winter*, 1777

Leicht ist's folgen dem Wagen,
Den Fortuna führt,
Wie der gemächliche Tross
Auf gebesserten Wegen
Hinter des Fürsten Einzug.

Ach, wer heilet die Schmerzen
Des, dem Balsam zu Gift ward?
Der sich Menschenhass
Aus der Fülle der Liebe trank!
Erst verachtet, nun ein Verächter,
Zehrt er heimlich auf
Seinen eigenen Wert
In ungnügender Selbstsucht.

Aber abseits, wer ist's?
Ins Gebüsch verliert sich sein Pfad
Hinter ihm schlagen
Die Sträuche zusammen,
Das Gras steht wieder auf,
Die Öde verschlingt ihn.

Ist auf deinem Psalter,
Vater der Liebe, ein Ton
Seinem Ohre vernehmlich,
So erquicke sein Herz!
Öffne den umwölkten Blick
Über die tausend Quellen
Neben dem Durstenden
In der Wüste!

III. LESSING

p. 123. from *Nathan der Weise*, Act III, Scene 5

Ein Mann wie du bleibt da
Nicht stehen, wo der Zufall der Geburt
Ihn hingeworfen: oder wenn er bleibt,
Bleibt er aus Einsicht, Gründen, Wahl des Bessern.

p. 124. ibid., Act I, Scene 2

> Begreifst du aber
> Wieviel andächtig schwärmen leichter als
> Gut handeln ist? Wie gern der schlaffste Mensch
> Andächtig schwärmt, um nur—ist er zu Zeiten
> Sich schon der Absicht deutlich nicht bewusst—
> Um nur gut handeln nicht zu müssen?

p. 124. ibid., Act V, Scene 5

> Was sollt ich eines Fehls mich schämen? Hab
> Ich nicht den festen Vorsatz, ihm zu bessern?

p. 125. ibid., Act III, Scene 1

> Wann war ich nicht ganz Ohr, so oft es dir
> Gefiel, von deinen Glaubenshelden mich
> Zu unterhalten? Hab'ich ihren Taten
> Nicht stets Bewunderung und ihren Leiden
> Nicht immer Thränen gern gezollt? Ihr Glaube
> Schien freilich mir das Heldenmässigste
> An ihnen nie.

p. 128. ibid., Act I, Scene 2

> Stolz! und nichts als Stolz! Der Topf
> Von Eisen will von einer silbern Zange
> Gern aus der Glut gehoben sein, um selbst
> Ein Topf von Silber sich zu dünken.—Pah!—
> Und was es schadet, fragst du? Was es schadet?
> Was hilft es, dürft ich nur hinwieder fragen.—
> Denn dein 'Sich Gott um so viel näher fühlen'
> Ist Unsinn oder Gotteslästerung.—
> Allein es schadet; ja, es schadet allerdings.

p. 141. *Nathan der Weise*, Act III, Scene 7 (*The Fable of the Three Rings*)

> Man untersucht, man zankt,
> Man klagt. Umsonst; der rechte Ring
> War nicht erweislich;—fast so unerweislich als
> Uns itzt—der rechte Glaube.

p. 141. ibid.

> Und jeder schwur dem Richter
> Unmittelbar aus seines Vaters Hand
> Den Ring zu haben.—Wie auch wahr!

p. 141. ibid.

> Das muss
> Entscheiden! Denn die falschen Ringe werden
> Doch das nicht können!—Nun; wen lieben zwei
> Von euch am meisten? Macht, sagt an! Ihr schweigt?
> Die Ringe wirken nur zurück? Und nicht
> Nach aussen? Jeder liebt sich selber nur
> Am meisten?—O, so seid ihr alle drei
> Betrogene Betrüger! Eure Ringe
> Sind alle drei nicht echt. Der echte Ring
> Vermutlich ging verloren. Den Verlust
> Zu bergen, zu ersetzen, liess der Vater
> Die drei für einen machen.

p. 141. ibid.

> Mein Rat ist aber der: ihr nehmt
> Die Sache völlig, wie sie liegt. Hat von
> Euch jeder seinen Ring von seinem Vater:
> So glaube jeder sich seinen Ring
> Den echten.

pp. 141-2. ibid.

> Wohlan!
> Es eifre jeder seiner unbestochnen,
> Von Vorurteilen freien Liebe nach!
> Es strebe von euch jeder um die Wette,
> Die Kraft des Steins in seinem Ring an Tag
> Zu legen! Komme dieser Kraft mit Sanftmut
> Mit herzlicher Verträglichkeit, mit Wohlthun,
> Mit innigster Ergebenheit in Gott
> Zu Hilf! Und wenn sich dann der Steine Kräfte
> Bei euren Kindes-Kindeskindern äussern:
> So lad ich über tausend, tausend Jahre
> Sie wiederum vor diesen Stuhl. Da wird
> Ein weiser Mann auf diesem Stuhle sitzen
> Als ich und sprechen. Geht! So sagte der
> bescheidne Richter.

p. 142. ibid.

> Nathan, lieber Nathan!—
> Die tausend, tausend Jahre deines Richters

Sind noch nicht um.—Sein Richterstuhl ist nicht
der meine.

p. 143. ibid, Act II, Scene 5

> Sind Christ und Jude eher Christ und Jude
> Als Mensch? Ah! wenn ich einen mehr in Euch
> Gefunden hätte, dem es genügt, ein Mensch
> Zu heissen!

p. 143. ibid., Act III, Scene 6

> Stockjude sein zu wollen, geht schon nicht,
> Und ganz und gar nicht Jude, geht noch minder.

p. 143. ibid., Act IV, Scene 4

> Ich habe nie verlangt,
> Dass allen Bäume *eine* Rinde wachse.

p. 143. ibid., Act IV, Scene 1

> Weil das einmal so ist,
> Wird's so wohl recht sein.

V. HERDER

p. 203. from *St Johanns Nachtstraum*

> Bin nicht zu denken hier! Zu sein! Zu fühlen!
> Zu leben! Mich zu freun!

p. 204. *Selbst*, p. 256

> Vergiss dein Ich; dich selbst verliere nie.
> Nichts Grössres konnt' aus ihrem Herzen dir
> Die reiche Gottheit geben, als dich selbst.

p. 204. *St Johanns Nachtstraum*, pp. 249f.

> Zu leben allein?
> Der leuchtende Wurm ist nicht allein,
> wird, was er wird,
> einst nicht allein sein!
> Und mich freun?—Allein?
> Niemand zu sagen, wie schön im Sommerliebesbrande
> Mutter Natur du seist!
> Schöne Mutter Natur!

Niemand zu haben, der mit mir
schwirren die Schöpfung höre! gehn
die leisen Räder und sehn den Engel fliegen
und denken Unsterblichkeit!
Vereint sie denken und fühlen
das Erdeleben vereint! uns drücken
an Freundesherz! o schöne Mutter Natur,
Dein edelster Funke!

p. 204. *Das Ich*, pp. 252f.

Willst du zur Ruhe kommen, flieh, o Freund,
Die ärgste Feindin, die Persönlichkeit!

Ermanne dich, nein du gehörst nicht dir;
Dem grossen, guten All gehörest du.

Was wärest du? Kein Ich. Ein jeder Tropf'
In deinem Lebenssaft, in deinem Blut,
Ein jedes Kügelchen, in deinem Geist
Und Herzen jeder regende Gedank'.

Jedwedes Wort der Lippe, jeder Zug
Des Angesichtes ist ein fremdes Gut
Dir angeeignet, doch nur zum Gebrauch.
So, immer wechselnd, stets verändert, schleicht
Der Eigner fremden Gutes durch die Welt.

Nur wenn uneingedenk des engen Ichs
Dein Geist in allen Seelen lebt, dein Herz
In tausend Herzen schläget, dann bist du
Ein ewiger, allwirkender, ein Gott,
Und auch, wie Gott, unsichtbar-namenlos.

So lasset dann im Wirken und Gemüt
Das Ich uns mildern, dass das bessre Du
Und Er und Wir und Ihr und Sie es sanft
Auslöschen, und uns von der bösen Unart
Des harten Ich unmerklich-sanft befrein.
In allen Pflichten sei uns erste Pflicht
Vergessenheit sein selber! So gerät
Uns unser Werk, und süss ist jede Tat.

pp. 207-8. *Die Schöpfung*, pp. 250f.

. . . die Schöpfung, itzt am Ziel
Harret, schweigt noch!—Ihr Gefühl

Wandelt in sich, und vermisst
Was Geschöpf und Schöpfer ist;
　　Suchet einen, der mit Geist
Schmeckt und was er ist, geneusst,
Suchet, der mit Gottesblick
Alle Schöpfung strahlt zurück!—
　　In sich, von sich. Und selbst sich
In sich strahl' und väterlich
Von sich strahl' und walte frei
Und wie Gott ein Schöpfer sei!
　　Sie den suchet, jetzt am Ziel
Gottes Schöpfung, wirft Gefühl
In sich dess, was sie vermisst,
Und der Mensch—der Gott—er ist!
　　Neu Geschöpf, wie nenn ich dich?
Gott der Schöpfung, lehre mich!—
Doch ich bin, ich bin es ja,
Dem dies Gottesbild geschah!—
　　Ich wie Gott! Da tritt in mich
Plan der Schöpfung, weitet sich,
Drängt zusammen und wird Macht!
Endet froh und jauchtzt: vollbracht!—
　　Ich wie Gott! Da tritt in sich
Meine Seel! und denket mich!
Schaft sich um und handelt frei,
Fühlt, wie frei Jehovah sei.
　　Ich wie Gott! Da schlägt mein Herz
Königsmut und Bruderschmerz.
Alles Leben hier vereint,
Fühlt der Mensch sich aller Freund!
　　Fühlt sich Sinn voll Mitgefühl
Bis zur Pflanze, bis zum Ziel
Aller Menschengöttlichkeit,
Eint sich liebend weit und breit,
　　Immer tiefer, höher. Ich
Bin's in dem die Schöpfung sich
Punktet, der in alles quillt
Und der alles in sich füllt!—
　　Bis zur letzten Schöpfung hin
Fühlet, tastet, reicht mein Sinn!
Aller Wesen Harmonie

Mit mir—ja ich selbst bin sie!
    Bin der eine Gottesklang,
Der aus allem Lustgesang'
Aller Schöpfung tönt' empor
Und trat ein in Gottes Ohr,
    Und ward Bild, Gedank' und Tat
Und ward Mensch. Der Schöpfung Rat,
Mensch, ist in dir! Fühle dich
Und die Schöpfung fühlet sich!—
    Fühle dich, so fühlst du Gott
In dir. In dir fühlt sich Gott,
Wie ihn Sonn' und Tier nicht fühlt,
Wie er-sich—in sich—erzielt!

p. 211. from *Maskenzüge*, by J. W. v. Goethe (Jubilee edition, Vol. 9,
    p. 350)

Ein edler Mann, begierig, zu begründen
Wie überall des Menschen Sinn erpriesst,
Horcht in die Welt, so Ton als Wort zu finden,
Das tausendquellig durch die Länder fliesst.
Die ältesten, die neuesten Regionen
Durchwandelt er und lauscht in allen Zonen.

Und so von Volk zu Volke hört er singen,
Was jeden in der Mutterluft gerührt,
Er hört erzählen, was von guten Dingen
Urvaters Wort dem Vater zugeführt.
Das alles war Ergetzlichkeit und Lehre,
Gefühl und Tat, als wenn es *eines* wäre.

Was Leiden bringen mag und was Genüge,
Behend verwirrt und ungehofft vereint,
Das haben tausend Sprach-und Redezüge,
Vom Paradies bis heute, gleich gemeint.
So singt der Barde, spricht Legend' und Sage,
Wir fühlen mit, als wären's unsre Tage.

Wenn schwarz der Fels, umhangen Atmosphäre
Zu Traumgebilden düstrer Klage zwingt
Dort heiterm Sonnenglanz im offnen Meere,
Das hohe Lied entzückter Seele klingt—
Sie meinen's gut und fromm im Grund, sie wollten
Nur Menschliches, was alle wollen sollten.

Wo sich's versteckte, wusst' er's aufzufinden,
Ernsthaft verhüllt, verkleidet leicht als Spiel,
Im höchsten Sinn der Zukunft zu begründen:
Humanität sei unser ewig Ziel.
O, warum schaut er nicht, in diesen Tagen,
Durch Menschlichkeit geheilt die schwersten Plagen.

VI. NOVALIS

pp. 240-1. from *Hymnen an die Nacht*, Bölsche, I, p. 30

Was sollen wir auf dieser Welt
Mit unserer Lieb und Treue—
Das Alte wird hintangestellt,
Was kümmert uns das Neue?
O! Einsam steht und tiefbetrübt
Wer heiss und fromm die Vorzeit liebt.

Die Vorzeit, wo die Sinne licht
In hohen Flammen brannten,
Des Vaters Hand und Angesicht
Des Menschen noch erkannten,
Und hohen Sinns, einfältiglich
Noch mancher seinem Urbild glich.

Die Vorzeit, wo an Blüten reich
Uralte Stämme prangten,
Und Kinder für das Himmelreich
Nach Qual und Tod verlangten;
Und wenn auch Lust und Leben sprach,
Doch manches Herz für Liebe brach.

Die Vorzeit, wo in Jugendglut
Gott selbst sich kundgegeben,
Und frühem Tod in Liebesmut
Geweiht sein süsses Leben,
Und Angst und Schmerz nicht von sich trieb
Damit er uns nur teuer blieb.

Mit banger Sehnsucht sehn wir sie
In dunkle Nacht gehüllet,
Und hier auf dieser Welt wird nie
Der heisse Durst gestillet.

Wir müssen nach der Heimat gehn,
Um diese heilge Zeit zu sehn.

    Was hält noch unsre Rückkehr auf—
Die Liebsten ruhn schon lange.
Ihr Grab schliesst unsern Lebenslauf,
Nun wird uns weh und bange.
Zu suchen haben wir nichts mehr—
Das Herz ist satt, die Welt ist leer.

p. 241. ibid., Bölsche, II, p. 142
    Wenn nicht mehr Zahlen und Figuren
Sind Schlüssel aller Kreaturen,
Wenn die, so singen oder küssen,
Mehr als die Tiefgelehrten wissen,
Wenn sich die Welt ins freie Leben
Und in die Welt wird zurückbegeben,
Wenn dann sich wieder Licht und Schatten
Zu echter Klarheit wieder gatten,
Und man in Märchen und Gedichten
Erkennt die wahren Weltgeschichten,
Dann fliegt vor einem geheimen Wort
Das ganze verkehrte Wesen fort.

pp. 243-4. from *Heinrich von Ofterdingen.* Bölsche, II, p. 107
    Die Liebe ging auf dunkler Bahn
Vom Monde nur erblickt,
Das Schattenreich war aufgetan,
Und seltsam aufgeschmückt.

Ein blauer Dunst umschwebte sie
Mit einem goldnen Rand,
Und eilig zog die Phantasie
Sie über Strom und Land.

Es hob sich ihre volle Brust
In wunderbarem Mut;
Ein Vorgefühl der künft'gen Lust
Besprach die wilde Glut.

p. 244. from ibid., Bölsche, II, p. 126
    Der Liebe Reich ist aufgetan,
Die Fabel fängt zu spinnen an.

Das Urspiel jeder Natur beginnt,
Auf kräftige Worte jedes sinnt.
Und so das grosse Weltgemüt
Überall sich regt und unendlich blüht.
Alles muss ineinandergreifen,
Eins durch das andre gedeihn und reifen;
Jedes in allen dar sich stellt,
Indem es sich mit ihnen vermischet
Und gierig in ihre Tiefen fällt,
Sein eigentümliches Wesen erfrischet,
Und tausend neue Gedanken erhält.
Die Welt wird Traum, der Traum wird Welt.

pp. 246-7. *Hymne*, Bölsche, I, pp. 73f.

Wenige wissen
Das Geheimnis der Liebe
Fühlen Unersättlichkeit
Und ewigen Durst.
Des Abendmahls
Göttliche Bedeutung
Ist den irdischen Sinnen Rätsel;
Aber wer jemals
Von heissen, geliebten Lippen
Atem des Lebens sog,
Wem heilige Glut
In zitternde Wellen das Herz schmolz,
Wem das Auge aufging,
Dass er des Himmels
Unergründliche Tiefe mass,
Wird essen von seinem Leibe
Und trinken von seinem Blute
Ewiglich.
Wer hat des irdischen Leibes
Hohen Sinn erraten?
Wer kann sagen,
Dass er das Blut versteht?
Einst ist *alles* Leib,
Ein Leib,
Im himmlischen Blute
Schwimmt das selige Paar.—
O! dass das Weltmeer

Schon errötete,
Und in duftiges Fleisch
Aufquölle der Fels!
Nie sättigt die Liebe sich.
Nicht innig, nicht eigen genug,
Kann sie haben den Geliebten.
Von immer zärteren Lippen
Verwandelt wird das Genossene
Inniglicher und näher.
Heissere Wollust
Durchbebt die Seele,
Durstiger und hungriger
Wird das Herz:
Und so wäret der Liebe Genuss
Von Ewigkeit zu Ewigkeit.
Hätten die Nüchternen
Einmal gekostet,
Alles verliessen sie,
Und setzten sich zu uns
An den Tisch der Sehnsucht,
Der nie leer wird.
Sie erkennten der Liebe
Unendliche Fülle
Und priesen die Nahrung
Von Leib und Blut.

pp. 252-3. from *Hymnen an die Nacht*, Bölsche, I, p. 14.

Hast auch du
Ein menschliches Herz
Dunkle Nacht?
Was hältst du
Unter deinem Mantel,
Das mir unsichtbar kräftig
An die Seele geht?
Du scheinst nur furchtbar—
Köstlicher Balsam
Trauft aus deiner Hand,
Aus dem Bündel Mohn.
In süsser Trunkenheit
Entfaltest du die schweren Flügel des Gemüts.
Und schenkst uns Freuden

Dunkel und unaussprechlich,
Heimlich, wie du selber bist,
Freuden, die uns
Einen Himmel ahnen lassen.
Wie arm und kindisch
Dünkt mir das Licht
Mit seinen bunten Dingen,
Wie erfreulich und gesegnet
Des Tages Abschied.
Also nur darum
Weil die Nacht dir
Abwendig macht die Dienenden,
Säetest du
In des Raumes Weiten
Die leuchtenden Kugeln,
Zu verkünden deine Allmacht,
Deine Wiederkehr
In den Zeiten deiner Entfernung.
   Himmlischer als jene blitzenden Sterne
In jenen Weiten
Dünken uns die unendlichen Augen,
Die die Nacht
In uns geöffnet.

pp. 253-4. from ibid., Bölsche, I, p. 18

Gern will ich
Die fleissigen Hände rühren,
Überall umschaun,
Wo du mich brauchst,
Rühmen deines Glanzes
Volle Pracht,
Unverdrossen verfolgen
Den schönen Zusammenhang
Deines künstlichen Werks,
Gern betrachten
Den sinnvollen Gang
Deiner gewaltigen
Leuchtenden Uhr,
Ergründen der Kräfte
Ebenmass
Und die Regeln

Des Wunderspiels
Unzähliger Räume
Und ihrer Zeiten.
Aber getreu der Nacht
Bleibt mein geheimes Herz
Und ihrer Tochter,
Der schaffenden Liebe.

p. 254. from ibid., Bölsche, I, p. 16

Sie fühlen dich nicht
In der goldnen Flut der Trauben.
In des Mandelbaums
Wunderöl
Und im braunen Safte des Mohns.
Sie wissen nicht,
Dass du es bist,
Der des zarten Mädchens
Busen umschwebt
Und zum Himmel den Schoss macht—
Ahnen nicht,
Dass aus alten Geschichten
Du himmelöffnend entgegen trittst
Und den Schlüssel tragst
Zu den Wohnungen der Seligen,
Unendlicher Geheimnisse
Schweigender Bote.

pp. 254-5. from ibid., Bölsche, I, pp. 15f.

Du kommst, Geliebte—
Die Nacht ist da—
Entzückt ist meine Seele—
Vorüber ist der irdische Weg
Und du bist wieder mein
Ich schaue dir ins tiefe, dunkle Auge,
Sehe nichts als Lieb' und Seligkeit.
Wir sinken auf der Nacht Altar
Aufs weiche Lager—
Die Hülle fällt
Und angezündet von dem warmen Druck
Entglüht des süssen Opfers
Reine Glut.

pp. 255-6. from ibid., Bölsche, I, p. 22

> Ein ewiges Fest
> Der Götter und Menschen.
> Und kindlich verehrten
> Alle Geschlechter
> Die zarte, köstliche Flamme
> Als das Höchste der Welt.
>
> Nur ein Gedanke wars,
> Der furchtbar zu den frohen Tischen trat
> Und das Gemüt in wilde Schrecken hüllte.
> Hier wussten selbst die Götter keinen Rat,
> Der das Gemüt mit süssem Troste füllte:
> Geheimnisvoll war dieses Unholds Pfad,
> Des Wut kein Flehn und keine Gabe stillte—
> Es war der Tod, der dieses Lustgelag
> Mit Angst und Schmerz und Tränen unterbrach.
>
>   .   .   .
>
> Mit kühnem Geist und hoher Sinnenglut
> Verschönte sich der Mensch die grause Larve,
> Ein blasser Jüngling löscht das Licht und ruht
> Sanft ist das Ende, wie ein Wehn der Harfe—
> Erinnrung schmilzt in kühler Schattenflut:
> Die Dichtung sangs dem traurigen Bedarfe.
> Doch unenträtselt blieb die ew'ge Nacht,
> Das ernste Zeichen einer fernen Macht.

p. 256. ibid., Bölsche, I, p. 24

> Die Nacht ward
> Der Offenbarungen
> Fruchtbarer Schoss
>
>   .   .
>
> Des Morgenlandes
> Ahnende, blütenreiche
> Weisheit
> Erkannte zuerst
> Der neuen Zeit Beginn.

pp. 256-7. ibid., Bölsche, I, p. 25

> Einsam entfaltete
> Das himmlische Herz sich

Zu der Liebe
Glühenden Schoss
Des Vaters hohen Antlitz zugewandt—
Und ruhend an dem ahnungsselgen Busen
Der lieblichernsten Mutter.
Mit vergötternder Inbrunst
Schaute das weissagende Auge
Des blühenden Kindes
Auf die Tage der Zukunft,
Nach seinen Geliebten,
Den Sprossen seines Götterstamms,
Unbekümmert über seiner Tage
Irdisches Schicksal.
Bald sammelten die kindlichsten Gemüter
Von allmächtiger Liebe
Wundersam ergriffen,
Sich um ihn her.
Wie Blumen keimte
Ein neues, fremdes Leben
In seiner Nähe—
Unerschöpfliche Worte
Und der Botschaften fröhlichste
Fielen wie Funken
Eines göttlichen Geistes
Von seinen freundlichen Lippen.

p. 257. ibid., Bölsche, I, pp. 25f.

Der Jüngling bist du, der seit langer Zeit
Auf unsern Gräbern steht in tiefem Sinnen,
Ein tröstlich Zeichen in der Dunkelheit,
Der höhern Menschheit freudiges Beginnen;
Was uns gesenkt in tiefe Traurigkeit,
Zieht uns mit süsser Sehnsucht nun von hinnen,
Im Tode ward das ewge Leben kund,
Du bist der Tod und machst uns erst gesund.

p. 257. ibid., Bölsche, I, p. 27.

Er stieg, in neuer Götterherrlichkeit
Erwacht, auf die Höhe
Der verjüngten, neugebornen Welt,
Begrub mit eigner Hand

Die alte mit ihm gestorbne Welt,
In die verlassne Höhle
Und legte mit allmächtiger Kraft
Den Stein, den keine Macht erhebt, darauf.

p. 257. ibid., Bölsche, I, p. 28

Lange Zeiten
Entflossen seitdem,
Und in immer höherm Glanze
Regte deine neue Schöpfung sich.
Und Tausende zogen
Aus Schmerzen und Qualen
Voll Glauben und Sehnsucht
Und Treue dir nach.
Und walten mit dir
Und der himmlischen Jungfrau
Im Reiche der Liebe
Und dienen im Tempel
Des himmlischen Todes.

p. 258. ibid., Bölsche, I, pp. 28-9

Zur Hochzeit ruft der Tod
Die Lampen brennen helle.
Um Öl ist keine Not.
Die Jungfraun sind zur Stelle,
Erklänge doch die Ferne
Von deinem Zuge schon,
Und ruften uns die Sterne
Mit Menschenzung und Ton.

Nach dir, Maria, heben
Schon tausend Herzen sich:
In diesem Schattenleben
Verlangten sie nur dich.
Sie hoffen zu genesen
Mit ahnungsvoller Lust,
Drückst du sie, heiliges Wesen,
An deine treue Brust.

.   .   .

Nun weint an keinem Grabe
Für Schmerz, wer liebend glaubt

Der Liebe süsse Habe
Wird keinem nicht geraubt.
Von treuen Himmelskindern
Wird ihm sein Herz bewacht.
Die Sehnsucht ihm zu lindern,
Begeistert ihn die Nacht.

Getrost, das Leben schreitet
Zum ewgen Leben hin;
Von innrer Glut geweitet
Verklärt sich unser Sinn.
Die Sternwelt wird zerfliessen
Zum goldnen Lebenswein,
Wir werden sie geniessen,
Und lichte Sterne sein.

Die Lieb ist freigegeben,
Und keine Trennung mehr.
Es wogt das volle Leben
Wie ein unendlich Meer—
Nur eine Nacht der Wonne
Ein ewiges Gedicht—
Und unser aller Sonne
Ist Gottes Angesicht.

p. 259. ibid., Bölsche, I, pp. 29-31

Hinunter in der Erde Schoss,
Weg aus des Lichtes Reichen!
Der Schmerzen Wut und wilder Stoss
Ist froher Abfahrt Zeichen.
Wir kommen in dem engen Kahn
Geschwind am Himmelsufer an.

Gelobt sei uns die ewge Nacht,
Gelobt der ewge Schlummer,
Wohl hat der Tag uns warm gemacht,
Und welk der lange Kummer.
Die Lust der Fremde ging uns aus,
Zum Vater wollen wir nach Haus.

.   .   .

Hinunter zu der süssen Braut
Zu Jesus, dem Geliebten!

Getrost! Die Abenddämmrung graut
Dem Liebenden, Betrübten.
Ein Traum bricht unsre Banden los,
Und senkt uns in des Vaters Schoss.

pp. 259-60. from *Heinrich v. Ofterdingen*, Bölsche, II, pp. 144-6

Uns ward erst die Liebe, Leben;
Innig, wie die Elemente,
Mischen wir des Daseins Fluten,
Brausend Herz mit Herz.
Lüstern scheiden sich die Fluten,
Denn der Kampf der Elemente
Ist der Liebe höchstes Leben
Und des Herzens eignes Herz.

Leiser Wünsche süsses Plaudern
Hören wir allein, und schauen
Immerdar in sel'ge Augen,
Schmecken nicht als Mund und Kuss.
Alles, was wir nur berühren,
Wird zu heissen Balsamfrüchten,
Wird zu weichen zarten Brüsten,
Opfer kühner Lust.

Immer wächst und blüht Verlangen
Am Geliebten festzuhangen,
Ihn im Innern zu empfangen,
Eins mit ihm zu sein.
Seinem Durste nicht zu wehren,
Sich im Wechsel zu verzehren,
Von einander sich zu nähren,
Von einander nur allein.

.   .   .

Und in dieser Flut ergiessen
Wir uns auf geheime Weise
In den Ozean des Lebens
Tief in Gott hinein;
Und aus seinem Herzen fliessen
Wir zurück zu unserm Kreise,
Und der Geist des höchsten Strebens
Taucht in unsre Wirbel ein.

.   .   .

o*

Könnten doch die Menschen wissen,
Unsre künftigen Genossen,
Dass bei allen ihren Freuden
Wir geschäftig sind:
Jauchzend würden sie verscheiden,
Gern das bleiche Dasein missen,—
O! Die Zeit ist bald verflossen,
Kommt, Geliebte, doch geschwind!

Helft uns nur den Erdgeist binden,
Lernt den Sinn des Todes fassen
Und das Wort des Lebens finden:
Einmal kehrt euch um.
Deine Macht muss bald verschwinden,
Dein erborgtes Licht verblassen,
Werden dich in kurzem binden,
Erdgeist, deine Zeit ist um.

p. 261. from the *Geistliche Lieder*, Bölsche, I, p. 61

Was wär ich ohne dich gewesen,
Was würd ich ohne dich nicht sein?
Zu Furcht und Ängsten auserlesen,
Ständ ich in weiter Welt allein.
Nichts wüsst ich sicher, was ich liebte,
Die Zukunft wär ein dunkler Schlund;
Und wenn mein Herz sich tief betrübte,
Wem tät ich meine Sorge kund?

p. 261. ibid., Bölsche, I, p. 61

Hat Christus sich mir kundgegeben
Und bin ich seiner erst gewiss,
O! Wie verzehrt ein lichtes Leben
Nicht schnell die bange Finsternis.
Mit ihm bin ich erst Mensch geworden;
Das Schicksal wird verklärt durch ihn,
Und Indien muss selbst im Norden
Um den Geliebten fröhlich blühn.

p. 261. ibid., Bölsche, I, p. 65

Unter tausend frohen Stunden,
Die im Leben ich gefunden,
Blieb nur eine mir getreu;

Eine, wo in tausend Schmerzen
Ich erfuhr in meinem Herzen
Wer für mich gestorben sei.

p. 261. ibid., Bölsche, I, p. 66

Wenn ich ihn nur habe,
Wenn er mein nur ist,
Wenn mein Herz bis hin zum Grabe
Seine Treue nie vergisst:
Weiss ich nichts von Leide,
Fühle nichts, als Andacht, Lieb und Freude.

p. 262. ibid., Bölsche, I, p. 65

Er starb, und dennoch alle Tage
Vernimmst du seine Lieb' und ihn,
Und kannst getrost in jeder Lage
ihn zärtlich in die Arme ziehn.

p. 262. ibid., Bölsche, I, p. 64

Greife dreist nach seinen Händen,
Präge dir sein Antlitz ein,
Musst dich immer nach ihm wenden—
Blüte nach dem Sonnenschein—
Wirst du nur das ganze Herz ihm zeigen,
Bleibt er, wie ein treues Weib, dir eigen.

p. 262. ibid., Bölsche, I, p. 63

Seitdem verschwand bei uns die Sünde,
Und fröhlich wurde jeder Schritt;
Man gab zum schönsten Angebinde
Den Kindern diesen Glauben mit.
Durch ihn geheiligt zog das Leben
Vorüber, wie ein selger Traum,
Und, ewger Lieb' und Lust ergeben,
Bemerkte man den Abschied kaum.

p. 262. ibid., Bölsche, I, p. 66

Wenn ich ihn nur habe,
Hab ich auch die Welt,
Selig wie ein Himmelsknabe,
Der der Jungfrau Schleier hält.

o

Hingesenkt im Schauen
Kann mir vor dem Irdischen nicht grauen.

pp. 262-3. ibid., Bölsche, I, p. 67

Wenn alle untreu werden,
So bleib ich dir doch treu;
Dass Dankbarkeit auf Erden
Nicht ausgestorben sei.

.   .   .

Oft muss ich bitter weinen,
Dass du gestorben bist,
Und mancher von den Deinen
Dich lebenslang vergisst.
Von Liebe nur durchdrungen
Hast du so viel getan,
Und doch bist du verklungen
Und keiner denkt daran.

.   .   .

Ich habe dich empfunden
O! lasse nicht von mir;
Lass innig mich verbunden
Auf ewig sein mit dir.
Einst schauen meine Brüder
Auch wieder himmelwärts
Und sinken liebend nieder
Und fallen dir ans Herz.

p. 263. ibid., Bölsche, I, p. 62

O! Geht hinaus auf allen Wegen,
Und holt die Irrenden herein,
Streckt jedem eure Hand entgegen,
Und ladet sie zu uns herein.
Der Himmel ist bei uns auf Erden,
Im Glauben schauen wir ihn an—
Die Einer Liebe mit uns werden,
Auch denen ist er aufgetan.

p. 263. ibid., Bölsche, I, p. 61

Ich sehe dich in tausend Bildern,
Maria, lieblich ausgedrückt,

Doch keins von allen kann dich schildern,
Wie meine Seele dich erblickt.
Ich weiss nur, dass der Welt Getümmel
Seitdem mir wie ein Traum verweht,
Und ein unnennbar süsser Himmel
Mir ewig im Gemüte steht.

p. 263. ibid., Bölsche, I, pp. 72f.

Die Augen sehn den Heiland wohl,
Und doch sind sie des Heilands voll,
Von Blumen wird sein Haupt geschmückt,
Aus denen er selbst holdselig blickt.

Er ist der Stern, er ist die Sonn',
Er ist des ew'gen Lebens Bronn,
Aus Kraut und Stein und Meer und Licht
Schimmert sein kindlich Angesicht.

In allen Dingen sein kindlich Tun,
Seine heisse Liebe wird nimmer ruhn,
Er schmiege sich seiner unbewusst
Unendlich fest an jede Brust.

X. STRAUSS

p. 371. *Westöstlich*

Ich wollte reisen, nun verreis' ich nicht,
Doch ob ich bleiben werde, weiss ich nicht.
Dass hier ich in der Fremde bin, ist sicher:
Wo meine Heimat sei, das weiss ich nicht.
Ich mein', ich hatt' einmal zwei liebe Kinder:
Ob dies nicht bloss ein Traum sei, weiss ich nicht.
Ein Weib verstiess ich, ob zu Hass die Liebe,
Ob Hass zu Liebe wurde, weiss ich nicht.
Sie sagen, Bücher hätt' ich einst geschrieben:
Ob's Wahrheit oder Spott ist, weiss ich nicht.
Ungläubig, hör' ich, nennen mich die Leute:
Ob ich nicht eher fromm sei, weiss ich nicht,
Nie hab ich vor dem Tode mich gefürchtet:
Ob ich nicht längst gestorben, weiss ich nicht.

(1848, *Gesammelte Schriften, XII*, p. 64)

p. 371.

> Wem ich dieses klage,
> Weiss, ich klage nicht;
> Der ich dieses sage,
> Fühlt, ich zage nicht.
>
> Heute heisst's: verglimmen,
> Wie ein Licht verglimmt,
> In die Luft verschwimmen,
> Wie ein Ton verschwimmt.
>
> Möge schwach wie immer,
> Aber hell und rein,
> Dieser letzte Schimmer,
> Dieser Ton nur sein.
>
> (29 December 1873, *Gesammelte Schriften*, XII, p. 226)

LIST OF ENGLISH TRANSLATIONS

Quotations in the text are from original works. For the benefit of readers we append a list of English translations.

JEAN JACQUES ROUSSEAU

The Social Contract. Discourses. Introduction and Translation by G. D. H. Cole. Dent, 1955. Everyman Library.

Confessions. Translated and with an Introduction by J. M. Cohen. Penguin Books, London, 1953.

Confessions. Dent, London, 1931. Everyman Library.

A Complete Dictionary of Music. Translated by W. Waring. Second edition, J. French, London, 1779.

Profession of Faith of a Savoyard Vicar. Translated from the French by Olive Schreiner. Eckler, 1889.

The Reveries of a Solitary. G. Routledge & Sons, London, 1927.

Eloisa or a series of original letters. Translated from the French. London, 1784.

On the Inequality of Mankind. Profession of Faith of a Savoyard Vicar. The Havard Classics. Vol. 34. 1910.

18 Letters from Jean-Jacques Rousseau to Mme d'Houdetot October 1757-March 1758.

GOTTHOLD EPHRAIM LESSING

A Translation of Eine Parabel and Other Writings by Lessing in Reply to Goetze. Edited by I. Bernard. Trübner, London, 1862.

The Education of the Human Race. Translated by F. W. Robertson. Kegan Paul & Co., London, 1896. Reprinted in *Anthroposophy*, London, 1927.

Nathan the Wise, in *A Selection of Lessing's Plays.* Dent, London, 1930. Everyman Library.

Also in *Dramatic Works.* G. Bell & Sons, London, 1888. Also translated by W. Jacks and introduced by Archdeacon Farrar. Maclehose & Sons, Glasgow, 1894. Also translated with an Introduction and Notes by M. G. Patrick Maxwell. The Scott Library, Vol. 99, 1892.

Lessing's Theological Writings. Selected and translated by Henry Chadwick. A. and C. Black, London, 1957.

IMMANUEL KANT

A Critique of Pure Reason. Dent, London, 1934. Everyman Library. Translated by F. Max Müller. Macmillan & Co., New York, 1927.

Another translation by Norman Kemp Smith. Macmillan & Co., London, 1929.

Religion within the Boundary of Pure Reason. Edinburgh, 1838; *Religion within the Limits of Reason.* Translated by Theodore M. Green and Hoyt H. Hudson. Open Court, Chicago/London, 1934.

Prolegomena. Simpkin and Marshall, 1819. Manchester University Press, 1953.

A Critique of Judgment. Translated by James Creed Meredith. Clarendon Press, Oxford, 1952.

Kant's Critique of Practical Reason, and other Works on the Theory of Ethics. Translated by T. K. Abbott. Longmans, Green, and Co. Ltd., London, 1927.

The Moral Law or Kant's Groundwork of the Metaphysic of Morals. Translated and with notes by H. J. Paton. Hutchinson's University Library, London, 1948.

NOVALIS

Hymns to the Night. Translated by Mabel Cotterel. German and English, Phoenix Press, 1948.

Spiritual Songs. Translated by G. Macdonald, London, 1876.

HEGEL

Lectures on the Philosophy of Religion. Translated from the second German edition by Speirs & Sanderson. English and Foreign Philosophical Library, 1877.

Lectures on the Philosophy of History. Translated by J. Sibree. Bohn's Library. George Bell & Son, London, 1890.

Early Theological Writing. Translated by T. M. Knox. University of Chicago Press, Chicago, 1948.

SCHLEIERMACHER

Christmas Eve. Edinburgh, 1890.

On Religion. Speeches to Its Cultured Despisers. London, 1893; Harper Torch Books, New York, 1958, with Introduction by Rudolph Otto.

The Christian Faith in Outline. Translated by D. M. Baillie. W. F. Henderson, Edinburgh, 1922.

The Christian Faith. Translated by H. R. Mackintosh and J. S. Stewart. T. & T. Clark, Edinburgh, 1928.

FEUERBACH

The Essence of Christianity. Translated by Marian Evans. Chapman's Quarterly Series, 1853; Harper Torch Books, New York, 1957, with Introduction by Karl Barth and Foreword by H. Richard Niebuhr.

STRAUSS

The Life of Jesus. Translated by Marian Evans. London, 1846.
Strauss' New Life of Jesus. Williams and Norgate, London and Edinburgh, 1879.
The Old Faith and the New. Authorized translation from the sixth edition by M. Blind. Asher & Co., London, 1873.

RITSCHL

A Critical History of the Christian Doctrine of Justification and Reconciliation. Translated by J. S. Black. Edmonston and Douglas, Edinburgh, 1872.
Instruction in the Christian Religion. Translated by Alice M. Swing and included in *The Theology of Albrecht Ritschl.* Longman & Co., New York, 1901.
The Christian Doctrine of Justification and Reconciliation. Translated and edited by H. R. Mackintosh and A. B. Macaulay. T. and T. Clark, Edinburgh, 1900.

INDEX OF NAMES

INDEX OF SUBJECTS